No Reason

Also by Clinton Callahan

Building Love That Lasts

Conscious Feelings

Cavitation

Goodnight Feelings (children's book)

White Witch of Tenerife

Rancho Campo

No Reason

21 Years With Western Baul Master Lee Lozowick

CLINTON CALLAHAN

Thoughtware Press
Boulder, Colorado

Photographs used with permission of Hohm Press and Hohm Sahaj Mandir.

Artwork Cover: Nara
Book cover, layout, and design: Anne-Chloé Destremau <annechloedestremau.org>
Photo of the author on the cover: Wolker Anders <volkeranders.de>

ISBN: 979-8-9854058-0-4

DISCLAIMER: This publication is designed to provide accurate and authoritative information regarding the subject matter covered. It is sold with the understanding that the publisher is not engaged in rendering relationship, emotional, or psychological counseling, medical treatment, or other professional services. If professional advice or expert assistance is required, readers are advised to seek the services of a competent professional.

Thoughtware Press
1724 Broadway, STE 1
Boulder, Colorado 80302
www.thoughtwarepress.org

General Memetics:
generalmemetics.org
clintoncallahan.org

There is almost a sensual longing for communion with others who have a large vision. The immense fulfillment of the friendship between those engaged in furthering the evolution of consciousness has a quality impossible to describe.

- Pierre Teilhard de Chardin

Table of Contents

THE END

If you're really listening here, if you're awake to the poignant beauty of the world, your heart breaks regularly. In fact, your heart is made to break; its purpose is to burst open again and again so that it can hold evermore wonders.

- Andrew Harvey

Yogi Ramsuratkumar never spoke to me. Until tonight.

It is 03:18 Sunday morning, 29 March 2020, nearly ten years after Lee Lozowick died. I am in the medieval German town of Ravensburg (if ever there was a logo for Lee Lozowick, it is a raven standing on a skull, as on the cover of his first Shri music cassette: *Accused*). I am in self-imposed lock-down to avoid expanding the death list of the COVID-19 Corona Virus. Farmland and low rolling hills surround this village. The Schussen River runs nearby, flowing carelessly south into Lake Constance.

During the past couple weeks, I experienced weird subtle stabs of pain behind my left rib cage. It scares me. I don't know how long I have to live. (Does anyone?)

On 24 March, the day before my fifteenth 53rd birthday, as a birthday present to myself, I call Sharron Ragan, the psychic in Atlanta, Georgia, who in the early 90s told me I would move from Arizona to Germany and write seven books, something I had, at the time, no evidence to believe could possibly ever become true. During the call she tells me about a friend of mine who might die early from an illness he is not yet aware of, yet says nothing of the sort to me.

I contemplate a quote I recently read aloud to Anne-Chloé Destremau from John Fowles' *The Magus*. Early in the story, the main character cannot sleep and reads an antique pamphlet which he finds on a dusty bookshelf near his bed:

ON COMMUNICATION WITH OTHER WORLDS

To arrive at even the nearest stars, man would have to travel for millions of years at the speed of light. Even if we had the means to travel at the speed of light we could not go to, and return from, any other inhabited area of the universe in any one lifetime; nor can we communicate by other scientific means, such as some gigantic heliograph or by radio waves. We are forever isolated, or so it appears, in our little bubble of time.

How futile all our excitement over aeroplanes! How stupid this fictional literature by writers like Verne and Wells about the peculiar beings who have evolved in the same way and with the same aspirations as ourselves. Are we then condemned never to communicate with them?

Only one method of communication is not dependent on time. Some deny that it exists. But there are many cases reliably guaranteed by reputable and scientific witnesses, of thoughts being communicated at *precisely the moment* they were conceived. Among certain primitive cultures, such as the Lapp, this phenomenon is so frequent, so accepted, that it is used as a matter of everyday convenience, as we in France use the telegraph or telephone.

Not all powers have to be discovered; some have to be regained.

This is the only means we shall ever have of communicating with mankind in other worlds. *Sic itur ad astra.*

This potential simultaneity of awareness in conscious beings operates as the pantograph does. As the hand draws, the copy is made.

The writer of this pamphlet is not a spiritualist and is not interested in spiritualism. He has for some years been investigating telepathic and other phenomena on the fringe of normal medical science. His interests are purely scientific. He repeats that He does not believe in the 'supernatural'; in rosicrucianism, hermeticism, or other such aberrations.

He maintains that already more advanced worlds than our own are trying to communicate with us, and that a whole category of noble and beneficial mental behavior, which appears in our societies as good conscience, humane deeds, artistic inspiration, scientific genius, is really dictated by half-understood telepathic messages from other worlds. He believes that the Muses are not poetic fiction, but a classical insight into scientific reality we moderns should do well to investigate.

'Coincidentally', in these same days I hear a man explain in a YouTube video how he 'spontaneously' recovered from cancer through connecting with the benevolent consciousness at the center of the Milky Way Galaxy.

Lying awake in bed in the early morning hours of 29 March 2020, I decide to see if I can jack-in to that benevolent healing force. I make sure I have my Center, my Grounding Cord, and my Bubble Of Space, and then send my request over to the center of the Milky Way as a probe. Almost immediately a blast of 'warm and good' energy returns causing my whole body to quiver.

After a few moments of enjoying pleasant healing vibrations, Yogi Ramsuratkumar slips in sideways and skyjacks my connection with the healers! As soon as He sees that I recognize Who is talking to me, Yogi Ramsuratkumar says, *"It is time for you to finish your book about Lee Lozowick."*

Tears well-up as my heart begins to ache. For no apparent reason I am softly crying. What Yogi Ramsuratkumar says makes no sense to me! I have not even started to write a book about Lee Lozowick. How could I possibly finish one?

I call up every rational argument I can think of against writing any kind of a 'Lee Lozowick book'. I say, "Listen, I am already trying to finish four other manuscripts! If you scan all of Lee Lozowick's students, I am <u>certainly not</u> one who would be authorized to speak about Lee's life, thoughts, feelings, actions, relations, intentions, etc. I mean, I lived in France most of the time! Lee only visited Europe for a few months each year, and when there He was mostly on the road and not at His French Ashram. I don't have the proper spiritual perspective. My work is not endorsed on any of the Hohm Sahaj Mandir websites. Plus! Lee is no longer here to confirm if writing a book about him is what He truly wants me to do." You know the drill. Blah, blah, blah.

Yogi Ramsuratkumar sweetly side-steps every argument by reminding me that it was I – during Lee's 1991 India trip with ten men – who opened the door for Vijay Fedorschak to write Hohm Press' first book about Yogi Ramsuratkumar. To balance things out, it is only fair that Yogi Ramsuratkumar now gets to tell me to finish my 'Lee Lozowick book'.

Bypassing my whining entirely, Yogi Ramsuratkumar starts detailing the contents of the book, chapter-by-chapter. Within a few seconds I am so inspired by His enthusiasm that I slither out of bed, open a Word file for a new book project on Ansible (my computer), and begin typing these words that you are reading now.

This book turns out to be a confession:

I confess how much I love Lee Lozowick. I confess how much Lee Lozowick gave to me. I confess how much Lee Lozowick unleashed potentials in me that would never have come forward except through His extraordinarily skillful unreasonable invitations to challenging experiences, combined with devastating feedback, and His radically-ever-present Love.

If this book works, it will not have been written by Clinton Callahan. It will have been written by Yogi Ramsuratkumar, Lee

Lozowick, and the Muse. Its purpose is to tell stories of a few facets of the life of Someone who overturned the spiritual scene 1 January 1975 with His seventy-one-page Spiritual Slavery book, and then skyrocketed lifelong through the world as the astonishingly radiant Lee Kepa Baul. I propose we use these tales as a chance to celebrate His blazing life together.

It is a bad time for me to write about Lee Lozowick. Corona Virus panic-buying has stripped bare every shelf in town of tissues and toilet paper. I am forced to use my shirtsleeves to wipe my nose and the tears pouring down my cheeks.

We go on.

Lee Lozowick

Lee Lozowick with the author, Clinton Callahan.

Lee Lozowick with his friend, Arnaud Desjardins.

"Auspicious snow lions victoriously holding aloft a tray of radiant dharma jewels."
Tattoo on the author's back.

Sample pages of Lee Lozowick's edits:

What the alchemist offers to the apprentice is the principles of his school: kindness, generosity, and compassion. "You can be that," he says. If we are honest, what we think is, "That is definitely not my style."

Principles are huge. If the principle shows up in the place where we normally are, then there would clearly be no room for us.

"How do we do this?" We think we don't know. But actually asking the question "How do we do it?" is a block against the action of just going ahead and doing it. If instead of asking the question and trying to figure out how, we were to simply move, we may suddenly find ourselves alive and well functioning in the crampless state.

Here are some indicators confirming that location. If we are not cramped, then we are not there. Instead of being our normal selves, we become a space holder. If we are the space holder, then something else can show up in that space. If we are committed to serving the principles indicated by the alchemist, then it is those principles that can show up, and what we become is the space through which the principles that we are serving can do their work. We become the principles in action.

Having experienced the crampless state, an apprentice will afterwards notice that it was impossible during that time for them to be offended (not to say that certain things weren't offensive, only that they did not react offensively to them), that they took nothing personally, that they were "being that which nothing could take root in," that they did not know what they were going to say or do next, that it worked anyway, as if by mystery and magic, that they did not know and it was okay, that they were standing on nothing, that they were present, being "yes," with a minimized "now," that they were not about problems or reasons, that they were massless and could turn at ninety degree angles even when going light speed, that they could not resent, could not blame, and that they had no face to lose.

The Mountain

In many traditions, the way is well paved, or at least marked with bold road signs that point in a clear direction and say, "This way!"

As already stated in prior sections of this volume, Alchemical Transformation is a tantric tradition. Everything is used, in whatever way it can help. The tantric path lies largely exposed to the elements, exists up above the tree line, contains more rocks than path, and represents the equivalent of "class five" free climbing. It is the sly way, using all methods simultaneously. At the same time, it is dangerous, because final decisions are left to the free will of the apprentice. Yes, you may get there faster, but take note: there are neither safety ropes, nor first aid stations along the way. And as has always been true, reaching the top delivers one of no reward. At all times, the apprentice is responsible for

668

every move he makes, and in terms of the struggle for transformation, is left to his own recognizance.

The upward journey may take more effort than we ever imagined. And it may often feel paradoxical, or impossible. We may be struggling for weeks, months, perhaps even years, climbing and scrambling in a direction that we think we remember was indicated to us by the alchemist. We don't really know for sure. Here we are, seeking what looks like the top, covered with dust, sweat stinging our eyes, snakes hiding within every crevice, scorpions and tarantulas scurrying about, biting flies, stinging nettles, poison oak, lightening, gusty winds, little avalanches from above, rocks that at first appear solid giving way as we grab onto them for stability. We are inching our way up the mountain. Muscles quivering from exertion, fingers scraped and bloody, we pull our eyes up over the final ledge, and there, to our utter amazement, sits the alchemist, as if he has been waiting there for ages.

He drinks mint tea in full regal splendor, completely relaxed, fully attentive and totally aware of our terribly precarious predicament—hanging there by our finger tips out over the edge of the cliff. The shock of seeing him there may surprise us. We may lose our grip, slip back down the cliff a few feet until we grab for a bit of scrub oak that barely holds our weight and hang on with total focus and concentration. We worked too hard to get here to let a simple surprise view of the alchemist knock us off balance. Slowly we scramble back up. Peering over the edge again we see the alchemist looking at us, perhaps giving us a short enigmatic smile, but making no efforts to help us up. Why doesn't he give us a hand? We are so close to the top! He could reach out and hoist us the rest of the way up with almost no effort. But he doesn't move, sitting as still as the stones. He looks at us and waits, patiently, as if he had nothing better to do than watch the sweat slip inexorably into our bleary eyes.

Hanging there we keep asking why? Why doesn't he help us up the last few inches? Then the answer becomes clear. He does not help us complete the last few inches because that would not be lawful. We would not have done it ourselves. Our being on the top of the mountain would then be a false accomplishment, not real, and therefore unstable. He *must* allow us to make it on our own. He *must* allow us to flop about and fail if we cannot succeed. Looking at it from his viewpoint, this must be his most difficult work, requiring the greatest of discipline. It must be painful for him, to sit there alone and watch us struggle so, begging for him to rescue us, and him knowing the cost and consequences of such folly.

So we pour every last ounce of effort into dragging ourselves up to the top. We get a toe up. A leg. Finally, nearly exhausted, enraged at the sacrifice and the amount of effort, we roll up and over, our chest heaving, crying out for more oxygen. A few minutes go by. The applause is already over and we hardly noticed. That is all to glory we get, those fifteen seconds. Now it is time to work again.

NOTE: These chapters do not include exact reproductions of my articles published in Lee Lozowick's Tawagoto magazine, or in Volume III and IV of the Hohm Sahaj Mandir Study Manual. I have taken the liberty of upgrading the text in several ways, namely: changing to the present tense, first person imperative 'you' form, dropping the 'Mr.' wherever I had written 'Mr. Lee', and adding bits-and-pieces here-and-there from what I have learned in the meantime. All I can say about this is: Jai Guru.

1. 1970: Tender First Steps

What I love most to hear from a person is stories about their initial steps along their journey towards becoming the person they are today. "How did you begin on the Path?" I ask. The twists and right-angle-turns are impossible to predict, but they make faultless sense in hind-sight. Their inconceivability substantiates legends of the ruthless compassion of E.C.C.O. (Earth Coincidence Control Office, per John Lilly).

My story is no different. It begins on the Palos Verdes Peninsula, a WASP (White Anglo-Saxon Protestant) suburb west of Los Angeles, California, in my 1970 Rolling Hills High School graduation non-ceremony. That is the day I legitimately escape from my parent's bubble.

The first moment my mother puts me in kindergarten at Silver Spur public grade-school, I know something is horribly wrong. The daily 'pledge of allegiance to the flag of the United States of America' is empty and scary to me. Something terribly important is fundamentally missing. Nonetheless I sense how satisfied my parents are that I have finally entered the school system, and that if I somehow refuse to go, it would become a significant problem. No one is there to hear the depth of the pain that I feel when my stuffed animals and plastic toy figures all inexplicably lose their life.

Since I am the first of three brothers, I copy my father's survival strategy and become a 'good boy'. Both of my brothers copy other relatives and became 'bad boys', smoking, drinking, partying, ditching school, and getting low grades. Our difference in survival strategies sadly forces my brothers and I to become adversaries. I remain mostly alone in my childhood.

I spend my free time reading science fiction novels, adventuring along on my elbows and belly through sewer pipes under the roads using a candle in a jar for light, learning to pick locks and make small bombs from watching 1960s American television: *The Avengers, Mission Impossible, The Man from U.N.C.L.E.*, and building a small laboratory in my parents' back yard using large wooden pallets I scavenge from my father's work. I roof it with aluminum sheeting used back then in the newspaper printing process. Fortunately, I do not blow myself up.

During the last year of high school, I am put into a history class. My teacher never speaks to me, until one day he says, "Hey Callahan." I say nothing. "Why is it that I get a paper from the head office listing all the gifted children in this school, and of all the students in this class only your name is on the list?" I don't know anything about this list. He continues, "And last night when the curtain goes up at the school play, you are the only actor on the stage!" No answer is required. "And here you are, the whole year in my class, and you don't say anything?" I understand things enough to know that he just answered his own question. He is an asshole. But I am a good-boy, so we are in a stalemate.

I skip out on my 1970 high school graduation ceremony by registering for a National Science Foundation Summer Science Program for physics and math entirely across America in Greensboro, North Carolina. It is as far away as I can get from my parents and brothers without actually leaving the country. I earn pocket money by roving the streets early Saturday and Sunday mornings, collecting aluminum cans and coke bottles that I turn in for cash, sometimes having to step around pools of blood and broken glass from the previous night's activities. By the end of summer, I arrive at my college campus: California Polytechnic State University at San Luis Obispo.

The lady at the registration desk say, "So, young man, what would you like to study?" I am shocked. No one ever asked before. I decide to tell the truth. "I want to learn magic, healing, transformation, metaphysics, para-physics…" She interrupts me saying, "We offer physics." I sign on the dotted line.

Sleuthing around campus I discover *The Bulletin Board!* One announcement particularly catches my eye: an invitation to learn Maharishi Mahesh Yogi's Transcendental Meditation (TM). An unexpected tingle goes down my spine. Finally, I get to explore something that actually interests me!

My mother provides thirty-five dollars per month for food at college. The cost of the TM initiation is exactly thirty-five dollars! For one month I collect fallen walnuts and apples, steal saltine crackers and ketchup packets from salad bars, and discover how to scrounge half-rotten fruit and vegetables from dumpsters behind grocery stores without getting caught. My diet is strange for a month, but it liberates enough cash to start my spiritual path. I begin practicing TM of TM in the AM and PM

(Twenty Minutes of Transcendental Meditation in the morning and in the evening). It goes well.

In 1974 the Cal Poly Bulletin Board opens up another doorway when I discover a flyer for a two-weekend workshop that promises to unleash my psychic abilities or they will give me my money back. It is an offer I cannot refuse. The workshop is called *Silva Mind Control* (named after José Silva, now called *Silva Method*). John Magera is my trainer. After the two weekends I do not ask for my money back. Being psychic is our natural state.

Much later I learn that simultaneously on the East Coast of America, in the town known as Orange, New Jersey, a man named Lee Lozowick – a professional stamp collector – is studying the ideas and practices of José Silva and begins delivering the same seminar that changes my life. Is this mere coincidence?

It is September 1974. I begin my final year at Cal Poly with the sadness and frustration that I am not learning what I came there to learn. My guts move me to try something completely different. I design and post mimeographed flyers advertising a weekly Thursday Night Meeting that would begin 9 January 1975 at seven pm. I sit in the back row as seventy-six students pack into the tiny room in the Student Union. I had never given a talk before in my life. I am sweating and shaking as my friend Roger Taber nudges me to go forward and say something. I don't remember what I said, but we start meeting weekly on Thursday evenings for the rest of the school year. As a result, five of us from the group spend Fall Quarter of 1975 self-organizing and co-creating an Unschool for ourselves on the southern tip of Baja California, Mexico, between San Jose del Cabo and Cabo San Lucas. It is heavenly there on the beach. We do experiments and go on adventures. The aliveness of our mutual endeavor inspires me still today.

Confident, I join a Los Angeles project to set up an experimental educational community on Roatan, an island off the Caribbean coast of Honduras. Within hours of everyone arriving on the island we all get arrested and sent back to the USA. I am in shock about how badly this turns out after my previous success. Clearly I have more to learn about navigating human collaboration in small groups...

With only fifteen dollars in my pocket, I ride my ten-speed Schwinn bicycle from my parent's house in Los Angeles south to San Diego where I work for a while as a lab assistant in an air pollution technology research firm.

In Los Angeles, 1976, I get to participate in a one-day seminar with José Silva himself, along with my parents. What I remember most is overhearing a 12-year-old girl brag that she can bend spoons with her mind. My parents and I go to Denny's Diner for lunch where I steal one of their heavy-duty stainless-steel teaspoons. Back at the seminar room I find the girl, hand her the spoon, and say, "Please show me how you can bend this with your mind." She sits down quietly on carpeted stairs, focuses on the spoon while stroking it with one slender finger. In about nine minutes she hands the spoon back to me, bent ninety-degrees on a tiny radius. I still have that spoon today.

In 1979 I 'accidentally' discover Paramahansa Yogananda's book, *Autobiography of a Yogi*. Even though it is a whale of a book I do not want it to end. When it does, I immediately contact Yogananda's organization, the *Self Realization Fellowship* (SRF), and pay for their fifty-two-week correspondence course. At the end of my year of Hindu meditation practice they send me a written test to complete before revealing to me the secrets of their core practice: 'Kriya Yoga'.

I fail their test...

The genius fails their test...

This is an eye-opener.

I take it as a sign from E.C.C.O. and stop my SRF practices to go sailing around the world. By that time, Brenda (my first wife, and later on, mother to our two daughters) and I figure out the long hard way that in order to go sailing into the South Pacific you do not need to build a boat. You do not even need to buy a boat. All you need is to be accepted as a crew member of a boat!

We quit our jobs, get married, buy one-way air tickets to Honolulu, and hike the Kalalau Trail on Kauai. By September 1981 we are hanging around Honolulu harbor searching for a sailboat making landfall from California with a crew who hates each other so much – due to the psycho-emotional reactivity from the forced intimacies of sailing – that at first opportunity they abandon ship. As the captain searches for a replacement crew, we would appear. We don't have long to wait...

Last minute I am running around Honolulu in a panic, having almost no time to pack before shipping out for the South Pacific with two other couples on the pink-and-purple hand-crafted 45-foot trimaran christened *Moondog*. My panic comes from having no book to read!

Panic leaves me open to E.C.C.O.'s influence, which directs me, oddly enough, to the Honolulu *J. J. Newberry's* discount book table. Frantically pawing through a pile of pulp-fiction, my fingers miraculously pull out a hardback copy of *In Search of the Miraculous* by P. D. Ouspensky.

How the hell did this get here? Another freak coincidence?

I devour this hefty tome during the entire one-month sea-crossing. Later I learn that Lee Lozowick is simultaneously studying Gurdjieff's *Fourth Way*.

While cherishing the last few pages in Sydney, Australia, our roommate's boyfriend – by mere 'coincidence' – saunters past. He glances over my shoulder, and casually says, "You like that book?"

"Yes!" I exclaim fervently.

"Then, you need to call Ron Bosanquet. Here is his number."

I look at him quizzically, but I call Ron Bosanquet. Ron quietly asks me a couple of questions and then says, "You can meet me at the café."

I explain what is going on to my wife, and then I go alone to meet Ron Bosanquet at the café. After a couple of minutes conversing, he says, "You can come. We meet Thursday nights at seven. Here is the address."

Thursday nights at seven? That is the same as our Meetings in 1975! Is this also mere coincidence? I will go to that address the next Thursday night at seven. There I have the profound experience that my life has not been in vain.

I find that the serious disparity I have felt my whole life between the vision and needs of my Being, and the spaces and gameworlds offered to my Being by modern culture, is not my own insanity. There are some parts of humanity – in this case, thirty Australian women and men – who also cherish learning the arts of practical transformation and procedures for evolving consciousness. Ron Bosanquet is creating and navigating the spaces of a living School.

During the Thursday night meetings, and through engaging the exercises they teach me to practice during the week, my life jumps tracks. After a week or two, Brenda tells me, "I need to come to those meetings with you."

"Why is that?" I ask.

"Because you are changing."

Try to imagine a woman speaking these words to a man born and raised in the capitalist patriarchal empire of the late 20th Century. What man do you know has actually ever changed? How much heart-break do women feel about trying to relate with uninitiated adolescents? Mostly women are forlorn, hopeless, and frustrated-as-hell about never seeing a man become more aware of himself than a dog.

The Gurdjieff Work provides Brenda and I with something truly extraordinary to stand on. Our Australian Tourist Visa is valid for six months. After Brenda is accepted into the School we decide to finish up our travels, earn some money back in the USA, and then emigrate to Australia to continue in the Work.

My, my… how plans can change…

Ronald Eric Giffard Bosanquet eventually went on to create Leonis School which still exists today outside of Sydney, Australia. Ron died 30 May 2017.

In 1983, after our two-and-a-half-year, round-the-world edu-vacation comes to an end, we find ourselves right back where we started from: California… with one strange difference: we are pregnant.

Our first daughter is happily home birthed in May 1984. I use every spare moment to study any Gurdjieff book I can get my hands on, but I terribly miss the magical transformational downloads and practices of Ron Bosanquet's living School in Sydney.

I search out and visit half-a-dozen Gurdjieff groups meeting around Northern California assuming that they too would be alive. Sadly, each one reveals itself to be nothing more than a cerebral debate circle. I eventually give up hope, trying to imagine how I could possibly have been so stupid as to have walked away from the only living School on planet Earth.

One summer afternoon in 1985 our little family drives from our home in Santa Rosa, California, to visit an outdoor Tibetan Fair in Berkeley. My wife takes off with her sister and our daughter. I meander around thinking about the next book I want to read: *Programming and Metaprogramming in the Human Biocomputer* by John C. Lilly. On a grassy hillside I spot two intelligent-looking women standing behind an unshaded folding-table strewn about with books. I stroll over, do not make eye contact with the vendors, push a few volumes aside and find: The *Human Biological Machine as a Transformational Apparatus* by someone named E.J. Gold. I think to myself, "This is it! This is my next book!" I find a second book titled, *Secret Talks With Mr. G.*, whom I automatically presume to be Gurdjieff. I pay for the books in cash, turn away happily with my treasure, and walk away.

Until one of the women shouts, "Wait!"

I pause and turn around, thinking perhaps there is some tax I had forgotten to pay. This does not appear to be her issue. Something else is afoot. I sense an imperative yet heartbreakingly wistful tone in her voice.

"What?" I ask cautiously, staying motionless.

"You cannot just walk away!" the woman wails from deep in her being. This does not explain anything to me.

"Why not?" I say testily, thinking to myself, Of course I can walk away…

She allows a teetering moment of silence, then reveals with surprising intensity, "You cannot just walk away. We have been standing here for three days. You are the only person to even come over and look at the books. You don't ask us any questions. You buy two books without hesitation! You think we can just let you walk away from here?"

I have no answer to her question.

She writes furiously on a scrap of paper, says, "Here! You must call Mike McDonnell!"

With trembling hands, I take the precious little note from her fingers, barely able to look in her eyes. Could this be real? Could this be happening? I am unable to speak with the women further for fear of bursting out in tears. I walk away treasuring this little paper more than anything else I own.

That evening I call Mike McDonnell. Mike says, "Can you meet me at the café?"

Oh my god! It is true!

I meet Mike at the café. After a few questions, Mike says, "Okay, you can come. We meet Thursday nights at seven. Here is the address."

Halleluyah!!! Holy Samolians! Thank Gaia! There is no way to express the depth of my joy. Life suddenly makes sense again! Magic lives! Someone is watching out for me! I am on my knees in gratitude to the whole Universe. I have just been guided to another living School!

Even now retelling this story after so many years, my chest swells, my throat tightens, and tears pour down my cheeks in unspeakable gratitude for the spaceholders of such Schools. They are so rare, so important in the big picture. My Being Celebrates the potential abundance of nonlinear Possibilities shared on an authentic path guided by the great Mystery. I love this Work.

Mike's Thursday Night meetings are fabulous, for four years.

One summer weekend in 1988 Mike brings Brenda and I to attend his teacher's *World Wide Work Circle* conference in Sacramento, California. We find ourselves in amphitheater-seating with Mike and some two-hundred of E.J. Gold's students.

E.J. himself sits behind a long white table down in front of us with two powerful gorgeous women sitting on his left, and two additional powerful and equally gorgeous women sitting on his right. The room grows quiet and a solemn tension arises. E.J. finally asks his burning question, "How many of you have read my new book?"

Barely a handful of us raise our hands. I myself am only part-way through it, a labyrinthian journey to be sure. E.J. erupts out of his chair, furiously gesticulating. "I spend months writing this book for your development as a harmonious human being and you do not even have the discipline to read it!" All four women now stand up with him. The five of them turn to their right, and without further explanation, silently file out the door to our left.

No one moves a muscle.

We hardly breathe. This cannot be happening.

The room is quiet enough to hear an angel fart.

Reality just slammed us irrefutably in the face.

No one knows what is going on.

This is unprecedented.

We have no place to put this situation in our mind.

The rug has been pulled out and we are in freefall.

E.J.… He just stood up and walked out on us… What is happening? He can't take it anymore? We failed him? There is no hope for us? The game is over?

These thoughts are horrible beyond belief, beyond imagination.

We wallow in disgraceful, embarrassing pain. How could we have done this to him?

Fifteen minutes go by. Sweat trickles down our faces.

Twenty minutes… Still nobody moves.

Down at the right side of the conference hall, a door gracefully opens. A tall feminine angel floats in and turns to her right. A second angel somberly enters. Then a thin, long-haired bearded man enters in sober silence, also dressed in white, also turning to his right. Two additional angel-women follow him in. They are all barefoot.

The five radiantly-white Beings stand elegantly behind the same table E.J. and his women had abandoned. They sit down in wordless unison, and gaze benevolently upon us. This, however, fails to alleviate any of our pain.

This is my introduction to Lee Lozowick: a piece of consciously performed radical transformational guerilla street theater.

No one can predict what will happen next in this space. Everyone's attention is glued on Lee.

Slowly, evenly, carefully, word by word, Lee builds out a bridge for us to cross over from where we are – spiritual ghosts in various states of shock, shame, outrage, fear of consequences, whatever psychological aberration we have not yet healed in ourselves – over to where E.J. invites us to thrive with him.

Someone gains the courage to ask a timid question. We start to put our hearts on the table. It might be frightening or painful, but this is the only way forward. Lee delicately fills in gaps with distinctions, stories, reasonability, and practical clarity.

During this conference Brenda decides she wants Lee Lozowick as her Teacher.

As you might imagine, that opens up multiple futures before me.

One future is where Brenda follows Lee to Arizona and I stay with E.J. Gold in Northern California. This, I estimate, would cause a fundamental divide.

Another future is where I bow before the forces of E.C.C.O. and join Brenda in asking to be a student of Lee Lozowick.

E.C.C.O. prevails.

It is Friday, 17 November 1989, the day before Lee's birthday. The Western Baul Appearance Day Celebration is in full swing at the Prescott Ashram. Brenda and I with our two daughters have just driven nineteen hours from our home in Santa Rosa, California, across Death Valley, to this sanctuary, deep in the high Arizona desert. The phrase, 'Yea, though I walk through the valley of the shadow of death, I will fear no evil...' cruises through my mind, but nonetheless I shiver in my shoes.

The hubbub of the Hohm Sahaj Mandir office surrounds me. Every desk and chair is occupied by someone doing something productive. I stand here agitated doing nothing. Each breath has a life of its own.

My nervousness comes from having just written a note on a scrap of yellow paper and placing it into Lee's empty mailbox just outside and to the left of the sliding glass doors into the greenhouse. Lee's mailbox is always empty. I cannot imagine how He does this.

The note I put there is not just any note. It is THE note:

DEAR LEE,
ARE YOU WILLING
TO ACCEPT ME
AS YOUR STUDENT?
—JAI GURU
CL

My world enters a cusp moment, a state of indeterminacy. It is madness to try to predict what the Guru will do. He might not answer. He might say, "Come back next year after you have read all my books." He might say anything. What would I do then?

Not knowing what comes next is tough for a physicist, being so out of control, without a model to use for predicting how this is supposed to go. I wobble there aimlessly in some galactic waiting bardo while the universe zooms on around me.

Brenda wanders into the office, possibly to find me after settling the kids into childcare. That is when Lee enters the space through the glass doors like a hurricane with a mission. He catches my eye, stops, and clearly says one single word, "Yes."

Brenda sees the interaction and says, "Did you just ask Lee to be a student?" I nod my head. She looks to Lee and says, "Me too!" Lee confirms Brenda's discipleship without hesitation, but I am too occupied with what just happened to me to notice what is happening to her.

By December 1990 we extract ourselves from E.J.'s School, sell our California house, move to an apartment near Prescott, Arizona, buy seven-tenths of an acre of buildable land across the stream and a couple hundred yards from Lee's Prescott Ashram, and start designing up a passive-solar rammed-earth home. We find an ancient sky-blue house-trailer to put on the land in the meantime and move our little family into it. I give my bio-medical instrument prototyping business (Computer Effects Company) to my electronics partner Alan Friedman. I dedicate 1990 to becoming 'financially independent' as a multi-level-marketer selling NuSkin products in California, Arizona, Vancouver, and Hong Kong, finally maxing out so many credit cards that the banks won't give me any more money. My fantasy world pops as debt overwhelms me. I go down.

Mr. Gurdjieff would say, "Good situation? Bad situation! Bad situation? Good situation!"

In this case, being insolvent is an extremely 'good' bad situation. My life plan is utterly crushed. I am, at last, destabilized enough from my self-commitment that E.C.C.O. can slide me sideways into circumstances that unleash my true life calling. This, of course, is only discernible in hindsight. In present time I teeter over an unnamed abyss.

I have become meek enough to accept an employment offer to work as a 'secretary' in a tiny Prescott, Arizona, training company run by one of Lee's long-time students, Purna Steinitz. He needs a new assistant because his previous one was recently seduced by a female training participant.

It is January 1991. I am too emotionally untrained to recognize the immense joy of my Archetypal Lineage.

2. 1991: Seeing Krishna

Sunday, 14 April 1991 – In the original Arizona Ashram Darshan Hall near Prescott

During several previous pre-Darshan rush-arounds I had grabbed a piece of fruit from our household fruit-bowl to give for Prasad. By doing this I learned the hard way that this does not energetically work. There is not enough consciousness in the gift. Prasad needs to be attentively selected, energetically cleansed, carried into the Darshan Hall with intention and forethought. Household fruit does not provide a clean enough bridge to transport divine energy between Teacher and student. Prasad is handmade or found or bought with the clear formulation that the object was already Prasad.

On this evening, Brenda and I get the kids and ourselves fed, cleaned, dressed and into the car early enough that we can drive to Smith's Grocery Store for a 'Prasad Run' without being late for Darshan. A large, plump, fragrant, perfectly ripe, red-orange-green mango finds its way into my hands to lay at the feet of Lee Lozowick tonight.

We arrive at the Ashram without incident and approach the Darshan Hall door. I carry my daughter inside in my arms because she sprained her ankle just before we left the house. Brenda is so tense from doing bookkeeping all afternoon combined with rushing to arrive at Darshan on time that her right shoulder is hunched a full two inches above her left. A humorless set to her face and eyes tells me she is near her limits. I am emotionally Cramped up, trying to be a 'good hubby', yet deeply worrying that last year's taxes are due tomorrow and I have completed neither the account books nor the forms. In this condition we hobble into the archetypal space of the Darshan Hall, a glorious celebration chamber with Lee's seating platform front and center, and a massive, hand-carved wooden Bodhisattva statue blessing us imperiously from the left-front corner of the room.

Surprisingly, it is early enough that I can choose where to sit rather than squeezing onto the only available cushion at the back of the room in my usual 'family man' entrance. I see that in one row on the men's side, the middle seat is taken by Bishwanath, the Indian Baul currently visiting the Ashram. Bishwanath is Sanatan Das' elder son, with whom I feel some kind of rapport after having had a short, pantomimed conversation with him the previous weekend during our annual *All Fool's Celebration*. To his left sits Abhi, his translator. The seat to the right of Bishwanath is vacant and I choose to sit there, completing the row, having the fantasy flash through my mind that I too am a 'real Baul'.

Bishwanath sits in full lotus position, meditating. I manage a half-lotus as I settle in next to him. Shortly the chanting begins. Lee Lozowick enters and takes his place on his low padded throne. I bow to the floor, still singing praises to the Master's sandals.

As I rise up from my bow something feels distinctly different. The space has transformed into some other kind of space, as if it has gone up an octave in frequency. Nothing is changed but everything is different. A tingling brightness impinges on my nerves. For some reason my attention is drawn up and to the right, to the space in the right-front corner of the hall above Lee Lozowick's left shoulder, exactly corresponding to where a second huge Bodhisattva statue would be symmetrically placed. Only, of course, there was nothing but air where I was staring.

Or was there?

A senior female student of Lee Lozowick, M., sitting on the floor at the front of the women's side of the Darshan Hall, begins singing in her richly feminine voice the devotional preamble to a chant. I glance leftwards to watch her sing, and out of the right corners of my eyes I seem to perceive a gigantic blue dude with black hair, red lips, and multiple muscular arms standing in the empty corner of the Darshan Hall.

I think, "Whoa!" which is not necessarily something to be proud of thinking in such a moment, but still, that is exactly what I think.

My eyes instantly dart over to the right side of the room to try to confirm what is going on over there, and, of course, I don't actually see any physical object there. The right-front corner of the Darshan Hall is as physically empty as it always has been.

Then my breath catches in my throat as my ears collect the voice of M. chanting Krishna's name. The sounds impinge on me with the full resonance of their call. A gigantic chill ripples up and down my spine, making the hair on my neck and arms stand up. I am unable to block an ear-to-ear grin from taking over my face. Something truly amazing and inexplicable is happening right here and right now in this Darshan Hall, and I am somehow witnessing it full blast.

I *never* see stuff like this.

I mean, I am a pretty regular kind of guy. I have a college degree in physics. I have two kids and a wife. I own my own car, my own house. I ran my own business. I traveled around the world for two-and-a-half-years through the South Pacific and Southeast Asia. I have seen *a lot of stuff...* but *nothing* like this!

All these Gods who are aspects of God identified and named in the Hindu traditions pretty much baffle me. They don't make sense to my scientifically-trained engineer-practical perceptions. I am not familiar enough with the Hindu cosmology to work with it, let alone incorporate it into my worldview. Yet here's this big blue dude staring down at all of us from his side of the Darshan Hall, perfectly visible with my 'energetic eyes', being with us as sure as Lee Lozowick is being with us.

The thing is, I know that I do not believe in Krishna. I don't even know what a Krishna is, what it is supposed to represent, where it comes from, or what it is supposed to do. I never read *Vallabhacarya on the Love Games of Krsna*. Yet, as weird as it seems, here is Krishna, standing plain as day, in the corner of our Darshan Hall in cowboy land!

I sneak a few glances around the Hall to see if anyone else is seeing what I'm seeing. I look at Bishwanath to my left. Now *this* guy is a real Baul, literally dragged straight from the hills of Northern Bengal. He's rocking back and forth, eyes half closed, clapping his hands and feeling quite at home singing the same chants as I am, the only difference being that he knows what the words mean. This guy probably sees Krishna *all* the time. I look away from Bishwanath, thinking to myself that we are of such vastly different cultures that there can be no comparison. Still I wonder: *Have I become him because I'm sitting so near to him? Is it some kind of cloud consciousness, a resonance field effect? Is that why I'm seeing this?*

I look up at Lee Lozowick, the gentle King, fully present with the space. *Does He see Krishna?* I wonder. This does not help. The sense I get at that moment is that *Lee Lozowick is Krishna.* This commanding blue energetic god-like presence and the collaborative flesh-and-blood Western Baul spiritual Master: the two feel the same. Each seems to be self-contained, protective, overflowing with knowledge and power that is dedicated to something greater than themselves. They are fully engaged in chanting praises of God, serving the space and the rest of us as stainless-steel space holders while simultaneously being as fluid as air, moving with or actually invoking the moods of this vibrantly joyous chamber. Lee Lozowick is Krishna's right-hand man, his incarnation of this moment in time in these ancient Arizona mountains. Lee Lozowick is Krishna for us.

I keep glancing away from Krishna, checking to see if I can see what the others are seeing. I get distracted by the words of the chants, caught up in my thoughts and emotions, wondering if this whole thing is real, or just a dream, some kind of parallel reality or perhaps a simple self-delusion.

Then I get this wild idea: Ask the Krishna! I turn towards the imposing blue effigy and begin to formulate a question in my mind. Without prelude, the full Darshan Hall sounds of drums, bells, and chanting fade to a background murmur. My vision tunnels so that my entire attention focuses on Krishna's face. At the same time I can almost identify the various weapons and implements He holds regally in his hands.

At that moment a war erupts inside of me at various levels simultaneously. My physical eyes inform me that I am not actually seeing anything standing there in the corner... yet there is some kind of after-image of a shadow. Then my being wants to bow down before a four-meter-tall spiritual warrior pirate magician king lover blazing away in blinding Technicolor turquoise blue. The mind fights back: "Don't be crazy. You are not allowed to see such visions!" A deeper and more substantial part of me contradicts the mind's opinions with actual experience, saying, "Oh yes. I am seeing exactly that. This is a coming out party! Welcome to your future!" At this, the mind freaks out again: "Aaaarrrrgggghhhh! No!!! This is NOT happening! C'mon now! Get real! Wake up! This is the 20th Century! Nobody sees stuff like this!"

While the various psycho-emotional parts of me battle insanely on, a message comes from Krishna. He answers my question directly. Without speaking He says that He is truly here with us and for us. The chanting is what is happening. He is paying attention to us. He has been here before and He feels welcome. He loves us all, supports us, protects us, and guides us, even if He might from time-to-time come across as a bit stern, powerful or over-willful.

I am filled with a feeling of joy to make contact with Krishna, although He was clear that it did not matter to him whether I or we could see him or not. What also came over is that it is good to have a guy like this Krishna on our side. He is one to be relied upon, although not in any personal kind of way. He is not there to be used, or even praised. He came here this evening simply to accompany us, to be with us.

How extraordinary.

The chanting flows in waves of power. To me it feels like it is our community's job to chant, and it is a pleasure to be powerfully chanting as one body. Later, during the Darshan Talk, Lee even comments that when the chanting is like this, He is tempted to formalize the Ashram into a traditional closed Ashram where we would spend our time sitting together and chanting the names of God, practicing all day. He says He would do this, except that we have other business to attend to. "Perhaps," He says, "after the business is taken care of ..."

Eventually Lee rises to his feet and heads towards his Darshan Hall exit. I put my forehead to the carpeted floor. When I raise back up into sitting position on my cushion, Krishna has vanished. The space where He – just a moment before – stood, is now empty, completely empty.

One by one students gather their things to leave the Darshan Hall. I remain seated, only smiling. Something in me is radically changed by this experience. A place behind my heart along my spine feels highly energized and tingly. I feel incredibly fortunate, immensely lucky for being allowed to participate in this living School, to be one of Lee Lozowick's children, students, friends, brothers. A stray thought meanders pointlessly through my unusually empty mind: "There is so much I don't know."

I suddenly realize that I MUST go to the tea space tonight – even if it means that I would risk Brenda feeling angry that I had not arranged this with her earlier, would not help get the kids to bed, nor work on our tax papers... but Brenda agrees lovingly.

I grab into the 'giveaway' clothing box and put on whatever I can find that is more suitable than my 'meditation whites' for the tea space. I wait my turn near the tea room entrance, silently push aside the velvet curtains, step into the soft-music hushed-voices candle-lit incense-filled tea room, turn left and bow towards Lee Lozowick. He sits calmly, regally at the head of his circle, as if He has already been sitting there for hours, although I know just a few minutes before He was surfing the Darshan Hall spaces together with us.

Lee makes a brief five-body eye-contact scan of me, nods wordlessly greeting what is there, and with his left hand, gestures to an empty cushion across from him where I should sit in his circle. I am convinced that somehow Lee already knows something happened to me tonight. Not only do I trust Lee Lozowick, but by now I also count on Lee to perceive authentic needs of people around him and act rightly without coercion or petition on anyone's part.

In other words, I am not surprised to be invited to sit in Lee's tea circle, however I am nearly bursting to ask what the hell just happened to me. How should I possibly wait all that time while others enter the tea space and are seated, then brought tea cups, and tea is poured? How can I sit still holding all this in until the proper moment arrives to ask my questions?

Elegance, my man! Remember your elegance.

Eventually Lee glances over at me, silently making an expectant but safe space into which I may speak.

I say, "There's a lot of stuff going on that I don't normally see."

Lee Lozowick nods his head slowly in simple confirmation of the obvious.

M. says, "Uh-oh."

I continue. "You know the big Bodhisattva statue in the left front corner of the Darshan Hall?"

Lee Lozowick looks down at the hand-woven wool carpet on the tea space floor and doesn't say anything.

R. glances over at M. and says, "He saw Krishna."

M. looks back at R. and says, "He saw Krishna."

R. laughs and says to me, "There are two Krishnas – a little one and a big one. The little one is about four inches tall. He is very playful. The big one is more stern and protective. Which one did you see?"

"The big one"

The silence of respectful awe towards the great Mystery fills our little tea circle, me thinking in amazement, "They've all seen him before?"

Hoping for some kind of further explanation, I eventually say, "I don't usually see this kind of thing."

No one takes the bait. I feel confused, frustrated, and scared about the magnitude of unexpected future unknown surprises that could possibly jump out at me along our further journey on the path. I try again, "Is that it? I mean, there's nothing to do? There's no explanation? It doesn't mean anything? I should just pay attention?"

Lee Lozowick says, "Just pay attention and write it up."

M. adds, "Lee says it didn't happen unless you write it up. And this is something you want to have happened."

There is only silence in our circle. I think to myself, "How can something as wild as seeing Krishna be so normal that it is no surprise? That it calls forth no further comments? How can there be no questions?"

On the one hand I am not being sent away to a lunatic asylum. On the other hand, neither am I made special. Who are these people?

M. smiles at me, then says. "You don't usually see this kind of thing until you see this kind of thing, and then you don't usually see this kind of thing again until you see it again."

So here it is. I've written it up.

Thank you, Krishna. I look forward to being with you again, although I feel like you are with me now. Always have been. Always will be.

I am left with the overwhelming sense that I will be dousing myself in significant portions of the *Assertion* practice of asking, "Who am I kidding?"

One thing I can assert: I'm glad that I am done writing this up 'cause man, it is long past midnight, and I really have to pee.

3. 1991: Three Days With Yogi Ramsuratkumar

November / December 1991 – Notes from the men's India Expedition

We are nine men plus Lee for three weeks in Southern India. Lee has set an intense travel itinerary for us. I arranged to travel with Johnny Cordova, one of the men in my Men's Group. Our flight had a nine-hour layover in Singapore. I love Singapore from travels there ten years before with Brenda, but when we landed at midnight the buses to town already stopped running. Johnny and I decided to walk.

Warm humid ocean air graces our faces. The eighteen kilometers tick by under our feet. As dawn paints the Eastern sky in pastels, we enter a busy temple district. The thousands of Singaporeans lining up for morning ablutions and blessings at diverse temple doorways – already a mixture of Philippinos, Indonesians, Malaysians, and Chinese – now include a couple of greenhorn gringos. With no idea of what might be coming, we bravely step through the carved-stone doorway and move along a series of stations, each one dowsing us with rose-water, sacred ash, thick incense, rose petals, a chant, a pat on the head, something sweet in the mouth, then out the door, and on to the next temple. As far as we could tell, we were the only ones temple-hopping. After the third or fourth indoctrination we understood why. We were both dizzy. Somewhere deep in our nervous systems there is some kind of conflict going on between multiple religious cleansing and blessing ceremonies trying to do their work on the same soul. We grab some street food and step into a bus back to the airport in time to catch our nine AM flight to Chennai.

The men's tour begins with a visit to Lee's friend Professor Rangarajan and his wonderful family who present us with trays overflowing with Indian sweets that are expected to disappear by the time we depart for a twelve-hour ride southwest to Kanya Kumari. Here is where three oceans meet at the southernmost tip of India. We take our shirts and shoes off for a men's only blessing in the ghee drenched Bhagavathy Amman Temple. We ride a ferry boat a short distance over shark-infested waters to Vivekenanda's island. By then we know the procedure of soaking in blessings from temples and tombs of Saints by making one circumambulation in the clockwise direction.

We spend Jayanti Day (Yogi Ramsuratkumar's Birthday, first of December) in full celebration with Pon Kamaraj presiding at the Yogi Ramsuratkumar Mantralayam, at Kanimadam. Nights are illuminated with gaudily colored fluorescent tubes. Loudspeakers broadcast the distorted voice of whoever is chanting at the moment throughout the compound.

During a few minutes of unscheduled time, I meander into the tent where the chanting originates. Immediately the Chanting Director seizes the opportunity – meaning me, a student of the illustrious Lee Lozowick – and thrusts the microphone into my hands. I do my best, but within one minute Lee Lozowick himself steps into the tent, wordlessly removes the microphone from my hands, and escorts me out of the tent.

Later that night our group is invited to participate in a formal blessing ceremony, one which has been done for millennia. It proceeds by successively pouring precious and sacred substances over a large stone Shiva Lingam – ghee, colorful kumkum nut powder, milk, honey, sacred water, curd, young coconut water, Vibhuti (holy ash), petals from the specific flowers favored by Shiva, mashed perfectly ripe bananas, sandalwood paste, fragrant oils and perfumes, Bael leaves... you get the idea. Between each bath the attendants wash off the Lingam stone with water, while everyone chants unceasingly.

As soon as our group arrives at the ritual tent, the head priest invites Lee to have his students take turns pouring the sacred substances around the Shiva Lingam. This is an immense honor and indicates the level of respect showered upon Yogi Ramsuratkumar's Western devotee: Lee Lozowick. I watch as Lee invites every other man but me to do the pouring. Finally, with visible hesitation, Lee indicates that I should step forward. I hold the jar carefully in both hands so it does not slip. I focus my attention in the best 'spiritual student' style, then begin pouring... and immediately Lee shouts, "No! The other way around!" I am destroying the ceremony by pouring counter-clockwise, when right before my eyes for the past hour everyone else has poured clockwise! I still cannot believe I was sleeping to that degree, but this is exactly what happened. To me it is a story of what the Guru must endure by accepting new students, and also that, no matter how smart a student considers himself to be, he may need to learn everything the long hard slow way.

The next day we view the as-yet uninstalled bigger-than-life-size stone statue of Yogi Ramsuratkumar. Then our hosts stuff seven of us large American men into an old army Jeep, along with one driver, and a skinny young man standing precariously on the Jeep's rear bumper, ceaselessly nagging us to chant "Yogi Ramsuratkumar!" with him. For fifteen hours we rumble along bone-crunching pock-marked roads northwest. Lee rides with two of the men in a car in front of us. We arrive at Papa Ram Dass' AnandAshram and listen to tales of how Papa Ram Dass gave Yogi Ramsuratkumar the final push into sainthood, but our visit with our own Guru's teacher awaits us, and our hearts are already there. Only the final three days of our month-long journey will be in Tiruvannamalai, sleeping at Ramana Maharshi's RamanAshram.

Early morning after a twelve-hour all-night bus ride due east from AnandAshram, we bounce roughly into the dusty dirt parking lot of the Tiruvannamalai bus station. Each of us is tired, stinking, thirsty, and hungry. Every muscle aches from the ceaselessly bumpy, 'Cramped' ride. Lee hops out the bus door as soon as it opens and takes off fast like a hunting dog on a scent, not saying a word to us, and not glancing left or right at the myriads of exotic and/or repulsive distractions found in every shadow of every Indian town.

We straggle along after Him, complaining in our gesture. Lee beelines to a small street near the copper-kettle hammering-works beside the gargantuan Tiruvannamalai Shiva temple. Without explanation Lee shuffles all of us onto a broad stone stairway and indicates that we should squat down and hide behind the railing. He tells us to be quiet and not to move until He comes to get us.

We know nothing of Lee's one-time rejection several years earlier by Yogi Ramsuratkumar at the green Sannadhi Street house that is located directly across from the steps. Lee is still shy and cautious, hesitant to make any intruding assumptions, trying to arrange not to be an embarrassment should this rejection happen again.

I cannot resist. I slide one eye above the railing and watch surreptitiously as Lee scuffles between onlookers across the narrow street to Yogi Ramsuratkumar's door in the shadows of the building. In a few minutes the door opens. I gain a brief glimpse of Yogi Ramsuratkumar quickly blessing the small crowd of onlookers, then Lee is let in and vanishes. Yogi Ramsuratkumar does not see us.

We wait there motionless in the hot morning Indian sun for an hour. Finally, an attendant peers out of the door and waves us over to come in. The grillwork outside Yogi Ramsuratkumar's front porch where we sit in a tight circle is engulfed with bunches of dried flower malas, tied one upon the other, keeping the porch cool and dark. It is a short visit. Plans are made to meet at Ganeshan's House the next morning. We depart. Lee is happy.

At the meeting, we men are invited to sit in a semicircle on hard bare concrete while Lee and Yogi Ramsuratkumar sit across from us chatting. Lee's stern instructions are clear. We are to remain absolutely still and silent. Ask no questions. Let Yogi Ramsuratkumar have complete control over how the conversation goes. Any questions from us would only distract Yogi Ramsuratkumar from His work.

Due to a lack of stoicism – or lack of calluses – each man squirms this way and that into new positions every few minutes, rotating his buttcheeks trying to avoid moaning in pain, while Lee and Yogi Ramsuratkumar sit blissfully still, holding hands, oblivious of any discomfort.

Yogi Ramsuratkumar forces Lee to sit on his right, thus taking Lee's left hand in his right hand. The etiquette of never giving Lee his culturally 'dirty' left hand forces Lee to take the position of superior status. By arranging such status-lowering for Himself, Yogi Ramsuratkumar is actually taking prerogative of the higher status. Lee acquiesces simply because it is his Father's Will.

Lee keeps trying to form Mudra configurations with his fingers to augment his openness and acceptance of Yogi Ramsuratkumar's blessings. Yogi Ramsuratkumar keeps slapping Lee's hands apart, as a teaching lesson to stop with the nonsense and just be present with him. Throughout the two days Yogi Ramsuratkumar repeatedly slaps Lee hard on his thighs, his shoulders and on his back. We have heard that this is how the teaching enters the body. It looks painful but Lee never once winces or makes facial reactions. He lets Yogi Ramsuratkumar reorganize his energetic body as needed.

In the course of the morning, Yogi Ramsuratkumar asks seemingly nonsense questions as if they are of the greatest importance and seriousness. He asks some of the men about the crows. "Do you have crows in America? Oh, really? Are your crows like these crows? Oh? Do they have the brownish feathers on their heads like these? What kind of crows do you have?" We can tell that He has asked these same questions of previous American visitors a thousand times. We can tell that He already knows the answers. But He asks these same questions over and over again, as if He just thought them up fresh for us, as if we had not just told him the answers He wanted a minute before. Something else is clearly going on besides these questions, but what is it?

Yogi Ramsuratkumar's idiosyncratic physical manifestations are repetitive and predictable, meaningless and totally effective in some functional energetic way. He sits cross-legged in his rags. When asked about how often He changes his clothes or bathes, He says that He would like to do so more often, but that He just does not have time for such things. This beggar with no job or business, no watch or time schedule, and nothing particular to do all day, does not have time to wash himself or to change his clothes. Yogi Ramsuratkumar's smoke-yellowed bushy eyebrows bounce up of their own accord as his mouth partly opens and closes. Like a fish out of water He makes a short quick inhale, mustache and gray-white beard flopping. He jerks his head to the right, eyes looking up, then jerks left and looks up that direction. He gets out a cigarette. After a while He digs out a tiny paper match from the matchbox. He is ready to strike the match, but stops, as if to say something to someone, but then does not say anything in words. He prepares his fingers to strike the match again, and hesitates again. Our attention is riveted on the whole process as if thinking, "Why can't He just light the damn cigarette and get it over with?" While our attention and ego are confused and distracted, something nonlinear is happening. We have no conception of what it might be.

Finally, the cigarette is lit. Yogi Ramsuratkumar carefully places the cigarette in the crook between his left thumb and pointer finger, then cups both of his hands together up to his mouth. It is a makeshift hand-made water pipe without the water. He inhales a short breath, eyebrows flying, head twitching, now and then his arms flying up, still clasping the cigarette between them. Sometimes the cigarette dies out because it is not smoked enough and Yogi Ramsuratkumar starts the cigarette-lighting procedure all over again. When the cigarette is burned to a stub, the next cigarette creeps out of its pack into his fingers. Match after match, cigarette after cigarette, pack after pack, day after day, Yogi Ramsuratkumar does his Work.

Chai is poured by Yogi Ramsuratkumar's devoted attendants. They are an example of impeccable invisible service. Yogi Ramsuratkumar refuses a porcelain tea cup like the rest of us are given, and drinks out of his coconut bowl. He uses the same bowl for curried vegetables at lunch.

After lunch, Yogi Ramsuratkumar begins chanting. He makes no excuse, gives no reason. It is the 'Shri Rama, Jaya Rama, Jaya Jaya Rama' chant in three-step waltz time, the sweetest most innocent and deeply-longing chant the Universe could ever sing. We chant along with him. It is an honor never to be forgotten, so simple, so immeasurably profound. He stops after a few minutes.

Yogi Ramsuratkumar tells us He will sleep now. He leans over to his right, towards where Lee is sitting, puts his head on his bent arm, closes his eyes, and within minutes is breathing deeply. The other men feeling the heat of the afternoon ask if they can nap too. Lee says yes. I silently refuse. There is too precious much going on to sleep. I choose to stay 'on guard'. In a few moments when all are settled down, Lee quietly stands up and walks to the other side of Yogi Ramsuratkumar, where the souls of His feet are now exposed. Lee sits down snuggled up close to his Father's bare feet and opens the palms of his hands as if to expose himself to the maximum possible radiation from the soul of this Saint, the Godchild of Tiruvannamalai. Thirty minutes go by. Lee sits attentive and motionless. As soon as Yogi Ramsuratkumar begins to awaken and stir, Lee pranams briefly, stands silently up, steps over to his original position on the concrete at his Father's right side. Yogi Ramsuratkumar sits up and arranges himself, completely ignoring anything that Lee might have done during his nap. There is an immense trust of Lee by Yogi Ramsuratkumar, born of their visible communion and common purpose. Soon the other men awaken and the voyage continues.

Lee brings up the question of obtaining Yogi Ramsuratkumar's permission to write a book about Yogi Ramsuratkumar's life. Yogi Ramsuratkumar is adamantly opposed. He has read other books of Saints and has been disappointed. When the book is about the life of the Saint, the book invariably reveals tainted parts of the Saint's life, casting shadows upon his brilliance and tarnishing his presence for the readers. Yogi Ramsuratkumar realizes that a Saint has a responsibility to the people, to offer them an alternative, an example of what is possible in a life moved by God. The dark side of the stories is too high a price to pay... not what it would cost Yogi Ramsuratkumar, but what it would cost His devotees to have to transcend their own disillusionment.

I am shocked by this conversation, not because it is controversial, not because it has consequences, but because even with Lee's clear injunction about not speaking out even one word or even hinting at asking a personal question while in the company of Yogi Ramsuratkumar, it is clear that I have a line to speak in the ongoing script.

I deny the invitation and remain silent.

For a second time the conversation between Lee and Yogi Ramsuratkumar comes back around to the book-writing consideration. The moment comes for me to speak my line. I again resist. My mind kills the possibility of trusting this unexpected and disobedient impulse. Speaking out is too big of a breach of the strict protocol in this space, too radically disobeying my Guru's instructions. The moment again passes.

Unbelievably the book writing-question comes around a third time! By now the line is burned into my mind like a hot tattoo and I finally speak it at the required moment. "Don't you think it would be valuable for people to realize that out of the mud grows a lotus flower?" Yogi Ramsuratkumar looks into Lee's eyes with childish delight and surprise on his face. He says to Lee, "Did you hear what he called me?"

Permission is granted to write the book.

Then without preamble Yogi Ramsuratkumar asks Lee, "Do you have a prayer?" Lee looks to the men and signals to Mathew to come forward. Matthew kneels down close before Yogi Ramsuratkumar and begins to recite the 'meal prayer' that Lee has given his students to use. Yogi Ramsuratkumar listens intently. Some of the words are unexpected. When Matthew gets to the phrase 'let us be annihilated in love', Yogi Ramsuratkumar says, "What?" asking Matthew to repeat the phrase over several times until Yogi Ramsuratkumar discerns every possible aspect of the meaning. Then Yogi Ramsuratkumar tells Matthew to repeat the whole prayer again, so Yogi Ramsuratkumar can experience its full impact. The moment Matthew gets to the phrase, 'All this is yours', Yogi Ramsuratkumar interrupts him excitedly and blurts out, "See! See! I told you I was right! It says right there in the prayer, all this is my Father's blessing! Everything is Father's! All is Father's blessing!" He is ecstatic. We laugh to think that Yogi Ramsuratkumar would have any need of confirmation from some American's prayer. He laughs delighted because His incessant declaration that 'All is Father' has finally been authenticated. We laugh too. It is a good joke. Yogi Ramsuratkumar's eyes delightedly dance and sparkle like shiny diamonds in clear spring water.

[These next two paragraphs are printed on pages 43-44 Tawagoto Vol. 5 No. 2 Spring 1992.]

Yogi Ramsuratkumar closes his eyes, gets a smile of pure happiness on his face, and leans his head joyfully onto Lee's shoulder, moving affectionately closer to him. Every now and then He raises his head to glance up at Lee's face, as if to remember his features forever. "Our friends are leaving for America at five a.m. tomorrow morning," the Yogi says to nobody in particular. "We don't know when we will see them again."

These two men who, in some ways, are so close, only get to visit together for these few short hours. The poignancy of temporary life in the body becomes apparent in the face of love. There they are, the two of them. Just for an instant, Lee abandons his usual stoic self, and rests his left cheek on top of the Yogi's head, returning the affection in a timeless moment. Suddenly He snaps his head upright, chuckles at himself with an embarrassed smile, and recovers his composure. It's just a little too much for him to make love while twelve people look on. But it's too late – we have seen, and we rejoice.

I arrange not to return to Arizona immediately with Lee, and instead take a two-week layover in Hong Kong to try to set up distributors for Tonic Gold, the elixir made by Lee's friend, the alchemist Petri Murian in India. I have been using Tonic Gold for a while and notice beneficial coincidences beyond all measure of probability falling into place in my life. I love the stuff. I keep deepening my understanding of how it works in calls with Tom Lennon, a student of Lee's in Boulder, Colorado, who went to meet Petri with Lee the year before.

I buy a Hong Kong 'burner' phone and rent a tiny flat, barely room for a bed. The shared bathroom is down the hall. I get access to a phone directory and make appointments all over Hong Kong and Kowloon with businessmen and businesswomen. They run seminar centers and health product distributorships, perfect places for selling Tonic Gold. All of them are respectful and kind to me, enthusiastic about their products and services, curious about my offer, and professional in their negotiations with me. Every one of them says, "No thank you." I wear out a pair of shoes pounding the Hong Kong pavement to no avail.

Rewind the story a few weeks. Almost from day one of my time trekking around southern India with Lee and the men I find myself spontaneously picking up and hand-washing scraps of cloth here and there. I sew up a sewing kit for myself (which I still have to this day). Two things are gnawing at me. One is the Sufi tradition – now part of the Western Baul tradition – of spiritual students having a personal handicraft they can turn to – and usefully occupy themselves with – during those times when the bottom falls out from under reality and all they can encounter is the raving groundlessness of the Bardos. The second thing is the Baul's tradition of hand-sewing their own patchwork robes by cutting up discarded Hindu and Moslem garments. Sewing the fabrics together is their way of transcending religious dogmas and unifying souls.

After a few days of seeing me bowed over my handiwork, Lee says, "Your shirt is looking good." I say, "It is not my shirt. It is your shirt." Lee says nothing. Later I get to ask Lee for some details about what He would like sewed onto His shirt. He specifies two things. On the front he wants Yogi Ramsuratkumar's right hand placed over his heart. On the back, two serpents, one going up, the other going down, eating each other's tails, to represent the Baul breath practice of circulating prana energy up and down the spine. On the India journey I get Lee's Baul shirt well-started.

Back in Hong Kong, my hopeful but naïve money-making plans disintegrate. A level of despair I have never before encountered settles over my being. No one knows where I am or what is going on for me. I sit on the bed in my three-by-three-meter flat with nothing to do but go crazy worrying about what I will do when I return to Arizona empty handed. I am not a hero anymore. The whole hero thing has been fake. I am totally lonely, totally lost in despair and hopelessness. By reflex, I pull out my sewing kit and sew the next part of Lee's shirt. Thousands of stitches, all day, most of the night. It saves my life.

The day before my flight home I have one last appointment. This one is at *Reflections Resource Center* with its founder, a stout Sekhem healer woman who stands as tall as my sternum, named Ruby T. Ong. She gives me the once-over look, then takes a case of Tonic Gold – on consignment – meaning she pays me if and when the Tonic Gold sells. (Many years later I return to Hong Kong with the Gaian Road Team to interview Ruby. Sure enough, as promised, when I arrive she hands me an envelope full of greasy Hong Kong dollars. All the bottles had sold!)

Then Ruby says, "You have to meet with Keith Varnum. Make an appointment with him for tomorrow morning." I say, "My plane leaves tomorrow. Who is Keith Varnum?" She says, "He is a psychic reader from Phoenix, Arizona." I say, "Yes, well… I am from Phoenix, Arizona. Why should I meet with him here?" She says, "Because you are both here together. It is not an accident! It only costs two-hundred and eighty Hong Kong Dollars in cash." I say, "I already arranged to have no Hong Kong Dollars in my wallet!" She says, "You have to make an appointment with him and pay in cash."

There is no arguing with Ruby T. Ong from Hong Kong. I spend the next morning raiding cash machines and my credit cards and return to Ruby's office on time. She says, "He is in there, waiting for you."

I step into the back room. A thin friendly-looking Western man indicates I should sit in the folding chair across from him. As I settle myself in, he starts laughing out loud.

I stare at him for a while, and then say, "What's so funny?" He says, "Well, I have been doing these readings for years. Each time when someone sits across from me like you are, someone on the other side appears to talk with them: Saint Germain, the Virgin Mary, Jesus, Krishna, Ram, Madame Blavatsky, Gautama Buddha, Maitreya, Confucius, Kwan Yin… someone. I am laughing now because you come in here and sit down, and they ALL want to talk with you! Who are you? And what is your question?"

I am stunned. I don't know who I am. I don't know what to ask. Finally the spirit guides just start talking to me on their own volition. Keith translates. "They say that the trainings you are doing…" I instantly interrupt him and say, "Wait! How do they know I am delivering trainings?" Keith just laughs, then keeps talking. "They say the trainings you are doing, you need to keep doing them. They are important. And this Tonic Gold you are distributing…" I interrupt again. "How do they know about Tonic Gold?" Keith laughs out loud again, then continues. "They say the Tonic Gold you are distributing has the same effect as the trainings you are delivering. It is liquid truth, sunshine in a bottle. It builds matrix to hold more consciousness. It is a living and awakened elixir, providing exactly what the user needs to integrate what they learn and take their next steps."

That is when I discover a real question. I demand, "If Tonic Gold is so obviously wonderful, why didn't anyone order any from me? Why has my trip been such a failure?" Keith laughs so hard he can barely sit in his chair. For a while he cannot stop. With tears in his eyes he finally says, "I am laughing so hard because all of them over there are laughing so hard! I've never seen this before."

After a while he continues. "They say you should just keep going. It will all work out. You are doing fine. You have your teacher and all of us behind you. Just keep going. You are doing fine." End of conversation.

I shake my head, wondering, How can things look so bad and be so good? I put my two-hundred and eighty Hong Kong Dollars (about $35 US) into Keith Varnum's hand, and fly home. Many years later I meet with Keith in Phoenix, Arizona, and interview him for the Gaian Road Team.

Back in Prescott, life is not easy for me. I have little money and it seems like I must invent each step along the way out of nothing. Time goes by.

Three months later I bow before Lee Lozowick in the Darshan Hall at the Ashram. As I sit up, Lee looks into my eyes and says, "Where's my shirt. I want my shirt."

I sew furiously on the shirt, barely getting it finished so I can hand it to Lee by Darshan of *All Fool's Day Celebration*, Sunday, 5 April 1992.

Lee takes the shirt into his hands and holds it up to see the details. He smiles. I sigh. Things seem to fall into their new proper places.

4. 1992: Yes

The most precious thing I possess is knowing the answer's "Yes!"
  - Mike Oldfield, lyrics from 'See the Light' on his *Earth Moving* album

8 December 1992 – A writing challenge from the Guru

Surrender your life to God. How am I supposed to understand this? What does this mean? The only hint I have is that my life has not turned out the way I imagined it would. There are so many things I am not. For example, I am not the lottery winner, setting up secret foundations that shape the cultural evolution of the human species for centuries to come. I am not the famous eccentric inventor, living with three wives in a secluded Earthship house built on orchard-studded country acres. I am not the friend and guest of flying-saucer-piloting aliens who consult with me on terraforming the local planets and take me to visit their families, waking up in the morning to the light of a different star. I am not the Samurai computer-hacker masterminding the revolution that transforms North America from a sleeping, corporation-controlled consumption machine to a sane-and-conscious ecologically-regenerative experiment in Humanity.

I am just this guy in a forty-year-old male body that creaks and aches in places I never thought existed. I wake up in the morning, pick my nose, take a pee, eat my bowl of oatmeal, brush my teeth, kiss my wife and kids, and go to work, just like everybody else.

Yet there is something else in my life also going on. And this little 'something else' is far more surprising and mysterious, far more magical and powerful, far more awesome and exciting than all of the above life-fantasies combined. It has appeared as a direct result of personally investigating John Lennon's little hint: "Life is what happens while you're busy making other plans." If the creation of my future is not in my control, then where is my life coming from?

To such a question I have no answer. What I do have is the intimate companionship of others who ask similar questions. Glorious and magnificent in all its simplicity, I am part of the Hohm Sahaj Mandir Sangha. I am a devotee of the Satguru.

I must have been ready because the Teacher appeared. And what this means in terms of 'my' life, 'my' future, 'my' evolution, is that I have been relieved of a tremendous though fictitious burden. I no longer must 'make something of myself'. All of that is in the Spiritual Master's hands now: it's His Job. My one responsibility in this situation is to show up as yes while relating to the Spiritual Master. Being a yes in action is neither as easy, nor as comfortable as it may sound. It means surrendering my life to God. It means acknowledging the actuality of my Spiritual Slavery. Yikes!

Once I read a book containing a collection of what the author regarded as the most Earth-shaking decisions ever made in the history of the human race. The part I remember most is the criteria by which the historian chose which decisions to include in his anthology. He declared that decisions in the negative – decisions that prevented changes or stopped things from happening, were uninteresting and unimportant. He said it is decisions in the affirmative which shape the future and make history, create possibility, and form the navigational landmarks in the evolution of human consciousness, both individually and as groups.

The fact that Lee Lozowick is having us consider yes as a practice at this time is not insignificant. His invitation may feel shocking… threatening even. If you could really know the full implication of what a deep and consistent practice of yes would do to your life, it would be terrifying. No exceptions.

(There is still time. You could stop reading right now, drop the magazine, and run like hell… This is a WARNING. *Proceed from here at your own risk. Who told you to listen to that voice anyway?)*

The Work is now requiring an upscale of practice from us as Hohm Community Sangha. Lee Lozowick has been telling us about it in excruciating detail, over and over again in Darshan and After Dinner Talks – every chance He gets. He is not fooling. His Work needs a few good Beings. The elite corps of Tantric Angel Janitor Slaves is heading into the front lines. For you to continue on in the company of the Spiritual Master, you are required to face your deepest, slyest, most horrific and gut-wrenching fears… and practice Yes.

Yes – as a position and an attitude – is the most foundational and profound of our Baul practices because it precedes all the others. Before you can meditate or study or exercise or stay on the diet, you must first be Yes to practice itself.

Until now you may have been thinking of practice as a process of saying no. Being no is not practice because it provides no way for the effects of practice to influence you (although it's better than nothing). You may have had such conversations as these in your own head: "No, I can't sleep late this morning; I must meditate and exercise. No, I can't go to the movies today; I must study. No, I can't eat chocolates and drink coke or coffee; they're not on the diet. No, I can't flirt with that woman or man; I'm supposed to be in a monogamous relationship." By trying to practice as a no (or even as a maybe) you demolish the ways in which practice could serve and feed you.

No is the voice of your psychological defense strategy, your 'Cramp'. Just consider all of the times you tell yourself no during the day. "No, I can't think this way or feel this way or act this way…" "No, this is wrong. This is bad. This is stupid."

Actually, being no is impossible for you to do, because in order to describe what you are saying no to, you would first need to recognize that in a particular situation there is, in fact, a possibility of saying something other than no. But the reason you say no is because you do not see the possibility of choosing anything other than no.

The problem is that the big-picture circumstances in which you say no are invisible to you. The typical assessment goes: "This is just the way things are. This is just how I am." The Cramp defends itself by convincing you that your only possible choice in the situation is no. "This is how it is and I can't do anything other than what I have to do." The survival-strategy denial-prison of the Cramp is built with bars made of no. You may think that the bars are there to protect you, to keep you from dying or being killed or punished or abandoned. It may seem obvious that death waits to pounce on you just beyond those bars.

And at one point in your life, that was possibly true. When you were a young child in the care of your parents, it was necessary to keep your hands off the wheel and leave the driving to them. The authority figures in your life painted a certain picture of reality for you, and if at first you didn't see it that way, then you soon figured out that your survival depended on learning to see it that way. Punishments and rewards forced you to drop all contrary experience and information. You developed a set of rules for yourself that allowed you to mesh with your caretakers enough that they would care for you. You developed your mask. You practiced your show. You manufactured your personality – the backbone of which is your Cramp. And you did survive.

However, you are not a little child anymore. Mommy and Daddy are not going to take care of you anymore. The situation is different now. In fact, a complete context-shift awaits you: to move out of survival entirely. The life of a spiritual student is not oriented towards surviving. It is oriented towards living.

Lee Lozowick is asking you to grow up.

The shift in lifestyle you are being asked to make is the same as the difference between a photographer and a painter. A photographer begins with whatever is present in their immediate environment and, using the camera's lens and the angle of the shot, eliminates from the viewfinder (says no to) everything that is not desired for the final effect. The photograph is limited to what is available out there.

The painter begins with a blank white canvas. On this 'empty' screen they create every detail. There is nothing until the painter puts it there, so there is no limit to what can be invented.

The foundation of photography is scarcity.

The foundation of painting is abundance.

You are being asked to shift your *Point of Origin* from being a Photographer: limited to choosing from what already exists, to being a Painter: choosing to create from the infinity of nothingness whatever is wanted and needed.

This shift in paradigm from no to yes is the Secret. And as with all Real Secrets, even though it will be spelled out to you right here in the greatest detail, in the simplest and clearest way possible, it will completely pass you by unless have previously built a matrix of experiential distinctions within your Being that has fine-enough detectors to catch and hold the Secret. A Real Secret cannot help but keep itself hidden, inaccessibly away from anyone who has not yet fashioned a Golden Key to release its powers in practical applications in their daily life.

Here is how big of a Secret this is: God said yes and there was Creation.

By its very nature, Creation is saying yes to you all of the time. When you stand in yes, you are synchronized with the Universe. When you are a yes and a job slides down the tube and lands on your bench, you have enough radical trust in the job – originating in radical clarity about the mechanics of Evolutionary Work – that you just do the job. (*We know you can get the job! But can you do the job?*) Not later. Not in just a minute. You do it right now, in a minimized NOW. The dishes need doing. The bill needs to be paid. The gate needs to be shut. A sign needs to be repainted. A recording needs to be transcribed. The vegetables need to be picked and stored...

Just This.

And in the irrefutable presence of Just This, your Cramp shrieks, "But I have other plans! I'm always stuck on childcare! I'm always stuck answering the phones! I'm always stuck cleaning glass cases! Why can't it be someone else?" That is how you be a <u>no</u>.

One transformational realization that integrates the procedure of being a <u>yes</u> is that if you seem to be stuck cooking, there is someone else stuck going to the movies with the Guru. And if you are stuck going to the movies with the Guru, there is someone else stuck serving food to the children. And if you are stuck serving food to the children, there is someone else stuck bookkeeping, or running errands, or typing on the computer, or fixing a leaky faucet, or pulling weeds... on and on and on. The most effective way of being <u>yes</u> is to do what's in front of you. No one can stop you from consciously engaging the invaluable alchemical-transformation-space that the entire Universe plus E.C.C.O. (Earth Coincidence Control Office) has custom-designed and dropped you into, for your own benefit. No one can stop you from giving your life permission to come out as it may in the Guru's hands. Neither can anyone else do it for you.

<u>Yes</u> means that wherever you look, you see the Face of God placing its countenance upon you, and you glory in that.

Serving in this way, doing the Work, and getting it moved on by letting the Work do its Work upon you, provides space for the next Work opportunity to show up on your bench.

A job will stay on your bench until you do the Work. It is the Law.

The Cramp must always be a <u>no</u> to nonlinear influences as a way of keeping things the same where the Cramp feels it can assure your survival. If your Cramp is not in control, it is afraid it will die, sure that if it dies, you will die.

By being <u>yes</u>, you make yourself available to the forces of Evolution (such as Lee Lozowick). You open yourself completely up to voyages in the Domain of Possibility. This is definitely a risk that the Cramp – by its nature and mission – would wish to avert. Your Cramp screams on-and-on directly into your nerves: "What if you fail? What if you make a fool of yourself? You cannot know what will happen next!"

Well, yay! It cannot be predicted! Instead, you get to explore through careful experimentation and clear observation. You get to test whether it is true or not that by practicing <u>yes</u> you are taken care of by Coincidence – even if 'being taken care of' includes being Evolved. Through being <u>yes</u> you get Evolved whenever it is necessary to That Which Puts Jobs On Your Bench and Needs the Work Done.

Lee Lozowick says that if you are <u>yes</u> to whatever He asks of you, you will be able to do it, even if you have never done it before, although you may need to show up in a different way in order to do it.

And to be clear: "<u>Yes</u>" is not "<u>Yup</u>," or "<u>Sure</u>." <u>Yes</u> is unreasonably committed, powerful, elegant, impeccable, and adult. In comparison, being a <u>yup</u> is being <u>no</u> in disguise. <u>Yup</u> is a childish, muddled bitterness, sourced by an unconscious, "You can't make me!"

The entire Universe is <u>yes</u>. It is only humans who come up with assumptions, reasons, stories, unfulfilled expectations, and conclusions that trigger their own 'no'.

It is also possible that you take a 'no' stand because of your unworthiness issues. Deep down inside, you may have a firm conviction that you are not loved, that you are not loveable, that you do not deserve to be in direct ongoing ecstatic relating with the radiant Divine. Here is where intelligent, persistent inner work shines.

Patrick Bellott, a student of Arnaud Desjardins, shares: "There are two stages of the path which Arnaud shows us: first, to build a strong ego through lovingly healing our own wounds and fragilities, yet being firm towards ego's lies. The nurtured, recognized, respected ego eventually relaxes and blossoms like a well-cared-for tree bearing fruit. At the same time, we confront the craziness of the mind with its negativity, criticism, superiority, and stories of separation. Otherwise we remain captured in the mind's insane little world of never-ending comparisons, accusations, judgements, and resentments. The possibility of both nurturing the ego and disempowering the mind emerges from developing a simple, clear, and resilient inner structure. Before Arnaud met his own teacher (Swami Prajnanpad), he met many other teachers. One amongst them said, 'What you need is to build a strong inner structure.' When Arnaud came to Swamiji, Swami told him, 'You are an amorphous crowd.' A person with a well-formed inner structure can be counted upon to walk the path, has the discipline to make real efforts, can keep promises, can proceed without breaking down over little things. A weak inner structure is like a house-of-cards that collapses under the least bit of transformational stress. Arnaud makes a very important distinction between 'ego' and 'mind'. The second stage is ego unfolding to become more-and-more open and comprehensive, so it ends up vanishing through merging with the universe, while the mind gradually fades into background noise. Then there is <u>no</u> more separation."

Being <u>yes</u> is central to both stages.

In addition to <u>yes</u> being profound, <u>yes</u> is also practical. For example, <u>yes</u> is the primary practice to use with people from the sleeping world. E.J. Gold demonstrated this to me in a way that I will never forget. It was a very special Easter weekend. Brenda and I had been invited to E.J.'s place in Grass Valley for a meal and a talk. I had never been there before, never spoken directly with E.J., and had never spent time in his intimate company. Just as E.J.'s students welcome us into the big house, E.J. needs to exit through the same front door. Because of the physical layout of the furniture, E.J. is forced to squeeze by me between the back of the couch and the wall. Looking directly into E.J.'s eyes in that moment of great intimacy, I cannot keep from mechanically blurting out the most important thing on my mind, which is: "*Happy Easter!*" Now, keep it in mind that E.J.'s background is Jewish... and he's decidedly <u>not</u> into the unconscious consumer mechanicality of American holidays. E.J. could have said anything to me. In that moment he could have torn me to shreds. What he does instead is speak just one word. He says, "*Yes.*" He agrees with the primate...

This is what Lee Lozowick means when He explains how He will never defend himself. Instead He simply agrees. By being <u>yes</u> with regards to a sleeper, you provide nothing for the sleeper to argue about, grab onto, butt heads with, or take root in. This is equivalent to a Toreador staying in contact with the charging bull but allowing him to rush harmlessly past to his side, putting his horns through his insubstantial Red Cloth rather than plunging deeply into the Toreador's guts.

<u>Yes</u> is also how to be with children. When a child asks you for something or asks you to do something, the Cramp wants to say <u>no</u>, often simply because it might be an inconvenience. Rather than thinking of reasons why you *cannot* give it to them, why it *cannot* be done, why they *should not* do it, instead figure out ways to help them do what they want to do. By holding a space of <u>yes</u> in which the children can unfold and become, they learn how to do the same for you and others. In <u>yes</u> there is relating, interaction, evolution, and life.

Practicing <u>yes</u> does not mean being naïve. Naivete begets betrayal. Not taking care of yourself makes you easy food for demons. Making the distinction between <u>yes</u> and naivete, and between taking care of yourself and <u>no</u>, requires the *Sword of Enquiry* and the *Shield of Discrimination*.

Integral to the practice of yes is plain and simple common sense. Do not kid yourself by implementing blind boldness, assuming that spontaneous reactivity is yes. Lee Lozowick may offer you indulgences to distract you from the Divine because that is included in his job. He will offer indulgences until you experience the distinction between the indulgence and Him, until you become a yes to Him… until you surrender your life to the 'just this' of God.

In each moment, you choose between invoking your Cramp and indulging in psychological dramas, or invoking Lee Lozowick and indulging in miracles. Early in the morning on July 15th, 1975, Lee Lozowick was given exactly that choice – a split-second opportunity to surrender his life to God, or not. His secret is that He lived in but one answer: YES.

(POSTLOG: I am in the Blue Baul trailer, a quarter mile from the Prescott Ashram. It is 7:30pm Wednesday evening December 8, 1992. I would normally be over at the Athanor office making calls this night to enroll people into the upcoming San Francisco Event training. Instead I am wrapped in a down-filled sleeping-bag in bed, shivering with a fever and a headache, stomach rumbling, aching in every part of my body. My two daughters play with their dolls, draw pictures, eat oranges. Brenda finishes up her second housecleaning job of the day in Prescott. I lie here longing for the painless oblivion of sleep.

The phone rings. It is the sixth time someone tried to call this evening. None have left a message. I groggily repeat myself to the kids, mumbling, "Don't answer it… It's probably some salesman." They obey.

We wait for the message machine to cycle through. We cannot imagine who it could possibly be calling us. This time the caller leaves a message. A clear, resonant and decidedly female voice says: "This is A calling for Clint. We are publishing a special issue of Tawagoto on the general theme of 'Practice'. Lee has given out article titles for writing projects, a kind of Work task. He's given one to you. The title is 'Yes'. He said, 'Clint will understand.' I need a copy in two to three weeks. Let me know if you decide to accept this mission. Goodbye."

I flop back onto the pillow, nodding my head with half-a-grimace and half-a-grin. I would definitely have unleashed a huge belly laugh if it would not have hurt so much. I do not call immediately back. The trap is already sprung. It is a done deal. I mean, Lee Lozowick does have a sense of humor, eh? He asks me to write an article about the practice of 'Yes'? You think I am going to say, "No"?)

5. 1993: 33 Hours With The Spiritual Master

19 February 1993 – A birthday party with Lee Lozowick

It is morning. I am working at Athanor, The Event training office. The phone rings. Becky is not in the office so I grab the phone and shift into my professionally neutral tone of voice: "Good morning, Athanor, LGB Music. How may I help you?"

"How's it going?" this deep, slightly hoarse male voice asks.

You have to realize that at Athanor we receive calls from all over the world, frequently from people we've never spoken to before. I don't assume that I know who I am talking to now. I say, "Great! How's it going for you?"

The response is, "This is your spiritual Master calling." He clearly gets it that I do not recognize the voice of my own spiritual Master.

My eyes get wide. There is one of those indescribable silences, so empty of sound, but so full of mind.

I grin in embarrassment. He does not see, of course. These are the days before video calls, if you can imagine that.

I bow slightly and say, "I am at your feet," every cell in my body expecting the unexpected. Regardless of how prepared I try to be, the thoroughly unexpected arrives.

"They're having a small birthday party for Claudio Naranjo in Berkeley. I'd like you to come along. We would leave at 8:00 a.m. Friday. I haven't invited anyone else."

"Okay," I say with my mouth, while my mind frantically scrabbles to piece something together and figure it out. Irrelevant questions tsunami my mind: Why me? I never spent more time than an accidental moment alone with the spiritual Master. What does this mean? Is this a test? Where will I get the money for the plane ticket? How will I get the time off from work? Is this a test?

On and on and on.

Machinations of the mind notwithstanding, the departure moment arrives, and all of the details have somehow mysteriously worked themselves out without any problems at all. *The Yes thing actually works!*

It's Friday, February 19, 1993, early morning in a cold, overcast, lightly raining Prescott, Arizona. I stand by the new Ashram van in the dirt parking lot waiting with Brenda. Lee strides briskly around the corner of the house, scanning to make sure things are happening as they should. "Is that all you're bringing?" He asks me, referring to the black nylon briefcase dangling from my fingers.

"Yes," I answer.

"Good!" He comments enthusiastically, toting his usual small well-used cotton bag over one shoulder. I feel relieved to somehow be in resonance with Lee regarding his 'travel lightly' practices, sharing his distaste for waiting around at baggage carousels. I didn't even bring a coat – just packed my toothbrush and planned to wear the same clothes tomorrow.

This is an auspicious beginning, I think to myself. Then I realize I just manufactured a conclusion in contradiction to Lee's oft proposed practice of resting in '*No conclusions mind*'. Of course, I immediately start reprimanding myself to pay better attention to avoid making conclusions, and when I notice this, I think, *Ho-boy! This could be a rough ride…*

I kiss Brenda goodbye and crawl way to the back of the van. Two women and a child join us for the ride to Phoenix where we will leave them with relatives. Lee starts the engine at precisely 8:00 a.m. I think *Lee is his word. I am indeed a lucky man.*

The Ashram gate is open. I prepare to jump out and shut the gate after we go through. I am certain Lee notices my move. I am accustomed to gate-shutting Sadhana. For me, keeping the gate closed is a kind of ceremony, a respectful and practical exercise frequently requested by Ashram staff, and Lee himself, helpful for keeping loose horses in and loose strangers out. It is an effective reminding factor for staying awake and paying attention, so simple and easy compared to some practices, yet frequently and inelegantly ignored with incredibly artful justification by Ashram residents and visitors alike. I ALWAYS shut the gate. Lee zooms through the gate, not even slowing down.

I am shocked. Less than one minute into this journey and already I am off balance. My mind machine leaps into gear again: What's the deal?

Was this for my benefit? He did not even look into the rearview mirror to see how I reacted. I could be in for some big surprises!

Lee navigates three minutes out of his way to access the gas station selling fuel for two cents cheaper per gallon than any other in town. I offer to operate the pump. He

accepts.

"How much shall I put in?" I ask.

He pauses for a second, then says "Fifteen dollars."

As I remove the gas cap I think, "I'll put in fifteen dollars to the penny because that's what He asked for."

I pump away, then *CLUNK!* The pump shuts down automatically sensing the back pressure of a full tank. I look at the pump display indicating that I only put in $14 .09. *Oh, no!* I squeeze the lever again. *CLUNK!* $14.47. *CLUNK!* $14 .62. *CLUNK! CLUNK! CLUNK!* I desperately try to top it off. *CLUNK!* The tank refuses to accept even one more drop of gasoline. I surrender to my failure, and squint at the gas pump meter one last time. My entire countenance sobers when I blink my eyes to double-check what I am seeing. The meter shows that I put exactly $15.00 worth of gas into the tank. It is clear that we have entered a different kind of space. But is it an extraordinary space? Or is it the Twilight Zone? I can't tell.

I pay with my own cash and climb back in. We move on down the road. The highway snakes its way out of the high scrub brush plateau into the low green saguaro-studded desert. Dramatic gray storm clouds fly across the wide-open sky. The air is saturated with the uniquely pungent scent of wet mesquite.

Lee wears black slacks and a long-sleeve white shirt, but He drives barefoot. I grin at this barefoot Baul who is my spiritual Master. Polished black shoes rest beside him in case He is forced to put them on, but this does not change the fact that He walks the streets a beggar.

A lively conversation ensues in the front seat. I cannot hear a word due to road noise, but there is laughter and smiling. Every now and then Lee checks his rearview mirror, sometimes holding my glance for a moment. I am definitely included in the space, even if I am not part of the talking.

I am forever grateful for these two hours of driving. I get a big question answered in my silent self-observation. My questions torment me. How do I make the best use of this rare opportunity of being so physically close to Lee Lozowick? How do I absorb the greatest concentration of evolution-inducing radiations? How am I supposed to be? What am I supposed to say? How can I be useful in His presence for so long? I mean, when Lee is not physically near me, I can simply regard Him and rely on Him and praise Him and surrender to Him. But what am I supposed to do while He is standing right next to me all day today and all night and all day tomorrow, and there ain't nobody else around to buffer this intensity or keep Him entertained?

An amazing possibility arrives by way of the warm laughter and bright smiles emanating from the woman sitting in the front seat next to Lee. She shows me the answer. It is so simple. She maximally enjoys Lee's good company.

What a completely obvious secret! Just relax and enjoy Lee's good company. *Just this! I can do that! I can be that!* I think to myself. *I can be a maximum enjoyer of Lee's magnificent company. I sigh and nod my head. This could create a new future!*

We pick up the relatives and drive to a deli in Tempe, Arizona, a wealthy suburb in the flat outlands of Phoenix. Lee expresses little interest in the couple who has joined us. He expresses a LOT of interest in his double-decker roast beef and pastrami sandwich on American rye bread. I feel a vague jealousy, some inner anguish, that hidden in Lee's sandwich-gusto is a life-energy-secret to which I don't have access. I wonder why that is, and what to do about it. Nothing comes.

We leave the in-laws and drive to the airport. Lee parks the van while I get our boarding passes. The timing is tight. I wait by the ticket takers at the jet. A man gets on our plane who has the same physicality and mannerisms as E.J. Gold! I am thrown into a space warp. How contrived is this trip? What if that really is E.J.?

The stewardess announces final boarding. I start to sweat. At last Lee arrives and I follow him through the gangway tunnel.

I usually try to bless a plane as I board, but with Lee in front of me it is obvious that the jet is already blessed. Almost all the seats are taken. Lee finds two spaces one in front of the other and is about to settle for that, but my body doesn't hesitate an instant to impose myself on the men sitting there and ask one of them to move so that Lee and I might sit together. They oblige. Lee seems pleased.

Our plane streaks off into the sky. A stormy desert drops away far below and we head northwest above the clouds.

I ask Lee a couple of questions. He answers matter of factly and without hesitation. I comment that I cannot look upon a crowd of people, such as those sitting around us on the plane, without sensing a tremendous amount of pain in them, without knowing that at least one in three of the women have been sexually abused, for example, and that a good many of the men are molesters, and that all of this suffering is masked by their psychological defense strategy. Lee nods in agreement. I mention Darshan, those moments when we approach Him, how during a single scan Lee recognizes our state. No amount of acting deceives His direct perception, and He responds from what his body tells Him is needed. I comment that my training comes from an intense year of working with Athanor participating in dozens of Event trainings with hundreds of different people. "Where did you get your training?" I ask.

"It's not training," He says. "It's internal self-clarity."

I recall the statement He made at an After Dinner Talk not long ago: "When you stop hiding from yourself, then everything and everybody becomes completely visible to

you."

I tell him that I sometimes feel shakti energy running through my body, but that my tendency is to suppress it and not allow it to manifest in jerky movements or strange sounds or mudras. I ask, "Is there any harm in this?" He says, "A better question to ask would be: Is there any benefit in allowing it to show up?"

This strikes me as a generalizable principle. I mention that I've been having a tingling ache in my left shoulder-blade area, that I've had a deep massage for it and that it hasn't gone away. He tells me I should continue trying physical means to alleviate the pain, but that if it doesn't go away, I should just learn to live with it. He leans his head back to take a nap. I can't help but feel that his accent was on 'LIVE with it', not as a kind of silent suffering tolerance, but as one spices up life.

The jet lands in Oakland. Lee exits immediately. I wait until the last passenger disembarks so I can get to the tail of the plane where a gift that Lee is bringing for Claudio Naranjo was stored during the flight. I imagine one of Claudio 's students meeting us at the airport, but as I walk up the ramp, I see that it is Claudio himself, and Suzie his companion.

Claudio and I shake hands. Claudio does not recognize me from a brief meeting we had at E.J. Gold's some years ago.

We all scrunch into a rusty 1970's vintage green Toyota wagon. Lee and Claudio sit in front trading stories about their latest publication endeavors, while Suzie answers my questions about their travels, the five languages she speaks, and her workshop on relating, while simultaneously giving navigational suggestions to Claudio as he's driving the wet California freeways. This is a foreign country to them.

Lee mentions that he's not sure how he's going to deal with being in a room with so many famous people. He says, "That's why I brought Clint along. He's the gregarious one."

I start laughing.

Suzie immediately asks me why I laugh.

"I'm laughing because I don't think I am gregarious at all! What am I doing here?"

Then Lee laughs. He says, "That's what H. M. always used to say. But whenever we'd get with a group of people, there she'd be in the center of everything, chatting up perfect strangers as if they were family…" just like I was doing now.

We arrive at Claudio's house in Berkeley. I must have driven by the place dozens of times over the years I lived in California, never knowing there was a Wizard living behind those walls.

Claudio shows us to our quarters for the night. It's a separate building from their house, the lower of two studio apartments. The room is cool and damp, and lined on all four walls with totally packed bookshelves. Esoteric artwork, prints, photos, sculptures, paintings and needlework fill every available surface. The room feels like a Work space, and indeed Claudio says he has lived there for a time, that various Tibetan visitors have guested there, and that the room has housed numerous meetings. He leaves us.

Lee and I have time to take a pee and look around a bit. Then Claudio returns and we sit down together to visit. Claudio describes a certain process he has been going through as a question to Lee. In Claudio's demeanor I clearly observe a tremendous respect and regard for Lee Lozowick. By Lee's response, his posture and tone of voice, it is obvious this respect is mutual.

Afterwards we walk over to the front house where Lee and I sit on a couch in their small living room. Half of the room is occupied by a grand piano upon which rests a sculpture of a couple in the midst of lovemaking. A large painting depicts a similar scene, and all remaining wall space is covered with bookshelves up to the ceiling. I can see into a back bedroom, and observe that it too is encircled in completely full bookshelves. Suzie serves us herb tea. Claudio sits across from us in an overstuffed chair. The mood is warm, comfortable and relaxed, yet engaging, not sleepy. It is a space of friendship. Into this space steps Arthur, an old friend of Claudio's who has flown out from back East for the party. He is pleased to meet Lee and, because he reads Tawagoto (our community's tri-annual publication) and one of Lee's books, has much respect for Lee.

Arthur comments that Lee's presence is one of innocence, and politely asks Lee to speak about that if He would. Without hesitating Lee says. "Innocence is pretentiousness completely unmotivated by self-interest."

While on the plane I had told Lee that I didn't know what Lee did when He was on vacation, not 'at Work'. At that time, He just nodded his head. Observing the space we are all sitting in together in Claudio and Suzie's living room, the pleasantness of the interactions I say, "Ah-hah! I found it! This is what you do for play!"

Without time delay Lee knows exactly what I refer to and responds, "No, I did not answer you before. My Work is my play. It's too intense to take seriously. If I was on vacation I would just relax. Except I never go on vacation."

Lee gifts Arthur with a number of books plus liars, gods & beggars cassette tapes to take home with him. Arthur is exuberantly grateful.

Other guests arrive to prepare for the evening, and soon it is time to drive through the rain over to the Berkeley Club where the party is to take place. This is an established, 'old money' building, perhaps built in the 1920's. I could imagine Humphrey Bogart doing a film in the place.

We walk upstairs to a large auditorium in the back. On the stage is a grand piano. Lee and I help Suzie arrange red carnations and greenery on the dozen round tables covered with white linen. Then we wait.

Lee selects a table for us, front and center of the stage. He sits down. He is visibly nervous: feet tapping, fingers drumming the table top, every now and then stretching and sighing deeply. I ask him about it. "I thought that after being on stage with the band and speaking to many thousands of people at conferences and gatherings in America and Europe, being at a friend's birthday party would be a piece of cake."

He says. "In those other circumstances my role is structured. There is definition. Nothing is being asked of me here. It's one-on-one with these people, and it's not a teaching situation. I am out of my element."

I just nod, thinking in amazement, There are so many facets of which I am not aware.

Sylvia from Argentina, one of Claudio's musician friends, puts on a CD of Baul music. I grin. This music, though unknown to most, sets the underlying tone for the entire evening as guests begin to arrive.

Claudio introduces us to the firstcomers. Lee and I shake their hands and engage in small talk. It is easy to get these people to tell us their stories.

Many of Claudio's guests are the original members of Claudio's elite Seekers After Truth (SAT) study groups, and true to their name, have in various ways continued to 'seek after the truth'. Lee comments that Henry Miller would have had a heyday writing about this evening's gathering.

I am tempted to begin enrolling these 'Seekers After Truth' in The Event training, but I keep one eye on Lee and He keeps one eye on me, and at the earliest possible polite moment Lee looks me straight in the face with a knowing glint in his eye and says, "Let's eat!"

Standing next to Lee at the round buffet table Lee indicates the roast beef au jus, barbecued chicken wings, sausage quiche-ettes, and skewered beef strips in pineapple sauce, raises his eyebrows and nods his head smiling at me as if to say, "Let's dig into this stuff!"

So here we are, seated around the most central table in the room: Lee, Sylvia (who sponsored Sanatan Das's Baul Music Tour in northern California), Ivan Laurie (E.J. Gold's Publicist from IDHHB) with Nancy Kristie and Avram Chetron (representing E.J. at the party), Suzie, and me. Claudio is busy doing the bumble-bee guest-of-honor thing going from table to table greeting old friends. And for the entire meal, no one else dares to come near our table. It is as if our circle is invisible to the others, as if we are listening to a different drum. It seems that the others pretend like we do not exist. Yet the energy column pouring into this space from over our table is so palpable I can almost see it shimmering silvery blue. I feel like I am being mildly electrocuted straight through my spine.

There is no denying that Lee is sourcing the table, and through the table, sourcing the energy in Claudio Naranjo's Birthday Party as his gift to Claudio and his friends. But none of this keeps either Lee or myself from going back for third helpings of the roast beef.

The eating is over. Or maybe it just begins. One by one the 'important' guests are being called forward to the microphone to heap accolades on Claudio and his life's accomplishments. Some manage this well. Some only manage to heap accolades upon themselves. Suzie takes the microphone and shifts the entire space with her beginner's mind statement, "I learned from Claudio's demonstration how it is far more important to love than to be loved."

Then Lee is called forward. He glances at me; all traces of nervousness have vanished. He is in complete alignment with the Universe now. He says, "I always thought that great men were arrogant, pretentious and oppressive, because whenever I feel like I am a great man I get arrogant, pretentious and oppressive. Claudio is none of these, obviously indicating that Claudio is a truly great man."

Lee launches into the story of the fly, who, while making love to an elephant, misinterprets and takes credit for the elephant's moan when it is actually caused by a coconut falling on her head.

After Lee returns to our table, Ivan Lourie says, "It's a good thing they don't really know what that means."

The cake is brought out. It is tasty but we each have only one piece. At that point, Kathleen Speeth, author of a book titled *The Gurdjieff Work*, approaches us and introduces herself, but remains standing. She's read something Lee wrote years ago. She wants to be sure that Lee does not think of himself as a teacher of a Gurdjieffian School. She asks if He knows what He is doing. To my astonishment, I suddenly interject. "I should be the one to answer that question. The answer is yes. He knows what He is doing."

She asks if I am an example of Lee's teaching. I say, "Your question should be answering itself right now." She leaves somewhat satisfied, gracing us with an enigmatic smile.

People begin scraping chairs and stacking plates, bidding each other farewell. Overhearing some conversations, I make the story that this party was a success. Lee is certainly pleased. Although I am not sure why He is happy, I am happy too because He is. That is enough.

We make our way back to Claudio's house and bid our hosts goodnight. Lee and I agree upon a time to wake up in the morning and I set my wristwatch alarm. Lee sleeps on a mattress in the corner. I sleep under a tattered wool Brazilian poncho for which I acquire unusual feelings of attachment. I remember no dreams.

When the alarm beeps, we both wordlessly arise, use the toilet, and do our morning practice. I sit while Lee does some kind of Chi Gung movements. Later I kick myself for not asking to practice the wild Chi Gung forms alongside him. I might have looked bad but learned something precious. I had taken the safe way…

After Suzie prepares bagels and scrambled eggs for breakfast, she and Claudio drive us across the bay to the San Francisco airport. We wave them goodbye. It feels good that we will see them again soon at the Arizona Ashram All Fool's Day Celebration in April.

We obtain our boarding passes, find the Phoenix departure gate, and sit down in a waiting space surrounded by women and children. I say, "Well, we've got twenty minutes to wait."

Lee says, "We've got fifty minutes. I didn't want to take any chances about missing the plane, so I said it left earlier than it really does. Do you want to read this Playboy when I'm done?" He pulls a thick glossy magazine out of his shoulder bag and flips to the centerfold.

Sheesh! It's a one-two punch to the solar-plexus! Lee Lozowick, my spiritual Master, has just admitted to lying AND reading Playboys in one breath. I am taken to the floor.

What erupts in me is my automatic good-boy program again. I say, "Oh, no thanks. I think I'll walk back to one of those shops and see if I can find souvenirs for the kids."

I am half-way down the hall before I realize what I have done. Lee just invited me to do something with him. I said no and walked away. Was what Lee invited me to do wrong? No. Was it bad? No. Was it dangerous? No. Was it stupid? No. He merely invited me to do something with him that was beyond the reach of my mechanical nature. Lee offered me a chance to expand my box, to have an experience of life with him outside of my box's restricting beliefs. I said. "No." Inconceivable!

I stop in the hallway, dazed. Fortunately, I know about 'Do-Overs'. I make a military 'about face' move and walk directly back to Lee, announcing, "I've changed my mind about the Playboy."

Lee does not bat an eye. He reaches into his bag and hands me the fat Christmas issue. "Here, you can read this one first." This is what the Guru carries in his shoulder bag? Playboy magazines? I would have bet a million dollars… and lost.

It is a mind-blower. Here I am, sitting IN PUBLIC, in plain view of the other passengers, right in front of mothers and children, this 'good boy' Callahan is checking out the mighty breasts and carefully combed pubic hairs of voluptuous Playboy bunnies in the company of my spiritual Master!

I surreptitiously glance over at Lee. Yep. He is really there. He is doing it. He's studying their little 'autobiographies' about what turns them on, how they like their men, and what their 'hobbies' are.

But I notice something else going on. There is an inner sensation of Lee seeing, feeding, and acknowledging a part of me that I had neither seen, fed, nor acknowledged for a very long time. It is the pre-civilized part, the original nature, with innate original wisdom. It is a fabulous feeling, a miracle, a healing. An old wooden door has been pried open revealing a vast treasure inside, and the key that locks the door has been thrown away. I want to jump up and run through the airport hollering *Eureka*!

Instead we swap Playboy magazines and laugh at the same articles the other has read.

Lee naps on the flight home.

We retrieve the van in the sweltering Phoenix parking lot. I would normally endure the sauna-temperature interior of the van all the way home because 'We Of The Hohm Community Do Not Use Air Conditioning'. Lee qualmlessly turns on the air conditioning full force until we get going and the breeze cools us off. I say nothing out loud. Inside I gaze upon my recently populated graveyard of false assumptions.

On the drive Hohm we swap Silva Mind Control stories, and talk about the magicians we love and are amazed about. (I never get to have a conversation like this with Lee ever again.)

It is late afternoon. Lee says, "I can't wait to get home and eat salad. Boy is that salad going to be good!"

He waits for me while I open and shut the gate. We pull into the Ashram parking lot. He looks at me and says, "Well, it was a very successful trip. I did it in two Playboys. Thanks for the company."

I say, "Thanks for the invitation."

6. 1994: 42 Years Of Foreplay

19 August 1994 – The discovery of Countenance

You got me. I did not think that You ever would. I might even have bet on that. After all, I am forty-two years old. Looking backwards, I can see that all the clues led me step-by-step to this point where my heart gets broken.

I did not think that it would happen like this, gazing. Just gazing, and drinking tea! I did not suspect that in that moment You were reaching for me. In actuality, there probably has never been a moment when You were not reaching for me. All these years You have been waiting, waiting, endlessly patient. Were You confident in the results? I doubt it. I would not have been. But without hesitation You have only waited, never ceasing to reach out for me.

Then unexpectedly, this one time, as I gaze, something slowly burns through the thoughts like the sun can burn through morning fog. It is the realization that You are reaching out to me, that even with all my imperfections, my human frailties, You completely want me and receive me.

The dawning reformulates my consciousness, like what happens when you study chaotic patterns in special posters. If you change the focus of your eyes in the right way, suddenly a three-dimensional picture emerges in plain view. The new image is always inherently there but the viewer must shift to perceive it. Somehow, I shift.

As I come to realize that You are completely open and intentionally inviting me to fully enter Your realm, a bolt of pure terror rips through my body. I am instantly and automatically blocked against that kind of surrender, that kind of intimacy. If I continue, then in a moment I would be closer to You than to my own mind. My eyes want to dart around the room, my mouth wants to chatter, my mind generates a million questions. I know there is something else I should be doing right now. Please let there be something else! Anything but this!

Yet somehow, miraculously, I do not make a sudden knee-jerk move that could 'accidentally' destroy the space. Somehow the mind does not interrupt me with 'interesting' or 'necessary' thoughts to distract my attention forgetfully away from You. Somehow, the five bodies around me have built up barely enough tolerance of the intolerable that I can stick around rather than run away. What is happening now is the result of having 51 percent vote to stay put on this extremely intense spot. Maybe it is only 50.01 percent. Barely there, hanging on by a hair, like a tightrope walker balancing on the line for the first time without a safety net, making it, but verrrrry wiggly.

Then I remember to take a breath, and coach myself, "Relax those knots between your shoulders. There, see? It is not so bad, is it?" I keep trying. I keep paying attention. I try to relax and let the presence of the presence grow. I cannot grasp it, so subtle it is. If I grasp, it vanishes like smoke. If I relax in total alertness without pressure it comes back again. I am thinking, "Just allow. Just notice. Just accept and enjoy. It is not going anywhere. If you stop going anywhere it will stay there with you. Breathe!"

Way back in there, somewhere, the mind is also screaming: "Hey! Stop this shit immediately! Let's get out of here! Are you crazy? We are going to die!!!"

But there is another, deeper part of me that is feasting, gorging itself on this endless supply of indescribably nourishing nectar. And this is the part, right now, that has its fingers guarding the controls.

And You just keep opening more and more, but with sensitivity, only as much as I can handle. You seem so relaxed, so comfortable, as if this were the most common thing in the world, while I am teetering on the edge of insanity.

It seems that without feeling like I deserve it at all, I am somehow being invited back into the Garden. It is the Garden that Archetypal Woman builds within the space held for that purpose by Archetypal Man. This is the Garden that Woman is, the Garden of Eden. Without explanation, without excuse, without warning, the door opens wider and wider. Something in me knows that if I accept the invitation, I will be subsumed in Paradise. You are initiating me into what it means to be ninety percent Woman.

Many forces urge me to be a thief, a vandal, to try to take all the goodies I can, then destroy what is left and run away. That would be possible because You are completely vulnerable. The great Mother is defenseless. But to stay here, to keep from being expelled, I must become a beggar, one who has nothing to offer but gratitude, and who appreciates in full consciousness and awe whatever is given. There is a fine distinction between what it is to be a beggar and what it is to be a thief.

To be permitted to stay I cannot lie, no matter how much face I lose. In fact, I must lose all face, and instead just feel what I am feeling – the truth, all my fears, all my sadness, all my excitement.

In Your embracing smile I see that there are no bad consequences to losing face. It is me you are offering to embrace, not my face.

As I begin to sink into the immense stillness of Your presence, to accept Your invitation to be-with You, I also begin realizing that nothing else could ever feel this good. Nothing else could ever be so satisfying, so nourishing, so healing, so fulfilling.

No kind of physical sensation, not touching the softest skin, not kisses, not orgasms, not swimming in the warm tropical ocean at night, not baking in the sun, not cool sweet mangoes, not homemade chocolate-chip cookies, not the most beautiful magenta-orange sunset or the most incredible movies or the most superb concert. As I relax into it – my body humming like a high voltage transformer – the only thought I have is a kind of attention which is monitoring my Gremlin. There is no way I want to lose my focus and let that monkey-mind take back control by asking fancy questions or cracking wiseacre jokes. No way. I keep calming the Gremlin while he squats muttering to himself at my left side on a very short leash. I keep trying to pay every kind of attention and yet relax.

I notice that I am losing my usual concerns about even basic human needs, like knowing what time it is, or knowing what happens next. I begin to wonder to myself, "Can you imagine resting in this? What if it could be like this forever?"

At the moment, this seems possible. Perhaps I already died and went to heaven? On and on and on it goes. Nothing else is important. Nothing else matters. Nothing else counts. It becomes clear that the whole purpose of human-realm life is to support the miniscule chance that there could be a moment like this. And You have been just waiting, wanting, aching to share this with anyone who will come, offering direct undiluted contact with You since forever! How stupid I am for not surrendering to this before, for not accepting Your offer. How could I have been afraid of being so totally welcomed and held like this?

I am scared to stop. What if this is it, my only chance to drink of You? What if...

And realization hits me like a hand smacking a mosquito. I have been had.

Here I have been given what feels like an endless source of pure ecstasy and after unreservedly jumping in I realize three things:

1.Once I have tasted Paradise, I can never not be hungry for Paradise.

2.I am going to have to stop ecstatically drinking of You like this at some point, and go off to take care of the mundane details of life.

3.I am not in control of whether or not, or how, or when You are ever available to me like this again.

I have been caught, like a monkey with his hand around an apple in a jar. No way will I let go of that apple. No way will the jar let go of me.

Now that I know what I have been looking for, You tell me that it is not permanent, and that the method for gaining access to it again is out of my control?

Well, that sucks.

And… I would not trade it for anything in the world.

And yet, for right now, I cannot stay here any longer. I must break from You. I stand up and walk away. I leave the space. I go about my business. My experience of You unavoidably drifts into the realm of memories.

That jungle of memories. Such a shame. So disrespectful that the most valuable treasure would sink into the same swamp with memories of pain, failure, and ordinary life. What else can I do? You are gone into the past. I am still in the present, and helpless.

Time goes by. Days. I breathe, walk, see, talk. Everyday life creeps in and normal overlays the Extraordinary.

But it does not overlay the Extraordinary all the way. I notice that there is something different now, some fundamental aspect deep within me is forever changed.

There is a place around my heart that aches.

It never ached like this before.

Why does my heart ache like this? Because I never used it before.

So tenderly, so insistently, my heart longs for a return, for another chance. Now that I experientially know what is possible for a human being, I also know what I am missing. I cannot deny this. And since this was a personal experience, neither can anyone dissuade me.

My old view of life has been irreparably shattered, replaced with direct knowledge of a world that is vaster, more alive, filled with a mysteriously wonderful heart-rending longing and awe. The aching remains, the ache of longing for You to visit with me again.

Now that I know what the most important thing is, I want nothing else.

I want to hoard You. I want to command You to return to me immediately, whenever I desire it. And, at the same time, I somehow know that You will never let me possess the key. You will come whenever it pleases You. There is no key.

Now it is my turn to wait. Can't You see? I have been had. I have worked all my life for this. My heart longs for the tiniest assurance that there will be a next time.

Please don't make me wait too long. Please.

I am still waiting...

7. 1995: Being Annihilated in Love

27 January 1995 – An evening of Tea

Piece by piece, a bit at a time, I am being annihilated in love.

I did not know what this meant before. I imagined it would be something that happened all at once – a big flash of sudden re-ordering sometime in the distant future, perhaps when I died – something like that.

But in meditation this morning I realized that is not the way it works. Rather annihilation is piecemeal.

Now that I know this, I can say that it feels more like I am being eaten by termites from the inside out.

What is being eaten are layers of my false self – the parts of me that work desperately to keep me separate and isolated and not in love, that keep me in control and intact.

'Intact' means 'untouched'.

Being annihilated in love is the opposite of being intact. It means being touched – in contact, in connection; touched by everything and everyone.

I have a vivid memory from around 1988. Brenda and I had somehow gotten ourselves invited to visit E.J. Gold's private residence in Northern California for Easter weekend. It was late morning. E.J. had not been around during all of the children's activities. I had just walked out of the front door into the midday Sierra foothills sunlight on my way to work in the vegetable gardens. Over to my right in the gravel driveway, standing in the partial shade of several giant pines is E.J., his back towards me, side by side and arms around the waist with several women senior students, together facing a couple of special visitors.

E.J. and the women are swaying slightly, hugged close together. It seems as if the guests are about to depart, but they can't – not quite yet.

They can't seem to bear to break the mood of the intimate contact they are so obviously sharing with the others.

The sunlight around the group seems to glow or shimmer. They are oblivious of anything going on around them. Deep inside me I feel an ache, a longing, a bodily wish to be a part of that group.

I stop, entranced by the scene, and just then for a precious moment I get to see E.J' s face as he turns to look in someone' s eyes. Here is the man who creates and destroys universes before breakfast, a formidable leader in the crazy wisdom spiritual tradition, an inscrutable teacher and master. I am stunned to witness that he is crying, tears rolling down his cheeks. Such vulnerability is something I never even conceived of as possible for him.

Perhaps they had been up all night together, ignoring the body's demand for sleep in favor of the spirit's desire for communion. And of course, in retrospect, E.J.'s sensitive openness would, of necessity, be highly developed. It is just that never before had I realized how deeply he could be touched.

And then there was one night in our evening gathering almost two years ago when Brenda and I were invited to sit in Lee's circle. It is a weeknight. Perhaps there are six or seven of us. The food served is simple: mint tea, pistachios, and medjool dates – the usual extraordinary fare.

But immediately upon settling cross-legged onto my cushion I sense a significant depth and richness to the space that I had never noticed before.

From time to time I gaze at Lee. He speaks almost nothing during the time He sits with us, but He does not need to speak – wave after wave of palpably rich blessing force permeates the room.

When He looks back at me, I can just barely tolerate the intensity of his receptiveness. We are naked beings sitting together.

It becomes all too clear to me that my psychology is doing everything it can to hide the fact of our nakedness, and Lee's is not. He cannot.

Now I am beginning to know why. Lee Lozowick has been annihilated in love.

And here's a paradox. Perhaps it's actually a Koan. When Lee goes to visit his Father Yogi Ramsuratkumar in India, every time He returns to us, we bodily recognize – impossible as this may be to conceive – that He is even more annihilated in love than He was before He left.

And we don't know how to regard it.

We only know we will have to deal with it somehow.

What a strange request: *"Let us be annihilated in Love."*

And to think of annihilation as a favor...
What is the special value of being annihilated in Love?
Why would anyone wish for such a thing?

8. 1995: What Is It Like To Be The Student Of A Western Baul Crazy Wisdom Master

27 January 1995 – Journal Excerpt at Phoenix International Airport:

It is an After Dinner Talk night. On Tuesday and Thursday evenings when Lee is not traveling, and there is no 'liars, gods & beggars' gig, or some Rinpoche or teacher giving a presentation locally which He wishes to see, Lee invites anyone who will be so responsible as to write their name down on a list inside the cover of a black plastic three-ring binder on a desk in the Hohm, Inc. office to join him for dinner in his own dining room ....

Two days ago, I mentioned to Lee that I noticed my 200-page journal was almost full and I was shocked to see that the dates from beginning to end spanned almost three years. The implication being that there is not enough journaling going on, not enough reporting. He says, "I'm looking forward to reading it."

Next morning I slide my *Decomposition'* book into his pigeonhole mailbox mounted on the greenhouse wall outside the sliding glass doors leading into the Hohm, Inc. office.

On returning home from work that evening there is a message waiting for me on my telephone answering machine. "This is Lee. Call me before 6:00 p.m. Call me even if it's after 6:00. I want to ask you a question."

Well, what could this be, I wonder? It must be something important. Lee almost never calls me. If He wants to talk, He usually just waits and catches me passing through the Ashram office or speaks to me during the occasional check-in chats we have. But this was a request for immediate attention.

I dial the Ashram number at once. When Lee comes on the line, He says, "I've finished reading your journal. Do you want it back? It's useless to me."

Whammo!

I feel the impact of the proclamation in all five bodies. The Master has made a 'call' – He has named it. He has said what it is.

The ramifications begin to whizz through my mind. CLICK CLICK CLICK like a wooden Jacob's Ladder flip-flop toy, the connections tumble down upon each other.

I think about my journal. I have written personal notes in it, some rage letters, condensed excerpts from After Dinner Talks about alchemical laws and transformational principles, practices recommended to me by my friends and colleagues. It is all important stuff to me. "Yes," I say. Lee hangs up the phone.

I think to myself, *I can write!* Almost everything I submit to Lee in writing gets published or used in some fashion. But Lee is very particular about journaling. Over and over again He has stressed to us the importance of this practice. Irina Tweedie's book *Daughter of Fire*, and John Mann' *14 Years With My Teacher* are constantly being held up as examples of what journaling is meant to be. My journal writing is like neither of these. In comparison with those books, what I have written is self-indulgent childishness. It serves only me, rather than serving the big picture. It contains only cryptic personal anecdotes rather than being a guide or a tool to be passed on to the future generations as a record of the life and spiritual work of Lee Khepa Baul, including encouraging stories and ruthless introspective self-honesty for others to consider when setting out on the great Path.

In light of Brenda's and my personal assignment to India as overseers of the construction of Lee's first overseas Ashram [a plan which changed, so that Brenda and Clinton went instead to France, as chronicled in Brenda's article in this issue], impeccable journaling is a crucial element.

Such a fault as inept or incomplete or inelegant or lazy journaling on my part is absolutely intolerable and unforgivable. The message is that there is no acceptable learning curve.

The demand / command (clarify which) is this: Get it. Now. No time for explanations. No time to figure it out. No time for fooling around or error or incompleteness, no justifications. This is it, your wake-up call.

You are lucky to get it. You will almost certainly never get another. Lee does not work that way.

Only the slightest hint or insinuation from Yogi Ramsuratkumar can completely change the direction or quality of Lee's work. Lee does not need it spelled out in big loud terms. Lee is listening. He is Paying Attention, and He is responsive. It is an awesome example to be inspired by.

So, how can I become a reliable journaler? That is the Quest.

From one perspective I spend very little time in the physical company of Lee Lozowick. So, what could I have to write about that would be useful or interesting?

This same voice continues on, murmuring in my head, *"When Lee is not around, nothing is happening..."*

But I know better.

Due to some foolhardy vow I took, some naïve wish I made in a magical Dakini connection space, Lee has been minding more and more of my business.

Oh, I can handle this, I think. It will be great serving the spiritual Master.

Yeah, it's all fine until He says, "Hey! Wake up! This is not acceptable. This is not in alignment with what I need. This does not serve. It is not useful," and then my whole system freaks out and goes into recoil.

New voices shriek in my head: But I am already giving as much as I can! There is nothing left to squeeze out of me! I have to sleep some time! I should be sleeping now on this jet to Vancouver! I got only hours of sleep last night and I have an important presentation to give tomorrow. I haven't seen a movie, or read for longer than sitting on the toilet, or had a positive checking account balance for weeks and weeks! What more could you ask of me? To write? Reliably? Sure.. okay... but how? And, when?

Only after two days of mental-emotional wash-machine churning on these considerations do I remember Lee's general admonition: *Don't take it personally.*

How does a Western Baul crazy wisdom Master work? He does not give my journal back to me. He gives it to my wife to give back to me. And He does not give it directly to her to give back to me, but instead publicly, at the After Dinner Talk, hands it to someone else to give to her so she can give it to me – like some rejected piece of contamination that everybody knows about and must watch out for. *But don't take it personally.*

There He is: Lee Khepa Baul, a living paradox, sitting at the head of the dining table, laughing at us mere mortals struggling with the impossibly enormous task of transcending the trivial, ludicrous, life-quenching effort of finding meaning in an ultimately meaningless situation, instead of just accepting what is, as it is, here and now, without judgment, and living.

We could be laughing with Lee at our panicked investment in the importance of figuring it all out – before it's too late – and living as an expression of integrity and enjoying the good company of the others in the Sangha, as He is – laughing at it all.

So much is communicated and expressed by Lee Lozowick's laugh. It is simultaneously a Benediction and a cat-o-nine-tails. It is an invitation to join him in chuckling at the ultimate folly which is human existence, and a chastisement for over and over again resisting doing so. His laughter is a completely vulnerable gateway into intimate relationship with the Godman who is also at the same time untouchably unwilling (or unable) to even dabble in the relative, fickle world of neurotic human psychology. He is so attractive and so far away. And there He stays at the head of the table, looking at us with those fiery, sparkling blue eyes, just laughing.

9. 1995: Arizona To France

25 September 1995 – Over the pond, into the fire

It has been said that if the Guru sends you to a foreign country, it indicates that you are half enlightened. What they neglect to mention is the eighty-twenty rule: It takes only twenty percent of your energy to accomplish the first eighty percent of a job, but eighty percent of your energy to accomplish the last twenty percent of the job. I was about to learn exactly what this means in practical terms.

In 1994 Lee asks Brenda and I to design and source the summertime Guru Purnima Celebration at the Arizona Ashram. The challenge is unprecedented. We accept. We decide to theme the Celebration around *Arrakis*, the desert planet in Frank Herbert's book Dune, a fat science-fiction novel that is required reading for Lee Lozowick students. Lee even named his Ashram house *Arrakis* to communicate how the degree of discipline required by the *Fremen* tribespeople living on *Arrakis* in the story is also the level of practice for living in his company.

Brenda and I propose a list of activities and environments for the Celebration. Lee accepts them all – except for the idea of holding a ritual where Lee as *Muad' Dib* – the main character in Dune – spits into a bowl of water that we can then all drink from. That one He crosses off the list.

Everyone comes to the celebration in elaborate hand-made costumes. The bustling crowd includes elegant statesmen and queens of the royalty, as well as Fremen wearing 'stillsuits' and carrying 'thumpers' to attract sandworms for crossing the great deserts. We walk in a parade around the entire Ashram. There is an underground alien bar, and the creepy Space Guild navigator who cannot talk or walk but who eats 'spice' that makes him able to bend space as he is pulled around in a wagon, protected by his cadre of punk-gothic guards. The Celebration is a success. Afterwards, one of the senior students whispers a comment to me. "It looks like Lee is training you for something."

For the 1995 summer Celebration, Lee asks me to build a life-size statue of Yogi Ramsuratkumar as the central decoration in a complete Indian village being built on the Ashram tennis court. I scramble together a team, asking for help from anyone willing. On a circular base I build a plywood cube two feet by two feet by two feet, all painted black. With heavy steel wire I shape a large lotus flower around the top of the cube. A team of women cover the wire frame with chicken-wire and paper mâché, then paint the lotus blossom in realistic pinks. Other women use electric tools they never had in their hands before to fabricate a back-board to be covered with flower garlands.

I use a four-by-four wooden post as a 'spine', and steel plumbing pipes to create Yogi Ramsuratkumar's shoulders and arms. His left arm would hold an authentic fan that Lee gives me from India – an actual version of the woven-leaf fire-tender fan Yogi Ramsuratkumar carries around with a coconut bowl which I make from a coconut I buy at Safeway. Yogi Ramsuratkumar's right arm is up in a blessing pose with the palm of his hand facing forwards. Lee gives me several sacred objects to attach inside Yogi Ramsuratkumar's 'body'. I then cover the 'skeleton' with chicken-wire to shape his clothing and hands. I ask Bandhu Scott Dunham, our Sangha glass blower, to make Yogi Ramsuratkumar's brown eyes. But what about the head? This scares me.

I buy a block of sculpture's foam and stare at it in dismay. It is two days before the Celebration is to begin. I am exhausted trying to bring this statue together while I work a job and raise a family. It is actually impossible. I want to cry and stick my head in the sand. Paula, the future wife of Purna, looks up with paper mâché covered hands. She sees me staring hopelessly at the headless statue and the block of foam in front of me. She slowly steps over to my side, looks at what I am looking at, then looks at me and says with certainty, "You can do this." I will never forget her words.

The head miraculously gets carved and painted. The eyes are inserted and a paper mâché beard is applied. His head gets wrapped in a turban of the perfect dark green color. With the fan and coconut bowl in his hand, He is finished.

At five the next morning Jim Capellini arrives with his little pickup truck. We carefully load Yogi Ramsuratkumar into the flatbed and drive him across the stream and through the Ashram gate to the tennis court. No one is yet awake. We secretly carry our statue into position and cover him with white sheets until the ceremony.

I miss the unveiling because I am shopping for every coconut in town to make coconut bowls to sell during the Indian village that morning. Me and Everett make and sell thirty coconut bowls to other 'villagers'. We donate the ninety dollars we earn to the Ashram. Lee sees we are raking in the dough in our little village business. But it is His village, so I am a lucky man to get to place the cash into His hands.

Later they tell us that Lee got tears in his eyes to see Yogi Ramsuratkumar suddenly appear there in front of him in 'the flesh' on the Ashram, a garland of fresh lemons around his neck made by Brenda. Lee said that Yogi Ramsuratkumar's eyes were perfect.

Seven years later Lee has the Yogi Ramsuratkumar statue burned in a Yajna ceremonial cleansing fire. I hear that the statue literally becomes the sun as it burns. The firemasters stir the ashes to make sure the fire is completely out. Nothing remains of the steel pipes, wire, screws or fasteners that I had used to build the statue. The only thing they find in the ashes are Yogi Ramsuratkumar's glass eyes. How does the physicist explain that? He does not.

After the 1995 summer Celebration, Lee calls Brenda and I into his living room to explain that our original assignment to manage building Lee's Ashram in Tiruvannamalai, India, has evolved into revamping Gilles Farcet's two-hundred-year-old family farm into Lee's French Ashram near a village called Saint Pierre de Maillé. My first thought is that I probably will not be using my new Tamil vocabulary much.

My second thought is a memory of my first date in High School. In eleventh grade there is a prom dance where the girl gets to choose the boy who will take her on a date. The Jewish girl who chose me was in my economics class where we played a two-week-long no-rules time-lapse investment game. Most kids invest conservatively for safe long-term gains. I take maximum risk, make wild 'investments' and became a multi-millionaire within the week. I guess this girl thought I would make a good husband.

I could drive, but I have no idea where to take this girl out to dinner before the Prom. My parents suggest a fancy French restaurant. I phone them up and make a reservation. When we arrive, I cannot read the menu, cannot understand the waiter, do not like the food, and spend all of my real-money savings on this one awful meal. At the Prom I cannot dance, and she does not even try to kiss me. Immediately afterwards I come down with a severe case of mononucleosis and spend my Christmas vacation moaning with fever in bed and gamma-globulin shots in my butt. My relationship to France is tarnished before our family even begins our

Hohm Sahaj Mandir French adventure. I cannot even pronounce the French word for 'hardware store'. (You try it: *quincaillerie*.)

There in Lee's living room I picture our beautiful mud-floored passive-solar rammed-earth house across the stream from Lee's Prescott Ashram that we just moved into. With Lee's new plans we pack everything into a storage area, preparing to 'temporarily' move with whatever we can carry from Arizona to France.

It is September 1995. Luckily our oldest daughter's sprained ankle means we have a wheel-chair on both sides of the Atlantic within which we can cram bags and bundles of odds and ends to manage our way through the air terminals.

La Ferme de Jutreau is a 'métairie', which means it is the house where the peasants associated with the mini-castle Jutreau would grow food and keep half of it, giving the other half to the owner. The quaint little Jutreau castle sits now on a separate property, and the stacked-lime-stone farm buildings – which are configured into a 'u' shape around a fabulous old maple tree centered in the courtyard – had not been occupied for twenty years. The previous inhabitants had removed everything they could on their way out, including the water heater and all the light fixtures.

We are four women (Brenda, our two daughters, Amethyst and Aurora, and Alrun, a German student of Lee's who volunteered to be 'the cook') plus myself, moving into a cold, dark, damp and dusty quarters (fully an inch of dust everywhere throughout the main house), with no working indoor plumbing. The weeds in the courtyard are so high that the women can take stove-heated outdoor bucket-baths without fear of being exposed. Lee wants La Ferme de Jutreau ready 'in the style of Arnaud Desjardins' Hauteville' for our Guru Purnima summer celebration in June 1996.

I get the idea to actually visit this fabled mystical place called 'Hauteville' to obtain at least some kind of 'blueprint' for what we are to build. Lee grants permission and travel arrangements are made. Brenda and I are met at the train station by Arnaud's son, Emmanuel Desjardins, and his friend and colleague, Thierry Martin. They are our age. The tour of Hauteville is overwhelming. The red-brick buildings with massive white marble stairways are immaculately cared for. The vast carpeted sitting hall defines the simplicity of elegance. Their fruit orchards and flower gardens delight angels who must certainly come there to refresh and repose. The unfathomable challenge of transforming La Ferme de Jutreau into Hauteville with no budget, alone, before next summer, is simply mind boggling. It is time to make dinner.

Emmanuel invites us to his apartment and begins preparing a salad. I feel hungrier than a salad can mollify. To speed up the process I volunteer to help in the kitchen. Emmanuel retrieves a large ceramic bowl from a cupboard and begins tossing in ingredients. Into a pile of washed and torn lettuce leaves he instructs me to add chunks of various kinds of cheeses, broken walnuts, dark raisins, chopped red apples, and slices of raw celery. I am sure he is making a mistake. I tell him so. He just smiles at my unrefined American sense of cuisine. I try to argue him out of it. My psychological perceptions of reality are freaking out. This is not a salad. This is blasphemy. In our School, mixing fresh fruit with greens and veggies is an absolute no-go. Lalitha Thomas said so! Nonetheless, accompanied by French baguette, French salted butter, and hunger, the salad proves to be delicious and satisfying.

Emmanuel and Thierry offer to show us our sleeping quarters for the night. We are honored with Alain de Rosanbo's room in the main house, and will be sleeping in his custom-built bed with the feet raised higher than the head.

The four of us sit down on the carpet at the foot of the bed to continue our conversation. Emmanuel and Thierry seriously provide the quintessence of formal hospitality from Arnaud Desjardins' spiritual school at Hauteville to their special guests from Lee Lozowick's Hohm Sahaj Mandir. The mood is uncomfortably proper for Brenda and I who are… merely Americans. The formality breaks my camel's back. Something in me snaps. I leap up, grab an armful of white feather pillows, heave them at Emmanuel and Thierry, then dive on top of them to wrestle. Without hesitation they respond in kind. The four of us have a Pillow Fight Royale! For ten ecstatic minutes or more we shout, throw pillows, wrestle around, and laugh our heads off. Luckily nothing gets broken except the formalities. We depart the next morning in good cheer.

Back at La Ferme de Jutreau, Arnaud's students generously travel from all around Paris to help us begin the work. We transcend the language barriers and become good friends. For weeks we burn scrap wood, moldy furniture, and literally tons of sunflower stalks that had been packed season-after-season for one-hundred years into barn attics as insulation to keep the cows warm in winter. We need the attic space to build out sardine-style sleeping slots for eighty guests, but it takes pickaxes to pull it apart and throw it down into wheelbarrows. Thick with sweat and dust I tend this huge Vajra fire – hot enough to melt glass bottles – burning away ancient Karma night and day.

I lose count of how many cement trucks full of concrete we pour onto the barn floor to make the combined dining and Darshan hall floor. We also pour cement to make floors in a food storage basement under the kitchen, more sleeping quarters in another part of the barn, and a roofed, outdoor dishwashing station so that ten people in parallel can wash, dry, and put away ninety people's dishes in less than twenty minutes.

On 1 March 1996 we establish a legal French cultural foundation named RAMJI Association (Association loi 1901 ou assimilé) to take over ownership of the property.

We build twelve wooden bunk beds and ten large wooden dining tables with twenty wooden benches.

We build hanging wooden shelves in the basement food storage room, and a full wall of wooden bookshelves in the multipurpose library / tea room / living room / RAMJI meeting room. We refit the big house's kitchen with stainless steel equipment, new cupboards, and an industrial stove / oven for inspectors to certify its sanitariness.

We dig a French-drain system uphill of the little house to dry out its floor and keep the white saltpeter crystals from forming throughout the rooms.

We order huge truckloads of gray-rock gravel and wheel-barrow it by hand down the mud driveway to fill in the thousand potholes.

We build up a productive vegetable garden with a greenhouse on the south slope behind the little house, plant fruit trees all over the property, have the septic system pumped out, build a small outdoor sink and shower house for the men, a multi-shower multi-sink covered bathhouse for the women, and a raised, concrete-floored, outdoor composting women's toilet using a scrounged grocery-store-shopping-cart-return house.

It must be said that relations with our new French neighbors are created by Amethyst and Aurora, our homeschooled / unschooled daughters. Their friendly communication skills, and their love of and talents with caring for horses and ponies save the day. Here is an example: Without permission Amethyst and Aurora fence off the two Jutreau castle ponies into a small corral and stop the caretaker from feeding them left-over baguettes. The caretaker complains to the owners who do not believe Amethyst and Aurora, thinking they are starving their poor creatures. Finally, a professional veterinarian is called to the scene of the crime. He examines these two frisky Scottish Highland ponies and declares to the owners that the girls have gone out of their way to save the ponies' lives. The ponies were dying from colic, a disease that comes from eating too much rich French grass and too many baguettes. Suddenly the owners and caretaker cannot praise Amethyst and Aurora enough. Neighborly relations flourish.

At one point, Amethyst, two and a half years older than Aurora, says, "Dad, I want to go to school."

I say, "Okay. Why do you want to go to school?"

She says, "I want to see what school is like. All my friends from the horse club are going to school." So we help her get picked up by the French school bus and she starts attending the local French public school.

Three months later Amethyst says, "Dad, I want to stop going to school."

I say, "Okay. Why do you want to stop going to school?"

Amethyst says, "Because none of the kids at school know what they want to do with their life. I already know what I want to do with my life. If I go to school, I don't have time for my life."

So she stops going to school. At the appropriate time, we ask both girls to take the GED exam to get their High School Equivalent Diploma. They pass with flying colors. They each decide they want to become certified French horse-riding trainers at *École nationale d'équitation* (ENE), home of the world-famous *Cadre Noir de Saumur*. They complete their studies, become fully certified, marry French brothers, buy their own farms, and live happily ever after with their families in France. I already have five French grandchildren. Who could have imagined such an outcome when I first met Lee Lozowick in 1988 as an electro-mechanical engineer in California? But I have gotten ahead of myself here...

One morning a French Police car rolls into our tiny gravel parking lot, slowly turns around so it faces back out the way it came in (for a quick getaway, if necessary), and both doors slowly open. Two armed cult police stand warily up out of their car. They keep their doors open and stay near their car, waiting to see what we will do. Luckily I am there when the car arrives, and luckily I have been prepared by Gilles Farcet about what to do. I walk slowly over towards the care with a big smile on my face and shake their hands. I invite them to come into our home for Pastis (the traditional French anise-flavored hospitality liquor) and coffee. According to social law, they cannot refuse. By the time Brenda scrambles to get some American-style coffee and cookies together, and the cult police taste the coffee – trying to be polite about our hospitality but hardly believing we would call this weak stuff coffee compared to French espresso – we are friends.

They tell us that the body of a dead woman was recently discovered in a forest not far away. Do we know anything about this?

I am unspeakably appreciative that these two men are undertaking such a gruesome task. I am literally in tears of gratitude that they had come to visit us and do their job. It is certainly something I would not want to do. We know nothing, but we promise to put our feelers out and let them know of anything we might discover. We make it clear that they are welcome to come back and visit us any time for no reason. Here is our telephone and email contact information. And they do visit us, once a year. But now they park their car the regular way.

On another day, Gilles Farcet's mother drives into the courtyard of La Ferme de Jutreau unannounced. She lives in Vicq-sur-Gartempe, where Gilles grew up, a cute castle-centered village nearby. Madame Farcet urgently reports that she has heard a rumor about the priest in San Pierre de Maillé. He is telling his congregation every Sunday at church that a devil-worshiping baby-eating sect has moved into their area and they must do whatever it takes to get rid of us. She suggests we do something about that immediately. Then she drives off.

Do something about that?

Immediately...

Try to imagine my mind as it faces into this problem. I am a white American idiot, bumbling unknowledgeably into the dark bowels of central France, cannot speak the language, do not know the customs or the lay of the land, and am forcefully accused of being a dangerous sect leader, an immediate threat to the peace and harmony of the villagers. *Do something about that such as what, for example?* The witch hunts and Inquisitions persisted in this area of the world for over seven-hundred years. It appears they are not quite over.

I can hardly sleep that night, imagining a growling crowd of foaming-at-the-mouth blood-thirsty villagers carrying torches and pitchforks overwhelming our property and burning the place down.

Next morning, I get into the car and drive to Saint Pierre de Maillé, chanting Yogi Ramsuratkumar's name out loud the whole way. The church is easy enough to find, although I have never seen it before. But where is the Priest?

This is Friday. I prowl around the property, trying to exude an aura of innocence. I find a small stone dwelling behind the church. I knock on the wooden front door. A nervous, black-haired, womanless-looking man about forty answers the door. In embarrassingly-destroyed pseudo-French I try to say, "Hello, my name is Clinton Callahan. I am looking for the Priest. Do you know where I can find him?"

The man says, "I am the Priest."

A truly novel kind of silence settles over me in that moment, a space one might only expect to find in that gap between insanity and death.

Grasping for anything to cling onto, I finally manage to say, "I am the sect leader. I live at La Ferme de Jutreau. I would like to meet you. Could I introduce myself? Could we talk?"

He looks me up and down – possibly searching for weapons. I make sure my hands are in plain view and do not move a muscle. He cautiously invites me into his hovel. Then he offers me a cigarette.

This is the first time in my life that I wish I smoked. I figure I would cough too much if I try a cigarette now, so I kindly refuse his offer. He lights one up for himself, takes a deep drag, then exhales fully in this tiny room.

I tell this Priest of the Saint Pierre de Maillé Catholic Church that I grew up in California, a place where everyone puts a tall fence around their yard and nobody knows their neighbors' name. The highest form of respect in that country is to stay disconnected from everyone so they can mind their own business. I tell him that I came to central France without learning that the first thing I should have done was come over here into town and introduce myself to the Priest. I tell him about Brenda, Amethyst, Aurora, and Alrun. I tell him about our garden and our remodeling work. I apologize sincerely for not coming to visit him earlier. I tell him that I have a lot to learn. I say nothing about the rumor I heard from Madame Farcet. I ask him if there is anything he would like to know about us. I am happy to answer his every question. I invite him to come visit us. And believe it or not, I say all this in French.

He pauses a moment, takes another drag on his cigarette, then asks, "Are you baptized?"

"Oh, yes. Certainly!" My parents told me I was baptized. I saw a certificate of my baptism once.

"Are your children baptized?" he continues.

I do not hesitate for an instant. "Yes!" I say. One time while Brenda and I were visiting some cathedral somewhere with the kids, Brenda took handfuls of 'sacred water' and sprinkled it over the kid's heads saying, "There! Now you are baptized!"

Then the Priest asks, "Will you start coming to my services now?"

My heart skips a beat before I find my way out of this trap. I say, "We are Lutherans."

"Oh," he says.

This is the end of our conversation. It is also the end of his horrifying tales to his congregation about the evils of the inhabitants of La Ferme de Jutreau.

And, somehow... through fiercely-creative collaborations and luck, La Ferme de Jutreau comes to life as Lee Lozowick's RAMJI Association Ashram. Working and playing together, we hold the first of many, fabulous and sacred, Guru Purnima celebrations in France.

10. 1996: The Road's Ahead

1 January 1996 – Entering reality at La Ferme de Jutreau, France

There are periods for me when I don't see the big picture, even though I am committed to the big picture.

What I understand now is that a lack of big picture vision does not confuse me as to what to do next, because first and foremost, I am committed, and therefore, it is clear what to do next. I do what is in front of me, that is mine to do, that is in alignment with the context of serving Lee and this commitment.

Little, big, possible, impossible, I like it, I hate it, I'm glad, I'm scared, I look good, I look bad, I have enough time and money, I don't have enough time and money, I have clarity, I'm utterly-confused, none of this matters. None of it. Just do the next obvious thing, and work smart. The how and why of it will come later, if at all.

I have been through this enough times already to know that sooner or later the sense of it all will slip into view just exactly when it does. Having some particular level of comforting certainty is more of a luxury than a necessity. Waiting around until everything is clear is how my psychology wins. I no longer need my psychology to win.

I don't need to understand everything before I can do something. I don't need to understand anything before I can be.

So, what is this commitment I made?

Something like this: Move with my family to France for an indefinite period of time while delivering trainings in Germany and Austria, and build up Lee's new La Ferme de Jutreau Ashram.

As impossible as this has been to create out of nothing, here we are.

Our arrival at La Ferme de Jutreau feels as exciting and as mysterious, as difficult and as tedious, as it would be to discover a sunken ship from an ancient culture deep in the muddy bottom of the Mediterranean

Sea. The farmhouse and outbuildings, smothered in ivy, are built of hand-hewn limestone, hand-sawed logs, and whatever they used for cement and plaster back in the 17th Century. Some modernizing improvements have been made, but everything was completely shut down. There is no electricity, no gas, no water, no heat, and no telephone.

Inside one of the small stone outbuildings, next to the spot where the water heater used to be, there is some kind of furnace contraption all hooked up with dual pipes to some huge tanks in the next chamber. I am mechanically skilled but have no experience with such a mechanism. When I push the 'ON' button, nothing happens. I have no time to figure this out now – especially with no way to even verify the effectiveness of my figuring. Why no time? Because we are cold. The weather is getting colder. There is a fireplace. There are dead trees in the nearby woods. I buy a small Swiss-made handsaw and a green-painted steel wheelbarrow. The kids and I set to sawing up logs to burn in the house to stay warm.

Here we go, chopping wood.

When we finally locate the main underground water valve and turn the water on, our illusory concept of 'simple fixes' vanishes in the watery plops made by the one upstairs toilet shut-off valve constantly dripping into a one-liter plastic bottle taped to the side of the tank. The bottle over-flows every thirteen and one-half minutes. We have no tools. At the least, repairing this leak requires locating and purchasing a replacement part and somehow getting a torch and gas for resoldering the copper pipes which are laid tight into a wallpapered corner. It is no easy job. In fact, given the circumstances, it could take days.

Either run upstairs every thirteen minutes, untape the bottle, dump its contents into the toilet (which we soon discover is stopped up more than a toilet plunger can unclog – as of this writing it still is...) and tape the bottle back in place for another thirteen minutes.

Or we turn the main water valve on outside every time we need water inside, keeping careful track of the cumulative drip time... Attention splitting exercises are great for building matrix, but they have their appropriate time and place.

We choose a third option instead. We decide to obtain all the water we need for drinking, cooking, washing, brushing teeth, and flushing the downstairs toilet from an outside hose spigot in a five-gallon plastic bucket.

And here we are, carrying water.

While packing up in Arizona to leave for France, I ask Lee if He would select three books that might be useful to guide me: one to portray his ideal vision for the French Ashram, another to help me through where I'm presently stuck, and a third just something He recommends I read. The next day I receive a message from the Ashram office that a package is waiting for me atop the mailboxes in the Arrakis greenhouse. When I retrieve the package I find three books, an invoice from the Ashram bookstore for $55, and no note indicating which book fulfills which request. The three books are: Idries Shah – *The Commanding Self*, Chögyam Trungpa – *Journey Without Goal*, and *The Way A Master Works* written by Ivy. O. Duce about her work with her teacher Meher Baba. It is this latter book which, four weeks later, is the first to find its way onto my lap on the return train from delivering an Event training in Freiburg im Breisgau, Germany.

As I open the cover and smell the pages, my whole body responds as if I have come upon a hidden treasure free for the taking, a feast ready to devour. I find myself caressing the cover and stroking the pages like my lover's bare skin. What is this? I wonder. Word by word, I find out. It is an exact guidebook for the work we are involved in at La Ferme de Jutreau. We have just entered what Meher Baba referred to as 'The New Life'. Leave everything behind. Go to strange new lands. Start completely from scratch. Beg. And under all circumstances, no matter what happens, regardless of how helpless you feel, how hopeless it may appear, how clearly pointless or ridiculous or problematical or embarrassing it all seems, be happy.

And it *is* hopeless.

There is far too much to do.

But you know those *Callahans*… you can't get them to stop doing. Do, do, do… All night long if they have to. They will do whatever it takes… *Oh! So you like to do? Here, do this!* There is so much to do around here that even just making a list of it all could put you into immediate physical, psychological, mental, and emotional breakdown.

This whole conversation unreels in my mind:

You are committed to doing it all, aren't you?

Well, yes.

But it is totally hopeless! Impossible even. You will never get it all done! You cannot succeed.

Well, yes, that is true.

And yet, we must succeed. It is necessary.

Well, yes, but, necessary or not, we are totally incapable to do it all. We do not speak the language. We do not know how the French culture, French money, French customs, or the French government works. We do not have the innate power to make things happen here…

Ahhh… Now isn't that interesting? This is exactly how Meher Baba described The New Life: a period of helplessness and hopelessness.

Clearly this is a purification phase.

November 17-19 is La Ferme de Jutreau's first public seminar, the same weekend as the Appearance Day Celebrations in Arizona and Germany. Our daily schedule consists of meditation, work, talks, work, meals, work. 'Work' in this case means to climb into the attic of the five-hundred-year-old barn and pry apart ancient matted bundles of dried sunflower stalks and dried grasses which are stacked three feet high across the beams as insulation to protect livestock from the winter's bitter cold. The fibers are so tightly settled that a two-handed pickaxe swung over the shoulder with full force bounces off. Every handful we tear apart and shove down through the rafters into the barn below produces clouds of choking black dust that sticks to our sweating bodies.

Inch-by-inch something old is being dismantled, energetically disassembled. As we cart these piles out into the field behind the barn and set them afire, half a millennium of energy is released, making room for something entirely different to show up in this place. Energy tied up in the ancient structures is consumed by the transformational properties of fire. And with the old structure gone, the vampire entities go too, for nothing remains to which they can cling. This is now our time here.

Such a massive amount to combust in a limited amount of time requires a specific approach. Our intention must be on maximizing the burn. We must pay close attention to details to produce such efficiency, to do what needs to be done. Not to dump in too much at once or we snuff the flames. Keep the ashes stirred to keep allowing fresh oxygen in. Don't let the flames die down or we have to build up burn momentum all over again.

This is precisely how Lee works with us. He calls it maximizing profit. Keep the fire hot. If there is too much feedback the student gets overwhelmed and it snuffs out the desire for transformation, wastes time, and all you get is whining. If the transformation gets too wild, sparks may drift into unprepared souls and the fire may get out of control. That's too dangerous. But not enough intensity and the transformation will be too small, too conservative to make a real difference. Always you must stir the coals and deepen the context, or incompletely transformed substances accumulate and fill up the internal furnace with a half-transformed mess. The metaphor is precise.

Fire is not selective. Heat is heat. If you're near heat, then anything that can burn will bum. The cleansing is deep. We've been feeling it. Incomplete and unexpressed emotional baggage, even from the very first days of my relating with Brenda, pop up at unexpected moments and flash into intense flames, burning what remains into dusty ash that the winds of time blow away. Not comfortable, though clearly necessary.

All this is easily understandable from some Dharmically practical perspective. The concepts are something the mind can tolerate, or at least chew on. But then there is this one little extra demand that seems totally insane. The all-inclusive one: *Be happy*. During all of this? Are you kidding? We're supposed to be happy? It's our duty?? Are you out of your mind?

Perhaps.

Or as Lee might say, "Hopefully!"

The fire boils it down to two choices.

Either you row upstream: "No, listen! Something is really wrong here! There's a problem! This isn't working! I can't do this! There has been a big mistake! I've got reasons. I'm tired – can't you see? I'm sick! I can't handle it! I can show you that this is not the way it should be. This is not fair! This isn't right! This cannot be happening! God did this? Well then, God screwed up!"

Or you row downstream: "Just This. It does not mean anything. There is no reason needed."

We each individually choose minute-by-minute which way to row. One choice makes you a victim, a viewpoint from which you can conveniently blame that to which you are playing victim on someone else, and resent it, and be right about it. The other choice destroys your ego's victim game and empowers your presence of Being.

You are never, in actuality, a victim, although you can pretend to be one if you wish.

Can you imagine how much power there would be if you conserve your energy and are simply happy about it?

I struggle with feeling excluded amongst people speaking intimately – even about me – in a language I do not understand. The students of Arnaud Desjardins who have been helping us set up La Ferme de Jutreau have a great old time, bubbling in conversation, laughing. I sit there watching a silent movie, noticing my own private inner victim movie tightening its grip around my heart. The self-observation arrests ego's progress, and as I hang there in the confusion, something other begins to emerge.

I recall the story of a blind man complaining to Meher Baba that he could not see, claiming to have such a disadvantage in the Work. (Victim!) Meher Baba's response is to state that all which is seen with the eyes is a distraction. He tells the blind man that He actually has an advantage by being not so easily fooled.

It begins to arise within me that perhaps I have the same advantage as the blind man by not being able to hear. Suddenly people's countenance shifts in appearance. A heretofore unnoticed warmth emerges from the group, and it becomes tacitly obvious that I am included and connected in a far deeper way than I would previously allow myself to experience.

And when it becomes 'impossible', when *we do not have what we need* to do what we have to do, then we have to ask for it. The practice is to avoid being entranced by whatever it is that looks like a wall, and instead look at the ways around, through, over.

Instead of lamenting not having what you need, you increase the size of your team and ask for what you need.

But isn't that egotistical? Self-centered? Asking for *what I need* seems so selfish. Yes, it may feel selfish, or even look that way. But from the overall perspective, if you are genuinely surrendered to serving the space, then asking for what you need is asking for what the space needs. (Can you kid yourself about this? You bet your sweet ass you can.)

At this moment, Lee Lozowick is selecting from among the people who have volunteered, those who will actually join him on this 'New Life' leg of his journey with us. Some of the people being considered are thinking ahead. "Let's buy Clint and Brenda a such and such… an espresso machine, a widescreen TV, a Cuisinart food processor… I am sure they really need some of this and that…" Then it may just so happen to work out that when these particular people arrive at La Ferme de Jutreau, these generous contributors will not have to endure certain particularly distasteful personal deprivations…

Listen folks – we are not going to be comfortable at La Ferme de Jutreau. We are going to France to teach people to be devotees. That Guru of ours – He is so sly! He knows that the best way to learn something is to teach it.

In France the demand to practice is absolute. There arises a camaraderie and intimacy out of such work together, even when, or, perhaps, especially when the Master is not physically present. Such communion is the hottest fire of all, yet it arises as a side effect of 100% commitment to the road. The beginning of such a commitment may sound approximately like this (excerpted from the *John T* rock-opera lyrics by Lee Lozowick):

Yes, now we do remember.

He did call all the shots.

But we're not sure we're thrilled with this,
If we're happy with our lot.
Well, the road's ahead.
Let's walk it.
We'll see what fate provides.
And remember John and Jesus,
And the words they did confide...

11. 1996: Stopping The World

15 October 1996 – The ground falls away in Crete

It doesn't work anymore. I dangle here in nerve-racking unsettlement, my full body noticing that things no longer hang together like they did even a few moments before. I am certain you know what I mean. You too have been here, where there is nothing to stand on. The floor drops away. The stage upon which life plays out its theatrics is utterly shattered. The shock is deep and beyond description. My nice, tightly formulated picture of who I am comes apart at the pixel level. What remains is invisible white noise.

Before this, the picture was seamless - everything melted into everything else and I glided through. Now there are seams everywhere, open seams. Between each object. Between each word, each movement. I frantically ask my mind to explain what made everything stay connected before? Some kind of glue? The glue is gone. Dissolved. Nothing is continuous anymore. Now I see that it never has been continuous. The seamlessness was a mirage. There are big gaps between everything.

I used to imagine that I had it all together, that things were fine, my kids, my ability to relate, our little family holiday to Crete. Where did I ever get that idea? It's so obviously not true. Look around. Look at this. Who am I kidding? Every motion I make is so mechanical, so robot-like, so predictable. Each of my thoughts is the same stale thinking I had so many times before, same attitudes, same opinions, same emotional reactions to being offended, same judgements, same expectations, each thought so tight and quick and final. They all fit a formula specifically designed to keep my survival strategy of being a 'good boy' safely in control, so comfortable, so separate, so asleep.

Seamless.

But not now. Now nothing works. Nothing is together. Everything is stopped. It's a real mess.

Who I thought I was – I don't even remember anymore, some vague image, a ghost, a cartoon. I feel immense sadness from losing my part in the charade. How can people still like me if I am not what they thought? If I don't fit into their movie anymore? How can people like me if I'm nothing? How will I function? What if I never come back together?

I invested years in manufacturing piece by piece this presentation of who I am – who I was. I sacrificed a lot to keep the image seemingly solid. So often I have done what my image dictated, what was necessary to maintain the character rather than what my Being truly wanted. I have paid in blood. I really tried to be good, to be nice. I tried to be sincere - Oh God! *How I tried!* A good child, a kind sibling, a perfect student at school, a strong friendly worker, a loyal trustworthy mate, a generous and compassionate father, a good devotee. I paid. I sacrificed. So many years of my life I used up and gave away, abandoning myself trying to keep the show together.

Now it is so obvious that all of that effort was a lie, a sham. I have been living in a fantasy world.

No, it's worse than that. I have been false.

I have been adaptive, trying to have on reserve at all times, good reasons for my behavior in case any authority figure wanted to know just exactly why I was doing what I was doing – even when there was no authority figure available. I spent my life trying to connect the next thing I was about to do with the previous thing I had already done, trying to make my life contiguous and consistent, to follow a reasonable progression. I have tried not to frighten people. Really. I have tried to be sane.

But now I see all this from a different perspective – something has shifted. The new view is extremely painful to endure. And I can't stop it.

I want to scream.

I want to hit somebody.

I want to run.

I want chocolate, doughnuts, cookies.

I want a drink.

I want to watch endless videos. Anything to stop this pain. Anything to get me away from all this confusion.

I ache.

I am alone in a foreign country, on holiday from another foreign country.

I am afraid.

NOBODY understands what is happening to me right now. Nobody knows what this feels like.

It hurts.

I am utterly raw. I'm cracked open. I'm naked. I'm ruined.

My whole life is a lie... In fact, the world is a lie. Everyone out there is still trying to keep it all together. They still believe things are seamless. They still act like they are standing on something real.

Do you want to know what's real? The evilness of women is real.

Nothing that women say or do is as they represent it. Always deceiving. More is always going on than they want it to seem. Women's spider-work is incredibly subtle and fast. They use their fear as a weapon, a tool, a way to control. They play shy, weak, helpless. But they are not. Oh, no! They know exactly what they are doing. They know who is watching what part of their body and who will be offended by a certain choice of words or tone of voice, an implied inclusion or exclusion. They know who has the power, who wants it, and what they are trying to do to get it. And they let the men play into their web of illusions so that it looks like the women are being controlled and dominated, when, in fact, the only time they play this game is when they are dominant and in control. Their invocation is always nonlinear, multidimensional and emotional. Anything else is so boring. They will never say "Yes," or, "No." They will never clearly and simply and directly ask for what they want because if they do, they lose. Such a move would be outside of their domain of power and they can no longer control the outcome.

And the stupidity of men is real. Men are so stupid!

They live in a dream thinking they have power and control and they do not. Oh, no! Show a man a bare breast or a sports game on television, or a plate of food, and see where his attention goes. The men make noises and threats with their brute force and stupid aggression. They play war games with nuclear bombs and machine guns, cellular phones and the internet. They own millions of dollars and conquer and pollute, but they are little boys in big bodies playing grandiose fantasy games. They make rules to control and impress the women, but women do not even acknowledge the domain of Rules. Men need to look good; they need to know. The women love this game. Instinctually, without even having to think about it, women devise and ask just the right question, perfectly suited to challenge a man's intellect and make him feel necessary and important, enhancing his self-esteem. But the instant a man engages the question at the level it is asked, the game is over. The trap snaps shut across his balls. She's got him wrapped around her little finger.

Men don't even know what hits them. Only the side effects indicate the effectiveness of this female ploy. The little boys make underhanded comments and rude degrading jokes behind mommy's back, while to her face they sometimes strike out brutally – at her or at the children – but more often He just shits in his pants. The women watch in disgust, or nag and complain, while the men diddle about, never claiming their real power. And a woman can't claim her real power until a man claims his.

That is what is real.

Seeing society's delusions crash and burn hurts to the core. I can feel it rip me open. Pretending to be sane and reasonable under the pressure of social rubbish has been a ridiculously shameful burlesquing of my life. Only the whole time I did not know to what degree I was pretending. I am very angry now about being fooled. Those fuckers!

But who fooled me? My parents? My teachers? They are just as fooled as I am.

Who fooled me then? No more lies!

The answer is: me.

I have fooled myself for all these years.

It was me.

But why? What did I get for this outrageous sacrifice? This outrageous performance? Why did I do it? To get love? To get attention? To get acceptance?

Yes.

Did it work? Did I get these things?

Yes - but not really. Those things were given to be, but I did not truly receive them. My act got these things.

My show reveled in its accomplishments, in its survival. I was left out of the equation. I got nothing.

But what do I have when I stop fooling myself?

Nothing.

Either way it's nothing.

That's funny…

So, then what?

Do I put the show back together now? Continue pretending? Act as if I haven't seen behind the curtain, that the crack in the cosmic egg passed me by? Go stupid again, as if I don't know the joke?

Is this what I have to do?

What else is there? How far does the nothing go? Who else is outside the prison with me?

Do I have the courage to avoid putting the 'Clinton' mask back on my face?

Do I have the courage to stay insane?

What would that mean?

Nothing would ever look normal.

Everything would be new and unique.

I could not function according to the same set of assumptions as those around me, so communication would be difficult. Every communication would be an act of creation.

I would see the shadow parts of what I was intending because I would no longer be fooling myself about this. But I would know the evil intentions of the others also.

How could I keep from being pissed off all the time at the petty power manipulations, jealousies, and fears?

I could only stay detached if my opinions and values as a person, an ego, never hijacked me again.

And that only happens like this, when I'm centered in the nothing.

But do I have the courage to remain here? Do I have the courage to rest in nothingness for the rest of my life?

It feels so lonely here. None of the petty satisfactions of life produce any resultant fulfillment. I can't even talk with someone or be touched by someone and have it mean anything real. Everything is empty.

On the other hand, it is equally true that everything is full... of nothing.

True responsibility comes from choosing the interpretation that empowers me.

If everything is full of nothing, then we are all the same, exactly the same. We are connected at a level below everything else.

But what about this endless sadness I feel in the center of my chest? The ache, the longing... it is so huge. What about that? Where does it come from? Where will it go?

Don't mix the two together!

There is sadness, yes.

It is sad to acknowledge the passing of an old position. The smaller view is subsumed; it dies. Grieve its death.

But don't confuse the grieving with the longing. That longing will never go away. It will only become bigger and more intense, more succinct.

This is supposed to be fabulous?

"May the heat of suffering become the fire of love."

I wonder what circumstances will be the excuse for the unconscious internal fantasy-generating machine to start rolling its gears again.

I wonder what would make the mists roll back over my perceptions, deftly smearing all of the parts back into a seamless whole so I can feel better?

Maybe asking this exact question is the start button.

Oops…

12. 1997: Radiantly Ordinary

1-4 September 1997 – In the car with Lee Lozowick from France to Spain and back

Thirteen playing cards whisper undecipherable secrets as they slide to a stop in front of me, one on top the other. I count points while arranging the cards into suits. The tally is concluded. Clubs, diamonds, hearts, spades, the hand is irrefutable. It is what it is. When the situation is completely known there is only one move to make. More often than we might expect, the choiceless choice is no action. "I pass."

How could it be that the most powerful thing to create is nothing at all? That the most useful thing to do is be still? The most appropriate thing to speak is silence?

In one stunning, actionless scene of the video, '*On The Road With Mr. Lee,*' made by Francois Fronty, a student of Arnaud Desjardins and an ardent fan of Lee's in France, we see Lee sitting, legs outstretched, arms crossed over his chest, leaning back in a hard wooden straight-backed chair in some nondescript yellowish kitchen. He is perfectly still.

Time passes.

Nothing happens.

Lee is like a fine bottle of Champagne with its cork worked halfway out ready to pop. He is like a fully-inflated balloon poised one-millimeter away from a steel-sharp needle.

There is no music. No sound. The mind starts going crazy trying to figure out what is wrong. Is the video tape stuck? What is the problem? What is the point of this?

Finally, with hardly a move, Lee looks straight into the eye of the camera, his face totally expressionless, and says - with a poignantly complex context that slams home only after a delay of some seconds - "A big part of the spiritual master's job is waiting."

Perhaps the most intense experience that a student can have in the company of the spiritual master is to be allowed to wait with him.

I am unexpectedly granted exactly this opportunity the first four days of September, 1997, when Lee invites me to join him on a long drive from the French Ashram at La Ferme de Jutreau to a tiny village tucked into the rambling hills of Northern Spain where his friend, Claudio Naranjo, gathers the participants of his three-year SAT program ('Seekers After Truth': a name with an air of mystery, pulled from the archives of spiritual lore, made famous when G. I. Gurdjieff used it for his study groups) for forty-days of intense training in various therapeutic modalities.

We arrive. Bright Spanish afternoon sun bounces off of stuccoed walls, making me nearly blind as I stumble into the shadowy interior of the old Spanish mansion that has been transformed into a seminar house. Eyes adjusting to the shadows, I already feel like I'm walking barefoot on the razor's edge.

I heard a rumor that Lee invited me along because I was the only person around who could speak some Spanish. (Where is Mr. Cruz, my seventh-grade Spanish teacher, when I really need him? Why did I spend so much time perfecting spit-wad technology instead of Spanish verb conjugations?) My Spanish has been buried under years of trying to learn German, and on top of that, French.

Standing in the entryway, grasping for words, I suddenly experience how seriously Spanish has become fossilized in my mind. I try to say, "Buenos dias," and introduce us, asking after Señor Naranjo. Instead my mouth locks half-open in complete mental chaos. Lee steps forward and gracefully handles the situation. As I fail to translate their answers from Spanish back into English, Lee already understands everything they say without my 'help' by connecting directly with people's hearts and listening to what they mean. I trot after him up the hall in no small amount of embarrassment.

A giant thunderstorm is raging all the way from central France deep into Spain. We drove all day in torrential rains. Greeting us, our hostess mentions that they had been having nice weather until today. Lee says, "I think it will be sunny again." Next morning it is a cloudless blue sky from horizon to horizon. I ask him what his intention had been when He predicted the change in weather. He says, "I was just wishful thinking."

On our drive to Spain we eat no breakfast and no lunch. When our host asks if we prefer to eat vegetarian, Lee says, "No, we are in Spain. We will eat meat. Lots of it."

Lee is invited to give a talk on each of the three nights we are there. The first night Lee wears mock-Teva sandals, navy blue sweatpants, his belt pouch, a gray T-shirt printed with the words 'Above The Line' on the left chest, and a brushed-denim 'SHRI' baseball-style cap worn backwards.

He makes it a point to instantly memorize people's Spanish names. A man he was briefly introduced to on the day we arrived raises his hand to ask Lee a question during the third evening's talk, and Lee calls on him by name.

Days are filled with round after round of training sessions. We sit-in with Bob Hall, a well-known American therapist trained by both Ida Rolf and Fritz Perls. Mr. Hall demonstrates methods in Gestalt Therapy. Since he already has translators at his side, one to be his ears and one to be his mouth, we understand what he says.

On our third day, after a particularly grueling session, Bob looks at Lee and says, "Let's get out of here." Lee agrees. We gather a few other people in a couple of cars and drive into the nearest village for a short reprieve. One of the women sees a sign that indicates a historically famous, beautifully restored sixteenth century monastery just outside of town, suggesting we make a detour since we are so close. Bob says, "I didn't come here to look at old buildings." Lee is instantly delighted in finding someone who understands his sentiments exactly. We sit together at tables under shade-trees overlooking a stream, drinking Spanish beer, cracking open salted peanuts in the shell, and chewing down black Spanish olives.

Back at the seminar house, some of the seminar participants approach Lee during a break with questions. One such conversation between Lee and a couple of men goes like this:

STUDENT: Do you have disciples?

LEE: I prefer to call them students.

STUDENT: How do you deal with the projections people act out towards you?

LEE: I have absolutely no sentimentality.

STUDENT: So, you don't care if they like you or not?

LEE: Right. I'm looking for results, not a personality cult.

STUDENT: The work is solo. Why does one need a guru?

LEE: Everyone must do their own work, but it's the relationship with the guru that gives you the energy to do your own work.

STUDENT: What about learning from being in the wilderness?

LEE: Nature can't give you feedback in human terms like a living human teacher can. Once the relationship is established, even if the guru dies, the influence continues.

STUDENT: Does the Devil exist?

LEE: Only in people's minds.

STUDENT: So, Tantra energy work is to remove the Devil from people's minds?

LEE: No. The energy work is to live better lives. One of the results of using more energy is that we have less illusions. So, in that sense, yes, the work removes the Devil from the mind.

Every evening we dine with the presenters, Bob Hall, Claudio Naranjo, Alexandro Jodorowsky, and others. We are served institutional food, not the fine Spanish cuisine Lee had hoped for. After eating thick potato soup with sausage, thin-sliced chicken-fried steak, and ice-cream, Lee makes a side comment: to me, "Dinner was great, but if I ate like that for forty days, they'd have to carry me out in a wheelbarrow."

Claudio arranges for us to stay in an elegant antique-filled villa nearby. Lee takes one look around and says, "They gave me enough towels here to last me nine months!"

Basically, what we are doing here is waiting for the evening talks. I am reminded of the cartoon of two very hungry buzzards sitting side-by-side on a power-line out in the desert. Nothing is happening. Finally, one buzzard says to the other, "To hell with this waiting around! I am going to go kill something!"

I decide to take certain risks. I pay attention as best I can to Lee's attention. I try to notice what He notices. Several people seem of interest to him, and whenever I can, I make gestures to open up conversations with these individuals while in Lee's company. I play the fall-guy, asking questions which take us to spaces I think Lee might wish to investigate. I back out whenever Lee takes over navigating. The conversations get pretty interesting pretty fast. I think I am doing fantastic.

During a pause while one 'interviewee' steps away to refill his coffee cup, Lee hunches over the table, looks me straight in the eyes, and whispers, "You want some feedback?"

"Yes," I say, the 'Elephant's Child' asking the Crocodile what it eats for dinner.

"Your questions are too obvious. They are too much about you. Address people where they are instead of about what you want to hear."

Ka-bong! How do I ask questions about what I don't know? How can I ask questions that are not obvious? How can I ask questions that are not about me? How can I be nobody and still ask questions?

Two years have passed since I accompanied Lee to Spain. All this time these unanswered questions have been sitting in my guts. Sitting in there – like a brick.

Now I know why.

The brick will not dissolve because for all my life I have been committed to being 'somebody', being right. I have been committed to knowing. Why have I hung onto this commitment with such life-and-death urgency? Why was I willing to let people fail around me rather than 'get off it' and serve them? That was the question I took to the last Event training which I delivered in Little Rock, Arkansas. ('The Event' is a weekend 'breakthrough' seminar which Lee invites his students to use for taking steps in dealing with their psychology.) This question was my Demand.

First Grade was rough for me. I felt like my mother completely 'abandoned' me to a class-full of unknown kids and this stranger, Ms. Pinoniemi, the teacher. She was kind enough, plump, eye-glasses, sweet voice. But she had three dozen six-year-olds to deal with, and it was her job to teach us what 'school' was all about.

Day after endless day I sat there, deathly alone, in those hard wooden chairs with built-on desks, learning that the only way for me to get recognition, love, attention, approval and acceptance, the only way I could figure out how to survive in this environment, was to know the right answers to Ms. Pinoniemi's questions. If I stuck my hand up and knew the answers, she would absolutely beam at me with one-hundred percent unreserved smiling acknowledgement, and then I was somebody. It was in that moment that I unconsciously made a core decision: "If I am not right, I am nobody."

Ahh, the key is just discovered to being nobody!

============================

It is an eight-hour drive from central France to the Spanish highlands. On the way Lee grants me permission to ask him whatever is on my mind, and to tape-record our conversation along the curvy rain-soaked roads.

Lee's gentle answers unreservedly shattered the fundamental assumptions behind even my first question. While transcribing now, I notice that between Lee's answers and my next question are often minutes of blank tape filled only with the sounds of splattering rain and the swish-swash of the car's windshield wipers. You don't hear those minutes in the transcript below, but those long silent lapses are the times when my brain patterns are struggling mightily to reorder themselves according to new data. In contrast, there is no time-delay at all between my questions and Lee's responses. It is as if He already knows what I will ask and has pre-prepared His explanations. Of course, this is not so. He just lives exactly what He speaks, radiantly ordinary.

STUDENT: You mentioned that for a while after the incident which precipitated your teaching work you had the impression that it would be only a matter of a few months before you successfully transmitted what had been revealed to you to all of your students.

LEE: To some of them, anyway.

STUDENT: I have been thinking that your main teaching work is about responsibility. You speak of 'already present enlightenment', and you say that the difference between you and us is that you have taken responsibility for already present enlightenment and we have not. Your work with people is creating the chance for us to take responsibility at a greater and greater level.

LEE: It's more like responsibility is the effect of the work rather than the point of the work. The work is about abandonment, rather than responsibility. If you genuinely abandon yourself to the will of God, then responsibility is an automatic effect of that abandonment. How you know if you are surrendered to the will of God is because you are acting in a way that is responsible for first yourself, then all of the rings out from there. The will of God naturally produces responsibility for its process in the world.

STUDENT: I always thought it was the other way around. Somehow you try to be responsible first, and then...

LEE: Abandonment is not something that you can do by an act of will, so while you are considering the nature of abandonment itself, you act responsibly as a gesture of commitment to the process of abandonment, a gesture of sincerity. You are showing your willingness to enter into the process of abandonment by acting responsible as an act of will, until you are driven to move in response to the will of God.

STUDENT: I always had the impression that in order to become more responsible, a person's 'Being' first had to expand to include awareness, or to include into one's world that 'something' for which you were going to be responsible.

LEE: It is not 'Being' that expands, it is consciousness that opens to that possibility. And then when consciousness opens to that possibility, 'Being' can evolve in a way that is kept minimized by not opening to that possibility in consciousness. So maybe you're using the word 'Being' the way I'm using the word 'consciousness'.

STUDENT: I don't think so. It's different.

LEE: You said, "Being expands to include...", what?

STUDENT: I said that I thought 'Being' expands to include more of the world, to include that which one can then be responsible for.

LEE: Well no, that is not a quality of 'Being'. 'Being' doesn't do that. 'Being' works within the world that you become more responsible for, as a catalytic agent, or as a generator, or a magnet for grace, or as a tangent point for the divine. 'Being' doesn't expand to include the world. It functions in the world.

STUDENT: So, consciousness expands?

LEE: Consciousness opens to reveal that which is simply waiting to be revealed.

STUDENT: So, previous to consciousness opening, consciousness is owned or shut down by ego.

LEE: It's defined by ego. Not as a definition, but as a boundary.

STUDENT: The process has to do with consciousness owning ego rather than ego owning consciousness?

LEE: Or consciousness defining ego rather than ego defining consciousness. You could use 'owning' in the sense of 'being responsible for', but not in the sense of 'ownership'. 'Managing' is a word I would use also. Consciousness does contain ego, but ego acts as if it contains consciousness. And consciousness responds to that activity, and allows itself to be defined that way even though in fact, it encompasses ego.

STUDENT: There is a distinction between intellect and awareness, because consciousness contains intellect.

LEE: Intellect is a tool of awareness.

STUDENT: Would awareness and consciousness be the same then?

LEE: I would say consciousness is the field out of which awareness arises.

STUDENT: So, awareness has a little more self-reflection to it?

LEE: A little more definition. A little more defined.

STUDENT: So, in already present enlightenment, consciousness is already there, shrunk by, or imprisoned, by ego.

LEE: Limited by ego.

STUDENT: And the surrender that can happen is a surrendering of the limits of ego into consciousness, a releasing of the limits.

LEE: Well, it shifts poles, from the center of attention being ego to the center of attention being consciousness. It literally shifts poles, so that all of a sudden ego is not the managing force. If your center of attention is consciousness, then ego is just something you are watching function, and which you are able to function in spite of. It is like in the beginning ego has traction. After the pole shift, ego continues to spin but it has no traction.

STUDENT: We are functioning in spite of ego if the poles shift, and consciousness has management power.

LEE: Consciousness is what defines behavior. In small ways, ego can affect behavior. But in important ways, ego cannot affect behavior, because behavior arises out of consciousness, instead of behavior arising out of 'Being', which is a totally different motive. The ego may never lose its motives. But if behavior is arising out of consciousness, the motives of ego can't get a grip. They can't do anything.

STUDENT: Is there a separate process whereby consciousness is subsumed by the divine?

LEE: I think we can equate, relatively speaking, consciousness with the divine. There are certain particular functions of consciousness that may look like they are more divine than other functions, but that's just projection.

STUDENT: So, when the pole shift happens, it really is just that? It's not a little bit this, and a little bit that. It is either this, or that.

LEE: Yes. There are certainly tensions in relationship to the pole shift that make it appear like movement is happening, or progress is going on, but really the pole shift is the thing. It is like falling into the domain of possibility. You don't do that gradually. It happens instantaneously.

STUDENT: I want to know how you can be so patient with people.

LEE: I don't consider myself very patient. It's not a matter of being patient; it's a matter of the physics of the situation.

STUDENT: Meaning it can't be otherwise, and this is it?

LEE: Yeah.

STUDENT: I guess what I mean is, how can you tolerate the intensity of the pain that's so ever-presently there in people.

LEE: The focus is working in relationship to it. The process itself creates a functionality. It's not personal. That's the whole thing; it's not personal.

STUDENT: A man named Bucke wrote a book called, Cosmic Consciousness.

LEE: Where he estimated the average age of enlightenment was thirty-three. Jesus, Walt Whitman... he took their average age when they woke up.

STUDENT: A lot of my world view has come from some kind of naive childhood fantasy about consciousness or the divine, and one of the things that I still cling to is the idea that people who had the pole shift occur for them would really be in communion with each other. The Great White Brotherhood, The White Hats, The Federation, whatever the fantasy is, and yet I don't see it. The closest I see it is you hanging out with Arnaud Desjardins and E. J. Gold and Andrew Cohen, and a few guys like that. Is that it?
LEE: That's as close as it gets. In the world of appearances, that's as close as it gets.

STUDENT: I guess I still don't understand why that would be. If teachers aren't in communion, I can only assume that there must be remnants of ego, remnants of competition...

LEE: That's just the play of ego in the world. It makes no difference. In essence, everybody has their own path. If there was no differential, there would be no Work. Nobody would be able to find their teacher or their path. Everyone would be lost in this New Age haze. Differences are very necessary.

STUDENT: So it's actually lawful?

LEE: Yeah. At a very refined level, there is more communion than we ever hear of on the surface. On the surface of things, there's just different clubs.

STUDENT: In the Bodhisattva Vow, about 'sentient beings', what is a 'sentient being'?

LEE: Well, there is some differing of opinion amongst Buddhists about that. Some say sentient beings are only human beings and some animals. I just finished a book by the Dalai Lama in which he said that plants were not sentient beings. Other Buddhists say that all of life is sentient.

STUDENT: For the Bodhisattva Vow to be fulfilled, doesn't it mean that all life would have to become Bodhisattvas?

LEE: The assumption is that the Bodhisattva denies himself or herself entry into Nirvana until all sentient creatures can proceed him or her. So, in essence, many creatures could enter Nirvana without being Bodhisattvas, without returning to the world of illusion to serve the process. They would just go in and stay there.

STUDENT: In Singapore there is a park full of statues and scenes called How Par Gardens or Tiger Balm Gardens, full of gruesome hell-world scenarios. Is this Hindu or Buddhist?

LEE: Buddhist.

STUDENT: So there is some deciding factor when a being dies whether they go to Nirvana or to any particular hell realm.

LEE: Mmm-hmm.

STUDENT: Is it Buddha who decides?

LEE: No. It's one's actions.

STUDENT: But who interprets the actions?

LEE: No individual interprets the actions. The actions speak for themselves. Every action has an inherent implication.

STUDENT: Objectively?

LEE: Yes, according to that tradition.

STUDENT: I was always under the impression that either people got recycled or they went to Nirvana.

LEE: In that tradition there are very definite and clearly defined hell-worlds – several different kinds. How you've lived your life decides which one you're going to. If you've lived your life graspingly and greedily, you go to the hungry ghost hell-realm.

STUDENT: In the Baul tradition, is there any such cosmology?

LEE: Not that I know of. Coming back, staying on the wheel is the hell-realm. Remaining in the grip of karma is the hell-realm.

STUDENT: Is it necessary for consciousness to have a map of what happens for the 'pole-shift' to occur?

LEE: What matters is intention. Faith.

STUDENT: So it won't happen without that? If we were speaking about voltage, is faith the 'electric potential' for having 'pole-shift' occur?

LEE: Yes. But faith can be conscious or unconscious. For the amount of faith required, most people are never conscious of that.
STUDENT: Is it faith almost to the point of certainty?

LEE: Yes.

STUDENT: Is this faith declared on the basis of nothing?

LEE: Yes.

STUDENT: There is no evidence for the faith?

LEE: None. You can look at historical examples of what we would call advanced individuals. But in the present moment, there's absolutely no proof. No evidence.

STUDENT: Does faith come more from intention or more from surrender?

LEE: Surrender. The one who got surrendered can't surrender himself. Intention is volitional. Faith is something that happens.

STUDENT: It would seem that if you magnified Basic Goodness, you'd have faith? If there was a radical reliance on Basic Goodness, could faith come from having one's self included in the Basic Goodness of the world?

LEE: Faith has to do with the perfection of the process. Basic Goodness has to do with everybody's individual 'alrightness' within the process as it is.

STUDENT: But perfection is a mathematical concept. Perfection of the process won't appear to happen in this realm.

LEE: That's why faith requires complete acceptance. That's why there's no evidence for this. This is the realm of the senses. All evidence is gathered by the senses.

STUDENT: That might be the whole purpose of a human being's ability to conceive of perfection: to have that faith. The possibility of transcendence can't occur unless you can conceive of something beyond what's obvious in terms of evidence.

LEE: One of the secrets is transferring from the domain of science, to the domain of the mind, to the domain of the heart. (Lee laughs) This is why most mathematicians never get to be saints. They can't make the shift.

STUDENT: (Thinking to himself about all the mathematics involved in obtaining his degree in Physics.) Hmmmmm…

13. 1997: Interviewing Alexandro Jodorowsky

3 October 1997 – During Claudio Naranjo's month-long training in Spain.

Alexandro is a guest speaker at the month-long *Gestalt Therapy* seminar hosted by Claudio Naranjo. Spanish is Alexandro's native language, so a translator helped us during the following interview.

CLINTON: I have been a fan of yours since I saw your movies *Holy Mountain*, *El Topo*, and *Santo Sangre*. I know that you have been working with people for many years. There is a lot involved in working with people. I want to ask you some core questions about your work.

ALEXANDRO: Go. Ask it.

CLINTON: What are you doing with people?

ALEXANDRO: What I am doing with people?

CLINTON: What is your purpose? Where are you going?

ALEXANDRO: What I am doing with people is I am doing people.

CLINTON: What does that mean?

ALEXANDRO: I believe that in our society we are not being who we are. The human being has infinite possibilities which have not been explored yet.

CLINTON: How do you know this?

ALEXANDRO: I feel it within myself. All I do with people is transmit experiences I have had with myself. I do not treat the experiences as if they were mine. I treat the human self.

I am a human being like you and her (*the translator*). I work with myself because it is the closest human being to me, and is the state of consciousness where I am. From here I have difficulties with the language.

Apart from working with people, I am working on myself with language. I have learned that in these fields it is impossible to think with language the way we have learned it. The first reaction of people who feel realized when they encounter this problem is to reject the language and to reject the intellect. Their work begins with the study of the body, which is life as it presents itself.

I have noticed that I have a mental intellect. If I have a mental intellect, it is sacred, and it is possible, by means of thinking, to situate yourself well in life. Having previously been an anti-intellectual, I am now working the intellect. For example, when I say: "The state of consciousness I am in now," this is the same error as saying, "God is in all places." When I asked yesterday, "Where is God not?" God cannot be, because there is a duality between he who is and the place. God is not. He is not in a state. You cannot use that language. I cannot say 'the state of consciousness in which I am now' because it would be a duality. I cannot, the consciousness, be in a state. It is very difficult to speak of this.

I prepare for the future a system where I will work with people exclusively in the intellect. I work with the body in the meantime. I work with the emotions and sexuality and acts which I call psycho-magic acts. These are acts which permit us to liberate ourselves from negative pulsations of the unconscious emotional and sexual residues. All persons who are on a spiritual path know that it is not to try to reach anything, but rather to liberate yourself from what is not useful.

I see that society is in bad shape. I do not think I can do anything if I try to change society. If I try to change society, I would have to have a utopian theory about society. What I try to do is first to work with myself, then with you, then with all of us. Out of this work the new society must be born. And this is what we want. We are trying to create a better world. To create a better world, I had to learn how to learn. To love the world after I die. To love the humanity which will come. To love the world I will lose. To love the prosperity of the rich from the vantage point of my poverty. In order to do this, one must get out of time and work knowing that in future centuries you will be the unknown soldier. You know the tree but you do not know the seed. That is all of it.

For that I think you do not have to have plans. It is not necessary to visualize the future society. You only have to work in the possibilities of humans and awaken them. But when I say awaken, they are awake. I would say they are covered by what is not useful. For me, to work with someone is like peeling a banana.

CLINTON: When you peel a banana, are you saying, "Okay now, banana, go in the world and peel other bananas?"

ALEXANDRO: I do not produce soldiers, nor do I produce monks. Neither heroes nor champions nor saints nor geniuses. I work for the human being. That is all.

CLINTON: If you are working for the human being and you are a human being, are you teaching human beings to work with human beings?

ALEXANDRO: It is very subtle. I like that you have asked that question because no one has ever asked me that. It is all a science – how to treat the other. At times I teach a course, and on Thursdays I teach thirty therapists. Usually I do not work with therapists but this class is for therapists. The therapist learns how to sit. How to sit when the person arrives. How to move their hands. The gestures He should not do. What He should not have in his hands. How to look. From where his voice should resonate when He speaks to the other. How to have a human attitude and not a rigid attitude.

For example, I would have changed your attitude last night. With your attitude you prevented your teacher from communicating better. I will explain. The teacher was sitting like this. Totally informal. Comical. Taking away seriousness. Laughing – about himself and about us. Understanding that God is here and there is nothing to say. And you were sitting there like this. All straight. All serious. All devotion. The teacher was not a clown anymore. He was a serious man in your estimation. You never smiled. And all the silly things He said voluntarily, you were taping them. One automatically makes a union between the master and the student, and the master, for us, becomes something false. Because how can this teacher, who is like this, produce a student like you? It is not possible. I would have taught you to sit like the master, to echo the master and to dress like the master, not in contrast to him. I teach what you need to do so the message will come through without obstacles.

That is how I work. I work respecting, for example, the objects of the other. All the blocks, mental and physical. At times I use them. For example, in the conference I gave, I played with Claudio's rocking chair. In playing with his chair, I played with Claudio. Playing with Claudio, I played with the 'Claudio' his students have inside of them. And then it was a very agreeable and amiable thing.

The voice must resonate differently in the head, in the throat, in the chest, in the base. According to the person's problem, I teach them the voice to use. I also demonstrate what you have to have inside when you direct yourself to a person. Where you should not commit. What you should give. Where does what you give come from? How do you give it?

Here, watch what I do. (He moves his hand towards my shoulder.) I did not touch you. I cannot touch you like this. (He grips her shoulder firmly, solidly, full contact.) Her (the translator) I can. But you I must touch sweetly. I cannot touch you hard, because you are a closed man. So it is different. I look for the communication. Do you know the Evangelist? The prophet, John The Baptist. He said, "I come to prepare the path. I come to plan the way for the other one. The other one is here, but I have to prepare the way so that the other can come without obstacles."

Now, the first grand technique which I have discovered after many years of working with people will seem strange to you. It is confirmation. The first thing I do is communicate that just the way you are is perfect. If I do not first confirm you, I cannot do any good. First, I have to accept you - that you are okay. After you are okay and I accept that you are okay, now let us see what you need. The way you are is perfect. You do not have to be like me. You are perfect. That is the first step. Then we are friends.

You may ask me, "Why do you do all this?" I suffered very much in the world. I came into a family of barbarians, merchants, working people in Chile. Chile was a country without a mystical initiation. I noticed I was not satisfied with the world. I noticed I could not change it, but I discovered that I could begin to change it. And I dedicated myself to begin to change it. The whole world!

CLINTON: How old were you?

ALEXANDRO: I am sixty-eight.

CLINTON: No, I am sorry. I wanted to know how old you were when you committed to change the world.

ALEXANDRO: I was immortal until I was eighteen. Then one night I was at a party with my friends. We drank a lot. It was four o'clock in the morning. I was standing alone in the street, and there I suddenly died. I had nothing. I did not have religion; I did not have beliefs. I had nothing. After that moment I was looking to console dying – to understand that. What was dying? I could not sleep at night knowing that I was mortal. I could not accept it. I looked at God as a criminal. Everything lost its value. Everything. And I fell into the nothing. And there my work began. I started to lift myself up, to educate myself.

CLINTON: And you committed to change the world at that point.

ALEXANDRO: It had to be changed. The world was constructed in a way which did not respond to things. I could not live in that world. I did not have anyone to talk to. For example, about the Tarot. After eight years studying it by myself, I understood the Tarot in a very special way. Afterwards, I had no one to speak to. As if I spoke perfect German and there was no one in the world with whom to speak German. So I began teaching Tarot. I did groups with the Tarot. Later I taught thousands of people. Then it expanded on the planet. Now I have many people to talk to.

CLINTON: I would say that you are a man who wakes up the creative part of other people.

ALEXANDRO: I try.

CLINTON: So you are a creator who is creating creators.

ALEXANDRO: No. I am a transformer who is transforming transformers. No creation. Transformation.

CLINTON: Okay. Transformation of what to what?

ALEXANDRO: It is going from separation to union. That is all. We are separated. Transformation is from separation to union. Not only union with the exterior but within yourself. This is what I am doing.
I am not interested in American Capitalism. I do not want it. It is a prehistoric system which will end in two centuries. Two or three hundred years and that is it. We have got only a short time to wait for that. So my

change is not to produce performing soldiers in this society or in the new liberated society. I would never collaborate with that.

CLINTON: People are really afraid of communion. Like I was afraid when you were coming to touch me.

ALEXANDRO: I do it slowly.

CLINTON: Yes. But still there is fear. How do you work with people's fear? The big fear?

ALEXANDRO: I respect you first. I respect you. I establish where I can go with you. When I perceive how far I can go...

CLINTON: Intellectually or energetically?

ALEXANDRO: In all places. Then I call you to the limit. I tell you, "Come to the frontier. To your frontier." And then we start to go inside you together.

CLINTON: You go inside me together - instead of calling me outside, we go together inside.

ALEXANDRO: I go together. Listen to this: I have a student who is autistic. I saw that they were trying to get the autism out of him. So yesterday I put him in front of the world and I made the world go into him. He is much better today. The world came into him. I did it in the reverse. That is all. It takes time. Little by little. There is nothing that needs to be taken away from you.

CLINTON: So by you coming to me, that makes me bigger or more conscious?

ALEXANDRO: No. It makes you accompanied. There once was a man in Mexico who I saw hit by the wheel of an electric train. He was thrown down, waiting for the Red Cross. I knelt and took his hand. That is all I did. I accompanied him. I noticed that that was essential. You die better accompanied. You are born better accompanied. When I go to you, I give you my company. You may not get bigger or get smaller, but you are accompanied. I have not thought about it, but now that you ask me, it is so.

CLINTON: I see you teaching people to accompany others.

ALEXANDRO: Yes, naturally. For example, the wife of the biggest French neurologist, Director of a French Hospital, was dying of cancer and she did not want any of the professors to be there. She wanted me to be there. What could I do there? I could only accompany her. She asked me, "What is the finality of life?" And I told her, "There is no finality. The finality of life is to live." And she said, "I appreciate that very much." And the following day she died. And she died well. She died accompanied.

I have a student who wrote a bestseller in France. She works in hospitals now and accompanies people who are dying. But in no way religious. Human. I think when we die within religion we die badly because we die in theories and superstitions, which prevents us from living the instant moment. Is this what you wanted to know?

CLINTON: Yes. I have more questions. Is it okay to keep going?

ALEXANDRO: Yes, keep going. I am very curious to see how I will respond and what I will learn about myself.

CLINTON: In order for me to be able to accompany others, I first have to be able to accompany myself, and I am afraid to accompany myself. How do you work with one's fear to accompany one's self?

ALEXANDRO: Very easily. You can accompany me. Perfectly. You take me into your arms and put my ear next to your heart. Your heart will beat with my heart and there you sustain me to where I need it. Your heart will accompany me, not you. I do not need to know anything about your psyche. Your heart is pure. It will accompany me. You can give your heart to whomever: to a child; an old man, a wise man, a fool, a saint. You take him to your heart and you accompany him. Why do you make a problem? Why should there be a problem?

CLINTON: I have a group of thirty people, sometimes seventy-five people, and they want something. I am with them and they want something. They are here to learn to be with people and they are together to be with each other, and yet there is so often separation, and so often fear.

ALEXANDRO: These are my hands. I do not reject anything of myself: my hands, my heart, my sex, my feet. I trust you. That is all. Difficulties? Pass through them. One has to observe a lot, with great gentleness. For example, this morning during breakfast, you made a very lovable gesture. You went to get ice cream and brought one for yourself and two for your teacher. And you gave this to your professor. You could have brought two, not three. But you brought something more for the other. That is the truth. You must give the other more than you give to yourself.

CLINTON: People think they do not have enough already; how can they give more?

ALEXANDRO: You have to show them that what they give they do not give themselves. The ice cream you gave was not yours. You are giving what you do not have. You have to teach people to give what they do not have. The Arabs say if you close your hand, you have a fist of sand. If you open your hand, the entire desert passes through your hand. With an open hand you do not have a desert. So, you are very generous. When you close your hand, you have something that is yours and then you cannot give. Do you know why those stories are so beautiful? Because I love them very much. I speak about what I love very much. What I do not like, it does not exist. What else do you want to know, my dear young man?

CLINTON: There is so much pain. I live in a nice place and I work in nice places, but in between those places there are many people with much pain.

ALEXANDRO: This is the pain of the world. And how well you live is part of the pleasure of the world. It is good that you live like that so that someone is happy. It is good. If all my teeth hurt and there is one that does not hurt, what a miracle. However, once you are conscious, you have to diminish suffering – but without sacrificing your suffering, because for some reason you got it.

I met a guru who did not get up from his bed because his body felt all the dreadful things occurring in the world. When there was war in Yugoslavia his leg hurt. He was full of pain. I thought he was a fool, because at the same time he did not feel all the miracles happening in the world in his body. He specialized in feeling the terrible stuff and he believed he was a saint.

To me he was a devil because he was putting suffering on top of suffering.

For example, if I see someone suffering, I do not suffer, because then I aggregate suffering. Inside my neutrality I can help them. And if I cannot help them, I do not do anything. I do not suffer because I cannot help them. The important thing is to help the other.

CLINTON: People get very angry if you do not suffer with them.

ALEXANDRO: Yes. If they get angry, I do not get angry too. They can be furious, but me, I do not care. It is not useful. The person has to know that what occurs to them, they have to handle it inside of them.

CLINTON: So how can you be in communion with them and not be affected?

ALEXANDRO: When you call them 'them', when you say 'them', you are talking of the illusion that is their shadows. I am not in communication with what they are not. I am in communication with what they are.

CLINTON: So you determine what they are...

ALEXANDRO: I don't determine anything. (To the translator he says: "Tell him he is talking with a humble person." Then he laughs.) "I am not determining anything."

CLINTON: Yes, I am speaking with a humble person, but a very confident, powerful and bold humble person.

ALEXANDRO: What is, is. Within craziness, sickness and death lies. The person that enters into this path, does not have to worry if they are crazy, sick, lying, pretending. He has to have the certainty of what he is doing. Where does certainty come from? From your interior. No one has to confirm that for you. You do not have to depend on anyone.

CLINTON: Many people are committed to the belief that certainty does not exist in them.

ALEXANDRO: Momentarily, yes. That is why we do this work. To take them to the certainty that they are useful.

CLINTON: Last night, I saw you in front of one-hundred and fifty people. I do not pretend to know everything that you were doing, but I saw you working with the energy of the whole group. Where did you learn that?

ALEXANDRO: I never learned that. I did it.

CLINTON: When did you 'did' it first? How can you teach that to somebody else? How can you give that away?

ALEXANDRO: One day when I was seventeen and an actor, I said, "I need to start to change the world." I loved to read Tarot cards. I went to a coffee shop and I told the owner, "I will read here every Wednesday from seven to nine at night. I will read the Tarot." He said, "Yes."

I did that. And then every week I gave a conference.

It is like this Chinese story. There was a mountain whose shadow covered a village. The people were growing badly because they had no light. One morning the oldest man went to the mountain with a teaspoon, and everyone said "What are you doing?" He said, "I go to the mountain to move it." They told him, "Look, old man, you will never do that with a teaspoon." He said, "Yes, that is true. I will never do it. But somebody has to start."

I started to change the world. My kind of mysticism, I learned that. My kind of therapy, I learned that. I do it. For eighteen years I am doing that.

Sometimes I have the flu; sometimes I am tired, but I do it. I committed to a contract with myself. I always will do that. To go and do it and to not get paid.

At first only a few people would come. Then more and more, six-hundred, eight-hundred. For me one-hundred persons, one-thousand persons is a person. When I was making movies in Italy, I would stop production and fly back to Paris to do the Tarot every Wednesday night.

CLINTON: What you are committed to is giving this away?

ALEXANDRO: I am not committed to anything. Nothing.

CLINT: But, you were committed every Wednesday....

ALEXANDRO: I committed to myself, but I did not commit myself to heal anyone. If I want to do it, I do. If I do not want to do it, I do not do it. I do whatever I feel. Because I do not need that. My ego is satisfied.

In art: I make movies; I make books. My ego is very happy. I am very well known. No problem. When I work with people, I am anonymous. Here I am a servant of Claudio. Claudio is the owner of that. Claudio is the start. Out in the world, I am very well known. Here it is Claudio. And he made me the enormous pleasure to let me do what I do. I am not the center. I can do something good. If I want to do, I do. If I do not want to do, I don't. I do not need that. (To the translator, he says: "Do you think he believes me?")

It is true. I am so happy doing that. I am also happy to work with my sons. I do not obligate them. They come; they like it too. They like what I do. I teach one of them, and they know very well. For me it is a great pleasure. They work. For me it is a big pleasure. I do not need to feel anything. A big pleasure.

My books are artistic. In Mexico I published 'The Gospel to Heal'. This I did for Mexico and Chile in order to heal Mexico and Chile because they are so Catholic. This side also is a little anonymous. Everything with the spiritual is anonymous. A little. It is not my business.

But if I earn money, I am very happy to earn money. I love money. I am not against money. What I am against is its exploitation. For me, money in this society is the most spiritual thing. When the other person wants to make a lot of money, I am very happy. It is good because it means prosperity; it means they will make many employees. That is good.

Is this useful for you?

CLINTON: Yes. It is good. Thank you for saying yes to this conversation with no hesitation.

ALEXANDRO: I want to know: Why were you so serious yesterday? Why are you so serious? Why? Why you never laugh once?

Tomorrow you go and take three ice creams. You give one to your friend [Lee Lozowick] and in front of him you eat two. One for him and two for you. You do not say anything to him. You put three and then you take two and you eat them quickly. Two at the same time. Why do you need to have less than him?

CLINTON: I am afraid of taking attention here. I am not here for me. I do not want to insult Claudio. I am a big guy. I take up space. I am loud. I lead trainings with lots of people. And this is not my training. It is Claudio's, and yours.

ALEXANDRO: Because you were like that, you forced Lee to be rigid and serious. You forced him to be like you. No one dared to make questions to Lee. When I work with people I need to open. And I need questions in order to open.

CLINTON: Okay. Thank you Alexandro. I will do that. [And I did.]

14. 1998: One

10 June 1998 – One morning during meditation at La Ferme de Jutreau

It is early morning. Thrills of wakefulness shoot up from the bottoms of my bare feet to the hairs on the back of my neck as I stride across the cold dew-covered grass. I am crossing from the cow-stall – our summer sleeping palace – to the rear entry-room of the big house, which we are still using as our miniature winter Darshan Hall.

We would have moved the Darshan Hall over to the big barn by now, except that the entire barn interior is heavily coated in dust and spider webs, still functioning as a woodshop and storage facility. Transforming the ancient stone and timber hay-barn into a formal Darshan Hall is but one of a zillion things which needs to be handled before the American Sangha arrives in five days. It's already Wednesday, June 10. The first wave of guests lands in France on Monday. That doesn't give us nearly enough time to properly prepare. You would think that by the third Sangha Summer we would have gotten ourselves more together than this...

Ducking into the small darkened meditation chamber I suddenly remember that I can relax this morning. Thomas is Pujari. He will keep his eye on the time and perform the familiar rituals and duties. I am free to just sit.

Stuccoed walls reflect the dim glow, barely enough light to see by. I am positioned diagonally behind Thomas, off to his right side. This situates the bulk of his Nordic body directly between me and the Puja table.

I breathe a deep sigh and settle onto the pillow, eyes closed, solid.

Shortly, I notice that there is a question niggling at me. It is a familiar question, one that I have been working with off and on for thirteen years.

E.J. Gold fooled around with this same question. He wrote that it was important to him, though he made no big deal out of it. I only saw reference to it once in his writings. On first learning the question, it didn't even make sense to me: *How is consciousness differentiated?* What separates individual self-awarenesses one from another?

I don't know why this question stuck with me all these years. Something about it must have intrigued me at a deep level – perhaps the fact that I couldn't relate to it at all. Or maybe my interest is only that E.J. liked it. The consideration is not something I've lost sleep over, but now and then I chew on it. Lately it has become more and more relevant. This morning it slowly forces my eyes open.

It is silent and still but for the birds chirping raucously outside. Three candles light the nine-by-twelve foot room. One is a tea light in a clear glass holder, resting at the feet of the green robed Vigraha of Yogi Ramsuratkumar on a table in the right corner. The other two are simple white candlesticks in Indian brass holders – half burnt sentinels standing at attention to either side of our Murti of Lee Lozowick.

I gaze at the Murti, which I can see clearly to the right of Thomas' head. In this particular photograph, Lee appears to look wistfully down-wards. He is not peering directly at us, as He does in some Murtis. The mood is shyly pensive, tender, vulnerable, though completely without weakness or uncertainty. I wonder what He was thinking about at the time the photo was taken. I wonder what He was experiencing.

I notice the two candles. I can see the candle on the right directly. The left candle is completely hidden from my view behind Thomas' head, yet its image – reflected in the Murti glass – is faultless. If I did not know about reflections, I would swear that what I was looking at was an actual burning candle.

It occurs to me that it would be possible to experience the reflection of that candle anywhere in the room simply by placing a piece of glass there to shine its likeness back to me. What a mirror does is take an invisible image that is available at one particular place and make it visible.

I could get a little wild and arrange to place, say, a hundred mirrors in this room! A thousand! From each mirror I set up I could get yet another reflection of the same candle. The only reason that I do not see these other thousands of views right now is that there is no glass there to reflect them back to me. Nonetheless, the images are potentially still there. Thousands and thousands of views of this one candle are completely fill-ing the room right now, even though I cannot see them, or even see the candle itself.

No matter how many mirrors I set out, they would not 'use up' or diminish the images radiated from the original candle. Each mirror would simply reflect back to me an image that is already there.

Even though there are nearly an unlimited number of possible images scattered all throughout the room, all of the images come from a solitary flame. One candle sources all the reflections, whether they are seen or unseen, reflected or not reflected. One single candle.

And that's it: ONE.

I feel the question about consciousness do a flip-flop in my body.

How is consciousness differentiated? The answer is that IT IS NOT!

Consciousness is NOT differentiated. It is ONE.

Consciousness is already everywhere, just like the images of the candle.

The candle image is already everywhere in the room.

God is already everywhere in the universe.

ONE! This is too obvious! Yogi Ramsuratkumar keeps saying over and over again, "All of this is my Father's blessing." This is no sweet poetry dripping from an old man's lips. He is being absolutely literal. The stones, the dust, the air, trees, ravens, concrete floors - problems - miracles - possibilities - everything manifests out of the ever-present consciousness that is God. From the tiniest to the greatest, from the nearest to the farthest, uncreated, everlasting, just like it says in the Vedas. Every-thing.

Human bodies just happen to be the things in this world that have sophisticated enough matrix that consciousness can become aware of itself. "What you are looking for is what you are looking with!" Self-reflecting consciousness only happens in human bodies, not in flowers or dogs. Flowers and dogs are not quite complex enough.

There are seven of us sitting in the room meditating right now. Each one of us is 'made in God's image', a 'reflection' of God. It is our bodies that act as the mirror to reflect that image. Godness is already everywhere. Godness only becomes apparent on the material plane when there is an object through which the Godness can function. The object is itself the Godness functioning. The more refined, complex, or evolved the object is, the more accurately and completely it manifests the Godness.

ONE? But why don't we automatically know this?! Why are we so completely convinced of our separation from each other and from God? Why can't we notice and experience the field of consciousness that is everywhere within us and around us?

Just because there are two images does not mean that there are two candles! Just because there are two bodies does not mean that there are two consciousnesses!

But why does the illusion of separation seem so real to us? Do you know how much unnecessary pain this causes? War? Jealousy? Greed? Hatred? Why is the true perception of reality so rare? Why are we so invested in maintaining a distinct identity? Why are we each in such survival and scarcity so often?

Oh. I see. It is because we have a body.

Of course. It has to be this way. It is mechanical. Identification is an inescapable side-effect of incarnation. The natural and obvious perception of who we are when we incarnate is that we are what we incarnate as. If we don't identify with incarnation, we don't incarnate. Incarnation happens through identification.

That's why the body seems so real. We experience pain, so we must be the nerves and tissues. We have thoughts and learn to speak, so we must be our mind. We experience strong feelings and emotions so we identify with these sensations. The body has a natural built-in commitment to survive. We are designed to use everything we can to protect ourselves with an impervious psychological defense strategy. It truly feels to us like this is who we are. We have no evidence for thinking otherwise...

That is, until we somehow start asking questions..., until we decide that we want to know the truth..., until we are willing to experience the full depth and intensity of our longing to go home, regardless of the cost.

When you pour cream into cream what you get is cream. Where is the balloon-ness after you pop the balloon and release the air back into the air? We sing about this every week in the Guru Gita. The description is exact. Lee has been talking about non-duality for twenty-three years. "Just this," He says. "Just this."

The truth can become evident in a whore-house or a shit-house, a dining hall or a meditation hall, on a battlefield or a baseball field, where or how is not important. Each lock has a different key. It's the unlocking that's important, the disidentification. The key is invited to appear when you begin to pray, as Phillip K. Dick wrote, "I wish to encounter a disinhibiting factor which will trigger my anamnesis."

It is so obvious. All of the cute little metaphors for awakening are true – and they don't matter. They don't help. All of the sophisticated models and explanations are correct – and they don't make a damn bit of difference for someone who is trying to figure it out. It cannot be figured out. That's what pisses me off. None of it makes any sense until you can experience it for yourself, and then it's as plain as day. The truth is nonlinear and unreasonable. Yet it is all around us, everywhere, all the time, in everything, always. It IS us!

Jeeeezus!

Is that it? Is that all there is to it? Is that the Big Secret that keeps itself hidden from everyone who is not prepared to receive it? E.J. Gold says we are awake dozens of times each day. What's the big deal? As Werner Erhard might say, "It's the so what of what's so."

Lee has been very careful to give us instructions about this. He says that it is easy to give people the experience of enlightenment. Put a bottomless paper bag on their face, for example. It doesn't take much.

But that's not the point. It's what we do with the experience once we get it that counts. Realizing ONE is only the beginning of spiritual Work. The real test is, how do we live the realization? Lee is very clear about that. He says: "Time will tell." He says: "We will see."

Three bells ring.

We bow. We sing Arati together. We receive blessings of the fire, and take Prasad. I walk unsteadily outside. The grass is not quite so cold, though it feels a bit odd. What is different?

Everything. And nothing. Just like normal.

Time to change my clothes. I have work to do.

15. 1999: Lee Lozowick In His Own Words

10 Sept 1999 – Notes from a Lee Lozowick Seminar at *Terre du Ciel* in France.

My seminars are about war. If you aren't at war with your illusions then my seminars are about starting that war. My wars are not aggressive or violent (like Christian wars). They are sacred and compassionate. I'm interested in the kind of war that has no winner and no loser. It's not competition. There is no enemy. This war is about exposing reality. When truth is the victor there is <u>no</u> loser.

The mind is not all that important. It doesn't eat. It doesn't have sex. The problem with most people's diet and most people's sex is that they are letting the mind do it.

The way I teach is to provoke emotions and feelings. The domains I provoke are often atrophied, so having them stimulated is often uncomfortable. Our muscles of truth and reality are atrophied. We've forgotten what it is to be real or true. I am a spiritual physical therapist.

I create circumstances where revelation is possible. This is not linear teaching. If I say something that makes sense to you and you assume that because it makes sense to you, you know it, that will be just one more illusion that will have to be destroyed. But if I am able to create an experience that will allow knowledge to spontaneously arise within you, then <u>you</u> will know it.

Two things are necessary for the transmission of grace to occur. The sender must have grace and the recipient must know how to receive it. If you are around me you get to learn the principles of the receptivity of grace.

The pure acceptance of this moment, as it is in this moment, has no relationship to the way things were in the last moment and the way they will be in the next moment. We may be neurotic in this moment but the law of reality does not say we have to be neurotic in the next moment.

It is the law of psychology that says the next moment is based on the present moment. The acceptance of what is redefines the domain from one of psychology to one of reality. The acceptance of what is here and now is the most powerful force of change in the universe.

The difference between psychotherapy and spiritual work is context. Psychotherapy takes 'the dream' to be real, takes the illusion of separation to be real, and assumes that a disturbance in the dream that can be recreated to be not disturbing fixes the problem. The unspoken assumption is that healthy psychology equals reality and is the truth. If you look at the technology of psychotherapy, it is not about the realization of reality. It is about coming to a harmonious balance within the illusion. It can be a valuable preliminary part of the path. We can't work spiritually if we are psychologically obstructed.

There are two contexts: ego and truth. When we live in the context of ego, truth can arise. But the experience arises and subsides back into the context of illusion. When we live in the context of truth, an experience of ego can arise. But it arises and subsides back into the context of truth. The path shifts context from ego to truth. Our experience may remain the same in form, but not in essence. One of the things the path does is turn difficult elements of our psychology into useful forces on the path.

If it bothers you enough you will be willing to take the necessary steps to resolve the confusion. People don't change because they love God. They change because they are in pain.

If you are moving towards God because God is beautiful, turn around. Find yourself a lover who can really cook - live, drink and be merry. If you are moving towards God and God accepts you, you will be thrown into a meat grinder.

If we make an action and the result of that action is to inspire others, then that is a creative action. If we make an action and the result of that action is to resolve our confusion, then this is merely distraction. Creativity is other motivated. Distraction is about ourselves. Most artists are glorifying what they believe is their own talent. True creativity moves in a positively influential way beyond our own circumstance.

All the clues are hidden and they are obscure. The Treasure is Yourself (God). The treasure is of such value that to throw it in your lap would be uninteresting to God. You have to pay for it with intention, commitment, and the willingness to go all the way. Trying to figure out the clues in a group is more likely to succeed than trying to figure it out alone.

This weekend was a learning forum. There may have been some information transferred and that was icing on the cake. It was intended for you to learn something that will help you on the path.

If any value was produced this weekend, something that continues to feed you over time, it was a common effort.

I do not work in a void. Neither do any of you.

16. 2000: Some Amazing Things (Psychologically Speaking...)

24 April 2000 – For Tawagoto

We live in such solid, perfectly defended little self-made prisons. This is a very personal and individual choice. It is not something we have inherited from our parents or society. We do it, under our own volition and free will. We are doing it right now! This is what is so amazing about it. We are the prisoners and we are the prison guards. We are the prison itself. (While dropping me off at the airport following our Monday 'Morning After' meeting, Sue Nestrud said, "Time after time during the Intensive I would desperately grip onto one of the bars of my prison as if to hold it in place as a solid piece of reality which I had always known and could count upon, only to suddenly discover that I had nothing in my hands!") We use all of our immense creative power not for the purpose of disassembling this prison so that something new can occur for us and others in our life, but rather to over and over again (every three seconds) reinvent an identical prison for ourselves so that everything in our life remains exactly the same as it was in the moment before. We consign ourselves to a life of solitary confinement with no chance of parole. We dedicate every effort to sustaining conditions as they are, because only then do we feel 'safe'. Only in this prison cell do we feel like we will survive. This is an amazing thing!

Here are some more amazing things. When we make an action, we are identified with that action. We have no separation from it. We act as if our action were true, as if that one particular action were the only possible solution to all of the problems at hand. We have no idea of the purpose we are serving through executing that action, and we are blind to any feedback about our action. We think the action is isolated and independent.

We think it is not mechanical. Most remarkably, we pretend ignorance of the possibility that our action is merely a piece of dramatic theater which we are generating as a way of creating an invocation around ourselves intended to suck everyone around us into agreeing that we are victims of the circumstances in this situation, and that we have no alternatives but to act as we do!

We invoke these detailed, intricate, involved, emotionally charged and irrefutably clever theatrical performances to attract our own attention away from our attention, so that we cannot self-observe and begin to notice our motivations and true intentions - which may not be as pretty or high-minded as we might like to think. Being thus identified we prevent ourselves from realizing that what looks like hard immutable circumstances are only solid-looking when viewed from a certain specifically chosen and unique perspective.

Our perspective frames up a set of interpretations which, when applied to the facts, twists them into enemies and permits us to assess that we are 'in' a situation, that we 'have' a problem, and that we are justified... no, we are forced to act as we act. We think we are prisoners, victims 'in' a situation, victims 'of' a problem, rather than seeing that we are ongoingly, moment to moment generating and directing that situation.

The truth is quite different from this. We are actually the source of our situations and problems. We spend our days (and nights) acting center-stage in a show that we wrote the script for and set the stage for, and for which we have rehearsed and played one or more parts repeatedly for most of our lives. It is our favorite show. We arrange things so we get to play out our best-loved characters. And we do not want anyone to know that we are having this much fun! Especially ourselves! (OWN IT!) This is so amazing!

Part of the show is that we develop and profess some opinion of ourselves, some self-image that concludes that we are perhaps to some degree creative, or maybe not very creative at all. We think some people are more creative than others. We might even consider taking a class to improve our 'creativity'. Yet every word we speak, every thought we think, every action we make, every energetic or physical gesture, every facial or tonal expression, every emotion we feel, the qualities of our every experience, every place we put our attention or fail to put our attention, every condition we see or understand, or fail to see, or fail to understand, every interpretation we make, is an act of creation made to serve a purpose. We are either conscious of the purpose we serve (High Drama), or we are serving unconscious purposes (Low Drama).

Serving conscious or unconscious purposes is neither right nor wrong, neither good nor bad. Serving conscious or unconscious purposes simply produces different results, and in either case, we are always creating, and it is all theater. All of this theater is overlaid onto a completely neutral universe. We create Low Drama so that we think that we must continue to put on the show as we have always put it on. This is the Defensive Context: Serving ourselves. Being totally dedicated to keeping things the same. The Expansive Context puts us always at risk by being responsible for serving something greater than ourselves, yet not knowing how, so always having to reinvent ourselves in order to create results. You can always detect if you are serving a conscious or unconscious purpose by the quality of the results which are created. None of this is based on beliefs.

It is amazing that we think we have no other choice but to act as we do. We create this illusion for ourselves by thinking we have an identity that is real, that is permanent and solid and cannot shift, and which has a fixed set of 'needs'. (Hah! It is all politics! Whichever 'Identity' happens to be in power in this moment gets to determine which 'needs' are real and which must be met! (Hint: To wreck the game, Name the Identities. Naming is a powerful alchemical act. If you want to change the 'needs' of the moment, change the Identity of the moment, in yourself, or others. This is a very fun game!)). We create the illusion of having no choice by failing to ask the question: "Who chooses to have no choice?" We train ourselves to ask no real questions, to not ask at all. Disallowing our awesome power to ask questions ensures that we will not discover who operates the levers behind the curtain. (Note: As a human being, we have the ability to make commitments and take responsibility at a level that is greater than our personal preferences, likes and dislikes, and comfort.)

It is amazing that we would think that we do not have enough time when we have all the time there is: we have all the time that anyone else has, and are choosing every moment what to do with it. Who do we blame for choosing what we make time for? What a game!

It is amazing how many of us hand over our lives to some little voice from our mind that says, "I'm tired! I'm exhausted! I deserve a break today!" and then choose to go unconscious, thinking that things should be some way else other than they are. It is amazing that we do not simply enjoy things as they are, or reinvent our experience of them if we want.

It is amazing that we pretend to be afraid of fear so as to continue the behaviors and attitudes which fulfill our addictions, reward us with our payoffs, feed the psychological vampire entities (good boy, nobody loves me, nice girl, outcast, victim, poor me, being right, being superior, fantasy life, etc.) which devour our hearts, our lives, and our loved ones, and fulfill our Hidden Purposes, yet at the same time we crave fear and pay dearly to experience it by driving unsafely, eating and drinking unhealthily, exposing ourselves to terror in the news and at movies, by lying, by engaging in gossip, by finding persecutors, even by going to Disneyland.

It is amazing that we glance over the dry, barren landscape, looking for minimalized, mediocre opportunities, rather than realizing that we, ourselves, hold up the veil which makes the infinite possibilities present in every moment and available from every chamber appear to be invisible and inaccessible to us. Rather than creating opportunities for ourselves and others out of available materials, or better yet, out of nothing (a material which is readily at hand, anytime, anywhere, for no cost - if we have the space for it!), we go around like crippled elephants at a fashion show thinking there is no opportunity to be found, and nobody loves us besides.

It is amazing that we have made ourselves afraid of the power of insanity. Insanity is where nothing is. Insanity is where nonlinear possibilities and orthogonal moves come from. Relating is always an ongoing act of nonlinear creation. If we do not have access to insanity, we cannot create relating. No wonder relating seems dead, and love seems possible anywhere else but here. Relating is always sourced through invention. Love is invented. Right here, by you, with what you have right now. Or your life is loveless, worthless as an outdated coupon for thirty-cents off a jar of 'Miracle Whip' mayonnaise, lying faded on the road.

Life becomes simultaneously horrifying and exhilarating, the most fulfilling of endeavors, in the moment you commit to being the source of relating and love in your life (or the source of love in someone else's life, or, if you are truly insane, the source of love in life itself) even though you do not know how. (You may think that you already know what this means, but consider the possibility that you do not. Consider the possibility that you do not even know that you do not know what this means. This is not new age philosophy. This is alchemy. There is a big difference. You can discover the difference.)

If you really wanted to be loving in any situation, who could stop you?

There exist many more amazing things.

If you don't discover them, who will?

17. 2000: An Evening In Arnaud Desjardins' Garden

Summer 2000 – At Hauteville, the French Ashram of Arnaud Desjardins

The buzz is that Arnaud Desjardins for the first time has offered to let students of Lee Lozowick ask him questions in a private meeting tonight at his patio at Hauteville. Every other year Arnaud treated Lee's students with grand hospitality, but dedicated all spaces to Lee Lozowick's speaking and answering questions. Yet Lee's standing instructions to us are that during meeting spaces at Arnaud's, and all public talks or workshops in general, questions are reserved for the guests, not Lee's students.

That makes this indeed a rare opportunity. But something becomes clear almost immediately to me. This is not a rare opportunity for us, Lee's students. This is a rare opportunity for Arnaud Desjardins. And there is a job for me to do. I mention to M. and A. that they should be prepared to take very good notes because I will be trying something a little wild tonight, and I will not be able to write. They agree.

As we gather outdoors on Arnaud's flagstone patio, Arnaud and Lee sit together on the low stone wall. It is the luxurious calm and balmy summer evening as only France can produce, perfect for growing sweet peaches and large juicy apricots. A dozen or so of Lee's students huddle at the feet of these two great friends. Silence descends upon us accompanied by an ancient, archetypally-formal teacher/student transmission space.

I place myself in the center of the group of listeners, sit cross-legged on the flagstones, and hold a strong intention to create a listening into which Arnaud can truly cut loose and speak from his heart about whatever he most wants to speak about. Although I direct most of my attention towards Lee and Arnaud, I reserve twenty percent of my attention to move my energetic center to my physical center so that I am centered. From there I make a grounding cord five times as thick as my usual grounding cord, which connects my center to the center of the Earth. I declare an energetic bubble of personal space around myself, and additionally I declare a golden cube of work space around the whole group. Then I call the Bright Principles of the Hohm Community into that space, namely Kindness, Generosity, and Compassion. This takes only a few seconds. Then I prepare my hand to shoot up into the air the instant Arnaud begins to ask, "Are there any questions?"

That moment arrives almost immediately. My hand leaps vertically and stays there unwaveringly. It is neither frantic, nor demanding. It is merely certain. Arnaud looks at me in the eyes and says, "Yes?"

I say, "Could you please tell us more about your teacher, Swami Prajnanpad?"

Arnaud's face breaks into this huge gentle smile, warm enough to melt the hearts of all who are present. "Yes," He says.

Arnaud Desjardins proceeds to ecstatically roll out story after miraculous story, lesson after wondrous lesson, all he can share from the years with his Master.

I don't remember a word that he says.

I am fully occupied being electrocuted by huge currents of shakti energy flowing from somewhere up behind Arnaud, through Arnaud into the space, then through me down my grounding cord into the Earth. This I arranged on purpose.

By continuously emptying the energy out of the space down my grounding cord, the space cannot be filled up with energy. An energetically filled space creates back-pressure on the speaker. With no back-pressure, Arnaud is free to continue downloading his insights and emotions, pouring full blessings onto everyone there. The listening in our group is effectively bottomless. Arnaud gets to be fully used.

Arnaud goes on speaking to us for forty-five minutes before he comes to a pause and looks to see how we are all doing, eventually asking for the next question. My nervous system is smoking from overdrive, crackling and sparking from the stress of conducting such a huge current of shakti. So many people benefitted, and I lived to tell the tale.

The experiment works.

It is a night to celebrate, and a night to remember.

Some time later, in Arizona, at the bottom of the stairs leading from the old Hohm Office up to Lee's private kitchen in Arrakis, I give

Lee the last hug I would ever give him. He has just returned from his last trip to India. His physical body is skin and bones, decimated by the disease, but his soul shines brighter than ever.

After the hug Lee looks me in the eyes while holding both of my shoulders in his hands and says, "Nobody asks questions like you."

I include this anecdote not to lavish praises upon myself, but rather to share with you a way I discovered of serving a speaker and a space, a way you could learn and practice. Imagine how valuable an experience it is for a teacher to be fully used, to speak into a listening that can receive all that he or she has to give. You can build that listening space for them.

18. 2000: Divine Alchemy Part 1

6 November 2000 – Contributed to Hohm Sahaj Mandir Study Manual III and IV

mAN TO MAN

The entire teaching of the Western Baul Tradition, as with the core distinctions of every true path of spiritual evolution, rests physically encoded within the body of every man. (It also rests within the body of every woman. Those considerations are written about elsewhere.)

Stated most simply, a man lacks nothing to becoming Man. Spelling the word 'man' with a small 'm' is intended to mean the quality of man as produced by modern culture – in other words, self-referenced man, problematical man, conniving, arrogant, patriarchal, uninitiated man. Spelling the word 'Man' with a capitalized 'M' is intended to refer to an authentically initiated adult man, the archetypally stellated King, Warrior, Alchemist, Lover… Man Number Four, Man On The Path, etc.

This is not referring to Enlightened Man or God-Man. This is merely referring to the designed-in, natural capacity which every man has for being responsible and having integrity, the basic prerequisites for being a spiritual student and apprentice to a Spiritual Master. The premise for this consideration of Man is that every factor and ingredient necessary for the transformation from man into Man is available in the body of every man.

The intention in this writing is to clearly outline those factors and perspectives so that readers can consider what is possible for themselves and also what is possible in relating with each other, Men with Men, and Men with Women. The capacities outlined below are ground zero; they represent the so-called 'first position' for Manhood. They also indicate precisely what the Spiritual Master can be expected to expect from a man at the outset of a mature Master-Apprentice relationship.

We must begin this consideration by looking directly and unreservedly at something you probably know to be true in your guts, but which you are probably unwilling to carry around with you in your day-to-day perspectives because it at first appears to be so disgustingly dishonorable.

We begin this consideration of man by fully acknowledging that man, as known and lived in Twenty-First Century Western cultures, is not Man. Patriarchal men live as selfish, lying, obsequious, insecure, self-hating, self-aggrandizing, weak-visioned, small-berried, will-less, momma-hating or momma-owned little boys. This includes all of your role models, political leaders, military leaders, corporate leaders, religious leaders, and popular entertainment stars, entirely without exception.

Upon reading such a scathing indictment you may at first feel insulted and defensive, readying your rebuttal with examples of personal exception. After understanding what is written below, I wager that another more concurring and sober perspective will emerge for you. I suggest that, rather than arguing now to defend your weak and unexamined position, instead you slog forth and keep reading.

Ask yourself, "After all these centuries of life, why would an intelligent Western culture promote and reward a man for being without dignity, clarity or power? Why would a man be trained to have unquenchable neediness and neurotic insecurities?"

Consider this answer: "Because when a man feels like he does not know himself, he can be manipulated, controlled, and marketed to."

In Western culture, if a man cannot be sold to, he is considered worthless to the multi-national military-industrial corporate machine which takes it upon itself to determine the values of anyone who does not consciously declare their values for themselves. (You might as well read that as 'everyone'.) Men have no option but to accept the massive proclamation of ineptitude because men have not been taught to live as anything different.

What we are suggesting is that transformation of boy into Man is possible through an archetypal journey that builds matrix to hold more consciousness through authentic adulthood initiatory processes contexted in radical responsibility.

ARCHETYPAL JOURNEY

Mommy will never cut the 'apron strings' that are tied to a man's brain, heart, testicles and soul. Never. As long as a mother regards herself as a 'mother', the mothering role requires that she always have children around her, regardless of how old they are or how old she is.

No amount of struggling, isolating, explaining, pleading, revenging, complaining, blaming, or fighting between a boy child and his mother will change the fact that for a mother, her boy can never become a Man. If he did, then who would she be? (No longer a mother.) And if she is not a mother, then she is without identity in the capitalist patriarchal empire of modern culture, which, as you know, is a terrifying state for an uninitiated psychology.

It should be noted that there exist procedures whereby a woman with children can actually graduate from the role of mother when her children reach the appropriate age of approximately eighteen years old. During this exquisite transition the woman elegantly eradicates her singular identification with the role of 'mother', automatically regaining access to her full repertoire of characters including friend, researcher, adult woman, wife, concubine, professional, adventurer, poet, teacher and also her real name. She frees herself from the tyranny of a single character's limitations in reality, thus re-declaring herself as Woman. By accomplishing this transformational self-surgery, a woman enters a vaster, less definite, and far more authentic relating with the Universe.

Annihilating the 'mother' script contradicts years of 'irrefutable' circumstantial evidence, and shatters a woman's long held and strongly reinforced self-image. As can be imagined, the procedure is not comfortable, and is therefore rare. On the other hand, nothing less than this will free a woman to also become a spiritual student and establish a Woman's relationship with a Spiritual Master. However, we digress. We were speaking of men.

The man must cut the cord between himself and his mother, or it will not be cut. The corollary to this is that if you have not consciously and completely cut the energetic umbilical cord to your mother, then it has not been severed, and you live as an addendum to your momma, answering to her every need whether you think you are or not. You should know that these quaintly named 'apron strings' truly exist, and, when viewed with eyes wide open to perceiving such things, are actually a bundle of stretchy, resilient, white-colored energetic lines that tie into various parts of your body and follow you wherever you go and whatever you do in your days and in your nights, even if your good old ma is long dead and buried. With the cord intact, she owns you, boy.

Males have learned under life-threatening circumstances to be 'Good Boys' or 'Bad Boys'. These personality traits are merely a shell covering over the pain and confusion of un-initiated existence. Neither defense strategy – 'good boy' or 'bad boy' – has an advantage in surviving the fire of what is to come, because surviving the fire, in the case of becoming a mature, adult Man, is the opposite of success. Burning is the way into Manhood. The question is, how does the burning occur? What burns? Where is the match? What serves as the equivalent of oxygen? What remains?

If the transition to adulthood was built into modern culture, or somehow occurred in the natural development of psychology, conditions for entering the Alchemistic 'athanor' oven of maturation would occur by themselves and we would not be having this conversation. Obviously, such conditions do not arise by themselves. Most of us men will play out our love-hate relationship to mommy, and, in a similarly ineffectual way to daddy, for the totality of our lives, never once setting foot into the world as Man, and never knowing except at a tormented unconscious soul level what we have missed. And then we will die.

To become someone who has the fierceness, clarity and balls to slice away contact with the only known safe refuge in the Universe, namely, the boobs, something devastating must occur. A man has to enter a domain in which irreparable damage is done to the 'good boy / bad boy' scam. Your survival game must be nuked in order to begin living.

Moving beyond the defensive context cannot be undertaken by oneself as one's self. The shift must be sourced from someone not controllable by your psychological defense machine, because the machine will never 'monkey wrench' itself. If a man does not find a way to liberate himself from the being-fetters of psychology before engaging a Spiritual Master, then the only work that the Spiritual Master can do with that man is to try to get him to grow up.

If you wonder why the Spiritual Master keeps giving you the same rudimentary feedback (or no feedback at all), guess where you are on the map of evolution. Though it may be painful to acknowledge, it is far better to learn where you are on the map than to continue fooling yourself into thinking that you are somewhere else.

Rather than tangling the Spiritual Master in a game of search and destroy, other men can be engaged. The purpose of your men's group must be declared at the outset and adhered to with a commitment beyond dissuasion. Such an agreement among men cannot generally be fruitful without a Man at the helm, acknowledged by the group in that role. Most men's groups fail to arrange this formality and are quickly lost on a psycho-emotional sea, foundering on rocks ingeniously placed by ego's hidden purposes of self-defense.

So again, how? How does a man leave the fantasy world that is held together by the presence of mommy? You cannot succeed by continuing with actions resulting from being attracted or repelled. Rather you must go where the floor falls out from underneath the whole mommy game, where you find yourself flailing hopelessly in an underwhelming whirlpool of confusion, rage, terror and grief until reality, as it has always been known to exist for you, is fully disassembled, until it is flung away, frame-by-frame, so that nothing solid remains intact, and everything comforting is seen for the mirage-veiled trap that it is, and lies charred, burnt black, or blowing about in little puffs of gray lifeless ash.

How can a man 'hit bottom' hard enough that the demolition upon impact is total?

Most of us, if we get this far in the consideration and even dare to ask such an insane and terrifying question, allow ourselves to remain stuck in the question of "How do I do this?" forever, never being truly willing to experience the answer. Because the answer to the question "How do I do it?" is itself utterly devastating.

The answer is: *you already know how*. For eons the way has been told. It is in our bones, explained by storytellers, wise-men, poets, witch-doctors, troubadours, and shamans. The journey from naivete to wisdom has only one beginning. Either by accident or by folly, the way begins by entering headlong into the dark cave of the Underworld, the corridor of madness.

What does this mean, going into the Underworld? What happens there? How does one come out again? Where is the Underworld?

You do not have to go far to find the Underworld, because it lies within you. The Underworld is, in fact, you. You function daily, minute-by-minute, in the service of Underworld demons, and yet you assume that you are just being your 'good' and 'righteous' self. You have concluded that life is like you have always known it. Such conclusions seem unquestionably obvious.

You think that what you have been doing is proper because it is the only possible way you could think of in the moment to respond to the problems that are incessantly battering you. Since you are identified with the character of yourself, and since you ongoingly justify your actions to yourself, the Underworldly nature of your daily activities completely escapes your perception. You must have a view from outside of the Box to notice your Box.

A fish says, "What water?" A human says, "What Underworld?"

And in your delusional blindness, the demons slurp down your life energy and the love of those dearest to you. They lick their lips smiling, take a little nap, wake up hungry, and use you to conjure up their next low drama meal. You have been calling this 'life'.

Going into the Underworld means having the world-shattering bodily experience of noticing that, moment-to-moment, your primary commitment, previous to any other commitment, is to create, and live in, hell.

Your first unconscious commitment is to serve your Hidden Purposes, motivated by scarcity, clouded in irresponsibility, created with low dramas, designed for survival, competing for limited resources, stopping at nothing, using the weapons of chaos, confusion, deception, self-hatred, betrayal, and destruction, causing yourself and countless other people deep and long-lasting pain, deriving great Underworldly pleasures at the other person's demise, or vowing endless revenge because of your self-created resentments. This is where you live. This is home. You unconsciously love it here, or it would not be sticking around.

Once in the Underworld, what must you do to come out of it? There is a shockingly familiar answer given by modern society, given by religion and 'positive thinking' philosophies. If the Underworld is in you, then, in order to forget it, more unconsciousness is required. To exit the Underworld you enter sleep, numbness, denial, arrogance, repudiation, superiority, and zombieism.

Once in the Underworld, what must you do to come out again? This is an interesting question, but never honestly asked. Instead you conceal the Underworld through denial, drawing the wooly veil of unconsciousness back over your eyes. You wrap up your heart once again in stainless steel and barbed wire, numbing your feelings with dullness and derangement. You place your soul back into hibernation. That is the common way to 'exit' the Underworld. And if you try going that way, there is little chance of ego ever allowing you to go near the entrance again. You have chosen amnesia over transformation.

There is another answer to the question, "What must I do to come out of the Underworld?" It is a transformational answer, something that at first may seem like a paradox. Success in a transformational Underworld journey is only achieved by never leaving the Underworld. Ever. Success in the Underworld journey occurs by irrevocably re-defining yourself as also including the Underworld in your daily awareness and daily experience, in yourself, in others, and in the society and institutions around you.

Success in the transformational Underworld journey results from remaining fiercely conscious of the full implications intended behind all of your evil, twisted, unconscious, and hateful thoughts, feelings and actions. Not giving up. Not giving in. Staying alert to your purpose in each thought, word and deed. Facing directly and incessantly into the horror of the situation.

Success in the transformational Underworld journey is realized through being radically responsibility for each of your conscious and unconscious irresponsibilities:

- As if irresponsibility were an illusion. (Irresponsibility is an illusion.)
- As if there were no such thing as a problem. (Problems are self-authored fictions. Regarding someone else's 'problem' as a problem is also self-authored fiction.)
- As if there were no enemies. (There is no enemy.)
- As if it were impossible to be a victim. (You arranged for this to happen. It is impossible to be a victim.)
- As if circumstances were irrelevant. (The reason is not the cause.)
- As if reasons were a joke. (Reasons are hilarious.)
- As if every interpretation, every meaning, and every story about a situation was nothing but a self-serving lie. (They are lies.)

…and stewing in it, experiencing full 5-body present-time experiential awareness, without self-judgment, without cynicism, without self-recrimination, without excuses, without escape, without self-pity, and without forgiveness. This procedure is what Lee Lozowick calls, "*Digging in the mud to get to the sky*," in His song *Philosophize*, on the L'Ange Brisé ('broken angel') CD album.

What hits the wall and explodes as you take conscious responsible ownership of the Underworld inside of you is the fantasy world that your friends are your friends, or that you are you.

We are human beings. We have parts. Whatever parts in yourself you have not taken conscious responsible ownership of, run your life out of your awareness. Staying blind to something does not make it go away. Ignorance of the law is no excuse. Things you may not be aware of can still seriously affect the quality of your life.

Taking conscious responsible ownership of your Underworld parts is a step in the direction of not being naïve around others or around society. Only through becoming aware of, and consciously responsible for having choice about enacting or not enacting the needs and reactions of your own various parts, can you see and be proactive about the Underworld character zoo that resides in others, whether they see their own parts or not. It is not a pretty sight.

If you scratch a stainless-steel fork hard against the dry surface of a chalkboard, back and forth, over and over again, never letting up, with every nerve cringing in the screeching intensity, yet you do not shy away from the experience, this is what it is like to own your Underworld.

There is nothing glorious about it. Nothing funny. Nothing nice. Nothing comforting. It is raw pain, dusty sand in the eyes, mouthfuls of bitter dirt, freezing snow down your neck, sharp stones in your shoes, a dead stinking rat in your lunch box, each incident finding an inconceivably rude way to let you know that the Underworld is alive and well at your core and that it will never go away. Lee Lozowick refers to this area of work as: "Just good, clean fun!"

FEELING THE WORK

Success in the Underworld journey means that you have lowered the bar for the level of intensity that it takes to feel pain. By lowering your numbness bar, things that were not so painful before suddenly hurt. When the bar disappears altogether, everything hurts. Everything is bullshit.

This is success in an Underworld journey. Failure in the Underworld journey is if you somehow manage to forget all this.

Of what value is this pain? Why feel pain? What is pain?

Let us investigate emotional pain for a moment. There are four kinds of emotional pain: anger, sadness, fear and joy. (The fact that there are only four kinds of emotional pain is very good news for the men. Then it is simple enough for us to understand and remember.)

These feelings arise in intensity between 1% and 100% intensity all day and all night not long. It is not a design error from God that we have feelings. Without a conscious working relationship with your feelings, you do not have the intelligence and energy to deliver the services of your archetypal lineage to the village.

However, there is a world of difference between 'feelings', and 'emotions'. Almost no one in the world knows this. But you can know it. You can upgrade your thoughtware. Using these maps will clarify your inner journeys and human interactions to a remarkable degree.

At the beginning, feelings and emotions feel the same. They feel like anger, sadness, fear, or joy. There are two easy ways to experientially distinguish between feelings and emotions. Making this distinction ongoingly will change your life.

The first way to experientially distinguish between feelings and emotions has to do with time: how long does the experience last? When feelings arise, they increase to a certain level of intensity. You are aware of what you are feeling (anger, sadness, fear, or joy) and you put the feeling's intelligence and energy to good use in your daily life. For example, if anger comes, you say, "Welcome anger. What do you have for me?" Then you write down what the anger tells you with the full force of its inherent intelligence and energy. Then you say, "Anything else?" and keep writing. When you are done writing you say, "Thank you anger," and the anger will have vanished entirely from your sensations within less than three minutes. The same is true for sadness, joy, and fear. These are immense inner resources of intelligence and energy for you.

On the other hand, when emotions arise, they start out feeling like anger, sadness, fear, or joy, but then they do not vanish no matter how hard you try to use their intelligence and energy. Emotions may stick around for an hour, a day, a week, or may remain to some degree continuously active in the background of your daily experience. Nothing you try to do with the emotions completes them in the present. This is because emotions do not come from the present or from the people in front of you. Emotions come from numerous sources that are not you and not now.

For example:

- Emotions come from copying or adopting the emotions of external authority figures (such as from your parents, teachers, uninspected cultural traditions, religious beliefs, political propaganda fervor, corporate brand-fidelity advertising programs, etc.).
- Emotions come from incompletely integrated childhood feelings (resulting in neediness, impatience, inexplicable fears or anger tantrums, etc.).
- Emotions come from your Gremlin (which is the part of you serving your Shadow Principles to defend your psychological survival strategy).
- Emotions come from various vampire demons and entities you may be carrying around with you as a way to disempower yourself so that you do not frighten your childhood caretakers and they continue to take care of you.

Of course, you are not a child anymore. You are probably not dependent on your caretakers. Your situation has changed, but you still have emotional reactivity because you have not gone through the authentic adulthood initiatory processes that would transform all this shit into the fertilizer for a useful adult life. Initiations were banished from civilization six thousand years ago. We are paying the price. Perhaps you are an initiator and, with this new clarity, you can now get back to work providing authentic adulthood initiatory processes.

The second way to experientially distinguish between feelings and emotions is that feelings are pure, and emotions may be mixed.

This is another thing that almost nobody yet knows.

When you mix combinations of two emotions you create intense emotional experiences. For example, mixing anger and sadness together inside yourself creates depression. Any time you want to feel depressed, mix emotional anger and emotional sadness together and feel the mixture. Any time you do not want to feel depressed, unmix your anger and sadness back into their pure form. There are straightforward procedures for unmixing emotions.

By mixing fear and sadness together inside yourself you experience despair, hopelessness, or isolation. By mixing together fear and anger together, you experience hysteria, or aggression. By mixing together sadness and joy you experience relief, nostalgia, or sentimentality. By mixing together anger and joy you experience 'schadenfreude', or 'damage joy', feeling glad when someone else feels pain as in revenge. When you mix joy and fear together you experience curiosity, recklessness, or gambling excitement.

By mixing three emotions together you experience even more intense emotional sensations. For example, when you mix the emotions of anger, fear, and sadness together – depending on the percentages – you experience jealousy, shame, guilt, resentment. When you mix the emotions of anger, joy, and fear together you experience envy, greed, or competitiveness. When you mix the emotions of anger, fear and the physical sensations of nausea together you feel disgust. All of these experiences can vanish in a short time through separating the mixed emotions into their component parts and using the separated pure-form emotions accordingly.

By mixing four emotions together you experience psychotic breakdown, collapse, burnout, or total suppression. Again, these conditions can vanish by unmixing the emotions.

Any of these mixed emotion sensations are not feelings. They are emotions.

Distinguishing feelings from emotions allows you to take responsibility for your internal emotional world.

Feelings are for handling things. Emotions are for healing things.

Now when you feel an emotion, or have mixed emotions together, you can simply say, "I would like an Emotional Healing Process. Would someone hold space for me?" A half-hour later you have found the transformational treasure in the emotions and can use your new experiential clarity to invent a radically new future.

Why do we call feelings 'pain'? At some level of intensity, all four feelings and emotions hurt. (Remember laughing so hard that your cheeks cramp up and your sides ache?) In a Man (capital 'M'), each of these four feelings is recognized as the emotional body's way of consciously communicating about everything that is happening all day long every day. Feelings are the gateway to the body.

Experiencing feelings is never a problem. Feelings only become a problem in spiritual work when we identify with them as if they are true. Suppressing feelings is like tearing up a book thinking the ideas will go away.

Ignoring feelings is like killing the messenger.

In a Man, feelings are owned and valued for their wisdom and insight. The basic ground of being in feelings is gladness, what Chogyam Trungpa calls 'Basic Goodness', and what Lee Lozowick calls 'Wise Innocence'. For a mature Man, it is quite normal, for example, to feel angry, and simultaneously to feel glad about feeling angry. The same is true of feeling glad about feeling scared, and glad about feeling sad.

However, as children we faced sometimes dire consequences if we experienced and expressed our feelings.

"Big girls/boys don't cry," we were told, over and over again, until we stopped crying and our sadness was turned off.

"Hah, hah! You are a scaredy-cat. Chicken! Weakling!" they said if we showed that we were afraid. Now we have secret panic attacks.

Being angry is 'not nice', 'not safe'; we all know this deeply in our cells.

Even expressing happiness is a sign of our childish naivete and lack of a serious grip on reality. "If he really knew what was going on he would not be laughing! He does not take life seriously!" they say.

It is not long before we shut off our feelings except to support our stories about reality. We then use our feelings and emotions to self-define.

STELLATING ARCHETYPES

We need our psychological defense strategy like a butterfly needs a protective chrysalis until we are about eighteen years (fifteen years if you are homeschooled or unschooled). At this age the deep masculine archetype structures which are hard-wired into our bodies are mature and ready to be switched on. Wrapped in plastic, waiting for batteries, the archetypes will sleep within us for the rest of our lives, untapped if we do not go through authentic adulthood initiatory processes from childhood to adulthood during which our archetypal structures are activated.

The process of activating archetypal structures is called 'stellating' as in being transformed from a planet into a star. If you think about the difference, a planetary body absorbs more energy than it radiates, and a stellar body radiates more energy than it absorbs. The transformation of a planet into a star is like starting the planet burning from within, changing itself from mass into warmth and light. Adult human beings are designed to stellate. We are designed to be turned on, to explore, to create and experience the fullness of life. We are designed to live out loud. How does stellating happen?

There are four archetypal structures available within every human body. Each of the four archetypal structures directly associates with one of the four feelings.

The Warrior or Warrioress archetype is associated with the feeling of anger because it is the energy of anger which is used to make boundaries, make distinctions, start or stop things, make decisions, say "Yes," or "No," take initiative, or Go!

The Lover or Communicator archetype is associated with the feeling of sadness, because it is through sadness that your vulnerability is revealed, that you discover the commonality between yourself and others, and you allow yourself to surrender into contact, to listen with compassion and intimacy. Sadness lets you forgive, accept, be present and vulnerable.

The King or Queen archetype is associated with the feeling of joy, because the archetypal good King or Queen blesses and shares with the people, inspires and leads with vision, and calls forth the joy of others to work together.

And the Wizard or Sorceress archetype is associated with the feeling of fear, because only by being okay with experiencing total fear and still being able to function can the Sorceress or Wizard step out beyond what is known into the unknown and invent by calling forth out of the nothing whatever is wanted and needed.

In general, the Warrior/Warrioress, Sorceress/Wizard and Communicator serve the King/Queen.

Someone trying to live without the powers and insights available through one or more of the stellated archetypes would be as severely handicapped as a King/Queen trying to thrive in their gameworld without Warriors or Sorcerers or Communicators, or, as is sadly often the case in the modern world, trying to live in a Kingdom without a King.

Stellating an archetype occurs when it is okay for you to experience and express one-hundred percent maximum intensity of one of the four feelings as an adult. Feelings cannot exceed one-hundred percent maximum experiential intensity. Experiencing one-hundred percent maximum intensity of a feeling does not make the feeling go away. The process of stellating is not about discharging energy (catharsis). Stellating is a process whereby you change your relationship to a feeling (cathexis). You then recognize through direct experience (rather than through understanding a concept) that you are bigger than the one-hundred percent maximum archetypal feeling, rather than being smaller than it. You contain the feeling rather than being contained by it. You own the feeling rather than being owned by it. During stellation you see that archetypal feelings never dissipate, that they live in the Underworld or Upperworld, and that they are accessible at anytime, anywhere, for no reason, to serve you, rather than you being in the service of the feelings (e.g. keeping them contained and bottled up).

One-hundred percent experienced and expressed anger is called rage. One-hundred percent experienced and expressed sadness is called grief. One-hundred percent experienced and expressed gladness is called bliss. And one-hundred percent experienced and expressed fear is called terror.

As a child you could tolerate neither the immensity nor intensity of one-hundred percent maximum feelings, so you blocked the terror, rage, bliss, and grief, locking it away somewhere in your body. Unstellated, these blockages remain intact for the totality of your life, often manifesting sideways in unexpected ways such as lethargy (think of how much energy would be used internally to keep the lid on the trashcan of your whole Underworld of unexpressed feelings), depression (depression is hibernating spirit, rage in the refrigerator), or as various debilitating physical diseases.

During stellation the nervous system and the cells in your tissues learn that they can tolerate the one-hundred percent maximum feelings and not disintegrate, short-circuit, or overload. On the contrary, you are fine, and attain tacit permission to come alive. Feelings are no longer re-jected but rather received. The relationship to feelings changes. Many stored energies once locked away suddenly become liberated, along with their integrally associated wisdom, insight, and perspectives.

Cutting loose with one-hundred percent experienced and ex-pressed feelings is so intense it can at first feel like liquid-fire, or insanity. After some indefinite amount of time in the liquid-fire state, experiencing raw uncontrollable meltdown begins to become your new normal.

This does not mean that the Liquid State becomes less intense. It means that you learn to function in the midst of breakdown. You learn simple things at first. For example, you learn how to be in breakdown and at the same time to breathe, or to raise your hand and scratch your head. Sometime later, you learn to brush your hair, make your bed, eat. Resolid-ification only ever occurs to about 25%, and this only for theatrical pur-poses. You learn to speak to another person from within breakdown, but every interaction becomes a conscious piece of theater, almost never pain-less. The only alternative is just being. And the only place to be is nowhere, in the nothingness gap between the inner-world and the outer-world, which is not any less uncomfortable.

Successfully stellating the archetypes results in you becoming whole, becoming redefined. You now include an Upperworld and an Un-derworld, and are capable of serving the light and the dark sides. There is no right or wrong about this. What determines your moment-to-moment actions are the results which you are committed to producing.

Success in the Underworld journey gives you only one thing that you did not have before: a choice. Who you are now includes the distinc-tion that every act of creation, every movement on every level, where you place your attention and where you do not, every thought, feeling or ges-ture, serves either conscious or unconscious purposes. You are the one who chooses which. If you are not choosing consciously, then you have chosen unconsciously. There is nothing for which you are not responsible.

Living at this level of reality gives a man the refinements of aware-ness prerequisite to holding space as a Man.

MEN AS CONTEXT HOLDERS

Men are nothing. This means that when a Man shows up archetyp-ically, he shows up as a distinction. To understand what this means, think of the zero. The concept and function of the zero was an Arabic inven-tion. ("Allah be praised! I've just invented the zero!" "What!?" "Oh, noth-ing, nothing..." from Saul Bass' 1970's short film titled *Why Man Creates*.)

In primitive counting systems there was nothing to represent nothingness. After the zero was invented, it was possible to name a context that had no content. You could see a zero while counting or figuring, and you would know that there was a place where a certain quantity could be represented. However, in this particular instance, there is no number to go there. The zero is not actually a number, but rather it functions as a spaceholder.

The same is true of Man. Holding context or holding space is man functioning as Man. It is Man in action. A man's neurosis arises through him trying to be something rather than being nothing. Man's power and service arise when Man knows himself as nothing but the context holder of each and every situation that arises. With this clarity, Man can declare the context of the conversation which can occur in that space. He can declare for himself and others the Principles to which the space he holds is dedicated to serving.

Since the assumptions inherent in a conversation determine the allowable limits of the associated reality, Man gains access to the power of shifting realities by shifting the context of the conversation.

And by being nothing, Man is massless. This means that he can go light speed, turn on a dime, or reverse directions, in an instant in order to serve the Principles which are doing their work in the space he is holding. These are high-level skills, but skills nonetheless, and therefore learnable through practice.

The unconscious negative manifestation of man is stupidity. Stupidity arises when man does not know that he himself is the context holder of every conversation in which he is involved, and instead acts as if he is the victim of the context of the conversation. As a victim he can be hooked, manipulated, and fed upon by any roving psychological entity who happens to be hungry and in his vicinity.

HOLDING SPACE FOR SELF

Since Man is nothing, the concept of self becomes negotiable. Rather than thinking that he has the needs of an imagined self, a Man can come to make the declaration, "I already have everything that I need." This suddenly makes him no longer needy. He then can enter a situation needing to get nothing from it, which then opens the option for him of giving rather than taking.

Rather than holding space for a fictional imagined 'self', a 'self' that is a superstition, what a Man discovers is that who he is, is the Bright Principles which he is serving. Bright Principles include kindness, generosity, compassion, reliability, acceptance, gratitude, faith, being yes, commitment, integrity, responsibility, possibility, clarity, dignity, sanctuary, elegance, service, relating, trust, transformation, and so on. Each Bright Principle represents a facet of the Divine, an aspect of the General Field of Consciousness, one of the ninety-nine names of God. A person takes birth into a Destiny, usually described by three to five Bright Principles. By choosing consciously to be the space through which the Bright Principles that he serves can do their work in the world, a Man becomes his Destiny in action right now.

Since Bright Principles are vast Archetypal forces of nature, when a Man knows himself to be the space through which the Bright Principles that he serves can do their work in the world, he is functionally serving something greater than himself. The Bright Principles move through his life, using him to accomplish their various ends. In this way a Man becomes valuable to the Bright Principles. He has learned the secret of creating necessity for himself through his service.

Bright Principles have jobs to do. By radically relying on the Bright Principles to provide for him whatever he needs in order to successfully accomplish their tasks, the Man is taken care of, almost as if he were magically protected, or exceptionally fortunate. People around him will not understand how this has come to pass, but the Man knows exactly what he has sacrificed to establish this kind of relating to the Universe. He does not usually tell anyone, because most people do not really want to hear about it. People don't look up.

In studying the relationship between archetypal Man and archetypal Principles, one begins to see that a Man holding space for Bright Principles to work in the world will be involved in an archetypal life, squeezed forward at the cutting edges of the evolution of consciousness, passionately concerned with establishing the possibility of transformation, expansion, learning, change, realization, and growth for many other people, holding space for God. In particular, he takes the stand for the Manhood of other men.

HOLDING SPACE FOR OTHER MEN

There is a story about a jogger who runs every morning at six o'clock along the same path through the forest. One night an insane man digs a hole in the middle of the path, six feet across, ten feet deep with poisoned barbed spikes at the bottom, and then covers the top of the hole with branches, leaves and dirt to make it look as if the path has been undisturbed. He makes this 'tiger trap' and then departs from the scene.

That morning, as usual, the jogger comes running down the path at six o'clock, falls into the tiger trap, and dies.

Question: Who is responsible for the jogger's death?

Answer: The man who dug the trap.

Question: Why is the trap-maker responsible?

Answer: Because he knowingly dug the dangerous tiger pit in the jogging path.

Alrighty, then. Here is the next version of the story. The same insane man digs the same tiger trap in the same jogging path and then departs the scene. Only this time, you are the jogger. It is six in the morning. For years you have jogged through this same forest at this same time. As you pass between the trees, a barely visible pattern triggers your jungle-warfare training and you reflexively leap horizontally into the air making a perfect dive, rolling smoothly and unharmed in the dirt on the other side of the discrepant pattern. Crawling on your belly, you inch forward, scrape away some leaves and peer into the pit, thinking, "My God! It's a tiger trap! I could have been killed! What is going on here?" You carefully arrange leaves and dirt to make the hole invisible again, back away, and go stand behind one of the trees to see what happens next. Soon another jogger comes down the same path, does not have the advantage of jungle-warfare training, falls into the pit, and dies.

Question: Who is responsible for the jogger's death?

Answer: You are.

Question: What makes you responsible?

Answer: You knew that the tiger trap was there and you did not warn the jogger about it. You could have stopped him from falling in.

Question: So, what exactly makes you responsible?

Answer: Awareness.

Awareness breeds responsibility.

As men we are letting other men fail around us every day. We know the tiger trap is there in front of them and we say nothing. We let them fall in and die. We think, "Oh, I don't have time for this. It is not my problem. It's their life. I am not responsible. I don't want to get involved."

But you are involved. You are responsible. You seeing the situation automatically and irrevocably makes you responsible for it. By not telling the other men about what you see, you let your brothers, your fathers, and your sons fail around you ongoingly.

Holding space for other men in your life means you stop withholding. It means that you care about the others, and you express your care in very specific ways. You say, "Hey, buddy. If I don't tell you about this, then I would be letting you fail, and that is out of integrity for me, because I care about you."

Such actions come from big Men, archetypal Men. And such communication is called 'feedback' and 'coaching'. You could also make proposals for nonlinear or unreasonable experiments.

'Feedback' is sharing your perceptions about what happened that is working or not working.

'Coaching' is delivering distinctions that unveil new actions someone could take to produce different results.

'Proposing' is making offers that contain new possibility, which if enacted would cause a changed relationship with the world.

We men of the Work, we men of the Sangha cannot afford to let our brothers fail around us. Avoidable mistakes are very costly for the organism of the School as a whole. The errors can hurt the School. The errors can hurt the Teacher. He feels it. (Stop kidding yourself about this. He knows what you are up to. Every time.) Letting men fail around you wastes precious resources. You may think you are making things easier for yourself by ignoring the problem and not getting involved, but this is the small self-centered viewpoint. You are involved because you are a cell in the organism.

Becoming aware of a fault, a lack of attention, a compromised distinction, a broken promise, or sloppy integrity, is not an accident. It is E.C.C.O. 'putting a job on your bench' (the Earth Coincidence Control Office, per John Lilly).

If you do not do the job, then essentially you are saying "F___ you!" to the Universe. The Universe remembers such things. See what kind of job you get next time. Avoid four or five jobs, let them pile up, and pretty soon the mouth of your workbench tube is fully blocked. No more jobs can arrive. Your Underworld selves may regard this as a clever strategy. But what purpose does it serve? A conscious purpose or an unconscious purpose?

ENTER THE GREMLIN

Human beings have parts. Sometimes you are identified with one part that speaks as 'I'. Sometimes another part speaks as 'I' with just as much certainty as the first 'I'.

Which 'I' is the real 'I'?

Is there a real 'I'?

Some of your parts are committed to serving unconscious purposes. These parts of you will do whatever it takes to keep things in your world the same as they have always been, to defend your survival strategy at all costs, even by making you right and the other person wrong, making you win and the other person lose, where you derive pleasure at someone else's expense (those 'harmless' little jokes and comments you make…). The part trying to keep your survival strategy 'safe' is called 'Gremlin'. Giving this part a distinguishing name is a powerful alchemical tool. It gives you a 'handle' to use for getting a hold of it. Without the handle, Gremlin does what it wants whenever it wants to do it, meaning: Gremlin owns your life. This could explain a lot about what has been going on for you.

Everyone has a Gremlin. Until such time as you get authentically initiated with regards to Gremlin, it will run your life. Gremlin initiations include: clear powerful experiential distinctions about what Gremlin is and is not, discovering the name of your Gremlin through a formal process, taking a month of serious self-observation to list out your Gremlin's fifty favorite foods and, once you have fifty, choosing five of these Gremlin foods to feed him (or her) on a regular basis. Figure out whether you have a Type 1 Gremlin who you established as the Joker at the center of your survival strategy, or if you have a Type 2 Gremlin who you decided was too dangerous to have around and suppressed or imprisoned to keep him or her out of your life. Then to do a Gremlin Reconstruction process.

Through study, practice, feedback and self-observation, you can identify your Gremlin by its gleefully irresponsible smug little giggle of thinking that no one will ever find it. (That giggle! Do you feel the smirk? Right NOW Gremlin is occurring in your body. MEMORIZE THE CHARACTERISTICS! That is Gremlin energy.)

Until you self-observe to the point where you make each subtle or overt Gremlin activity conscious through sensing its purpose before it emerges, then Gremlin's activities will be unconscious. Your Gremlin will eat the possibility of intimacy by making assumptions that you think are true, which changes the assumptions into expectations. Then when one of your expectations is not met by your partner (business partner, life partner, it does not matter) then your Gremlin feels resentment and has a Gremlin feeding frenzy plotting revenge, while you starve for intimacy. Your Gremlin will destroy the possibility of being a stand for serving Bright Principles because he or she is afraid that your survival strategy might change. Allowing Gremlin to run free dedicates your life to remaining trapped inside of your Survival Strategy and serving Shadow Principles.

Even twenty-year spiritual students who have not made the Gremlin distinction can be counted upon to create nothing but Gremlin games with the people in their life. Sadly, their Work never becomes authentic and reliable because the Gremlin keeps its foot in the back door, never allowing the internal chambers to seal and heat up. No matter how much reality confronts that person, the internal heat and pressure can never get hot enough to ignite genuine remorse because Gremlin blows it off with a joke or a comment, or goes whistling unconsciously along its merry way. Without the intense lasting pain of conscious remorse nothing changes. By not giving these men immediate, specific, consistent feedback and coaching about their Gremlin creations, or worse yet, by playing along with them and allowing their Gremlin to call out your Gremlin, you let Gremlin win, and let the Work possibility in these men die.

How else can you identify Gremlin at work? Here are some characteristically Gremlin activities: flirting, masturbating, playing video games, internet sex, eating candy, ice cream, doughnuts and 'snack' foods, not lifting the toilet seat to pee, breaking time agreements (arriving even a few minutes late, even if you have a 'really good excuse' or if you apologize), pretending to be a victim, forgetting appointments or promises, playing practical jokes, stealing insignificant things (pens from work, grapes at the grocery store, airline blankets, special leftovers from the refrigerator, etc.), driving even a few miles an hour over the speed limit, not exercising, trying to cut ahead in line, cursing at other drivers, destroying energetic spaces even in small ways (e.g. making yourself visible while walking through a meeting space, inelegantly opening or closing the door, coughing, yawning, looking out the window, moving the chair, fidgeting, dropping your pen, conspicuously drinking from your water bottle at delicate moments, etc.), having little accidents or breaking something and not cleaning it up or telling anyone, littering, sneaking, swearing, sleeping in, trying to get more than somebody else, returning the car with the gas tank on empty, talking to keep the attention, leaving floating turds in the toilet, over eating, not replacing the empty toilet paper roll, reading other people's notes, sleeping during talks, sleeping during meditation, going through other people's drawers, lying, making jokes or comments about other people, reading other people's mail, gossiping (talking about someone when they are not there), triangulating (complaining about someone to someone else), feeling resentful, and so on ad nauseam.

As you can see, these activities are quite familiar, indicating that you have an entire Underworld Ecology thriving within you, determining the quality of your life day and night. It is your responsibility to learn the hierarchy of creatures feeding upon each other, upon you, and upon those people who are dearest to you. An unconsciously functioning Underworld subsumes the entire purpose of your life. In the company of other Men you have a chance to help each other take your lives back.

Once you have the distinction 'Gremlin', name these activities for what they are whenever they occur – as a service to each other, Man to Man. Gremlin creations are far easier to spot in someone else than in yourself. This is one way that Men can serve each other and hold the space for the Man in the other: calling the Gremlin by name when you see it. A Man will not let his brother's heart and soul be devoured by Gremlin. When you have accomplished the ability to hold a mature but not stiff-and-dead Gremlin-free space, only then have you developed enough integrity and subtlety to enter the domain of holding space for Woman.

HOLDING SPACE FOR WOMAN

Step one of holding space for Woman is assassinating the patriarchal delusion in yourself that Woman needs space held for her by a man. She does not. How pedestrian. How brutish. How self-serving for a man to think that.

"Woman, yeah. You gotta hold da door open for 'em cuz dey's so dainty... nyuk! nyuk!"

Neanderthal conversation reality is so corrupted that there is no chance of even beginning to transform it here. Most modern culture males will never escape the Standard Human Intelligence Thoughtware given to them by their parents and the patriarchy. Most modern culture males will remain unconsciously committed to adolescent reactivism and spiteful tyranny over the feminine. What are you going to do if you have been considering such an individual, my friend?

The archetypal purity and unbearable lightness of the feminine being may grate so severely against your deeply ingrained patriarchal constructs that you ferociously dedicate yourself to horrific and ruinous revenge on the feminine. Right now, a part in you may be redoubling its efforts to crush these clarifications. If this is you (and you know if it is) please return to reading your graphic novels, and never come back here. Continuing this investigation could result in a kind of madness you probably do not yet have the matrix to navigate.

This is a warning.

It is not trying to sound superior or arrogant. Perhaps just a little protective.

For so many centuries the patriarchy has contaminated and spoiled the pearl-essence of feminine sanctuary. Calling in enough archetypal feminine right now to speak about this can only happen in a personal and private chamber.

Before trying to make it possible to enter a preciously sacred chamber together it must be clearly stated: No pigs are allowed. No comments at all. Listen. Hold your mind. Be still... so still that the warm breath of woman, the subtle movement of her chest rising and falling as she breathes while watching you askance, the breathing so richly experienced by her, so careful of all its implications and possibilities, moves you to an awareness expanded well beyond and excluding everything male.

Power, pride, wealth, competition, possessions, reputation, strategies, these have no place here. They are the toys of angry vicious little boys. So foolish. So temporary. Let them fall away from you without trying to figure out how life can work without them. Let yourself trust the feminine beyond reason and be drawn forth into a freshness and tenderness so raw that words are too rough to be spoken. Yet, continue. Let it in. The beingness of Woman awaits you.

She invites you into the feminine world, so patiently. It is a world not reserved for women but reserved for receiving, for sensing, for perceiving, for being touched to the degree of having a full experience of its value. There is no way to disable or decrease the heart-rending impact of this touch. This journey cannot be undertaken without a partner to share the gifts, to accompany you on this voyage of sensual exploration beyond the limitations of normal senses.

A man can awaken to an intensity of refined attention that merely observing subtle gestures of a woman's wrist sends chills of pleasure down your spine. Unbeknownst to you how this could occur, you still have this capacity, far vaster than you can conceive. It will probably frighten you to the core, a core you dare not acknowledge.

Woman can welcome you into an immensity of homecoming that you have never before imagined, a healing so sweet and wholesome that your soul would reveal its wounded imperfections and bask in her radiant warmth, never wanting to leave. You do not know of this because your masculine attention is so crude. Yet you have a capacity to learn.

Regardless of your skill, Woman waits, hoping you will snap out of your cold, rational, defendedness. What are you defending? You attack while she holds the door open. Instead, try letting yourself fail. Let the wall crumble back into the ancient dust of wounds out of which you made it. Woman wait, arms open, hoping you will yearn for connection with the source, and not just once.

There is a wondrous doorway so rare and precious that it can only be accessed through honoring the feminine with impeccable attention. If you lack a reference point for that miraculous doorway in your life, then you will have missed the invitation to notice its existence a million times. That is a pity. You have wasted so much heaven, along with the millions of other uninitiated adolescent boys.

Anything that hints at the breathtaking openness and vulnerability inherent in the nature of Woman could perhaps establish a liquid link, a desire in a Man to look at her, to see her with more than respect, more than admiration, to see her as if he could breathe like her, noticing how she tilts her head so as to catch the light in her hair, to inhale the warm rich scent inviting him to move just a little bit closer and to adore her. To adore everything of the lake of her.

Look where she has placed the flower vase. Sense how it honors the space. How can she know how to do this? It is not thought about. It is not figured out. She places the vase as an invitation to appreciate all of her. Not the true part, but the real part.

When a Man has purified himself of his impatience and greed, when you no longer care for logic and reason, then you can allow yourself to accept the feminine invitation into a garden filled with ambrosia, more than you deserve, more than you can buy. She has been placing vases like this for years, years you have let pass you by.

Why? Why would a man refuse so much holiness? There is no answer, only disbelief, only regret, only awe that Woman has not yet retreated from your inexcusable inattentions.

Woman still invites. Woman notices the vast moments sliding one into the other. Nothing is happening, yet everything is here with her. Nothing is missing because the allness of her encompassing nature has nothing to hide, nothing to lose. Where would it go? How could it disappear or be lost when she is Everything?

Is she frightened to make the invitation? Of course. But she is willing to feel her fear and go on its journey so that it does not stick in her, so that it does not threaten her world. The fear flows in her, and can vanish with one sparkle in her eye, one curve on her lips. The tinkling brook of her voice sounds so appropriate in this sacred space, watering the tangled roots of the masculine mind so it wants to go nowhere else.

I could go on, but this description stops here.

Thank you for visiting.

Once a Man knows of this dimension of Woman, he could never disregard Woman again. You become willing to sacrifice immature masculine to enter her world whenever she invites you. It is perhaps the most precious of all worlds to protect with your dignity and power. You hold as a precious treasure the distinctions allowing you to establish the context for spaces clear enough to permit a woman to drop her worries and exude that feminine universe, also for herself. Then you receive the blessings of a satisfied Woman.

Relating is ongoing actions of nonlinear creation. Yet when the water faucet is dripping, it is the Man's responsibility to see that it gets promptly repaired. Otherwise, the Woman's attention can go nowhere else but to the pain about the dripping water. If there is a wasp or mouse in the house, the Man's job is to move it somewhere else. If something needs to be taken to the attic or the basement or the recycle bin, the Man carries it. If a light bulb needs to be changed, the Man replaces it. The Man faces the villains in the darkness by taking out the garbage, making boundaries with the neighbor about their dog, and keeping the bicycles safe and in good working mechanical order with brakes, tires, and air pressure. A Man makes the bed each morning with great care to getting the corners and pillows correct as a way of building Drala in that sacred space. Flowers now and then are not a bad idea either.

ONE HUNDRED PERCENT COMMITTED

For a Man to hold the space for Woman he must learn the intricacies of honoring and respecting space, like a gardener prepares the soil for his garden. A Man is the distinction called 'the garden wall'. Inside the wall is the garden. Outside the wall is not. The Man is the trellis, the stepping stones, and keeper of the compost pile. He knows when to bring in mulch, when to prune the roses and fruit trees, when to take out the bulbs to protect them from winter frost, and when to put them back in the ground for spring. But he is not the garden.

Woman is the Garden. Well cared for in these ways by Man, Woman can grow and blossom and fill the space with nature's abundant and nurturing wonders. She abounds in colors, wild scents, plump juicy fruits, laying forth a bounty of sustenance-giving vegetables and grains. The Man moves carefully through spaces in the Garden, never assuming he knows how it happens to grow, only that it is a Miracle, a Mystery, and that there may come a time for him to prop up branches, pull weeds, and trim back growth that becomes unwieldy.

Specifically, what this means is that, after shaving or trimming nose hairs, the Man washes away every last bit of whisker or hair and wipes off the faucet and mirror, leaving no souvenirs of his having been there. He dries himself off in the shower rather than slogging wet across the bathroom, leaving no drips or puddles, and rinses the tub or shower stall after himself. He folds and puts away his clothes in drawers, or the laundry basket, not leaving them about. Same with reading or writing materials, tools, play things. He learns to be a good guest in the Woman's space.

Every man has an energetic space within himself for his mate. You can visualize this energetic space floating out in front of your chest, a foot away, about eighteen inches tall, a foot wide, a foot thick, flat floor, curved ceiling like a temple, white, like an altar chamber. This is your relating space for your mate.

To proceed, ask yourself what is in there? It can be filled with many things. You must look carefully and ruthlessly to inspect its contents. Things tend to become invisible if they have been there for a long while, but they are still influencing the level of sanctuary that is possible in your relating space. Like in any sanctuary, even small things can denigrate the perfection. Are you still holding on to old letters from your previous lovers? Postcards? Are they still listed in your address book? Do you have a stash of old photographs remembering good times with other lovers? Flirtatious memories with the secretary at work, or a client, or your mother? Little mementos or gifts tucked away in the back of a drawer or a box in the closet? A tie? A t-shirt? Cuff-links? Old sports equipment in the garage? Dishes? Knick-knacks? Do you have poster pin-ups of movie stars? Singers? Artwork from the artist? Center-folds? Videos that betray a fantasy life in your mind? If so, your relating space may be cluttered seventy percent full of riffraff.

Here is an idea. Get rid of these things permanently. Cut them off. Terminate them forever. Burn them. Don't give them away to friends or family. Take them to the dump, or donate them to Goodwill. Burning is best. Participate in a relationship space cleanout process, which is loud and emotional, pulling demons out by the roots. Toss the shit into the black hole and the creatures into the white light. Purify and cleanse your sanctuary. Scrub it clean. Patch the holes, repaint the walls, and lay down new carpet. Refill gaps with Golden Pearls of your own purified energy and information. Prepare your relating space to receive your true beloved.

Because if your sanctuary for your mate is only thirty percent available, the rest being filled with this or that energies from surrogate mates, then you will find a partner who is satisfied relating to you only thirty percent.

This means that the back door of your relating space will never be closed. Like an alchemical blast furnace, the door will never seal, so the furnace can never get to temperatures hot enough for meltdown and transformation. You will never truly know what it is like to be in a long term committed relationship. With your sanctuary contaminated, you will never be able to attract a mate who wants to commit to you at one-hundred percent.

Only in a purified and cleansed sanctuary can commitment seal the door. The pressure can build, the heat can rise, and the true alchemical transformation processes of a long-term committed relationship can begin. In waves the thermal chaos builds, each new level of intensity vaporizes a new level of illusion. It bursts into flame and burns cleanly away. If you know that this is the natural evolutionary progression of a mature relationship, then you will not need to be discouraged about the smoke and flame periods. Only by repeatedly entering the fire together will you discover that which cannot burn.

Holding the space for Woman does not mean understanding her. Even on the spiritual path, the mind of Woman is unfathomable for a Man. That is why women are drawn to this Work quicker. Men see Clarity as Power. Modern culture is set up so that men achieve success because they attain things.

Women know inherently that Principles activate possibility. So if you are to climb up into the domain of Principles as Man, then you must have access to your own Femininity, because through Feminine receptiveness you can access your Bright Principles. For women, accessing Bright Principles is inherent in their being.

It might be that the only time you honor Masculine and Feminine space is when you get together consciously. The only time you honor the Bright Principles held in the Feminine is when you are having a conscious conversation about it. The rest of the time your life occurs in uninitiated chaos contaminated by systems and data and information and technologies. You take these as operational systems for 'living'.

What is being introduced here is the possibility that the operational systems for relating are not Masculine Distinctions and Technology from the domain of Clarity, but rather Feminine Principles from the domain of Power.

During fire and brimstone times in relating, when sparks are flying, and the fat is spattering and popping like bacon in a hot iron griddle, there are four powerful distinctions Man can rest in that will allow him to serve his Woman, the relating space, and God all at the same time. Remember, distinction-making takes place in the Being, not in the mind, and distinction-making occurs through intention.

The first distinction is how to listen as a space. If Man is nothing, then any identification he has with what is being projected onto him in any situation is merely illusion. He can keep his point of origin in the illusion, or he can relocate his point of origin into the clarity and power of being a space. If you choose space, then be space. When listening, this means that you do not need to understand what is being said; you do not need to agree with it; it does not need to be reasonable or logical, or even right. You can still hear it. You can be the space into which it is spoken, and not have to do anything with it.

Specifically, you do not have to fix it, find a solution, go out and change anything. All that you need to do is listen. Listening as a space is listening for her, not for you. You are being the space into which she can speak anything. You are the workbench upon which she can work complex things out.

Within the listening sanctuary that you are providing, her speaking takes stuff out of her mind and brings it into the world, where she can hear it herself; she can hear it being listened to. Through you being the space of listening she encounters no resistance. On your workbench of listening space she can create what she is speaking about, or reinvent it as she speaks. You make no comments, no judgements, no criticisms, and most importantly, you ask no questions (even to 'make it more clear for her', even if you think that your questions are 'for her own good'). Now and then you nod your head. Now and then you say, "Hmmmm…" so she knows you are not sleeping.

If there are raging emotions and killer energies mixed in with her communication, you simply create a black hole in the floor like a drain in a bathtub, peel the information out of the communication, listen to the information (part of which may be the information, "I am mad as hell at you!") and allow the charged up energies to get sucked down the drain into the Earth (who eats it as fertilizer).

Opening the drain as a tool is the second distinction. You no longer have to block communications due to being afraid that it might have too much energy for you to handle. Now you can extract the information by distinguishing the information from the energy of the communication, receive the information, and ground out the energy.

It is well known in communication theory that a communication will persist until it is received. Having increased skills in listening will allow you as a Man to receive communications from your Woman which have probably been delivered to you in one form or another over and over again for years because you have never before been able to hear them. Now that you can receive these high energy communications, their mission gets completed. You may then discover that new messages will originate in your mate and your relationship can get unstuck and continue flourishing.

Distinguishing the energy from the information in a communication does not mean that when you hear the message you are not affected by it. Quite the opposite is true. No longer having to defend yourself against the onslaught of the emotional charge of a communication means that you are more open to hearing its message. The message gets in.

And when the message gets in, it hits home. You feel the pain of it deep in your soul. In hearing the message, you cannot help but perish. Your old self, the formulation of who you were – previous to receiving the communication – has been forever changed. You have heard the message and you are pierced by it. You have been killed.

The problem with this is that your Woman will feel so delighted, acknowledged, and in love with you for now being able to really listen to her, that when she is done with delivering the communication, she may well want to take your clothes off and go to bed with you.

We all know that you cannot make love with a Woman if you have died. Here is where the third distinction comes in handy. You can learn to be killed, but not die. After allowing the message to have its full impact on you, stay silent for three seconds. In those three seconds the lethal blow will fade into the far distant past of three seconds ago.

All the sound echoes will have vanished from the space. Stay in a very small NOW. This small NOW allows you to keep being reincarnated into the present moment. Take a deep breath and let yourself be reborn into the new NOW. In those three seconds you have become a transformed you. She is a new she. You were able to be killed and not die, because the killing happened three seconds ago and you are not there anymore. It is celebration time! You are here with her. She is here with you. Together you get to meet and start over!

The fourth distinction is that no matter what your Woman says to you, no matter how childish, how misinformed, how evil, how destructive, how unconscious or self-referenced you may think it is, it is not your Woman speaking to you. It is her Box speaking. The distinction is that your Woman is not her Box. Your Woman is Woman: God's beauty, gateway to the feminine world, your personal guide to Paradise. If you cannot be dissuaded in your commitment to experiencing who she really is, then neither can she. But when you can, she can. You can have it any way you want it.

Let us be excruciatingly clear on this point: If you have dismantled your resentment by identifying the assumption you made, which you then changed into the expectation that your partner then did not fulfill, thus causing the resentment in you, but the feeling of resentment has not instantly gone away, then your Gremlin is at work. The next emotional healing process you need to do is not with your partner. It is with someone who has a sharp enough sword of clarity to put your Gremlin's Hidden Purpose irrefutably on the table in front of you, and indicate that you have given your life over to your Gremlin who is feasting on Shadow Principles at the expense of your relating. Only you can tell your Gremlin to stop.

HOLDING SPACE FOR CHILDREN

If you relate to your children as if they are mature, responsible, sensitive, strong, loving, coordinated, beautiful, intelligent, communicative, radiantly happy, team players, passionately involved in fulfilling their Destiny and living a life that really matters to them, then that is who you will get to live with for eighteen years.

Some men insist that child-raising is more complicated than this. It is not. The reason a father wants it to be more complicated is so that he does not have to experience the painful introspection of taking responsibility for having trained his children to be like they are. The father wants to blame someone or something else and pretend to be an innocent victim in the situation. If he maneuvers to abscond from responsibility, of course, then that is how he teaches his children to raise their own children. New possibilities only arise when a father stops pretending he knows how to be a father, and starts asking seriously vulnerable questions.

The following ideas unfold as specific answers to the question, "What conditions give my child optimum opportunity for health and happiness?" Many of the suggestions are for newborn infants, because this is when a child downloads most of their 'human thoughtware' about who they are, who other people are, and what to do in a world like this with people like them.

If your children are already older than three or four years, look for the attitudes behind the practices discussed below, and find ways to incorporate these attitudes in relating to your children whatever their age.

What is offered below is a 'Child-Raising Wish List' of best practices. They are fairly unjustified proclamations. Conformational research and study materials abound, so here we present the condensed version. Also, many of the suggestions apply directly to the mother. What the Man can do is support the Woman in her choices both by helping with details, and standing certain in the energetics, holding space for her to proceed even in the face of concerned neighbors, overbearing parents, and mass

media who has no idea how to promote human evolution of consciousness, and in fact is terrified of the simplicity of true human contact and
human relating. Here we go.

Breastfeed your baby - no matter what anybody says. Your Woman
may need to change her familiar self-image for the next few years - but
with your support she can do this. She can then look in the mirror and see
herself as a breastfeeder and feel good about it! Her body wants to.
Breastfeed your baby on demand day and night no matter what for at least
two years. Feed them only breast milk for their first six months, gradually
adding solid food after that. There is NOTHING that can replace the nurturing, life-supporting experience of skin-to-skin contact between baby
and mother during nursing time. We could speak for hours about the
virtues of naturally breastfeeding your baby. Fortunately, there are already
excellent books and resources available for your reference.

Have your child sleep with you in a big 'family bed' until they decide to sleep in their own bed around the age of three to six years. Imagine
how fear of the dark, fear of lightning and thunder, fear of nightmares,
or fear of abandonment could all resolve themselves without residue if
there was certainty about a Mother's or Father's arm to snuggle into all
night long. Families have been sleeping together for over two-hundred-
thousand years. Putting a baby to sleep 'in their own room' or even 'in
their own bed' is a recent modern-culture neurosis development with serious social and psychological side effects. On the other hand, sexual
abuse also has serious social and psychological side effects. If you cannot
not sexually abuse your children, skip the family bed idea. And immediately go get serious long-term professional help as a criminal.

Do not put a 'pacifier' in your child's mouth. Putting a piece of
rubber in your baby's mouth delivers a very powerful negative message to
them. They realize that what they have to say is not wanted or needed.
When a parent disempowers their own child by preventing them from
speaking, the child knows things are not as they should be. They begin to
view the world as unsafe for them. Instead of providing security for the
child, rubber sucking devices deliver insecurity. Your child is already a person. Gagging your child for your own comfort is devastating for them.

Begin to look seriously at your family's use of smartphones, television, the internet, and video games. What purpose are these activities
serving in reality? What value are they creating for your family? What else
could be happening during the times spent staring at the screens? Actually,
you have no idea…

Here are instructions for how to modify a television for family life. There is a tail on your TV. Pull the tail out of the wall. On one end of the tail is a panel (the TV) and on the other end of the tail is a small lump (the plug). Measure ten centimeters (five inches) back from the small lump. Cut the small lump off of the tail with scissors. Wear the small lump around your neck as a victory talisman. Use the flat panel as a tray for serving fresh fruits and vegetable slices to friends during neighborhood picnics.

Some families simply get rid of their televisions altogether. Other families keep the TV packed away in a closet, and bring it out to watch transformational videos now and then. Moving the TV out allows you to think of something else to do with your precious family time. Play music together, read stories, draw pictures, shuck walnuts, have plays, weave baskets, sew costumes, cook exotic meals from foreign lands, play cards, or just hang out and relax together as a family. Years later you will look back at these TV-less days as the best of times. Guaranteed.

Read out loud to your children every day. Be it children's books, adventure stories, Shakespeare, poetry, spiritual literature, or historical fiction, read to them. Do not read the news, murder mysteries, or overtly sexual material.

Striking, hitting, shaking, slapping, yanking, spanking, pinching, whipping, beating, or jerking your child – ever, for any reason – is a sign of your own deep wounds. Go get your wounds healed through professional emotional healing processes, immediately and ongoingly, before you become a criminal causing wounds to your own children.

When an adult tries to solve their own problem by physically abusing their child, this is time to call for immediate professional help. Yes, you can arrange to have more rest and less stress, calling someone for support, joining a parenting support group, and getting into therapy or a 'Twelve-Step' program. Your reactive aggressive behaviors will not change through positive thinking. Stop fooling yourself. Your own deep emotional wounds need to be healed before your behavior will change. Violence to children is a serious infraction and cannot be dealt with alone. Pay attention to your habits of behavior under stress. Do you terrorize your baby as a way of dominating, controlling or manipulating them? If so, get help. Now.

On the other hand, be real with your child. Create relational reality. For example, if a child hits you, notice what their intention is. A baby may grab your hair or nose and try to bite it, and this may hurt or be annoying, but that is different from hitting with the intention to hurt. If they are just exploring, gently unpeel their fingers from your nose and give them something else to explore that does not cause you pain. But if the child hits with the intention to hurt, then even though you are a fully grown adult Man, and, of course, the hit does not really hurt you, act as if it did. Say, "Ouch!" seriously, loudly, as if the child's intentions had been fulfilled and it makes you afraid. (Important note: Do NOT make a game out of this!) When the child sees that they have hurt their father, and the father says angrily, "No! Stop that! That hurts me! Don't do that! Stop it NOW!" just like one adult would say to another, then clear communication is happening, and relational reality has been established.

Put away the clock and be on your baby's schedule. These first few years are precious and go by very quickly. Babies do not care what time it is. They have an internal clock of their own. When they are hungry, they want to eat. When they are tired, they want to sleep. Why fight them when you can join them? Rather than rushing around trying to get all of your unfinished chores done when the baby naps, you can nap too. And if the middle of the night turns out to be play time for a while, relax. One thing to always remember about the stages of a child's development is that, no matter what this stage is, sooner or later it will move to the next stage.

Wear your baby! Strap your baby onto your body. You can obtain a few different kinds of front or back baby carriers – many are available these days – and learn how to use them. When you wake up in the morning and get dressed, you can put on your baby like you put on your shirt. This gives you two hands free to go about your daily business. Let your child see what it means to be a human being by watching you live your life. Wash the dishes, hang out the laundry, mow the lawn, rake the leaves, sweep the floor, go shopping. (Talking on the phone and doing desk work is generally neither active nor interesting enough for the baby, so try to minimize these activities.) The baby is used to the mother's natural rhythm and movement from being in the womb, and will sleep for hours in a back or front carrier, often with one finger somehow touching your skin. Let your baby touch your skin! Let your baby have physical skin-to-skin contact. When your baby is ready to get down it will tell you. Many cultures never put their babies on the floor for six months. Westerners often leave their babies alone every chance they get – as if carrying a baby were a nuisance rather than an honor! – and they wait a long while listening to a baby cry hysterically before going to pick him or her up. Do you like to be left alone to cry hysterically for help, for someone to be with you? Why are you torturing your child? Because it was done to you? Does this make it right? Why do you think the baby is crying? Why would you be crying if you were the baby? When a baby is left alone to 'cry themselves to sleep' the experience is life threatening for them. During those few moments is when a baby makes life crushing decisions, such as: "Nobody loves me. I am not good enough to be loved. Everyone has forgotten me. I cannot trust anyone to take care of me. If I want to live I have to do everything for myself. I have been rejected," and so on. Pick up your baby immediately and listen to them.

A commonly held idea is that babies are stupid. Such an attitude is shockingly false. Babies are learning at a tremendous rate. And in terms of what the baby is experiencing, recall some of your first memories. Can you remember how you first regarded yourself as 'me'? Did you experience that 'me', then, any differently from how you experience this 'me', now? Most people do not. Regard your child with infinite respect as a full-fledged Being.

Talk to your children, and listen to them as if they were fully cognizant individuals deserving your complete attention. You are training them to communicate. Every sound the child makes is an effort to communicate. If you ignore your child's vocally expressed communications to you by thinking that it is meaningless baby prattle, then so it will remain for a long time, perhaps even into their adulthood. And vice versa; every sound you make to your child is something the child wants to understand. If you speak to your child in meaningless 'baby talk', then your child's efforts to learn verbal communications through imitating you will long be frustrated, because they are imitating nonsense. Listen to your child and understand what they are saying to you, even if it is not proper language. Whenever they ask for it, give your child your full one-hundred percent attention. Then they will gain confidence that they can have your attention when they need it and will not develop the habit of having to nag you for your attention, or even use their Gremlin part to get negative attention from you, because negative attention is better than no attention at all. Respond to your child in clear, complete sentences. In this way your baby learns that the world makes sense, and that they can communicate. Out of communication grows trustworthy relating.

What do you say to your child? Keep pointing out and repeating the names of things: wall, chair, potato. Sing to them; describe experiences; recite poetry; make up stories. Don't just talk to make noise, but rather talk to share the wonders of life. Every night while brushing their teeth, I would count from one to ten in as many different languages as I could, one language for each section of their teeth. Now the children both speak two languages fluently, and want to learn others because they experience it as fun and interesting. Vocabulary, knowing the name of a thing, is a life-long gift that you can give to your children. Do not talk about your problems at work or with your spouse, your sexual escapades, or your worries about politics and the world of news. Your child will get to those things on their own when they have built the matrix in their Being to deal properly with those things.

A child needs a Dad who protects them, sets boundaries, asks for what he needs, tells them how it is, listens to them, leads them into practical relating with a magical wondrous world, and demonstrates integrity, impeccability, love, and possibility. A child also needs a Dad who is a total "Yes!" for them. So much of the world is already a "No!" expressed as laws, procedures, rules, schedules, grades, expectations, limits, and so on. Our parents were often a "No!" for us. Without knowing it, many of us are an automatic "No!" for our own children.

There is a way that you can be, in general, such that who you are for the child is in support of their existence. They can get that you are voting "Yes!" for them. Being "Yes!" for your child does not mean being a doormat. Being "Yes!" for your child means to commit to your child's commitment, whatever it is.

When a child starts climbing on the furniture, instead of shouting "No! Get down from there! You are going to break your neck!," notice exactly what the child is committed to in their actions. Is it the physical challenge? Is it to get attention? Is it because they are angry? If it is the physical challenge, consider squatting down next to your child and saying something like, "You really like climbing around, don't you?" By doing this you have acknowledged their commitment to expand their physical limits. Then commit to that so they experience your commitment as authentic. "Let's go outside and I can help you climb that tree." Or, "Maybe you would like to take a gymnastics class with a trampoline or a climbing wall?" If their commitment is to express their anger, consider squatting down next to them and saying, "It seems like you are feeling something big. Are you angry?" If they say yes, then you can listen to them say what they are angry about. Listening to them does not mean that you try to fix anything, or change anything, or defend anything, or explain anything. Their anger is not your problem. You just listen, and repeat back that you hear they are angry and precisely what they are angry about. They experience themselves as being heard, and that you were the "Yes!" to their anger.

DO NOT tickle your child, and DO NOT let other people tickle them. Tickling is a form of physical abuse. Most times, when someone is tickling a child, they are trespassing into the child's sexual energetic 'space' without the child's permission. Tickling is a form of rape. Since the child is defenseless, the world becomes dangerous if they are tickled. Many people tickle children to try to change their mood or to control them. Tickling is often hidden aggressiveness. It is not for the child's pleasure but rather to manipulate the child for our own selfish satisfaction of having the child smile or laugh for us and give us their attention or do what we want.

Keep your promises. Do not make promises you do not keep. This is one of the most powerful relationship tools you can own. If you tell your child that you are going to leave for the park at two o'clock, and at one fifty-nine the phone rings and it is your mother who likes to talk for fifteen minutes, just say, "I'm sorry, Mom, but I cannot talk right now. We are going to the park at two o'clock. Can you please call me back tonight?" (Notice that the Dad takes full responsibility for making and keeping the promise and does not play victim to the child by saying, "I cannot talk now because Johnny will get mad if I do not take him to the park.") If you tell your child that they cannot have a lollipop because it is too close to dinner, do not give in and give them a lollipop because they get angry with you or because they start whining. If it is bath time, it is bath time. There is no need for the father to be forceful, angry or aggressive about it. The father can have infinite patience, be creative and inviting, be consistent and gently firm, because he is already certain of the outcome through holding the space for their child having a bath.

Children run out of energy when they are tired, hungry, not feeling well, too cold, or too hot. You can easily learn to recognize the indicator signs when your child is about to run out of energy. I call it 'going over the edge'. Just before going over the edge, the child may get silly. Their tone of voice may shift. Their attention span may shorten. Timing in their speech patterns may speed up. They may become short tempered or demanding, or lose their sense of humor. Learn to notice and recognize these indicators, and train yourself to redirect activities in order to take care of your child before they go over the edge. Without making a big deal out of it, just feed them, just bring them in for a nap, just adjust their clothing, or give them quieter activities so they can rest, whatever is needed and wanted. Do not have a debate about it. You can even be talking about something else entirely. Just handle their true needs. Many fathers never learn to read these signs, and over and over again continue their selfish agendas rather than shifting plans mid-step to take care of their children. Then everybody has a hard time. Here is another great idea: Create a bedtime procedure, and go through it every night with your children. Transition to bedtime is a wonderful time to be together and to connect while changing into bedclothes, washing the face, flossing and brushing the teeth, and reading a chapter in a favorite book.

Trust your child's judgment of character, even if it is inconvenient. One time we were at a friend's wedding with our first daughter who was less than two years old. She disappeared for half an hour and we could not find her. Finally we found her off to the side of the crowd sitting on a bench next to an elderly gentleman we neither knew nor recognized. He was smoking a big cigar and apparently philosophizing to her about everything that was going on. We resisted and did not interrupt their communion. It went on for over an hour, she being totally enraptured with this stranger. When she was finished, she came responsibly back to us. We noticed a clear expansion in her worldliness and self-confidence after that.

Another time my partner and I had arranged a rare date for us to go out together as a couple. When the baby sitter arrived the children were not wanting to stay with her. Rather than rushing out the door anyway, we stopped and changed our plans, paid the babysitter, sent her home, and spent the evening together with the kids. Our lost date was a smaller wound than would have occurred if we abandoned our children to a stranger they were uncomfortable with.

We have watched seemingly intelligent fathers observe their child fall down, scrape their knees, come to their parents in tears looking for comfort and understanding, only to hear the father say, "Nothing happened. It does not hurt. There is nothing to cry about." What a horror! Here is the child, who is in real and undeniable physical pain, coming to their father who is like a god to them - all knowing, all powerful. When the child receives the communication from the father that 'nothing happened', it is in such total contradiction to the child's experience, that the father's message can cause a split in the child's psychology.

Such a message is psychological abuse, and can contribute to conditions known as 'borderline', 'schizophrenic', or 'psychotic'. It causes the child to mistrust their assessment of reality, and it also causes them to mistrust you.

All that the child needs is to be heard. When the child approaches the father, the father can ask, "What happened?" In recounting the incident to a listening father, the child can safely experience and express their big feelings, and heal themselves of the shock of the incident, all in a matter of moments with no scars, and then run back and keep playing. No 'make wrong', no 'warning', no "Did you learn your lesson?" Nothing else from the father is required. Just listen, acknowledge that something did happen from their point of view, and confirm the child's experience without dramatizing the situation into something bigger than it is.

One of the most important things our children learn from us is how to raise children. We learn child-raising practices without knowing it largely from experiencing how our own parents raised us. Our parents learned child raising from their parents, who carried on the child raising traditions given to them by their parents, and so on. The chain has been unbroken, handed down from generation to generation, possibly for thousands of years. This result is that you may be using very old child-raising thoughtware.

Through seriously questioning your own actions and motivations and choosing what purposes you serve when being with your children, you can create the possibility of shifting your behavior and your attitudes. You can take a stand and declare that, "The chain breaks here!" Then you can do something entirely different. This is important work. By making the effort to improve your parenting, and by being consistent, you can make a real difference in the quality of your child's life. Not only that, but by blessing your children with kindness, generosity, and respect, you are influencing the ways children will be raised for many generations into the future

HOLDING SPACE FOR COMMUNITY

There is no top end to holding space. The context of spaceholding expands and matures as the Man does. After holding space for your 'self', then expanding to hold space for other Men, then expanding to hold space for Woman, then expanding to hold space for children and family, the next spaceholding expansion is into the domain of community. A Man's spaceholding ability expands at the same rate as his matrix, and when matrix expands into the level of community, Man experiences himself as becoming one with the body of the community. His priorities naturally and automatically shift, his considerations have a new intention behind them. Not only is he attentive to his own practice, his relating, and the wellbeing of his children, he now experiences the practice of other men, the quality of other relationships, the wellbeing of other children in the community, and the wellbeing of the community at large with equal responsibility. Not because he thinks that he should, but rather as a manifestation of expanded awareness. This will result in new and different gestures on his part.

Rather than not noticing that a particular man has been out of relating with the other men in the community and may be in pain, a spaceholder of community will reach out and make contact to listen for what is going on with that man, no differently from reaching out to examine an ache on the side of his own foot. Rather than leaving the cars parked in haphazard congestion around the driveway entrance, a spaceholder for community will bring the issue to a meeting, propose signs and a parking system, and organize a work-weekend to layout new parking spots the way a Man would comb his own hair or neaten up the contents of his closet. Rather than being numb to – or a victim of – general tensions about the community in the nearby public indicating imminent danger of certain actions being generated unconsciously by a member of the community through their gossiping, drama making, or jockeying for power and position in their place of work, the spaceholder for community will connect with that community member and have a conversation that brings to their attention the dire consequences of continuing their actions for the whole community and the immediate necessity for changing their behavior.

The experience of 'being a community' or 'being in community' is a side effect of a group of people providing their services to the village. If you strive to make the goal and purpose and outcome of your gameworld to be 'community', this would be like trying to stand up when you are already standing up. It is very unsatisfying. Your gameworld exists to provide its value, and through the teamwork of providing that value, the experience of community naturally emerges.

19. 2001: Some Thoughts On Service, Sanity and Magic

17 April 2001 – For Tawagoto

After years of training yourself to live as a Westerner in a Western society, you unconsciously perform the acted-out role of being civilized and sane by the standards of the dominant culture. You have been taught that 'sanity' makes you seem 'good', 'nice', and 'safe' to others.

Then you enter spiritual life – in a crazy-wisdom path, no less – and you fail to realize that your assumed 'sanity' is merely an adaptive mask, a convention. You may also fail to investigate to what degree your fake 'sanity' has value to the crazy-wise Teacher or to the School itself.

You were taught to regard yourself as authentically sane, and to strive for the appearance of 'authentic sanity' – but in actuality your 'sanity' is a thin veneer of denial, like the crust of the Earth, no thicker than a hair on a basketball. Beneath the candy-coating is a gigantic uncontrollable roiling hot molten Underworld – your magma core. (Uncontrollable, but not unmanageable. Underworld management is, however, a separate consideration.)

Spiritual work, including aspects such as being a student, striving to become a devotee, a life of practice, obedience, service, and so on, often involves the practical aspects of being sensitive, sensible, impeccable, on time, and paying attention to energetics and spaces. In other words, spiritual work seems to require behavior that falls into the realm of being civilized and sane – but in the context of this Work and this School, spirit lives in service to something greater than itself. Although this may appear to be a paradox, it is not. There must be a way to discriminate between the self-deceiving unconscious act of pretending to be sane, civilized, and a 'good spiritual student' (a variant of merely following the status quo, irresponsibly and unconsciously 'just following orders'), and truly being of service. Embodying objective service is very different from following a neurotic, fear-based, impulse to gain acceptance or social status. How can you make the distinction?

Here are some possible approaches. The difference between acting sane and of service, and being sane and of service, is that authentic service is never enacted according to a rule.

Service is alive.

The expression of service is unique and specific to each circumstance – it is never actually the same as it was the last time, or the last moment, although the repetition of actions may be what is wanted and needed.

For example, the actions of setting the table with plates, napkins, glasses, cups and cutlery elegantly placed and completed well before the last minute, may appear to look the same every time because that is what is wanted and needed. But this does not require the table setter to be dead or mechanical. Actions in a space that are mechanical, no matter how much they may look like service, could as easily destroy the space as serve it. You may have noticed someone lighting candles before a talk and experience that even though the action seems appropriate, the space feels more contaminated than cared for by that action. Hello ego.

If you are sensitive, sensible, impeccable, on time and paying attention to spaces according to rules – because you think you have to – then the service is not service as you are considering it. It is ego's strategic posturing, ego's pretense.

This is why you may find it impossible to put your shoes onto the shoe rack by the door. You think that such behavior is following a rule instead of an action that is of service. Your ego is too much an 'individual' to follow rules, but this too is being at the effect of one's psychological knot.

The difference between pretending to be a practitioner and actually being of service, is that service is not sane by conventional standards. From the point of view of ego, service is completely nuts.

Service radically ignores the concept and philosophy of 'me' by functioning under the declaration, "I already have everything that I need."

From ego's perspective, this idea is untenable because it instantly and irrevocably disempowers all of ego's coercive force. In the face of real service, ego wants to holler, "Hey! Wait a minute here! Service? What are you, crazy? I have needs! Who will take care of me? My needs must be fulfilled too. This is America, after all! I have rights!"

How can ego present a convincing argument on its own behalf, anymore, if all of your 'needs' have been preempted by already present satisfaction? Real service to the other or the environment ignores the entire context from which 'me'-oriented considerations arise.

What this all means is that you cannot truly be of service unless it is okay for you to feel insane by the standards of the surrounding culture.

Attaining the discrimination between ego's acting sane or civilized, and real service (or real appropriateness and true sanity) forces you to acknowledge that real service is also an act from ego's point of view. Both 'pretending to be sane' and 'being of real service' are theatrical gestures as far as ego is concerned.

(Perhaps we could only have such a conversation within the context of a left-handed Tantric 'crazy-wisdom' school.)

Real service feels normal and becomes natural and organically innocent only when ego is not there to argue about it. In the meantime, it is valuable to notice that real service feels just as much played out as ego's pretend 'socially acceptable' sanity, except that you are much more familiar and comfortable with ego's standard show.

Real service feels awkward and insane to ego because you are moved from a motiveless context, which is unfamiliar and unsettling. You can only be of real service if you are willing to tolerate the intensity of slipping into service's context, and function there, even though you do not understand it.

Real service is never restricted to 'our' preferences, but originates as improvisation in the moment, according to what is objectively wanted and needed.

Real service is distinct experientially from behavior performed according to 'how it is supposed to be done'. You can learn to recognize this felt difference through becoming cognizant of and responsible for your purpose.

Ego is happiest in the domain of rules, because within the webwork of reasons and causes, ego can always find exceptions, loopholes, and justifications for doing what ego wants to do, or avoid doing what ego does not want to do.

If it is true that there are no rules about service, and you are still one-hundred-percent radically responsible, then there are also no excuses to hide behind or reasons to argue about. Only the results: did it serve, or did it not serve? Objective service, or hospitality, is considered to be the highest practice because there are not any rules. Hospitality works from magic, from invisibility, from tone, from mood, from timing, from radiance, from radical reliance on the guru and on Divine Influence – and to ego, this is insanity.

So you must at some point come to see that there is a part of each of us that is insane, magical, totally unreasonable, and alive in the moment. Part of your unfounded background feelings of confusion, rage, or grief may derive from tacitly recognizing that the world (the context of ego and worldliness) is so dead, and that this deadness is so unreal, so unnecessary, and such a waste of God. Your horror, pain, and unconscious revenge lashes out when you experience that you have granted the dead world such dominance in your reality for so many years.

What the guru offers you as the way through seems equally insane. He proposes another apparent paradox: the necessity of obedience.

The mechanics of the necessity of obedience may go something like this: Before you become responsible and reliable at the level of insanity and magic there is still service to perform. If you have not recovered the bodily sensitivity to detect what is wanted and needed to serve the present space – because you are too identified with psychologically generated emotional reactions (internal noise that is louder than the delicate signals of service), or if you have not recovered the ability to turn right angles while moving at light speed to serve the present space – rather than your projections on the space – because you keep trying to appear sane in the standards or ordinary modern culture, and you continue to carry psycho-emotional baggage (judgments, criticisms, beliefs, opinions, assumptions, stories, expectations, unfulfilled childhood needs, etc.), then how can you serve?

As you probably by now have noticed, it can take years, lifetimes perhaps, to work through the psychological quagmire maze into simple basic adulthood. Only through adulthood is the archetypal reached. But right now, service is needed. Without the capacity to be responsible at the level of insanity and magic, the appropriate action is to find your way into the company of someone who does have this capacity, and then to follow their lead. Gaining the ability to simply follow instructions without distortion, without recoil, following through to completion and cleaning up after yourself along the way – practicing obedience, especially obedience to reality – will take you a long way towards becoming responsible at the level of insanity and magic.

20. 2001: Divine Alchemy Part 2

26 August 2001 – Contributed to Hohm Sahaj Mandir Study Manual III and IV

NOTE: Lee Lozowick made editorial changes in the sections of the writing below that were taken into Volume III and Volume IV of the Hohm Sahaj Mandir Study Manual. After publication Lee arranged that I receive a printout showing his original hand-written edits on my pages. Lee's changes are so edifying (and entertaining) that I include them here using the following code: What Lee crossed out is shown as ~~crossed out~~. What Lee added is shown <u>with an underline</u>. I imagine that including these details here is exactly why Lee gave them to me.

DIVINE ALCHEMY (Part A)

This will be an exploration of the metaphor of 'apprenticing to a Master Alchemist' as a possible model for the student-teacher relationship. Viewing the spiritual path from the perspective of Alchemical Transformation reveals aspects of practice, service, and the Great Process of Divine Evolution which may prove invaluable for a spiritual aspirant.

Let us begin with the word 'alchemy'. What is inferred by using the term 'alchemy'? Alchemy is the science of sublimation (making things more sublime), specifically the technology of transforming base substances of lesser value into refined substances of greater value.

To understand this further, it can help to remember that there are two forms of transformation. Transformation with a capital 'T' can be envisioned as vertical motion into a new plane, a radical change of context from dualistic to non-dualistic. Vertical Transformation is the ultimate intention behind certain alchemical gestures. However, it continues to prove valuable to use the word 'transformation' with a small 't' to indicate change of a non-linear nature, even though the change may be lateral rather than vertical. Like hopping from one lily-pad to another lily-pad, 'transformation' with a small 't' indicates lateral translation from one stuck state to another stuck state, as compared to Transformation with a big 'T' which implies taking to the air.

The reason I will continue to speak about lateral shifting in this consideration of Divine Alchemy is that the necessity to 'get off it' built into lily-pad-hopping provides specific stresses and energetic nutrients needed for building an internal matrix which, over time and through repeated exposure of longer and longer duration, can sustain the sudden ultimate Transformational 'pole-shift' into the non-dual context. Unless otherwise indicated with a capital 'T', the word 'transformation' in this writing will refer to common lateral translations.

If alchemy is the technology of transformation, what then is Divine Alchemy? To understand how alchemy can function in relating with the Divine, it is necessary to take a closer look at alchemical transformation itself. This will be a rather long consideration, and I will not get back around to mixing the Divine back in with alchemy until after exploring a number of other pieces of the puzzle.

ALCHEMICAL TRANSFORMATION

In general, alchemical processes involve three phases. The initial phase, of course, is the set of present conditions. You might depart from the relatively known and stable present conditions and enter into a middle phase as a result of accepting certain invitations. The middle phase – 'the in-between the lily-pads state' – is where changes take place. Finally a third phase is entered where the new conditions stabilize – keeping in mind that the new conditions may allow for a completely different functionality from the original state.

After some degree of stabilization or digestion has occurred, you re-enter the first phase or 'ready' position again, but in a changed condition, with changed perspectives, options, and capacities. It should be noted that this is a cyclic process with no top end.

After some cycles, you may discover that the most effective time to re-enter the in-between state is just before the solidification in the third phase is complete, which may feel like just before you are ready. As an apprentice to an Alchemist, you do not have to worry so much about the timing of when to begin the process again, because arranging such things will generally be handled by the Alchemist.

For an example of the three phases, imagine a handful of gold coins. The coins are relatively hard and solid. Undisturbed, they would retain their shape for thousands of years. If your purpose is to transform the functionality of the coins from money into invocational art by reshaping them into a statue of a saint, the three phases of transformation become clearly visible.

In the beginning you hold the separate, individually minted and dated coins, each with its own history, having been used for hundreds or thousands of monetary exchanges, and then later kept for their value as antiques, or historically important relics. These are the original conditions.

Then the invitation to transformation arrives, in one form of discomfort or another. Perhaps the most straightforward gateway to the in-between state is placing the coins together in a crucible and melting them in a blast furnace (the equivalent of a formal study group, or an intentionally formed household of apprentices). Sparks fly; slag bursts into bright-orange flame and smokily burns away. One by one, the unique shape of each coin is released as the heat and chaos disorganizes its solidified structure and it gains fluidity. At last the gold no longer retains its various separate identities, flowing easily together into a single puddle of liquid metal.

Now that it is molten, the gold can be poured into a mold having the form of the saint, and then left to cool. The cooling is the third phase of the transformation process. In a short time, the mold can be removed. What remains is the same gold that had previously been coins, but which now has a new form that gives the gold unprecedented qualities. What at first appears to be total destruction of the coins simultaneously reveals the origin of a statue of a saint. Such typically dramatic manifestations during the transformational process leave us with the impression of having experienced a miracle of archetypal dimensions, nothing less than the 'death and resurrection show'. This is an accurate assessment. It is also simply how the process works.

Of the three phases, the second phase (liquefaction) is the most interesting because it is the most feared. (Even more interesting is the ability to create the possibility of the transition from the first phase into the second phase, while considering elements of timing and mood so as to promote sustainable change.) Words that are commonly used to describe being in various forms of the in-between state include: chaotic, confused, breakdown, fluid, uncontrolled, existential crisis, deconstructed, standing on nothing, destabilized, disoriented, unknown… meltdown. As rough as it may sound, the purpose and necessity of the in-between state are clear. Change cannot occur without it.

Since a system's form determines its functionality, if a function is to change, its form must change. (Insanity is sometimes defined as expecting different results when continuing the same actions, the equivalent of expecting different functionality from the same form.) Predispositions must reorder to allow something new to occur. Because it is so integral to the transformational process, let us more closely examine the Liquid State.

THE LIQUID STATE

Let us be practical. You can expect that the length of time spent in the Liquid State will vary, from a few moments in the beginning stages of alchemical transformation, to longer and longer times later on. After a fairly predictable series of evolutionary steps have occurred, one begins to shift from being primarily occupied with reassembling and defending solidified 'lily-pad' positions and learning to suffer through the intense sensations often associated with melt-down, to being primarily occupied with exploring processes of continuous expansion, where solidity becomes an inconvenient but temporary layover like St. Louis or Frankfurt.

The shift from regarding the Liquid State as a terrible misfortune to regarding the Liquid State as standard operating conditions represents a total context shift from the Defensive Context to the Expansive Context, two totally different modes.

The Defensive Context is positional, based on beliefs, committed to defending itself against changes and to keeping everything the same. A survival strategy is formulated in childhood. You adopt mechanisms of habitual attitude and behavior to replicate the strategy in your world and in relating, and then your psychology develops around sustaining these mechanisms, backed by a survival imperative. Your individuated psychology instinctively recognizes this approach as necessary and workable in the long run. Indeed, most people live out the totality of their lives confined to the set of possibilities defined by their Defensive Context strategy. You live out an ordinary human life, try to pass on the best of your strategy to your children, and then you die.

In contrast, the Expansive Context is process oriented rather than position oriented, based on distinctions and Principles, and committed to the evolutionary expansion of consciousness without limit.

Human beings are designed to relate to the world from the Expansive Context.

Trying to compare the Defensive Context with the Expansive Context is like trying to compare the experience of seeing written notes for a children's song with the experience of hearing a Hindu chant sung by a group of ardent devotees in praise of God. What is the difference between a jail cell and the wild free sky?

Though the spiritual journey may have no end, it does have a definite beginning. It begins in the moment when you are willing to release control of your experience of life and let life itself begin to lead the way. This opening catalyzes a shift of context from the Defensive to the Expansive context. Lee Lozowick calls this shift the 'Sacrifice Of Peace Of Mind'.

If you do not consciously understand at the outset that to be involved with an Alchemist or a School Of Alchemy means that you are devoting yourself to the purpose of evolving from the Defensive Context to the Expansive Context, then at some point you will become quite confused, frustrated or anxious. Old habits intended to sustain positionality no longer serve you when your work revolves around the entirely different purpose of sustaining groundlessness.

On the way towards sustained groundlessness, the shift from solid to liquid and back to solid again cycles through many, many times. It helps allay panic to learn that the intense sensations that may arise during disassembly and slipping into the Liquid State are quite normal and do not indicate that anything is wrong or broken. On the contrary, as unexpected as it may seem, the void that begins to appear through the cracks in what you once thought of as 'the real world' is none other than reality itself. Soon you may notice that when a brick vanishes from your defensive wall, rather than being terrified of the vulnerability you can immediately locate yourself on the map of alchemical transformation and note, "Ah, yes. The Liquid State again!" You can begin to appreciate the accompanying superfluidity, freshness of perspective, and lightness of being. A further way to consider this process involves introducing the concepts of 'psyche' and 'essence'.

PSYCHE AND ESSENCE

A person raised in the context and customs of Western cultures is for the most part preoccupied with doing things and having things, and thus identifies themselves with their psyche – the egoic personality – because it seems obvious that through implementing ego's imperatives, you can accomplish your doing and having. Just as when in a movie theater you tend to ignore the quality of the upholstery and the richness of light fixture design as soon as the show starts, you also tend to ignore your more subtle and unfathomable 'Being' or essential nature whenever personality steals your attention and performs its show - which is almost always.

You can observe the difference between psyche and essence by imagining the differences between someone who has grown up in the city with rapid transit, billboards, high-rise apartments, and shopping malls, as compared with someone who has grown up in the countryside with farm animals, vegetable gardens, fresh-water streams, and wide-open space. The fun-loving 'city slicker' usually lives in a verbal reality with clever repartees and a sharp sense of humor. The 'country bumpkin', though more outwardly reserved and sedate, rests in common sense wisdom, unshakeable beliefs, and deep long-lasting friendships. This is not naming either psyche or essence good or bad. This is about making the general distinction between the two orientations to indicate that what is possible is a changed relationship between the two, such that psyche functions in the service of essence rather than psyche running your life pretending like essence does not exist, as is perhaps your present condition.

Since entering the process of alchemical transformation involves both psyche and essence at the most profound levels, it is wise to have some foreknowledge of what this is going to entail. The process nurtures development of an internal matrix that can sustain a 'pole shift' in which essence replaces psyche as the predominant ~~presence~~ mechanism of motivation. The appropriateness of this radical shift has been understood for millennia and has been illustrated by the classic diagram of ouroboros, the snake, worm, or dragon eating itself, tail first. Like the chick who is still in the egg eats the egg whites to grow and mature before it can peck its way out of the shell, essence actually devours psyche bite by bite to establish a solid experiential foundation in a foundationless territory. If you and the Alchemist accomplish what it is that you have set out to do together, then this is what is going to happen to you. Thinking the process through, you might regard it as entertaining to consider what remains when the meal is finished.

The value of becoming intimately familiar with the experience of 'the snake taking bites out of its own tail' is that when it is occurring to you – when you notice big internal holes in your worldview where before you could have sworn was an understanding that was solid and real – you can try to relax. Play around with the deconstruction rather than trying to defend your 'self'.

You can rest in a modicum of reassurance that even though you may be extremely uncomfortable and unfamiliar with what is transpiring, things are proceeding as they should. With your increasing internal navigation experience, you learn that fear, recoil, contraction, and resistance are less in order during the Liquid State than neutral observation, persistent practice, and a kind and generous sense of humor. Forewarned is forewarned.

Even if you are familiar with the unavoidable sensations, terror easily arises when slipping into the groundless Liquid State, and a fear-motivated question easily takes precedence in your consciousness. A quivering voice squeaks out from the corner of your mind: "How do things come back together?" In asking this question you have just discovered the value of a School.

SCHOOLS

Tens of thousands of years ago, when the first human beings began asking themselves "Who am I?" or, "What is the purpose of life?" or, "What happens when I die?" the first small groups of people assembled to investigate possible answers to such questions.

Like a corporation, association, club, or culture, a group can begin to take on a life of its own that is bigger than the life of any one individual within the group. In this way, an organization can be considered to be alive, a living organism. A biology of groups could be formulated, so as to better understand the various species of groups, how they grow and evolve, how they reproduce, what foods they eat, what ecological niches they interact with, how they protect themselves from predators, and so on.

If we were to classify all the various types of human organizations, from sewing circles and football teams, to political factions, movie-star fan clubs, and religions, we would discover a small class of groups that exists to serve the purposes of Divine Alchemy. Rather than calling themselves a 'band', 'team', 'squad', 'academy', or 'association', such a group refers to itself as a 'School'. Though structurally and functionally a School has many things in common with other groups, their purpose and methodology are unique. One distinguishing characteristic of a School is the context in which it rests.

Most human organizations are dedicated to stasis, to sustaining and protecting a particular system of beliefs. They function within the defensive context.

True spiritual schools are not based on beliefs of any kind, but rather are dedicated to self-knowledge and Transformation. They therefore function within the expansive context.

These two contexts, the defensive and the expansive, are so different from each other as to seem like different universes. As could be expected, by functioning within an expansive context, a spiritual school involves a different set of relationships and procedures than most organizations with which you might be familiar. Why is it that you are interested in such a thing?

ON BEING A BLACK SHEEP

The false sense of sanity that is common to any institution dedicated to the defensive context results from the group defending their positionality with systems of belief. In such an environment, personal beliefs are regarded with reverence. When someone expounds upon what they believe, the beliefs are given credence as if they meant something important or carried some weight.

The fascinating quality of beliefs is that the human mind can believe anything about anything. (Read a book on comparative religions or cultural anthropology if you have any doubts about this.)

If you dare to inspect the faculty of belief closely enough you will discover that beliefs have no relationship to reality. There can be no objective conversation about beliefs. The only rational response to the expression of a belief is, "Oh…," pronounced in a slow, southern-drawl.

As part of the Defensive strategy we human beings ordinarily surround ourselves with 'like-minded' neighbors and friends, and attend religious or social gatherings with people of shared beliefs. This dynamic is so epidemic as to be invisible and unnoteworthy in normal company. If you happen to suddenly notice its deleterious effects on your creative potential and feel moved to discuss your discovery in public, the locals might quickly start regarding you askance, as if you are a bit eccentric, perhaps even slightly paranoid.

Shocked to find the disbelief of others liberally applied to the results of your empirical experiments, either you immediately inject yourself with a huge dose of your favorite soporific (chocolate-chocolate chip ice cream, screaming fights with our mate, five action videos in a row, an on-line mail-order shopping spree, you know what I mean…) and try to forget about it all, or, over time, you discover that a nagging, niggling sensation is building somewhere around your solar plexus. That feeling is panic. Or rage. Or both mixed together, better known as hysterical aggression.

And were you to clearly elocute the cause of this sensation you would have to admit that you are terrified that if you do not continue investigating the 'anomaly' you have discovered then you are not being true to yourself. At the same time, you may be outraged that nobody ever told you about this before, followed by another wave of fear from a growing certainty that if you do continue investigating the anomaly you will be shocked and horrified 'beyond belief' at what you will learn about reality.

In this dilemma you are solely responsible for making the choice. You who are reading this book have already chosen. Like in '*The Wizard of Oz*', the little black doggie exposes the feeble old man pulling levers behind the curtain when we realize that even though everyone around you seems to find comfort and certitude in a specific set of beliefs, you do not.

It is worth noting that this black sheep business is well-known to the Bauls of Bengal. It's the *ulta* path, which flows contrary to the current of conventional culture, in all aspects of life. However, as you enter into a School of black sheep, you may simultaneously experience a fear-based instinctual resistance to identifying yourself to the general public as a non-believer. Terrifying words begin floating through your subconscious mind, every now and then gurgling up to the surface shouting: *Heretic! Blasphemer! Heathen! Infidel! Outcast! Renegade! Black Sheep!*

Applying these horrific words to yourself is not uncalled for because in a social organization dedicated to stasis, being identified as a Black Sheep has often resulted in rejection, expulsion, abandonment, excommunication – in other words, inquisition, torture, and death.

Upon recognizing your precarious circumstances, your nervous system immediately prepares itself to hide from view or dodge flying rotten tomatoes and stones. Your awareness of danger is so deep that it must be cellular. The threatening image of an angry lynch mob looms into your mind's eye. If you stay true to yourself rather than subscribing to a false reality based on beliefs, then there is a sizable chance that you will literally or figuratively be killed! Now, ain't that a kicker?

Faced with so great a quandary, you may well live a secret life for many years before a certain courage and stamina matures within you strong enough to withstand the stresses certain to be involved in seeking direct knowledge of your true nature. When you are ready to begin, an intelligent approach to the problem might be to find someone who is already an expert in the arts and sciences of the transformative journey, an Alchemist perhaps, and then to apprentice yourself to them. How do you do that?

THE DISPOSITION OF APPRENTICESHIP

From the linear perspective it seems obvious that the first step in becoming an Alchemist's apprentice is to find an Alchemist to whom you can apprentice. But this is not true, and this is where many spiritual aspirants get stuck. Looking for an Alchemist is a completely different set of tasks than apprenticing yourself to an Alchemist.

Searching for an Alchemist to apprentice to before you are an Alchemist's apprentice is like looking for a Ferrari 9000 to drive at Le Mans before you have your driver's license, or, running for the office of President before you have acquired the abilities, the charisma, and the popular backing of a world-class politician. It is self-referenced, naïve, erroneous, and can waste a lot of irreplaceable time and energy, unless, of course, your true purpose is not really to apprentice to an Alchemist on the path of transformation but instead to be a dabbler...

Here is a huge secret: The first step in becoming an Alchemist's apprentice is to commit to being an Alchemist's apprentice.

It is this simple, and this difficult.

Committing to be an Alchemist's apprentice is not something that you can decide about in your mind. It is a change of state in your five bodies, a shift of identity, a modification of your self-experience. Becoming a commitment of this magnitude is something you choose and declare and walk into before you know what it means or how you are going to manage to do it – because the truth is, you cannot know these things beforehand. A commitment of this scale results in an all-inclusive new way of being.

Becoming an Alchemist's apprentice before being accepted into the company of an Alchemist is a non-linear approach. It is comparable to providing value into a 'money-loop' before you have a signed contract with a client. Somehow you intuit that 'what goes around, comes around', so to initiate the flow, you launch something valuable so it starts going around.

To deepen the analogy, it is radically obvious yet contrary to common thinking, to assert that you do not actually have to 'make money'. You do not have to make money because there is already more than enough money in the world. Everywhere you look there are trillions and trillions of dollars represented by the organizations and associations that create, sustain, and dispose of the objects and services of your life. This wealth flows abundantly from bank account to bank account in money loops.

Most of us relate to money as victims. That is, you wait around for some money-loop to come discover you and, of its own volition, start flowing money through your personal bank account for no particular reason.

But this is not how money works. Money needs a reason to flow through your bank account. The most irresistible reason is value. Value is irresistible to money no matter how tight the money-loop is constructed, because if value is received in a money-loop, the cost of the value will be less than the worth of the value.

The linear approach to providing value into a money-loop is to hope that a money loop discovers the value you can provide, and then invites you to deliver your value. This is called *advertising*.

The non-linear approach to providing value into a money-loop is to discover and refine your ability to deliver your value yourself, go find one or more money-loops in which the value you provide makes a difference and is valued, and then without asking permission, without marketing yourself or negotiating a deal, start providing the value into the loop. This is called *invention*.

The energetic law says that if value is received then it will be paid for. As soon as your value is received by the loop, you will start getting paid. Voila! You have just been included in the money-loop. It does not cost the money-loop anything to flow some of its money through your bank account too.

The universe works like this.

Therefore, the same non-linear approach works for becoming an Alchemist's apprentice. Alchemical work is flowing all around you in life all of the time. The strategy of waiting around for an alchemy loop to come find you, guarantees that you remain energetically classified as a seeker. A seeker acts needy, wounded, or incomplete and is constrained to looking around for something to fill the need, heal the wound, or produce completion. The seeker is a victim looking for an Alchemist to make a rescue.

The disposition of a seeker repels alchemical energy, and instead, attracts predators. Being a seeker is very different from being an Alchemist's apprentice. It is the same difference between someone watching a football game from the grandstands compared to someone playing as a team member on the field.

By committing to the disposition of being an Alchemist's apprentice now, first, before there is evidence to support that story, you will of necessity discover myriads of specific and real ways that you can begin practicing as an apprentice in your daily life, thus providing real value into the alchemical energy loops around you even if you do not see them. If you are providing real value into a loop, then sooner or later you will be compensated in the coin of the realm.

As obvious and straightforward as this methodology may seem, making the shift from being yourself to being an Alchemist's apprentice is not necessarily easy because nothing in your environment is designed to support your new identity. Your declaration is orthogonal to (perpendicular to) every other element of your present life. It does not, however, have to remain this way.

Right now you can start practicing as an Alchemist's apprentice. The first practice is to attain to the apprentice disposition regardless of the evidence that may indicate otherwise, regardless of your physical, mental, or emotional circumstances. You begin to function as if the disposition of apprenticeship comes first in every moment of your life.

For example: read biographies of spiritual teachers. Learn the difference between whole foods and processed foods. Pay back all debts. Inventory all of your possessions to see which objects give you energy and which objects suck energy away from you. Get rid of the energy suckers. Travel into foreign and third world cultures to expand your flexibility as a space traveler and learn how to be a good guest. Do emotional work to improve your inner navigation skills, your communication skills, and your ability to make interesting offers in relating to other people. Volunteer regularly at service organizations. Perform random acts of generosity and kindness without recognition or reward. Take harmless risks that cause you to lose face. Attend the public lectures of speakers on the spiritual scene and ask them real questions. Make friends with the local neighborhood children and contribute to their well-being. Get into a women's or men's group and regularly ask for feedback and coaching. Take Aikido classes for a year with a reputable teacher. Consistently practice learning new skills like bicycle repair, organic vegetable gardening, patchwork quilting or masonry. Learn to prepare and host an elegant meal for fifteen guests. Write articles for publication in newsletters and magazines. Learn to tell a few good jokes. Commit to making a real difference in the life of your boss and your colleagues at work. And so on. In other words, engage life with transformational intentions. These activities provide positive stress and contribute to building your matrix so it can hold more consciousness.

No one can predict how long it will be before the Alchemist you have apprenticed to will actually appear in your life. What can be counted upon is the principle that says: when the apprentice is ready, the Alchemist appears. How does E.C.C.O. know if you are ready or not? The answer is simple and irrefutable. If the Alchemist has not appeared, you are not ready.

It is counter intuitive but true that an authentic commitment to the disposition of apprenticeship on the path of alchemy is a powerful force which actually creates the necessity for an Alchemist to show up.

This remains true even after you have found your Alchemist. It is the so-lidity of your commitment and the quality of your apprenticeship actions that call forth the teaching level of the Alchemist. Your commitment comes first.

Think of a sailboat. On first examination you may think that a boat sails through the water because it is pushed by the moving air, but this is not true. A sailboat is not pushed. It is pulled. The sail is up and the wind is blowing past the sail forming a vacuum on the far side of the sail. Rather than being pushed across the sea by the wind the boat is sucked forward by the vacuum of necessity. Through placing yourself in posi-tions of necessity your transformation occurs by reflex, because it is nec-essary to that which you are serving.

Learning to create necessity for an individual or a group is a basic skill for an alchemist's apprentice.

It can be useful to remain aware that by making the commitment of apprenticeship to an Alchemist, you immediately become attractive to all variety of entities and energetic vampires. (God did not rest on the sev-enth day…) There exist all kinds of people out there who regard them-selves as 'teachers of alchemy' or 'servants of transformation', but who are no such thing. No Alchemist Certification Program exists, or could be trusted if it did. It is left to the apprentice to discern for themselves the level at which an alchemist is practicing. It is your job to detect the authen-ticity of the energetic Principles any possible 'alchemist' is serving. What are their Bright Principles? What are their Shadow Principles? There are many, many false 'alchemists' in the world.

One dependable way to investigate the verity of an alleged Al-chemist is to study the qualities, skills, and relating skills of their current apprentices. A false alchemist will tend to surround themselves with fol-lowers who give their center away to the alchemist and exhibit adaptive behaviors. Having collected other people's centers makes a false or Grem-lin Alchemist feel more powerful and important. A true Alchemist will surround themselves with powerful inspired individuals fully on their way to becoming true Alchemist's themselves. A sham alchemist makes fol-lowers. A true Alchemist makes more Alchemists.

People representing themselves as alchemists will be functioning somewhere along a spectrum ranging anywhere from 'Self Service' to 'Serving The Divine As Master Alchemist Of Alchemists'. And this is only on the positive end of the spectrum. There is a lot to be cautious of. Let the apprentice beware!

THE WARNING

At some point it is obligatory that a person seriously involved in investigating the nature of reality be warned. There exists a line, which, once crossed, changes everything forever. You must be aware of this condition so as to be fully cognizant of what is at stake if you proceed past the line. Moving from one side of the boundary to the other must be a totally conscious decision as it is perhaps the most impactful decision you will ever make in your life. The consequences affect everything, and it is approximately impossible to return things to how they were before. How can you reverse evolution? How can you recompress an expanded consciousness? How can you become unaware of something you have already become aware of? The classic warning 'ABANDON ALL HOPE ALL YE WHO ENTER HERE' is quite appropriate.

Consider the process of becoming a surgeon. The transition from being you to being a qualified surgeon takes at least ten years of your life, costs a significant amount of money, requires total commitment on your part, dedicating your intention and energy to do the work that needs to be done to learn and practice whatever is necessary and required to serve as a surgeon. Along the way something permanently changes in you. Your relationship to the human body will never be the same. As a surgeon you will see things and experience things that normal people do not, because in your training you acquire a deeper understanding of the surgical principles and truths involved. When you look at a body you see the texture of skin and know just exactly how difficult each skin type is to slice through. You become alert to the placement of veins and arteries. You have a map for how various tissues lay into one another, how they glide as you probe, the color difference between a healthy spleen and one that is in trauma, the best way to saw skull bones and sew tendons back together, the tension of making life and death decisions for people, and the heavy experience of guessing wrongly.

Consider the process of becoming an airline pilot. The transition from being you to being a qualified pilot takes at least ten years of your life, costs a significant amount of money, requires total commitment on your part, dedicating your intention and energy to do the work that needs to be done to learn and practice whatever is necessary and required to serve as an airline pilot. Along the way something permanently changes in you. Your relationship to flying will never be the same. As a pilot you will know things and experience things that normal people do not because in your training you acquired a deeper understanding of the aerodynamic principles and truths involved. When you as a pilot board a jumbo jet, you stroll back into the cabin and tell the passengers, "Sit back, relax, and enjoy the flight." But in your own cognition are the radio frequencies of the triple back-up satellite navigation system, the failure rate of various brands of hydraulic pumps, and the raw hard awareness of the little black box under the control panel that records your last words should the plane go down.

Now consider the process of becoming an Alchemist. The transition from being you to being a skilled Alchemist takes at least ten years of your life, costs a significant amount of money, requires total commitment on your part, dedicating your intention and energy to do the work that needs to be done to learn and practice whatever is necessary and required to serve as an Alchemist. Along the way something permanently changes in you. Your relationship to reality will never be the same. As an Alchemist you will know things and experience things that normal people do not because in your training you acquired a deeper understanding of the principles and truths involved. When you enter a conversation, you will know without a doubt that all considerations raised are illusion. You will feel the immensity of wasted potential in each moment caused by the irreducible mechanicality of every individual, the resilience of identification with emotions and positions in psyche's self-created separative reality, and the unbelievably vicious, sly, and twisted commitment with which ego retains a grip on a human being's consciousness. Reality will never be the same for you. Oftentimes this is neither comfortable nor fun. You have now been warned. Proceed at your own risk.

ENTERING A SCHOOL

Being able to contribute usefully to an Expansive Context School begins only after radical shifts in your socially-indoctrinated worldview. For this reason, schools of alchemy usually design themselves so as to allow for beginners to enter and commence with their work without being thrown into an impossibly steep learning curve.

This arrangement can easily be imagined as a series of three concentric circles, with the outer circle representing the 'exoteric level' of the School, the middle circle representing the 'mesoteric level' of the School, and the inner circle representing the 'esoteric level' of the School. Each level, through natural selection, contains fewer and fewer students. And each level involves its own array of practices, conditions, and circumstances, graduating from the more obvious and physical to the more refined and energetic.

The movement of an apprentice from one level within the School to the next is regarded more or less as a formal procedure, signifying the construction of inner matrix along with an appropriate evolution in the integration of inner practices with visible manifestations in daily life.

Not everyone would of necessity enter the School at the exoteric level. The School is inherently wise and does not waste or ignore appropriate matrix that has been built under circumstances previous to encountering the School. On the other hand, the School never functions from a disposition of survival, maintaining a perspective of centuries or perhaps millennia, being in no hurry to put someone whose reliability is untested into a position of responsibility except as is necessary for teaching purposes.

Thus, when an individual approaches the School (or in rare cases, when a couple in a committed long-term relationship approaches the School, or in even rarer cases, a stable, mature family) some guidelines should be considered.

Entering the School means only one thing. It means becoming an apprentice to the Alchemist. The relationship between apprentice and Alchemist is *always* formal. It may not always appear to be formal externally, but it always is formal. If a person is approaching the School and they have not established a formal relationship with the Alchemist, then that person may be fooling themselves into thinking that they are in the School when in fact they are not. ~~For whatever reason,~~ For reasons that should be obvious by now, some people fool themselves in this way for a long time.

A formal student-teacher relationship with the Alchemist is created in the same way that a person would apply for entry into any school or university. Inherent in the student-teacher relationship of a School of Alchemy are promises and agreements just as binding as a legal contract. (Some would say that the agreements are even more binding than a legal contract.)

The person wishing to become a student makes an application, pays the 'registration fees', and then waits to see whether their application is rejected or accepted. In essence, and perhaps in actuality, the person is going to the Alchemist and asking, "Will you take me as your student?" The wise person, desirous of being accepted as a candidate for apprenticeship might say something like, "Will you take me as your student? If there are no places left, do you need a janitor, a dishwasher, a sweeper?"

There are three possible answers to this question: "Yes." "No." or "Maybe, if you meet the following conditions." Such conditions could well be to participate in a study group at the exoteric level for several years, never set foot on the property of the School unless directly invited by the Alchemist, purchase all available study materials (and study them!), begin the basic practices of the School, and so on. These prerequisites are set forth not so much for the satisfaction of the Alchemist as they are intended to protect the potential student. Should the applicant, once the entry conditions set forth by the Alchemist are engaged, change their mind and decide that approaching the School was merely <u>impulsive romanticism, or</u> an aberration in their behavior after overindulging in anchovy pizza and cheap beer – no more than a glitch of temporary insanity – then getting out of the contract is of much less consequence before it is signed.

If an applicant is accepted, the communication will be clear and direct from the Alchemist. In those first few moments the new apprentice should pay utmost attention. Beginnings are the most delicate of times to make sure that balances are correct. Generally it is during their ~~first few moments~~ <u>early involvement</u> in the School that the apprentice is 'assumed' by the Alchemist. The manner in which the Alchemist delivers his response is also full of subtle communications. We can see that as soon as the student-teacher agreement is made, even while it is being made, the learning begins. <u>On the other hand, there is no reason to 'make mountains out of molehills' by reading deep implications into the Master's facial tics.</u>

HE DOESN'T LIKE YOU

An authentic Alchemist does not agree to take you on as an apprentice because he likes you. That would be the act of ~~a charlatan~~ <u>someone who clearly does not know themselves very well, or is blind to the laws of the Work and therefore incompetent or unprepared to teach</u>. Neither will the Alchemist send you away because he does not like you. Likes and dislikes are not part of the equation. They arise from a context completely different from the functionality of Alchemist. What is true is that the Alchemist makes decisions based on one factor and one factor alone: is it or is it not profitable for the Work? All other considerations are secondary, ~~and basically ignored~~ <u>and may factor into the eventual equation in some small way, but are not pivotal.</u>

Sooner or later the apprentice must come to grips with the absence of such a common social qualifier. So many of your actions and gestures are manipulative contrivances contexted in ego and motivated by your psychological needs to be liked or disliked, to get positive or negative attention directed at you. You may not realize that the deep-rooted confusion, panic, or frustration that you may be experiencing when you are in the company of the Alchemist could easily be the result of you failing to accept the shocking realization that: he doesn't like you. He may not even want to hear what you have to say, no matter how important you imagine it to be.

At the same time, after being around the Alchemist for a while, you may observe certain behaviors ostensibly indicating that the Alchemist has some favorites amongst the apprentices. They receive special attentions or particular favors far outweighing what random allocation would allow. You can assume that such observations are accurate, at least in the domain of external manifestations. What is also accurate is that, except in the psychological domain, this favoritism is irrelevant. Laws of gesture and response, real efforts, and practice on the Alchemical path are immutable and will in no way be affected by such trivialities. Yet still, the favoritism apparent inequities will be noticed. If you are not one of the favorites, you can be grateful for the opportunity to practice with such a clear distinction between interactions based on psychological drivers factors and essential interactions qualifications. If you are one of the favorites, you must pay special attention to how you are dealing with the special attention, not letting it create feelings and actions of superiority, or the demeanor of those less fortunate, or unfortunate, as the case may be.

A second occasion during which what might appear to be favoritism is exhibited by the Alchemist is actually a time when what could be called 'First-Aid' is being administered. At certain crucial points in the evolution of an apprentice, a specific form of shock must be delivered to carry the apprentice across some chasm of doubt, or through some swamp of delusion. On these occasions the Alchemist may place the afflicted individual directly across the table from him at a meal, or at his side during a drive or a movie. In this way the needed energetic nutrients can be transfused intravenously, and the nervous system can be fortified or repaired, or even altered. Should you find yourself as the recipient of such treatment, the suggestion is to try not to 'wiggle'. Definitely do not beat yourself up because the treatment is required. It is best to assume that you do not necessarily know the real purpose of the Alchemist's actions (which may, in fact, have nothing to do with you) and let the thing take place uninterfered with. An Alchemist's purposes are generally multi-dimensional, non-linear, and often not even conscious. Let the Alchemist do his work with you, and don't assume that every time you sit near him, that you are being operated on.

Whether you are confronted with too much attention, recognition, special regard, or favors, or not enough, the best overall recommendation is to *not take it personally*. The Alchemist doesn't like you and the Alchemist doesn't not like you. The Alchemist is doing his job. You do yours.

There are two corollaries that follow from the statement, "*He doesn't like you.*" The first corollary is that since he doesn't like you and doesn't not like you, then there is no one there. The second corollary is that everything the Alchemist does is an act of theater. And both corollaries are totally subjective anyway.

BUILDING MATRIX

What is ~~the~~ matrix? Matrix is a substrate for the intersection between Divine Influence and your body, an accumulator for *baraka*, the scaffolding ~~around your being~~ that allows transformational construction work to proceed, the degree to which you are able to shift context from self-reliance to God-reliance in everyday life, the conditioner that permits you to tolerate the intensity of higher experience without getting burned out, fixed points to hold onto so that you do not get lost in the world, the joyful spirit of discipline and ruthless self-honesty, a refined form of matter which comes from outside of your normal experiences of space and time but which is real and very important, the energetic web which informs everything you are, a center point, the internal lattice-work for the teaching to hold onto, an intelligent and interactive protecting groundedness, the muscles formed when you exercise your body of practice, that which remains ~~after losing face~~ allows you to lose face without losing focus, an evolving openness that connects duality with non-duality, spiritual bones, the framework of understanding upon which essence or being can grow.

Matrix is the soul's house.

Building matrix takes time and intention. ~~Expanding~~ Solid and reliable matrix is crucial to maturing on the path. Matrix is nurtured by certain nutrients and radiations such as being in the presence of living Teachers and sacred shrines and artifacts, and is fed by exposure to specific kinds of stress such as right practice, doing what you do not know how to do, nonlinear invention, and unfamiliar or uncomfortable behavior like enduring the unpleasant manifestations of others, providing hospitality, especially when it requires you to 'go the extra mile', or when you might dislike the guest or guests, caring for sanctuary properly, and being a good guest, especially when you might dislike the host or hosts.

The kinds of efforts that build matrix include behaving in ways that honor the School or the Alchemist, providing something for someone else without reward or recognition, submitting gratefully to feedback from men's or woman's culture and using it well, noticing the way your Gremlin part or scared needy child part wants to react and not letting it show on the outside, keep trying to do what the Alchemist has asked of you even if you are not succeeding, overcoming self-indulgence, and self-doubt, and not least of all self-loathing, cleaning up your messes impeccably (physical, emotional, financial, sexual, and energetic), doing tasks which your comfort zone does not like and generating another mood than is your psychologically mechanical tendency, observing self-judgement and cutting it off, welcoming others into your territory without getting tense, being consistent in subtle commitments, being more interested in continual resurrection than in the little deaths, consciously trusting the Teacher, even under what to you seems like questionable or illogical situations, not gossiping about yourself or others regardless of the invitation, not worrying, staying focused and avoiding getting distracted until the job is done, noticing your imagined self-limitations and keeping going, asking for help, being willing to admit how much you enjoy the simple company of others, choosing a different emotional reaction than your chronically habitual ones, forgetting about sleep or food for a while, making choices that are orthogonal to the predominant space, making a mistake and not feeling bad and being willing to go on, being the source-person for sacred space even if the source-person job is not fairly distributed to others, writing for publication and submitting it, putting things back in their rightful place (e.g. picking up litter now and then even if you did not drop it), being a yes for children and your mate, cleaning out your drawers, calling your parents for no reason and telling them that you love them, refusing to be an exhibitionist, a voyeur, a sadist, a masochist, a score stealer (or a husband or wife stealer) or an effete artiste.

Most apprentices amazingly regard matrix building as a burdensome pain in the ass. The truth is that building matrix is a privilege and an honor - or (dare we say it?) an exciting adventure!

~~We build matrix together. One apprentice encountered major resistance to sitting practice and stopped coming completely. After a while a friend called. The apprentice explained all the reasons why it was so difficult to sit. The friend patiently listened, and finally said, "That is okay. We will just go on building matrix without you." With this new perspective, the apprentice had no problem being on the cushion the next morning.~~

RAPID LEARNING

The purpose of a school is, of course, learning. Since a School of Alchemical Transformation functions within the expansive context rather than the defensive context of traditional culture, the word 'learning' refers to a set of experiences which could be vastly different from what you have come to understand 'learning' to mean from your life previous to now. Setting aside preconceptions, <u>judgements, expectations, so-called needs, and at times even rational thinking,</u> is in order.

Because there is so much to learn, the optimal form of learning in an Alchemical School is Rapid Learning. While the name of the learning method used in an Alchemical School is 'Rapid Learning', this does not mean to imply that the learning that is taking place happens over a short span of time. To the contrary, it is not infrequent that the Alchemist delivers a communication to the apprentice that may take one year, five years, ten years, or perhaps even twenty years for the apprentice to receive. The term 'Rapid Learning' refers only to a specific form of learning. This same form will apply whether you are learning in the intellectual, physical, emotional, energetic, or archetypal body. You can try to resist the efficacy of Rapid Learning by several methods, however, no matter how effective your avoidance technique, the Rapid Learning process will continue to operate on you for as long as you remain within the context of the School.

Rapid Learning is a simple, elegant, three-state process that commences when you follow the only instructions given to you by non-duality. The instructions are: "*Go!*" As you begin to engage Rapid Learning, you may sometimes notice that you get stuck at *Go!* You freeze up; you hesitate to do the experiment; you procrastinate, and you do this in very clever and deceptive ways. For example, you can get stuck at *Go!* by imagining that you are already *Go*ing when you are not. You may fantasize about how it would be to *Go!* You may talk about *Go*ing. You may speak the dharma about *Go*ing. You may think about *Go*ing. <u>You may even rapidly move your feet or spin your wheels.</u> But after some time of living in this delusion about *Go*ing you must eventually face the reality of the results that you are creating that show you that you did not *Go!* You probably do not *Go!* for very good reasons.

The problem with *go*ing is that if you *Go!*, you will immediately be given feedback. Getting feedback is the second state in the three-state Rapid Learning process.

Fortunately for an apprentice, it is not difficult to get feedback. The world is a giant feedback generator. Your environment automatically and instantaneously responds to your every action and inaction by delivering ~~you of~~ feedback <u>to you. Of course, you have to get the feedback, ingest it, and then act on it for it to actually be feedback.</u>

Although you may think that inaction is 'not *Going*', and by not *Going* you can protect yourself from receiving feedback, the inarguable truth is that the various forms of not *Going* (such as withholding, withdrawing, isolating, thinking that you do not want to get involved, that it is not your job or that it is not your responsibility, and so on), are only variations on the infinite number of possible ways to *Go!* And they each and every one call forth their own forms of feedback.

Please note that this comment about not *Going* is *not* intended to insinuate that not *Going* is bad or wrong. Not *Going* is often the most effective, powerful, and appropriate gesture to make when taking into account all of the given circumstances. Regardless of what you may think (or hope), not *Going* does not avoid you being delivered of feedback.

Getting feedback does not have to be so terrible. Consider this: there are only two categories of feedback. Typically they are thought of as 'positive feedback' or 'negative feedback'. In order to avoid the implied connotations involved in using the terms 'positive' and 'negative', you can use the following alternatives. When you receive 'positive feedback', see it as feedback telling you "This is working!" and the invitation to 'keep *Going*'. And when you receive 'negative feedback', understand it as a '*Beep!*' which means: "Stop! This is not working! Here is how or why it is not working."

Due to your previous training, you may have the strong tendency that as soon as you receive negative feedback, you create an energetic sidechamber called 'The Swamp', and dive right into it. Reinforcing sentences begin ripping through your mind, down-spiraling you ever deeper into the bog. "I am bad. I am wrong. I am not good enough. <u>The Teacher will be furious with me.</u> I will be punished, criticized, whipped, shunned. I am stupid. I am a failure. I am not lovable. I quit. I will never do that again! They don't like me. What do they know anyway? Those idiots! They don't care about me. They are jerks! I am taking my ball and going home!"

Once you dive into the slimy, stinking swamp as a result of getting a *Beep!*, you may find it so rewarding, satisfying and familiar in terms of fulfilling your Underworld, <u>self-hatred</u>, unconscious, or hidden purposes, that you stay in that state for hours or days, sometimes months or years.

If you distinguish the swamp, both intellectually (by giving it a name: 'The Swamp'), and experientially (by repeatedly observing your internal state to notice your various sensations and reaction patterns, and noticing that this experience usually occurs upon the occasion of your receiving negative feedback, supported by internally judging that receiving negative feedback is not okay), you can locate the swamp on your map of Rapid Learning. Once the swamp is on your map, you have clarity about it. This clarity gives you the power to recognize when conditions arise under which you have usually entered the swamp, and therefore provide you with the option of choosing whether to enter the swamp right now or not. Upon receiving negative feedback and seeing the swamp gates open wide, even though it may be very familiar and attractive for you to go there, you no longer have to. The way to not go there is simply to give yourself the instruction, "*Don't go ~~there~~ into the swamp.*" And then use your discipline to go somewhere else. Where you end up if you do not go into the swamp is having to face the reality of the feedback.

Some of the negative feedback that you receive will be useful, and some will not. The way to tell the difference is that the useful feedback will strike an uncomfortable resonance deep within the heart of your established view of reality. The inaccurate feedback will not. (Taking into account, of course, the possibility that not experiencing the resonance could easily be a manifestation of your tendency towards denial, that the feedback gets lost in your extensive denial system.) Since it is almost guaranteed that you will not immediately and automatically understand the negative feedback (e.g., it will seem crazy to you, at first.) your guide must be the physically-felt sensation of 'taking a hit'. Feedback is feedback precisely because it comes from outside of your rationality box. You have to be careful not to dismiss feedback as not useful just because you do not at first understand it. Such discrimination calls for an open mind. Useless feedback may come from projections, expectations, or assumptions, ~~etc.,~~ on the part of external viewpoint, and can be allowed to slide away without recriminations, knowing that the giver lives in the same expansive context universe as you do, and that the fact that the feedback which they just gave to you did not land as a 'bull's eye' is a *Beep!* to them about their feedback to you. It is up to them to learn from that, if they want to.

Feedback has tremendous value as a tool to use in disassembling the automatic mechanisms of your mechanical defense strategies. Specifically, feedback contains the insight and wisdom that informs you as to precisely what to shift so that you can modify your efforts to better accomplish your aim. 'Shift,' then, is the third state in the three-state Rapid Learning process. To shift means to shift identity, to shift some quality about the way you are being, to shift who you are. By shifting who you are being, you will automatically shift what you are doing and therefore what you are creating.

The Rapid Learning process is a loop. Immediately after Shifting, you *Go!* again. *Go!* Get your feedback. Shift according to the feedback and your aim. Then *Go!* again.

This is the same process by which airplanes fly from Los Angeles to Philadelphia. Ninety-nine percent of the time they are off course, not flying in the right direction. Using the Rapid Learning model of *Go!* Feedback. Shift. *Go!*, they efficiently arrive at their destination.

Imagine that you have a treasure map of an island. Even though you know that you are on the island, and the map shows you where the treasure is buried, you still need a third piece of information before you can use the map. What you need is the little 'x' that says "You are here." No matter how accurate the map is, no matter how big the treasure is, without this little 'x', the treasure map is useless. It is Feedback that gives you the 'x'

Here is the interesting thing about feedback: It does not matter where the 'x' is. It does not matter if you look good or bad when you discover the actual position of the 'x' on the map. Once you know where you are, you can see exactly how far and in which direction you need to go in order to reach the treasure. Feedback is this valuable to an apprentice Alchemist.

To progress along the path of becoming an Alchemist, you require a constant source of reliable feedback so you can make the necessary shifts without wasting precious time and energy going further and further off track. Fortunately in this School we have exactly that resource in our fellow apprentices, and also sometimes directly from the Alchemist himself. You can make best use of this wealth of wisdom if you become reliable with respect to <u>both</u> feedback, <u>and owning the new contexts that you discover</u>.

USING FEEDBACK

One way to become reliable enough to receive feedback is to distinguish feedback from praise and blame. Both praise and blame are forms of conditioning. They are delivered with a non-revealed purpose of manipulating the recipient into modifying their behavior so as to continue or to stop certain actions. Becoming aware of the existence of the intent to condition behavior allows you to see the wisdom of relating to others (including your children) from the disposition of 'no praise, no blame'.

The distinction between praise and positive feedback is especially important. If the Alchemist gives you some positive feedback, and you interpret it as praise, and you say, "Thank you," as you have been taught to do, so as to be polite, or <u>if you are feeling self-congratulatory or over smug</u>, then the feedback lands differently in your body. It becomes ineffectual if not harmful, and you prove yourself to be unreliable with respect to receiving positive feedback. The Alchemist can no longer give you a "Go ahead!" signal because instead of receiving it as instructions to keep going as you have been going, you turn it around to imply that the Alchemist is saying, "You are good. I like you. I approve of you." Making this internal transposition of purpose of positive feedback into praise is the action of someone being adaptive and looking for approval and acceptance outside of themselves.

Adaptive students drive Alchemists crazy! <u>Well, at least they are very expensive, and the Alchemist's expense account is not open ended.</u> What can an Alchemist do with an apprentice who is doing everything they can to not be themselves but rather to be who they think the Alchemist wants them to be? Only when an apprentice is being himself or herself – all distortions included – can the Alchemist work with them to create the possibility of being something different. <u>(Yes, it is *something* different, and not someone different. If all one wants to be is someone different, a good therapist will be adequate.)</u> When an apprentice is being adaptive, the only thing the Alchemist can do is wait until the apprentice learns that it is not only okay, but also necessary, to get back into their body, own their own center, and be themselves, however that manifests. It may look like the Alchemist is being patient, waiting for apprentices to show up. But it is not patience that allows an Alchemist to wait. It is clarity about the mechanics of transformation. If you are not there, he cannot work with you. Period. Remember, ~~it does not matter where the "x" is~~ <u>everything is workable</u>. Consider that, if the Alchemist has not worked directly with you in a while, it may be because you are being adaptive around him, <u>or that your attention has wavered and is now on distractions, or seductions away from your apprenticeship</u>.

On the other hand, this is not an invitation to give free reign to your internal chaos-generating Gremlin when you are in the vicinity of the Alchemist, or to not make efforts to pay attention and remember what spaces you are in and the protocol that serves them. Learning what it means to stand in your center and not be adaptive are basic apprenticeship skills. An Alchemist will sometimes suggest that an apprentice study Aikido, Tai Chi, or some other form of martial arts, or may send them to go work in the gardens <u>or into business</u> in order to gain these skills.

Making the distinction between feedback and conditioning is equally important for *Beep!*s as it is for *Go!*s. If you interpret negative feed-

202 | No Reason

back as blame, accusation, failure to please, or disapproval, and the internal voices start churning and you start shutting down, withdrawing, making excuses, justifications, or profuse apologies, or you start beating yourself up internally – or externally by having 'accidents' or physical ailments like back aches or diseases so as to receive what looks like kindnesses directed towards you rather than negative feedback – then you make yourself unreliable with regards to negative feedback. The Alchemist will disallow negative feedback for you if you are just going to get sick or plot revenge.

If you are unreliable with regards to positive or negative feedback, then the Alchemist has no recourse but to let you wallow in your delusions until you are ready to participate in life at a more authentic level. This is called 'giving us rope'. An Alchemist has a hefty supply of rope that he will loan you so as to 'hang yourself' or tie yourself up in knots if you want to. Once you are in the predicament of 'dangling by the neck', or some other part of your anatomy ~~(There is no accounting for tastes.)~~ perhaps you will 'hit bottom', come to your senses, and will be willing to get real about what you are doing as an apprentice in a School of Alchemical Transformation. Until then, there is nothing for the Alchemist to do but wait and <u>crack jokes (not, however, at your expense).</u>

To establish reliability for receiving feedback, all you need to do is to use feedback as feedback rather than as food for your psychological creatures. You can easily train yourself to recognize either positive or negative feedback as being just feedback, and acknowledge its receipt by saying simply, "Okay."

Imagine that you are driving down the road and the map reader says, "You need to turn left here." You do not respond by saying, "What do you know? ~~anyway, asshole!~~" You say, "Okay." Likewise, if the navigator says, "Keep going straight," you do not say, "Oh, thank you so much! I am so glad you told me that!" You say, "Okay." It is just feedback, delivered to help you get to where you want to go. You say, "Okay," to indicate that you have received the communication. And that is all.

Something else to watch out for is if you *Go!*, then you get feedback. Then you *Go!* again. Get feedback again. *Go!* again. And you wonder why you keep receiving the same feedback. It is because you forget to roll through the third state of Rapid Learning: You forget to shift.

You may also have a habit to *Go!* Get Feedback. *Shift*. And then wait, hesitating after all of that intensity to loop back up and immediately *Go!* again. It is the *Going* again that puts the shifted qualities into action to build matrix and habits in the new domain. So, keep looping.

Consciousness expands when you lower the bar of your tolerance for experiencing pain (of every sort and on every level). Then you notice things that you did not notice before. Once you are more conscious you naturally modify your behavior so as to be more responsible. How quickly can you learn?

POSTS

Members of the School serve the School by holding specific job functions, or posts. If you are not 'assigned' a post in the School, then you can serve the School by serving someone who is holding a post in the School. If you cannot serve someone who is holding a post in the School, then serve someone else who is serving someone who is holding a post in the School.

'Master Alchemist' is one of the posts. One Master Alchemist is required in each School. What the Master Alchemist says, does, chooses, and disallows does not derive from their personal preferences, as some apprentices fantasizing about having that job may think. The Master Alchemist job description combines functions of antenna, transformer, and speaker. Like an antenna (or lightning rod!) they receive transmissions from the Divine. Like a radio circuit they transform signals from the Divine into language which can be understood by human beings. And like a loudspeaker, they deliver the received and transformed communications in the times and places when that communication is most needed.

Without a Master Alchemist, there is no School. At the same time, the post of Master Alchemist is just a post. It is no more or less important than any other post. Without apprentices the Master Alchemist is just an academicist. Like an animal without a brain or a heart obviously cannot live; less obviously, it also cannot live without a pyloric sphincter, (the valve at the base of the stomach). All the separate posts work together, and they work together best if they relate to the Master Alchemist with a certain regard and protocol that is appropriate to the Master Alchemist post. Imagine the brain saying to the hand, "Please write this note," and the hand saying, "Oh, I'm too busy to do that right now." Or the heart saying to the foot, "Here is some fresh oxygenated blood for you," and the foot saying, "No thanks. I'm full." The organism could not function effectively. In the same way, the School could not function without respecting, honoring, and paying attention to the Master Alchemist in ways defined by the job descriptions.

MORPHOGENETIC FIELDS

There is a further question useful to answer, namely, "How do things come back together once you enter the middle state during processes of alchemical transformation?"

In short, the answer, which has been derived experimentally over thousands of years of work in Schools, is that you do not have to worry about it. Reassembly happens all by itself, as if your various pieces have a natural, gravitational attraction to more elegantly align themselves with each other.

A deeper explanation includes the *Theory of Morphogenetic Fields*, which explains how, during the reassembly phase of a transformational Liquid State, the pervading morphogenetic field determines the shape of your new form.

'Morphogenetic' means 'shape making'. A morphogenetic field could be compared to a magnetic field. Imagine sprinkling iron filings onto a white sheet of paper held over a bar magnet. The filings automatically line up with each other into arcing patterns on the paper for no apparent reason. In this example, the invisible magnetic field coming from the bar magnet beneath the paper functions as a morphogenetic field shaping the randomly falling iron filings.

After several iterations through the alchemical transformation process, one begins to notice that the Bright Principles of the School serve as a morphogenic field, uncannily influencing the reassembly and resolidification of your ego structure into something able to sustain more refined awareness. The Bright Principles of the Hohm Sahaj Mandir are Kindness, Generosity, and Compassion.

DIVINE ALCHEMY (Part B)

It is now possible to say how *Alchemy* becomes *Divine Alchemy*. A School of Divine Alchemy is a School which the General Field of Consciousness functions as part of its morphogenic field. In such a School, the Divine is the force field that influences the second phase of the transformation process during which time previously crystallized psychological and essential elements become mobile with respect to each other, and reorder the nature of the apprentice <u>who</u> is in the Liquid State. The Divine rearranges these elements in accordance to laws of the Divine, just as the magnet rearranges iron filings in accordance to the laws of magnetism, or a coach gives advice to a soccer player in accordance to the laws of soccer playing.

It is the Master Alchemist who, through his commitment, serves as the space holder for the Divine's influence in the School. The School's Divine context provides the morphogenic field for all processes taking place under the auspices of the School or in the name of the Master Alchemist and his lineage.

BECOMING RELIABLE

To participate in the functioning of a School, an apprentice must aspire to becoming reliable. What does this mean?

A chess player needs all the various pieces on the board to play chess. He needs all of the pawns in the front row, and he also needs all of the specialized pieces in the back row, the king, the queen, two bishops, two knights, and two castles, along with their associated abilities. The full set of pieces is required in order to play the game, <u>at least to begin playing the game.</u>

In the same way, a Master Alchemist needs all the posts filled in the School. It does not matter to the Alchemist who, in particular, holds each post. He simply needs the post well navigated.

This becomes an interesting observation for the apprentice. All posts are available to you if you can fulfill the requirements. It does not matter how old you are, what previous experiences you have had, how long you have been in the School, which culture you come from, your education, race or religion. Your present qualifications, however they have been attained, place you in the front or the back row on the Alchemist's playing board. The Master Alchemist's choice of who holds which post is not personal. Acquiring the necessary attributes to fulfill a particular post is completely the responsibility of the apprentice.

One of the crucial attributes of a back-row apprentice is *reliability*. An Alchemist's capacity to work with a student upscales in direct proportion to the apprentice's ability to be reliable. Reliability can be defined as dependability, <u>tenacity</u>, consistency, steadfastness, and trustworthiness.

With regards to the relationship between an Alchemist and their apprentice, being reliable specifically involves paying attention to details on multiple levels at the same time without excuses, following instructions exactly – including the parts of the instructions which are not specified, having common sense even in situations when everyone around is being self-referenced and silly, sensitivity with regard to the protocol of spaces and timing, infinite respect for people and things without being adaptive or naïve, and being radically responsible for everything not somehow mentioned or implied in the above list.

True, reliability is rare. The fact of the scarcity of mature reliability is neither a pity nor a shame. Rather, it has to be this way due to the mechanics of the situation, <u>the physics of incarnation</u>. A person can only be as reliable as their psychology allows them to be.

Realizing that our psychology can potentially interrupt the flow of blessings incessantly gushing through the Alchemist-apprentice relationship avails us of some valuable hints. If a person is only as reliable as their psychology allows, and if you are attempting to become more reliable, is it efficacious to work with psychology? Every Alchemist answers this question with a different spin, but in general, the answer is, "Not necessarily." The reason that dealing with psychology to alleviate an effect of psychology may not be most expeditious has to do with context. Psychology is psychology. Psychology can never become what it is not. Psychology can never become reliable in anything other than being psychological, and therefore must obey the laws of egoic-identification and self-preservation. Reliability derives from something other than psychology. It derives from <u>objective</u> clarity <u>and objective conscience</u>.

One bit of clarity is that, if an apprentice wishes to become more reliable, then, they must begin to rest in something other than a psychological context. In other words, your purpose motivating each gesture must derive from something other than a psychological context. Since the psychological context includes such a vast percentage of the territory that you have been trained to survive in, and are intimately familiar with in your life, (for example, "I am right; you are wrong." "I win; you lose." "I am good; you are bad." And vice versa, and so on.) the consideration that there might exist something other than the psychological context can be startling and unbelievable. Where is it? What is it? How do I get there?

When you finally ~~culture~~ <u>cultivate</u> a necessity to have the answers to such questions, then you have entered the possibility of finally hearing what it is the Alchemist has been talking to you about for all of these years. You are coming into alignment with what the Alchemist wishes for you. The Alchemist wishes for you to become more reliable because the more reliable the apprentice is, the more the Alchemist can give to the apprentice, thus the more completely the Alchemist can do their job and fulfill their commitment to God. When the apprentice has created a listening that can hear and receive everything that the Alchemist can give, then the Alchemist has succeeded. It is up to you, as an apprentice, to receive the education that allows you to become that listening.

AN EXAMPLE

To illustrate what is meant by reliability in the relationship between apprentice and Alchemist, here is a true-life example of reliability in action. (The names have been changed to protect the guilty.) Interspersed with the details of what actually happened in this example are some of the internal considerations and principles influencing decisions made to take the selected courses of action (or, as may often be the case, the selected courses of inaction). The flow of incidents begins with the Alchemist suddenly calling out for a specific apprentice who is in the middle of a conversation with a small group of other apprentices, "Wayne!"

Without hesitation, yet without being adaptive, abrupt, or mechanical, Wayne drops what he is doing, stands up, and approaches the Alchemist, saying, "Yes?" In other words, Wayne regards the Alchemist's request for his attention as important enough to stand up and walk over to the Alchemist and give the Alchemist his full attention, rather than staying sitting with his friends, turning his head and shouting back, "What?"

Wayne's response also reveals an additional important principle, namely, the principle of *splitting attention*. No matter what conversation or activity with which the apprentice is involved, while in the Alchemist's company the apprentice has at least some percentage of his attention split off and available at the Alchemist's disposal. Days, weeks may go by without that dedicated bit of attention being called upon by the Alchemist. Yet the instant the apprentice is asked for, he responds with elegance and dignity because he was being attentive to the Alchemist. Attentiveness is an implicit element of the Alchemist-apprentice relationship.

Splitting your attention and keeping some percentage (three percent is usually enough) of your attention on the Alchemist no matter what the activity, serves as a very powerful method for the apprentice not being identified with and coalescing into a hookable form. Paying attention to the Alchemist also acknowledges the presence and availability of the Alchemist in the apprentice's life at all times and under all circumstances, even when the Alchemist is not physically present. It is so easy for psychology to assume that when the Alchemist is away then he is not there, and therefore can't call upon the apprentice or pass on jobs. Think again. Functioning under the 'out of sight, out of mind' assumption is ordinary. Functioning in opposition to this assumption is reliability, and is extraordinary. An apprentice who tacitly rests in the certitude of his connection with the Alchemist can be used to perform high levels of service, and becomes a useful player on the Alchemist's gameboard, a working extension of the Alchemist's body. Being a back-row playing piece requires a direct awareness of one's connection to the non-physical presence of the Alchemist.

Continuing with the current example, the Alchemist asks Wayne, "Will you be calling your wife soon?"

Now, Wayne knows that while traveling with the Alchemist, it is the Alchemist's preference that news of the trip not arrive back home before the Alchemist does. Wayne also knows the importance of frequent communication in nurturing a healthy, committed, long-term, loving relationship with his wife, and actually has a mental plan to call her the next afternoon. There is a part of him struggling with the apparent conflict between maintaining a gossip blackout, as the Alchemist wishes, and communicating with his wife, also as the Alchemist wishes. This struggling part wants to somehow create a wiggly story that does not admit his plans to call, and also does not deny them. He also knows that the Alchemist wants the clarity of a "Yes" or "No" answer, and that actually the Alchemist sees everything happening in the moment, including his internal struggle. He also knows that the Alchemist recently said, "He who hesitates, communicates," and in thinking all of these things, he has been hesitating. The apprentice says, "Yes, I plan to call her tomorrow afternoon at one pm."

The Alchemist says, "When you call her, will you please ask her to call Betsy for Bjorn's number so I can give it to Sam?" Sam is a fellow Alchemist, who happens to be sitting in the group talking with the Alchemist and overhearing the entire conversation.

The apprentice says, "Okay." And that is all he says. The conversation is over. Nothing else need be said. The apprentice does not ask any unnecessary questions to extend the interaction, thus disturbing the 'wah' (a Japanese term referring to the present spiritual mood or energy) of the chamber that the Alchemist is working. He <u>does not become obsequious, trying to score points, by asking if he should call sooner, or some other unnecessary question.</u> He does not try to distinguish himself to make other apprentice's jealous of his interaction with the Alchemist, or to impress them with his importance. His wish is to serve the Alchemist invisibly. So he says only, "Okay," and then instantly fades back into the fabric of the space once again, as anonymous as a wall lamp.

This does not mean to imply that all is quiet on the apprentice's internal battlegrounds. Many well-intentioned voices are busily offering their 'assistance'. One voice is afraid of losing face and demands that he handle the task now rather than taking the chance of accidentally forgetting to ask for the requested information when making the call at the stated time tomorrow. Another voice wants to look good and please the Alchemist by acquiring the information immediately so that the Alchemist can fulfill his wish now rather than having to wait so long, <u>even though he didn't ask if this would serve.</u> Hearing such loud and 'reasonable' voices, the apprentice is tempted to change his plans and call his wife immediately... very tempted.

However, this particular apprentice has made such mistakes before and knows the consequences that would automatically ensue. He resists the temptation to gratify the voices by following their suggestions, and waits until the following afternoon like he said he would. This course of action and intentional inaction reflects intimate knowledge of two crucial alchemical principles establishing reliability.

The first principle is to follow the Alchemist's instructions exactly as they are given. If this principle is practiced, then after some time, the Alchemist begins to learn that when he gives you an instruction, he can count on it being carried out as he intended. Performing self-modified instructions, no matter what the reason, would be like being in an orchestra and playing whatever music you wanted to play rather than the music the conductor is leading. Yes, you might get noticed, but your solo performance, no matter how perfect, is self-serving and unconsciously intended to destroy the workings of the band as a whole, <u>not to mention completely dissonant to the smooth working of the space.</u>

The second principle is about establishing the reality of your speaking. What the Universe wants to know is, is your speaking real? Or is it just hog farts? When you make a promise, no matter how big or small, your speaking is an act of creation. The speaking itself sets up energetic circumstances which have as much impact and consequence in your life as signing a contract. Most of us make many promises every day without realizing that this is what we are doing. The unfortunate thing is that by not seeing that you have made a promise, you do not see what it costs you to not keep it.

The cost of not doing what you say you are going to do is that you teach the Universe that it does not need to respect what you say. If you do not keep a promise, no matter how minor it may seem, then you do not honor your own word. If you do not honor your own word, why should the Universe? When you do not keep your small promises, or you forget that you made them, or instead of fulfilling your promises, no matter what, you spend your creative efforts inventing clever justifications to excuse yourself to those you are breaking promises to, then your word becomes worthless. The Universe can ignore you because you have proven that your spoken gestures have no substance and your word has no consequence.

On the other hand, if you do keep your promises, then over time, this transforms your promises into a force of nature. A promise from you causes the Universe to align to you even as you speak the words. (The assertion *"Avra kadabra!"* is sometimes translated to mean *"I create as I speak!"*) When the apprentice said that he would call tomorrow at one pm, and he handled all of the unknowable and unforeseeable circumstances that did arise or could have arisen such that he did indeed call his wife at exactly one pm, the Universe sat up and noticed. More importantly, the Alchemist noticed too. Through the process of making a promise and keeping that promise no matter what, the apprentice reinforced the assertion that his word has power. What he said was going to happen is exactly what happened. Exercising consciousness of this principle establishes reliability not only with the Alchemist, but with the Universe as well.

When Wayne spoke with his wife at one pm she, in turn, promised to find the required telephone number and fax the information back that evening. Because Wayne's wife is a practicing apprentice and is aware of the principle of honoring her word, at seven pm that evening she sent a fax addressed to Wayne.

It was clear from Wayne's communication that the Alchemist had asked for the number, and that Wayne's wife *could have* addressed the fax directly to the Alchemist, but she did not. It was also clear to her that the number was for Sam, so she just as reasonably could have addressed her fax directly to Sam, but she did not. Reasonableness was not the critical measure in this instance; following the Alchemist's protocol was. She addressed the fax to Wayne, because the implied instructions from the Alchemist were that Wayne should give the number to the Alchemist. <u>Some assumptions may have been made, but if so, they were based on years of exacting observation and feedback as to the reliability of such assumption making in these people's or this person's case.</u>

Interestingly enough, when the fax did arrive, Sam himself was sitting in front of the fax machine making another call. Now, we do not know whether or not Sam actually read the fax as it came in. It is certain, at least, that he read to whom the fax was to be delivered, and also by whom it was written, and from these bits of information could easily have deduced that the fax was the very same number that was asked for by the Alchemist to be given to him. It would have clearly been logical, in a linear sense, to decide that since he now had the fax in his hands, he could consider it delivered by Providence, and simply inform both Wayne and the

Alchemist that he had received the required information. However, this is not what he did.

Sam was honoring the principle of reliability, which in this application meant that since the fax was not addressed to him, that he not read it, and also that he deliver it forthwith to the proper addressee, who happened to be Wayne. On his way back to his room, Sam found Wayne and gave Wayne the fax.

Again, the moment Wayne had the fax in his hand he knew it is from his wife, and he knew it contained the number for Sam, who was standing right there in front of him, handing him the fax. In this moment, neither Sam nor Wayne allowed ego to take over. Neither asked the other a question, nor made a comment. No conjectures were offered. No conclusions were jumped to. No shortcuts were taken to make things 'easier'. Sam said simply, "Here is a fax that came for you." And Wayne simply said, "Thanks."

Knowing that the Alchemist had already retired for the evening, and knowing that this was not an important enough communication to disturb the Alchemist after he has retired, Wayne waits until morning practice is over, then wordlessly hands the fax to the Alchemist. The Alchemist glances at the fax, sees what it is, and then hands it to Sam who receives it with gratitude, making no comment or energetic gesture about having had it in his hands the evening before.

As complex and unnecessary as some of these maneuvers may seem from an 'ordinary' perspective, this is a simple though authentic example of reliability in action. It can take years of work to build the matrix in your Being where such behavior is manageable without psychology stepping and stealing the show. Any Alchemist would be overjoyed to have his apprentices behaving with such reliability.

Nonetheless, a fax is a simple matter with which to become reliable. Let us consider another three-letter word that ends in 'x', something a little more challenging: sex.

PSYCHIC SEX

Remember trying to imagine whether or not it was even possible for a person to live as a vegetarian because meat was so common in your diet? Perhaps at one time you were also quite accustomed to using drugs or alcohol, smoking cigarettes, eating cheese and dairy products, drinking coffee, tea and sodas, having desserts with every meal, watching television, chowing down on snack foods, especially fried and salted and artificially flavored greasy ones, reading the daily paper, especially the sports, obituaries, and crime statistics, and listening to the local radio station, especially loud and jarring music. For most of us at one time or another, these things were quite normal for us to do with our time and our energy. If some of these activities have gradually come to fall away from your life it does not mean that you have excluded yourself from life or humanity. Neither does it necessarily make you unique or strange. You have simply refined your level of practice.

At the level of body knowledge, you already know everything we are going to consider here about psychic sex. The fact that you already know does not matter. If you are anything like most of us, you have not yet been willing to own at a conscious level what your body already knows – and for a very good reason. Once you become aware of the depth to which you are involved in psychic sex, it can ruin your day, and create messes you would NOT want to clean up! Yes, this means *you*.

Psychic sex. *If you are not consciously not doing it, then you are doing it.*

This consideration of psychic sex has nothing to do with interpretations of right and wrong, or good and bad – psychic sex is not a moral issue, with judgements about 'should' or 'should not'. Psychic sex becomes significant to an apprentice as soon as you discover that it leaves a long-lasting telltale energetic residue – a stain on your psychic bedsheets, so to speak. You wake up about what you are doing only after you notice the depth to which psychic sex karmically entangles you with other people.

Gradually along the spiritual path your perceptions mature until the moment comes when dead-ahead, out of the night, looms an immense iceberg on the dark, calm sea. You experientially discern energies and connections that you were totally unaware of before, and suddenly, there it is: Psychic Sex.

This moment may well occur later in your work than you might expect it to. Ego easily delays you getting to this point of realization by keeping denial mechanisms in place because psychic sex has so many pay-offs, so many pleasures, so many advantages, at least immediate and temporary. For example:

1) You can do it in public and be 'invisible', because everybody is doing it and nobody is talking about it. There is an unspoken agreement to look the other way.

2) There is no physical proof! No lipstick smudges or perfume residue, no stains, except psychically, and often psychologically… but these may take years to actually become problematical.

3) There is no danger of pregnancy.

4) You can do it with almost anybody, <u>any sex, any animal, any keyhole,</u> anywhere, anytime, even in your dreams.

5) There is no chance of contracting dangerous venereal diseases or AIDS.

6) It is quick. No foreplay is necessary. Success is almost guaranteed. Failure is not a problem.

7) In the moment you are doing it, it feels fantastic. It is very rewarding to ego, <u>and can really swell your pride, vanity, urge to power and cruelty, or your shame and perversity.</u>

Previous to hitting the iceberg, your casual ongoing involvement with others of the opposite sex (or same sex, as the case may be) is so common personally and so rampant culturally that it goes almost unnoticed. Only when you begin feeling the deep and long lasting effects of psychic sex, and, as a result, start consciously confronting the mechanisms of sexual substance exchange at their own level inside of you, does the submerged ninety-percent of the iceberg become apparent.

At this level, unwanted psychic sexual interactions are suddenly experienced as an interference in your work, perhaps even as a contamination. Only at that point will you be motivated to make the sacrifices and efforts necessary to shift your behaviors in this area. Only when you consciously experience the true costs will you willingly suffer the discomforts of changing unconscious habits.

Expanded awareness of psychic sexuality is a natural evolutionary occurrence on the spiritual path. As your investigation of the energetic subtleties of being experientially localized in a human body gradually matures, it becomes apparent that you have been unconsciously or semi-consciously exchanging sexual substances with others for almost as long as you can remember.

By waking yourself from your cultural somnambulance, you can become fully aware of the pervasiveness of psychic sex, both in your personal lives (each of your various psychological identities has its own perversions of psychic sex going on), and in the Western world at large. Consciously experiencing the immediate and long-term ramifications of a daily (or nightly) habit of exchanging sexual substances with numerous known and unknown individuals, will indelibly shift your perceptions of the reality and your understanding of the purpose of human relationships.

The seeming innocence of a momentary glance will vanish with the shock wave of a hand-grenade blast when you experience what you are truly creating for yourself and the other. Shared smiles <u>full of unspoken and often unconscious implications</u> take on a devastating implication.

No longer will the fleeting fantasy of full or partial nakedness leave such a sweet after-taste upon your nervous system. When you start to feel the true impact of psychic sex in your life it can be a shattering and easily depressing realization. Hopefully, things can no longer stay the same, certainly not if you are truly serious about your work on the Alchemical Path.

What is psychic sex? Think back and remember the last time you were strolling along in a shopping mall or through the center of town. Part of your mind may be occupied with thinking about what it is that you intend to accomplish there, whether it is window shopping for shoes, or remembering to pick up a bottle of shampoo while you are buying vegetables. Although most of your conscious attention may be involved in these intellectual considerations, a deeper and more broad-band 'animal' part of you is energetically scanning the environment for a possible partner with whom you can exchange sexual substances, usually subtle, but often the conscious urge to maintain discreetness is a moral, rather than Work choice, therefore not a choice that has true power or effectiveness. Unless you consciously obstruct scanning the sex channel, it happens of its own volition automatically. Unless you intentionally override the program, it proceeds to unerringly complete its designed-in purposes.

You notice when someone notices you. You turn your head and catch someone who was looking at you just as they look away, pretending they were not looking at you.

Others notice when you notice them. They turn and look directly in your eyes from across the space for no reason except that they could feel you checking them out, and you look away in that instant pretending you were not.

If the mutual noticing of each other, which can occur in an instant, reveals a ripeness of conditions, then 'shwing', the deal is done. A momentary 'zzzzztt' through the eyes, briefly imagined possibilities, and it is accomplished. You know what I am talking about. Everyone knows about this.

Through beginning to pay attention to the increased awareness of sexual substance exchanges, one apprentice said, "I discovered, that I was a total sex-junkie, and that psychic sex was the oldest and most difficult drug I ever had to face. Like every real addict, I was capable of throwing away everything for a chance to satisfy my addiction. When I smoked, I might walk a mile in a rainstorm during the night to get my cigarettes. I saw that I would sacrifice almost anything for a little quickie sex. I think that there is no drug in the world where the abuse of it creates more terrible results with respect to the loss of human dignity as in the case of psychic sex."

How do you stop such behavior when there is a large part of you that is adamantly convinced that *this is the best thing that you do in our entire day*? When it produces your greatest fulfillment? Your most stimulating aliveness? Your most enjoyable feelings of satisfaction, <u>that smug sense of showing a secret that only you hold?</u>

The Alchemist's answer is, "Fake it." Pretend that this is not who you are anymore. Declare that it is not so for you. Be different, suddenly, without warning, for no reason. Give no explanation. <u>Don't talk to anyone about it. Don't confess.</u> Be suddenly yet entirely different as an act of volitional theater. There needs to be no gradual or rational step-by-step procedure for changing behaviors. Just fake it until you make it, until it becomes reality for you.

Psychic sex may be one of the most cherished experiences in your daily life. The truth is that sexual substances from others are a drug no different from sugar, caffeine, nicotine, adrenaline (released into your system by the adrenal glands during a life-drama), endorphins (released by the brain into your system when you overeat), tetra-hydra-cannabinol (marijuana), alcohol, and so on. Stopping the use of this drug may eliminate pleasures which you have taken for granted and cherished for years.

It is not uncommon for an apprentice making moves towards stopping psychic sex to experience withdrawal symptoms of deep grief as if having lost a close friend, and to ask themselves questions about the purpose of life without the satisfaction of savoring <u>subtle</u> sexual substances from acquaintances and strangers, <u>although they are not always as subtle as you'd like to think.</u> The degree of pain experienced is the degree to which you indulge in nostalgia. The pain arises out of wishing for the ignorant bliss of the unconscious good-old-days.

A common mistake is to confuse psychic sex with communion. There is a vast difference between the two. In psychic sex there is an exchange of substances, <u>an illicit exchange.</u> In communion there is no exchange of substances, but rather an acknowledgement of mutual recognition of what is, <u>the radiance of being, recognizing the radiance of being.</u> Profound communion results from acknowledging deeper levels of reality. It is a recognition without exchange. Psychic sex involves – at least momentarily – getting inside of another person's space, <u>a space in which you do not belong.</u> In communion, the sanctuary of the other is honored with infinite respect at the same time that absolute commonality is implicitly understood. In psychic sex the other is devoured whole without respect for anything.

After subtle sexual exchange you can feel the foreign sexual substance in the back of your mouth, the sides of your tongue, going down your throat, and as a whole-body titillating, tingling sensation, or as a sweet sticky fluid. The reverberation can be retained for months, for years even. Foreign sexual substance in your body artificially fill the void of existential aloneness, at least in your addictive mind, a void which is natural and needed as an internal resource of nothingness out of which to create.

If you examine your life very honestly you can probably remember such exchanges from the recent past – only days or weeks, or moments ago. Further recollection brings up exchanges from years ago, perhaps even from childhood. Some of these incidents may have been turning points in your life during which time you made up stories about yourself, about others, or about the world at large, stories in which you still believe. Why can you remember these exchanges? Could it be because you are still carrying the substances that you received, substances which effectively poison your full ability to Work, to Practice?

There is not much difference between an exchange of psychic sexual substances, and an exchange of personal mementoes. If a woman gives a man a necktie by which to remember her, and in exchange that man gives the woman the gift of ear-rings, they will each be connected to the other through these objects until such time as they return them to the giver, or dispose of the objects completely, not just physically but also mentally and emotionally. The same is true for sexual substances, the only difference being that sexual substances are 'stickier' than material objects. They are subtler; they cling more firmly, and are far more difficult to get rid of in the same way that you cannot simply drop a memory into the ocean and it is gone forever. The harder you try to get rid of a particular memory, the more you think about it.

Even though it may have involved only a moment of time, a sexual energy exchange can last forever – the exchange creates karmic ties and bonds which can only be undone through specific forms of cleansing and completion. This is particularly true when you are seriously engaged in a process of alchemical transformation, and in fact, the karmic ties that are created become even more amplified and therefore stronger, especially when you strengthen them through repeated reinforcement.

You don't normally acknowledge out loud that psychic sex has happened. Nobody has seen it. Nothing can be proved. You think that you can get away with it. But the truth is that there are no secrets. Your psychic sexual substance exchanges are completely visible to your mate, to your children, to your relatives, and to your friends, should they ever care to look, and certainly to the Alchemist and the Universe.

An exchange of sexual substances can take place in as short as one-half of a second, and it can occur through glass. It can happen while you are driving slowly down the street and exchange glances with a pedestrian. It can occur at a subway stop when you exchange glances through the window with someone sitting in another train going in the opposite direction.

Psychic sex can occur through the breath. It happens while talking or breathing with the mouth open. ~~You can observe sexual exchanges through the mouth between movie stars at the cinema. (This is especially visible with Val Kilmer in the movie called The Saint.)~~ Psychic sex can occur through fantasy (advertising, movies, computer sex, phone sex).

~~One apprentice confided, "There are sudden moments when a woman looks into my eyes and grips me down to my balls. If I look at her I have no chance to defend myself, or to close the gate. She owns me totally, my skin, my hair, and she knows it, and she knows that I know it. I hoped that continuing with my No Sex practice would make it disappear automatically, but it didn't."~~

Building a 'no sex' wall and completely withdrawing from the world around you is not the answer to protecting yourself from psychic sex. The goal is to refine your sensing and your acts of creation to the point where you can be attentive on the level of sexual energy in a small 'now', with consciousness and purpose. When someone offers to exchange sexual substances with you and you notice the offer and do not wish to exchange sexual substances with them, it can become the same as someone offering you a cigarette when you do not smoke. You do not have to energetically ~~kill~~ reject the other person for making you the offer. Neither do you have to become ~~dead~~ isolated or insular yourself. What you can do is work to develop a sensitivity of tone and mood and timing which generates awareness on the same level that psychic sex takes place. When you are aware of what you are creating and what is happening in the moment you are creating it, then at that point you gain the precious opportunity of making a conscious choice.

~~Here are two practices that apprentices use to protect themselves from contamination and wasting energies.~~

~~The first involves timing. You can train yourself to differentiate between acknowledging someone's presence and exchanging psychic sexual substances with them. The key is to notice that acknowledgment~~

~~through an eye-glance can occur in one-tenth of a second, but psychic sex through the eyes requires a minimum of one-half of a second. This means that you do not have to totally ignore people. You can learn to acknowledge someone without having psychic sex with them by making eye contact for more than one tenth of a second but less than one half of a second. This takes some practice, but is very effective.~~

~~Another very powerful practice for protecting yourself from inadvertently exchanging psychic sexual substances through the mouth and breath is to press the tip of your tongue up to the roof of your mouth just behind your front teeth. Again, remembering and using this excellent tool can become an invisible habit.~~

~~One practitioner said, "Stopping psychic sex is much harder than stopping smoking. Using the practices is changing my daily interactions with woman completely. It is very hard for me not to be able to look directly into a woman's eyes while I am talking to her. The hardest thing is with friends or community members."~~

~~Another apprentice said, "The same is true with not taking women into my arms for a hug while saying hello or goodbye. Suddenly there arises a big fear in me when out in the streets or together with people, the fear that I am in 'enemy territory'. If men are there, they automatically become friends, even if they are the worst assholes."~~

The energy used by psychic sex exchanges is needed by an apprentice for other purposes. For example, beginning to deal with the 'Cramp'.

THE CRAMP

During the process of Alchemical Transformation, both the Alchemist and the apprentice will be working with the same set of conditions, namely the apprentice's psychological defense strategy, ~~which the Alchemist refers to as~~ in this School we call the 'Cramp'.

From the Alchemist's perspective, Cramp is a context. It is the Alchemist who formulated the name 'Cramp', because the Alchemist experiences the context of Cramp as a squeezed-down subset of the infinite possibilities available every moment in the real universe. The Alchemist sees the Cramp as a smaller, tighter, and more rigid space than the space he inhabits. In contrast to this, the apprentice experiences their own Cramp with some certainty and cockiness as being the full and complete limits of known reality, a self-contained and self-sustaining universe – all there is, not only for that person, but as objective truth.

The way context influences an apprentice's life is that context determines content. The content of your life – who you like, who you do not like, what you can or cannot do, where you live, all of your abilities, how much money you can earn or save, what opportunities you can see and make use of, your state of health, all of your relating, your capacities to be responsible, to have integrity, to communicate, to commit, to care – are all determined exclusively by your context. You think inherited capacities or external circumstances determine your quality of life. They do not. Your life is determined by context. One of the fundamental principles of alchemy is that consciously or unconsciously, moment to moment, you determine the context in which you will function.

Context is like a fishing net. The shape and size of the fishing net and the size of the holes in the netting determine which sorts of fish the fishing net can hold. For example, if you have a fish net that is an arm's length in diameter with holes the size of tennis balls and scoop it through the world there are certain things it will catch and certain things it will not catch. The net will not hold things which are too big such as a tractor, a pine tree, an elephant, or a house. It will also not hold things which are too small, such as apricots, diamonds, gold coins, or marbles. After scooping this particular net through the world, you would end up with things like roller skates, watermelons, books, and squirrels. What the net catches is determined by the form of the net.

In this same way, the life of the apprentice contains only those things allowed by the shape of the apprentice's Cramp. Anything else is either inconceivable to Cramp, invisible to Cramp, or disallowed by Cramp.

There is no such thing as a good or bad Cramp. Some Cramps are dedicated to being in abundance and having too much, some to being in scarcity and having too little. Some Cramps are dedicated to being big and loud and happy, others to being small, quiet and sad. Some Cramps are dedicated to manipulating, controlling and dominating territory and space, others to being invaded, abused, betrayed and abandoned so as to justify revenge. Some Cramps are dedicated to there being no problem, everything is fine, just being happy. Others are dedicated to the idea that there is a problem, nothing is fine, and being convinced of the importance of being ongoingly ~~pissed off~~ angry about it.

It must be understood, <u>once again,</u> that none of these types of Cramps are good or bad. They are all simply the context of Cramp. Cramp is Cramp. And the Cramp is not going to go away – ever. Having a Cramp is not a problem. Noticing your Cramp does not mean you are broken, or that you need to be fixed in any way. <u>It is simply part of what is.</u> When engaging work with an Alchemist the apprentice is invited to consider the possibility that *there is nothing wrong*. You may even be invited to consider paying attention to your Cramp, developing some appreciation for your Cramp, perhaps even loving you Cramp. In this way, the wealth of skills and abilities acquired through the Cramp can be absorbed into and put to use in your life of practice, turned toward serving something greater than can be included in the context of your Cramp.

Cramp is the normal and natural set of conditions generated by an intelligent psychology identified with the illusion of an individuated body as being ~~itself~~ Reality. While acclimating to life in the body, you develop a unique and effective strategy that allows you to survive in the perceived circumstances. You could live out a 'good life' well protected by the powerful buffers inherent in the Cramp's tenacious defenses. Most human beings will do exactly this. There is no reason not to, <u>as long as you have not discovered the Work.</u>

Any real Alchemist will tell you to your face (more than once) that if you can continue to live your life subject to the requirements of the context of Cramp, then you should continue to do so, rather than engaging the evolutionary offers of the Alchemist. The world-shattering experiences inherent in the processes of Alchemical Transformation are so disturbing and uncomfortable as to not even be something to wish on your mother-in-law. An Alchemist is careful only to accept apprentices who declare that, <u>as E.J. Gold said when asked how he got into the Work,</u> ~~except for the Work~~ *"There is nothing else to live for."*

CREATING

In the context of Cramp, when circumstances arise, you habitually respond with what you consider to be the only possible solution to the problem created by the circumstances. If there were another apprentice in the identical set of circumstances they would most likely respond to those circumstances in a different way from you, but they would be just as committed to the certainty that their response was, again, the only possible solution to these circumstances.

To deal with this seeming paradox, an Alchemist invites apprentices to work under conditions of providing service together. In order to be of service, an apprentice must have access to more degrees of freedom than are allowed in the limited context of their Cramp. And in the requirement of working together, the contradictory instructions delivered by Cramp to each of the apprentices rub up against each other creating an evolutionary friction much like the conditions in a rock tumbler. The work together slowly grinds off sharp corners of each of the apprentice's

Cramp, eventually revealing a polished jewel. The Alchemist consistently works with apprentices to create these kinds of possibilities.

Through diligently paying attention and observing the machinations of mind, emotions, and purpose in numerous, varied situations for some period of time, you must at some point come to discover that every internal and external gesture is an act of creation. Everywhere you place your eyes, every word you speak or do not speak, every thought, every feeling, your posture, your breathing, your moods, your tone of voice, every gesture, every touch, is an act of creation. Every creation serves a purpose. You may be conscious or unconscious about which purpose you are serving right now, and now, and now, but you are serving it nonetheless.

How do you become more conscious of the purpose you are serving? Here are two very strong clues. First, you can notice that if you are not conscious of the purpose you are serving right now, then you are serving the unconscious purposes of your Cramp.

Second, to find out the purpose you are actually serving, look at the results you are creating. What you have is what you want. Results do not lie.

For example, you may think that you wanted to be on time, but if you show up even two minutes late, your true purpose was to show up late. As the Alchemist is fond of saying, "Reality is hard and fast, and kicks you in the butt every time."

In making this observation, the apprentice, ~~must~~ if you are practicing rightly, will inevitably come to the realization that out of all the possible forms which you could create for yourself, the ~~form which is~~ forms that are most comfortable and familiar to you, and the forms you habitually create, ~~is our Cramp~~ are created out of your Cramp.

SHIFTING CONTEXT

One of the most stunning principles of alchemy states that it is always possible to shift context, because every space is connected to every other space. Metaphorically speaking, there are stairs out of one context and into another, handholds, elevators, doorways, rope ladders, fireman's poles, horses to ride, rockets to fly in, tunnels, and so on. The Alchemist, if you would care to notice, is continuously indicating these to you by immediate demonstration, and through his manner and inference. In respect to us there is no direct bridge from here to there, but there certainly appears to be.

You are of no use to the Alchemist when we are serving the context of the Cramp. You are simply then part of the circumstances to be dealt with, a problem to handle, a piece of the furniture to avoid bumping shins on, part of the landscape, <u>and at best, vast potential yet to be realized or utilized. However, as long as you are functioning unconsciously, mechanically, you are not actively available for service; you cannot be of help, although there are always plenty of dishes to be washed, albeit even in this domain you may fall down on the job and fail to complete it to the Alchemist's satisfaction if you wash the dishes unconsciously.</u> Either the Alchemist leaves you to ~~your~~ <u>this</u> mechanicality, or he gives you hints. Either you pay attention to those hints, no matter how uncomfortable this may be, or you blindly and belligerently continue to ignore them.

An exercise you can use to discover the depth to which the context of the Cramp subsumes your life is to intentionally do nothing. Block the manifestation of all the urges to 'do' for a specified period of time, such as an hour, or a full day. The force of your normal Cramp-motivated intentions to do things will then run into your essence-motivated intention to not do things like a bull runs into a wall. Be aware that this will deeply piss off the bull. You can follow each discomfort like a sonar wave back to its source deep in your Cramp, locating your original purpose that motivates each gesture you have stopped doing. More often than you might like to admit as a civilized human being, the motivation will be Underworldly and uncivilized. It is not a pretty sight. Do not do this exercise if you have a weak stomach. It will ruin your day.

Through this and other similar efforts, the apprentice must encounter the fact that you are making choices in every moment about your context. The choice is between form and formlessness. The choice is between ground and groundlessness. The choice is between reason and unreasonableness. It is not, "*Form follows function,*" but rather, "*Function follows form.*" Whatever form you identify with is the manifestation of your Cramp.

What does this option of being something other than Cramp mean? How can it happen?

What the Alchemist offers to the apprentice is the Bright Principles of his School: in this case, Kindness, Generosity, and Compassion. "You can ~~be that,~~ <u>function that way, and it is the higher way,</u>" he says. If you are honest, what you think is, "That is definitely not my style, <u>at least not all the time.</u>"

Bright Principles are huge. If the Bright Principles show up in the place where you normally are, then there would clearly be no room for your Cramp.

"How do I do this?" You think you don't know. <u>You turn it into a quest, a goal, a future possibility.</u> ~~But~~ Actually asking the question "*How do I do it?*" is a block against the action of just plain going ahead and doing it. If instead of asking the question and trying to figure out how to do it, you were to simply move, simply comply with the flow of Baraka, you may suddenly find yourself alive and well-functioning in the Crampless state held aloft by the beneficial forces of God.

Here are some indicators ~~confirming that location~~ <u>suggesting this principle</u>. If you are not Cramped, then you are not there.

<u>Werner Erhard has said, "*All invention comes out of nothing.*" By 'invention' he means creation as you are speaking about it, creation that is unique and real in the moment, not artificial and mechanical manifestations.</u>

Instead of being your normal self, churning out mechanical content, you become ~~a space holder~~ <u>context</u>. If you are the ~~space holder~~ <u>context</u>, then something else can show up in that space which just previously was fully occupied by your 'personality'. If you are committed to serving the Bright Principles indicated by the Alchemist, then it is those Bright Principles that can show up, and what you become is the space through which those Bright Principles that you are serving can do their work in the world. You become the Principles in action.

Having experienced the Crampless state, an apprentice will afterwards notice that it was impossible during that time for them to be offended (not to say that certain things weren't offensive, only that they did not react offensively to them), that they took nothing personally, that they were "*being that which nothing could take root in,*" <u>as Lee has instructed</u>, that they did not know what they were going to say or do next, that it worked anyway, as if by mystery and magic, that they did not know and it was okay that they did not know, that they were standing on nothing, that they were present, being 'yes' with a minimized 'now', that they were not about problems, reasons, <u>doubt or confusion</u>, that they were massless and could make ninety degree turns even when going at light-speed, that they could not resent, could not blame, <u>that they were free of projection, expectation, editorializing, shame, or self-hatred,</u> and that they had no face to lose.

THE MOUNTAIN

In many traditions, the way is well paved, or at least marked with bold road signs that point in a clear direction saying, "*This way!*" <u>Though as well-paved as it is, it is often not used by much traffic.</u>

Alchemical Transformation is a Tantric ~~tradition~~ process. Everything is used, in whatever way it can help. The Tantric path lies largely exposed to the elements, exists up above the tree line, contains more rocks than path, and represents the equivalent of 'class 5' free climbing. It is the sly way, using all methods simultaneously, <u>though each in its own time and place</u>. At the same time, it is utterly consequent, because final decisions are left to the free will of the apprentice. Yes, you may be attracted to the idea of 'getting there faster', but take note: there are neither safety ropes, nor first aid stations along the way, <u>and Coca-Cola is non-existent here</u>. And as has always been true, reaching the top delivers you no reward. At all times, you are responsible for every move you make, and in terms of the struggle for transformation, you are left to your own recognizance.

The upward journey may take more effort than you ever imagined. It may often feel paradoxical, or impossible. You may be struggling for weeks, months, perhaps even years, climbing and scrambling in a direction that you think you remember was indicated to you by the Alchemist. But you don't really know for sure. Here you are, seeking what looks like the top, covered with dust, sweat stinging your eyes, snakes hiding within every crevice, scorpions and tarantulas scurrying about, biting flies, stinging nettles, poison oak, lightening, gusty winds, little avalanches from above, rocks that at first appear solid giving way as you grab onto them for stability. You inch your way up the mountain. Muscles quiver from exertion, fingers scraped and bloody, you pull your eyes up over what seems like the final ledge, and there, to your complete astonishment, sits the Alchemist, <u>sipping his Coca-Cola</u>, as if he has been waiting there for ages.

He drinks mint tea (<u>to help digest the Coke</u>) in full regal splendor, completely relaxed, fully attentive and totally aware of your terribly precarious predicament - hanging there by your fingertips out over the edge of the cliff.

The shock of seeing him there may surprise you. You may lose your grip, slip back down the cliff a few feet until you grab hold of a bit of scrub oak that barely supports your weight, and hang on with total focus and concentration. You worked too hard to get here to let a simple surprise view of the Alchemist knock you off balance. Slowly you drag your way back up. Peering over the edge again you see the Alchemist looking at you, perhaps giving you a short enigmatic smile, but making no efforts to help you up.

Why doesn't he give you a hand? You are so close to the top! He could reach out and hoist you the rest of the way up with almost no effort at all. Wouldn't this be kindness, generosity, and compassion? Wouldn't this be brotherly love? But he doesn't move a finger, sitting as still as the stones. He looks at you and waits, patiently, as if he had nothing better to do than watch the sweat slip inexorably into your bleary eyes.

Hanging there you keep asking yourself, "Why? Why doesn't he help me up the last few inches?" Then the answer becomes clear. He does not help you complete the last few inches because that would not be Lawful. If you do make it, you do not make it. If he rescued you, your being on the top of the Mountain would be a false accomplishment, and therefore unstable. He must allow you to make it on your own. He must allow you to flop about and fail if you cannot succeed. Looking at it from his viewpoint, this must be his most difficult work, requiring the greatest of discipline. It must be insufferably painful for him, to sit there alone and watch you struggle so, begging for assistance, and him knowing the cost and consequences of such folly.

So, you pour every last ounce of effort into dragging yourself up over the ledge to where he sits. You get a toe up. A leg. Finally, ~~enraged at~~ nearly exhausted by the sacrifice and the amount of effort, you roll up and onto the ledge, your chest heaving, crying out for more oxygen. A few moments go by. The applause ended and you hardly noticed. That is all the glory you get, those fifteen seconds of applause.

You look over to get the Master's acknowledgement, hoping for a little commiseration. Maybe he will give you some coaching as to how you could have made it an easier climb. Maybe you two could sit side by side for a while and look out at the incredible view together. But again you are shocked! He is not even there!

What you see is a gray-flecked slab of quartz and feldspar. And, shocked again, this is not the top of the Mountain at all! It is only a tiny plateau blocking the rest of the Mountain from view.

The Mountain towers high above you, curving up and out of sight. A scrap of yellow paper rustles in the breeze at the base of the next cliff face. (There is always a breeze at this altitude.) The paper is the inside wrapper from a package of Nag Champa incense. There are words written on it in the Master's own handwriting. "Keep climbing," it says.

An eagle swooshes by below you as you turn to face the rock.

Dramatic? Yes, and also a fair metaphor for the, at least inner, effort that this Work requires. That is why all Schools issue the warning: "*If you won't finish this task, better not to even begin.*" Yes, for there is no value to going part way, none at all (well, perhaps a small bit of 'good' Karma, but you can get that by helping someone across the street through busy traffic).

A MAP

While 'climbing' you may draw on the wisdom and information of a map because it is useful. There are as many maps of the Mountain as there are paths. One such map has been documented by Carlos Castaneda as given to him by his teacher Don Juan. (*The Teachings Of Don Juan: A Yaqui Way Of Knowledge*, by Carlos Castaneda, pp 82-87, Penguin Books, London, England, 1970). You use a map because it explains relationships between an Alchemist and his level of practice in a way that makes alchemical sense. NOTE: We have extended this model slightly beyond Mr. Castaneda's original explanations.

The model being referenced is that an apprentice alchemist – a person dedicated to becoming a 'man of knowledge' in Don Juan Matus' terminology – working to defeat his four natural enemies as he progresses along the path of self-discovery and transformation. Defeating one enemy allows him to enter the domain of the next. Each domain builds upon and supersedes the previous domain. When an apprentice first enters a domain, he has one relationship to it. Over time and with efforts, that relationship changes in unexpected ways. What at first appears to be an entry way into a new domain eventually becomes a trap from which the apprentice must escape through sophistication into the next domain, which itself then becomes a trap.

Before you can have the idea that there might exist other realities than the one you are given during childhood, you are confronted with your first enemy: Fear.

Up to the moment that you engage the idea that there might be something beyond the limits of your present reality, your psychological defense strategy has functioned to protect you from exactly this knowledge. The strategy has worked so far.

Your current reality is known to provide sufficient safety for survival at your quality of life. You know this due to the simple fact that: you have survived. Any change in your strategy throws the entire equation into unknown circumstances, which your psychology relegates to the category of 'a very bad idea'. Seeking change opens you up to the possibility that you might make a fatal mistake. Fear stops you from trying like poison spray stops ant spray on an ant.

Even if you are enthusiastic about learning something new, as soon as you begin making gestures in that direction, the learning process and the learning itself are so different from what you fantasized it to be that you immediately mistrust yourself for making the decision to begin, or you mistrust the experience of learning, being certain that it will not succeed, and you become afraid. Very afraid.

How could everything be so new, so contrary to your expectations? How could you know so little? How could it be so difficult? How could it feel so dangerous? The challenge becomes overwhelming, and your original boldly adventurous purpose becomes a boxing ring for a fight to the death between 'Dr. Yes' and 'Dr. No.'

Fear reigns. You are stymied at every turn. If you give up and head for sanity, peace and safety, the game is over and your enemy has won. Your urges to discovery are crushed by scattered attention and frightening confusion. You settle back into your normal routines and try to forget about such craziness. <u>You realize, of course, that this entire process we have just described is often played out within your unconscious. On the outside you may simply look like you are procrastinating, or like you have lost interest and are attracted to some other pursuit. But make no mistake, on the inside this process is real and exact.</u>

Nothing can aid you to defeat and overcome Fear because Fear is undeniable and will not go away. Encountering Fear is incomprehensible. It is almost unheard of that a human being consciously chooses to work at the level of Fear because fear is so frightening. Yet this is the key that starts the whole process of evolution. Facing fear initiates everything. At some point in your life you get frustrated enough with fear to say, "This stuckness is too painful for me and I'm willing to deal with Fear because it's a tradeoff. Either I cower in front of Fear and continue being dead, or I face Fear even if it feels like I will die."

Struggling against your inner resistance and inner motivation you accidentally begin encountering influences from the next domain up the Mountain. Brief glimpses of new possibilities flash into your mind. Somehow a distinction lands in your Being. It becomes tacitly obvious that you cannot conquer Fear through force of will or numbing denial because the way out of the grips of Fear is through Fear itself! What a new idea! You try some different kinds of experiments, such as being afraid and not fighting it, simply staying in Fear and going ahead anyway.

After some time in the midst of Fear you experience a re-wiring in your mind. You detect that all along you have had the 'red wire' connected to the 'blue wire'; you had it cross-wired so that the experience of fear means: "This is bad. Something is wrong. I am broken. I am going to die." You decide to rewire the Fear memes in your own brain. A new thought pattern emerges. After the re-wiring you have the 'red wire' connected to the 'red wire' so that the experience of fear means: 'Fear'.

This is astonishing. Suddenly the entire universe of fear collapses into one simple profound bit of clarity: *Fear is fear.*

That was the totality of your problem with Fear: you had it cross-wired.

Clarity solved the Fear problem in an instant. You start feeling more sure of yourself. Fear does not go away, of course, but it no longer owns you. You are free to feel afraid without being overwhelmed or misled about what it means! You get your aliveness back!

Your relationship to Fear has changed, and Clarity was the key. Now when Fear comes, you surprise yourself by saying, "Welcome Fear! What do you have for me?" You write down the intelligence of your Fear, and suddenly have your Fear's mighty energy at your disposal. But it is you who makes the decision about what you will do. Not your Fear. You got your life back from fear, and Fear has become your ally.

The terror of gaining radical knowledge – knowledge that is beyond the comprehension limits of your birth culture – no longer stops you. The archetypal journey has begun. You get the notion that Clarity has allowed you to conquer your greatest enemy – Fear – and the rest of the way up the Mountain is now free of obstacles. Clarity has become your secret weapon. You begin filling your notebooks and bookshelves with distinctions like a hungry man with a gold card fills his shopping cart in a grocery store.

Your mind is blown wide open. The adventure begins. You have discovered that Fear is only a feeling, that there are four feelings (anger, sadness, fear, and joy), that it is okay to feel those feelings, and that you are not your feelings! Feelings used to be so important to you. Now feelings are not enough. Clarity reveals that feelings result from stories you create to self-define and to hold the world still. Now you create feelings on purpose to serve your Destiny.

You can reinvent yourself and reinvent the world through emotional healing processes. You learn how to use feelings as a map leading to transformational treasures and you can anticipate the Liquid State before it occurs, welcoming it boldly as a path for bringing in new Clarity.

Procedures for solving both interpersonal and group conflicts become available to you like an open box of tools, and you learn to use them at home and at work, internally and externally. As you distinguish your own purposes, the purposes of others become obvious, and upon this empathy you build a castle of understanding, patience, kindness, and ultimately compassion.

You are no longer hooked by people's low drama games. You are no longer a victim. You can do anything you please. The world seems radiantly bright, clear and sharp. Nothing is concealed. You think, "Clarity is fantastic!" And it is. Clarity is a sparkling gateway into a magical kingdom where you can pull out a magic wand and declare, "Something completely different from this is possible right now," and all of a sudden, there is Possibility. Previously unnoticed doorways open up and you gain access points to different realities through Clarity. You relate to Clarity as if it is gold. Clarity is the way. Great joy arises in you as Clarity becomes yours.

You start to become a Clarity machine. You see people ~~without~~ who lack Clarity everywhere in your life. You try to ~~use~~ offer the tools to develop Clarity ~~on them~~ and they rebel, calling you ~~cold-hearted, militant, distant,~~ manipulative, aggressive, arrogant and superior. They say that they come to you for help and you 'kill' them with your ~~Clarity~~ intensity. They are afraid of you. You have made new distinctions and developed healing and problem-solving technologies out of Clarity, making the domain of Clarity your own. It was hard work, precious enough that you value the sword of Clarity more than your own life, and then, perhaps this: You make Clarity the most important thing, using the same tools over and over again to solve the same kinds of problems. You find yourself using clarity to defend your positions. Clarity provides answers and answers destroy Possibility. Rigidity sets in. Insights which were once fresh, each one reordering reality for you in profoundly unexpected ways, soon become a requirement; you become very attached to 'your' Clarity.

You get addicted to the ego-gratifying experience of having a new insight, seeking insight for the sake of insight as if insights were important. Insights are personal and you enjoy the experience of a new insight happening – click, click, click, click, click, reordering happens – this is extremely rewarding for ego. You experience a new insight as if it is an achievement. Many people get hooked into what they think is spiritual work or a spiritual path by going from place to place to place, from book to book to book, from teacher to teacher to teacher, looking only for more insights, thinking that insights are the key. You dedicate yourself to possessing ideas, collecting them, defending them. You have become them. All the brilliance and certainty provided by infallible Clarity begins to blind you.

Slowly the reality of the situation begins to seep into your awareness. It is inconceivable that you are encountering your second enemy, and that the enemy is: Clarity!

How bizarre! How uncanny! What at first functioned for you as the harbinger of halcyon days has now closed in around you as the barrier to your evolution.

What at first served to help you get unstuck and to do incredible new things, now serves your Gremlin's clever, almost evil defense strategies.

You cannot see how this happened. You could never have imagined that you would encounter this condition. Try as you may, you cannot use the technologies of Clarity to free yourself of this riddle and move happily ahead. No matter how great your frustration, Clarity will not undermine itself.

You have climbed up through the entire mountainous domain of Clarity and are nearing the lower borders of another domain, a domain you did not suspect existed until now, because when Clarity was King, nothing else was necessary. Now you have become a beggar again. You must start over, noticing, waiting. Some new factor must eventually enter the scene! You have no idea what it might possibly be.

Your experiments become wilder. You risk failing in bigger ways. Feedback becomes more necessary, yet more devastating and direct. You let some new kinds of information wobble into your system as a last resort in the battle with Clarity for our lives. You experience yourself as beginning to lose your mind.

Mind is no longer enough when your authenticity is at stake.

Relationships hang over a knife edge. Without relating you cannot do your work as an apprentice alchemist. Without relating you keep killing the patient because your sword is too swift and heavy-handed. You must put the sword of Clarity in the hands of something other than your mind, something greater than yourself, something you do not own, <u>cannot dominate and cannot think your way around.</u>

Blundering ahead into unknown territory, regarding the Clarity toolbox with skepticism and newfound suspicions, almost as if Clarity were a mistake, gradually, accidentally, a vast and broad perspective subsumes your actions.

You no longer disconnect from the other to do your surgeries. You are moved by a force that includes the other with you indivisibly, indubitably. You are amazed at the unexpected gracefulness and fluidity arising as you surrender your personal certainty into the service of a Bright Principle that is common between you and the other, a Bright Principle that is common to the both of you. The other person or their problem no longer represents an adversary to be transformed or subverted through

Clarity, but rather a friend in pain, lost alone on a cold wintery night, who takes the risk of knocking on a stranger's door, hoping to be welcomed into light and warmth and not to be told ~~they should get~~ "If you had been more responsible you wouldn't be in this situation now," and then have the door slammed in their face. Astonishingly, these new ways of being and relating actually produce valuable outcomes.

Without warning you have bounced into the next domain up the Mountain, the domain of Power, a power so vast as to be undefeatable. You see that Clarity is not enough. Clarity comes from knowing. But you need the spaciousness of not knowing for the Bright Principles to function within your life. You see that Power is not a tool but instead is a force. You are relieved beyond measure to discover the value of something you do not yet understand, and which, in fact, may not be understandable.

Relating unexpectedly starts to blossom. Your relationships were at risk because you thought of them as problems that you could solve through Clarity. You used to think, "I have done work with Feelings and I have a reference point in my body for Feelings. Now I have Clarity about how relating works."

If you were interacting with your partner, you would begin a Box-to-Box mind-war by striking against their distinctions with your distinctions. The result can only be breakdown because no one was calling forth the Principles of Relating. You were stuck in what you knew, but Bright Principles arise in the space of not-knowing.

Your Clarity had become rigid and you begin offering your insights and your ideas about how relating should be. But relating is not just male/female (male over female), solved like an equation. Relating is a vast space of Possibility. Relating falls into breakdown at the level of insight and Clarity, and it stays in breakdown until you move up the Mountain into the fluidic power of Bright Principles.

Archetypal Principles of Masculinity and Femininity live in the domain of Power. You used to attack your conflicts in relating from the domain of Clarity rather than dancing in the Bright Principles that 'the Feminine is everything' and 'the Masculine is nothing'. It becomes visible how the Masculine holds space and the Feminine abundantly fills that space. Engaging relating from the domains of Power and Space makes a world of difference.

You may use this Power, ride on it, let it take you anywhere, but you do not own it. Bright Principles cannot be owned, because Bright Principles are the archetypal ninety-nine faces of God. Bright Principles exist beyond human life. Consciousness at large becomes your ally, and you start moving as it directs.

Clarity does not go away when you enter the domain of Power. Your context has expanded and Clarity is now seen for the tightly structured reality that it creates. Yes, Clarity works in that domain. But now you have a far greater domain to explore called Power. And in this domain, reality is nonlinear. Everything is possible. Nothing is a barrier.

You take care to keep yourself in resonance, to live a life of practice, while Power functions through you. What a pleasure. What a servant you are. A little voice in your head says, "Well, I've got power now. I can be fluid now, and flow stuff around. I can call a new Bright Principle into a chamber and it harmonizes, balances, and heals things." You ~~think~~ know that this Power is significant, and you begin to think that it is your own private Power. You start ordering the universe around to satisfy the Bright Principles as you perceive them. You start making rules for how things should work. And you stand on the secret assumption that there is nothing to worry about – ever. You forget that this is a temporary condition. You start to think that you are immortal, a co-creator with god Himself.

Oh, dear! ~~God! No!~~ Not again! The domain of Power starts to go sour. Again the Gremlin rears its evil furry little head and hijacks your hard-earned capabilities within a domain. At first you had the innocence, caution and wakefulness of a beginner when dealing with Power. As you became more and more familiar with its function, you made assumptions, you nodded off to sleep. And in those increasingly common moments, the Gremlin turns Power towards serving its own ~~dark~~ autonomous purposes.

When Clarity pulled you up out of the crippling shadows of Fear you were so overjoyed to discover an entirely new domain where Fear was not suffocating your life. Clarity entered the scene with so much refreshing delight. Then when Clarity, which had saved you, evolved into your betrayer, your prison, your neurotic enemy, you were nearly devastated. Your longing and desire to learn were almost rubbed out forever. Until you encountered the next domain and were saved again.

Now it is Power that has become your enemy. Its spaciousness is too relaxed. There is no urgency, no qualifiers, no challenge. You are too familiar with having it work out your way, too addicted to controlling the outcomes. This must be the upper range of the domain of Power.

There is something else? What could be further up the mountain than Power? You must become a beggar again to defeat your new enemy? Oh, no!

By now the bones are creaking, the joints ache. Journeying up the Mountain takes a longer time and much more focused effort. Entering new domains is stressful. Such transformational excitement is for young apprentices!

You glance in the mirror and see wrinkles where before there was smoothness, a sagging butt and breasts where before there was perkiness and bounce. Time is ticking away and you are getting older. Worse than that, now you are lost again, precariously lost, begging for a way out of the tyranny of Power.

Power is not enough. You need something more ~~significant~~ <u>transcendent and impersonal than</u> Power. But what could that possibly be? The ground is pulled out from under your feet. Freefall is happening, and freefall from such a high altitude can only be treacherous.

In rare private moments you catch quick glimpses of hollow eyes staring at you. It is a most chilling image. In a flash you recognize this familiar countenance.

It is Death.

Death has been vaguely circling around you like a vulture waiting to feed, wishing to consume everything you have worked so hard to fashion into a functioning whole.

Death wants to eat you. It waits hungrily around every turn. In the tension of this looming ever-present threat, your overabundant spaciousness vanishes and a critical urgency arises. The imminent presence of Death squeezes you reflexively into the next domain up the Mountain: Old Age.

The wise counsel inherent in Old Age reorders your feeling-filled Aliveness, your diamond-sharp flaming sword of Clarity, and your irrefutable Power into a new level of coordination and alertness. Old Age is a new factor, a new force. Old Age knows the timing of things. It knows urgency, and once again you can work with effective diligence!

Old Age knows that there is no place in any of the four domains that is safe: you can lose your Work in a moment on any level.

The wisdom of Old Age also knows that you can never conquer the enemy form of Old Age, because Death will one day win. Nonetheless, you can let the transformational form of Old Age enter your five-bodies as a context with a vast overview, and welcoming compassion towards the frailties of the human condition and the strictures of the Path.

The battle continues. You face the archetypal vastness of the overview while your Gremlin incessantly squeaks out its whining justifications for procrastination. It wants you to relax the pace, take more 'private time' and let things out there take care of themselves. "You deserve a break to-day," it purrs. "Take a rest. Just lie down and relax, forget it all for a while. You are feeble and old."

You pat your old Gremlin on his head and say, "Sit here, old fellow. Sit at my side. I will handle things. Don't you worry."

Old Age defeats its last enemy: Power, through transcending temptation. You have lived well by dying over and over, so many times, and in so many ways, that death itself stands at your side laughing with you. All enemies heretofore have been defeated, and yet, *there is no enemy*.

You have not retreated into complacent surrender. You have retained aliveness, clarity, presence, kindness, generosity, and compassion until the end. The Mountain stands more glorious than ever, radiant with the ancient Path-walkers strewn about its peaks, chuckling at their good fortune, and still secretly concerned about the next generations, so easily ambushed by sun-glasses, smart phones, Standard Human Intelligence Thoughtware, and social brainwashing media.

THE ALCHEMIST'S WORLD

Alchemy is transforming base substances of lesser value into refined substances of greater value. The subject of an Alchemist's experiments is himself. That is, the Alchemist uses his or her internal and external world as their primary laboratory for doing their work; they are the entire world, even the Universe, both gross and subtle, including themselves, as the Sources for collecting data to work with optimum efficiency. An Alchemist's purpose, in one form or another, publicly stated or not, is to offer something up the evolutionary ladder of beings which is attractive to and consumed by essences of higher levels, who then, as a byproduct, a waste product actually, generate what to us are refined substances that are carried back down into the human planes and are experienced as being of tremendous value. In ~~short~~ other words, we could say that the Alchemist creates and delivers food for higher beings, then collects their defecations for use on lower levels.

As could be expected, reality from the Alchemist's view is vastly different from reality viewed as a human being with no idea that such perspectives exist. The differences are subtle and yet so profound that there is no comparison between these two views, as if aliens living in universes which functioned under very different laws of physics tried to explain things to each other. Only approximate communication is possible until one of the explorers is able to go to the other's universe and experience the laws for himself.

If you were to be in the company of a Master Alchemist and had the good fortune of observing him or her during their daily life, you might begin to notice that the world responds to them differently than it responds to most other people. Why is this so? How could it be that one person's magic is another person's technology?

Even though our Western culture is quite committed to a franchised, homogeneous, white, Hollywood <u>and Madison Avenue</u> reality, this does not preclude the existence of other realities. It only decreases the probability that an individual will encounter them. Slipping free of culturally induced mental fetters takes vigilance, courage, will, a spirit of adventure, and a sense of humor. It really helps not to take one's self so seriously.

Below are included a few short descriptions of reality as seen from the Alchemist's perspective. Reading these sentences will be like peering into an Alchemist's toolbox. What is revealed may seem fascinating, even alluring. You may be attracted and want to understand and use the new tools. Here is the trap: In the same way that a student of Zen must change before they can unfold and receive the benefits of a koan, alchemical technology, no matter how clearly it is revealed, becomes practically accessible only after you change in such a way that you can take radical responsibility for further evolving the tools.

Changing who you are so as to be able to further develop an Alchemist's tools, distinctions, thoughtmaps and processes may be out of your immediate reach, because such change is generally only achieved under the personal tutelage of an Alchemist, within the context of a School, in the company of other apprentices, and after years of study and practice. As daunting as these prerequisites may seem, this should not prevent you from perusing the catalog of orthogonal possibilities, as an explorer ponders maps of as yet unexplored territories, as an experimenter roughs out designs for her next experiment, as a riftwalker combs through his gear to lighten his load in preparation for entering his next drop zone.

REALITY
Reality is what it is.
As the Master Alchemist says: what is, is *"Just this."*
There are only two things in life: bullshit and nothing.
Bullshit can be extremely useful, but only in the domain of bullshit.
Life is empty and meaningless, and it is empty and meaningless that it is empty and meaningless.

If you do not own the meaninglessness of that unfillable void of emptiness in your guts, then you do not have the necessary resource of nothingness out of which to create your life.

What is, is completely neutral. Emotional charge comes from your story about what is.

Human beings are story makers. We live in our stories of reality and interact with each other through the gameworlds we create and agree to play in together. We do not live in reality. This means that if you change your story, you change the way reality works for you.

The context of the gameworld determines the rules of that reality.

When making stories unconsciously, the only purpose of your story-making is to self-define and self-preserve.

Any story about what is, exists in time. In the present, there is no time. If you are in a story, you are not in the present.

Stories only have power if you give your authority over to the story rather than standing in your own radical responsibility regardless of the story.

It is impossible to be a victim.

There is no such thing as a problem.

Clarity about what is, can only be created now. Distinctions can only be applied now.

The opposite of scarcity is not abundance. The opposite of scarcity is creating.

Creation only happens now.

Two creations cannot occupy the same space at the same time unless they have the same purpose.

In a conflict of creations, the creation that is most fluid prevails.

Responsibility is consciousness in action. In other words, responsibility is applied consciousness.

RESPONSIBILITY

The world is rich in evidence. In every circumstance, there is enough evidence to substantiate any story. You may tend to position yourself as a victim in your story-making because of the tremendous payoff you get for being in ~~such a~~ any predicament and having it not be our fault, thereby eliciting sympathy and attention (even negative attention is still attention) from others. From the Alchemist's experience, it is impossible to be a victim.

You create everything about your <u>psychological</u> life, either <u>sub</u>consciously or unconsciously, and you create it to be exactly how you want it. You can have it any way we want it, ~~albeit strategically, not consciously.~~ If you would like to know how you want it, all you need to do is look at how you have it. What you want is what you have.

Making an accurate assessment of current reality requires ruthless self-honesty. Though it may be uncomfortable, current reality is where ~~an Alchemist lives~~ you live, and the 'domain of possibility', as Werner Erhard calls it, or 'Drala', as the Tibetans say, is where the Alchemist lives.

There is no such thing as a problem. Problems derive from a point of view. The same exact circumstance viewed from another perspective is not necessarily experienced as a problem. A problem is only a story, although there may certainly be struggles or stresses to be dealt with.

There is no such thing as being in a dead-end situation. Being in such a situation is simply a matter of conversation. If you claim that you are in ~~a~~ this type of situation then you insinuate that you are a victim of the circumstances, and that you are not responsible for creating the circumstances. Irresponsibility is ~~an~~ just another illusion.

If you change the conversation you change your world, and conversely, the world.

MEN AND WOMEN

~~Men are~~ Man is nothing. This is why when compared with a woman, a man's ego seems so insubstantial, pretentious, and laughable because men are always instinctively torn between their psychological and biological 'man-ness' and Essential Man (the 'Man of the Work', in Gurdjieff's language). A man's ego is a thin illusionary veneer over vast nothingness. Men's neuroses arise from trying to be something.

~~Women are~~ Woman is everything. This is why when compared with a man, a woman's ego seems scattered, confused, overwhelmed, and hysterical because women are caught between their psychological and biological drive to 'exclusivity' and Essential Woman. Women's neuroses arise from trying to be one particular thing out of all the things they could possibly be, yet a woman's ego demands that since she is everything, she must therefore control everything. This shows up as unconsciously staking out her energetic and relational territories in every situation.

Men like one big thing. Women like a lot of little things.

When a man owns his pre-primal energetic nothingness, then he has the capacity to be a space holder, ~~a zero,~~ a context for possibility or invention. A man can function in the world as the space through which the Bright Principles (the facets of God) which he serves can do their work. A mature man lives in the service of something greater than himself.

When a woman owns her pre-primal energetic everythingness, then she has the capacity to know all, be everywhere, and feel everything all at once. A woman can fill the space held by a man, in the same way that flowers, fruits and vegetables grow to fill a well-defined garden.

It is important to know that the man may need to trim back the plants in the garden of woman now and then, and a woman may need to bring the man 'down to Earth', here and now. As Robert A. Heinlein said, "*Women are the practical ones.*"

There are two kinds of shit.

1. There is bullshit, which is saying things that are ~~very, very~~ relevant, but completely untrue. This is what men do.
2. Then there is cowshit, which is saying things that are inescapably and undeniably true, but completely irrelevant. This is what women do.

The negative unconscious manifestation of the masculine is stupidity. The negative unconscious manifestation of the feminine is evil. (What a great combination for juicy Low Drama story-making: The stupid fly meets the evil spider! Low Drama supreme!)

When a woman cuts loose with a tirade of evil cowshit, the man's automatic, stupid, response is to return a volley of bullshit, and vice versa. This instantly creates an egoic Gremlin feeding-frenzy from which there is no escape but egoic Gremlin satiation. Valuing energetic resources too much to waste in such frivolous exchanges forces an Alchemist to discover nonlinear ways to spin out of the normally inescapable vortex.

It is well known that a communication persists until it is received. If what the woman is saying is not authentically heard by the man, then she must continue to deliver it. (Men, if you are wondering why she keeps saying the same things to you over and over again, consider the possibility that it is because you have not yet heard her.) The man must learn to listen to piercing truths unerringly delivered by precise, broadband feminine perceptions, to let the truths in and receive the full brunt of their impact. In allowing himself to be hit by the arrows of truth, a man cannot help but ~~die~~ surrender. What the Alchemist learns is the specific skill of how to 'die daily' and not be killed. If after unloading her full quiver of cowshit into the man's heart the man is killed, meaning depressed, isolated, exhausted, spiteful and mean-spirited, where is the spaceholder of her life for her to make love to?

Women must choose the results they wish to create. Do they want to live with a disempowered ignorant brute or with an attentive empowered man? In everyday life there is always an abundance of evidence to support either story about a man. When one woman receives the feedback that she is making her man wrong, she replies, "I am *NOT* making him wrong. He *IS* wrong! I am just pointing it out to him!"

In the same way, every man chooses who he lives with. Is she a cold-hearted, nagging mother-substitute, or is she the gateway to heaven on Earth? There will *always* be evidence to support either story. An Alchemist was once heard to say, "I have been living with the same woman for thirty years. Each morning I wake up, and I don't know who she is."

POSSIBILITY

What an Alchemist values most is Possibility. Having a conversation about the conversation creates the possibility of Possibility.

Every space has its own inherent set of possibilities. Alchemists have the disturbing knack of shifting spaces to domains where there is greater Possibility.

A lack of possibility is a lack of consciousness. An Alchemist continuously aims to create spaces that can sustain greater consciousness, or we could say, more Work potential, or a higher Being or Essence quotient.

Having more possibility means having more options. The trick to ~~retaining~~ optimizing options is to not get enrolled or hypnotized into the possibility limits of any given space. Alchemists develop an acute sensitivity to the qualities of spaces, and use the irreverent nature of their consciously initiated 'Gremlin' to go orthogonal to the assumptions of the space whenever necessary. Since a Gremlin respects nothing, it has the capacity to destroy any space at any time for no reason. Used responsibly, this impertinence protects an Alchemist's options from being subsumed by anyone else's ordinary assumptions about the possibilities of a space.

Alchemy becomes Divine Alchemy in the moment when the Alchemist sacrifices all of the vast varieties of possibility (including the possibility of creating Possibility) in exchange for the one immutably present ~~possibility~~ task of serving the Divine.

Imagine a pyramid of Possibilities. At the lower levels of the pyramid there exist many, many possibilities, accompanied by an extravagant number of loopholes. Distinctions are quite fuzzy. Consequences for breaking the rules are relatively inconsequential. The farther up the pyramid you explore, the fewer possibilities that exist, and the more stringently the requirements for functioning within those possibilities are held.

At the pyramid's peak there exists only one possibility, which isn't really a possibility but is rather a necessity, and that is to be the will of God in action in each moment. The only way to stay at the peak of the pyramid is absolute inherence in this one ~~possibility~~ <u>function</u>. It is an ongoing choice that the Master Alchemist is constantly making, <u>therefore a choice-less choice</u>, a way of Being.

LIGHT SPEED

Feedback comes in many forms. In general, feedback is generated directly through your relationship with the results you are creating in the moment. Most often you function as if there was a time-delay between the gestures you make and the feedback which they generate. This time-delay between action and reaction is generated in your mind by your mind. In reality there is no time-delay.

An Alchemist functions in the Present where there is no time – only NOW. In this circumstance, the Alchemist is in direct and immediate contact with the space and therefore sensitive to energetic flows, exchanges, and transformations. An Alchemist experiences her every gesture through the ripples and nuances they cause in her surroundings, providing her with ongoing and immediate feedback for use in navigating the spaces. Actually, the cause and effect relationship between gesture and ripple vanishes because the cause and effect occur simultaneously in NOW. Functioning in a minimized NOW allows an Alchemist to make navigational decisions in the Present moment (decisions made in the body, by the way, not in the mind, because the mind is far too slow), which permits her to seemingly speed up. Alchemists navigate spaces as they *Go!*, without time-delay. This can be referred to as 'going light speed'.

An Alchemist cannot go light-speed and make course corrections if she has any mass. Imagine trying to turn Her Majesty's Ship Titanic. You might have the wheel cranked all the way over, she might even be facing in a new compass heading, but the ship's mass continues moving in the original direction for quite some time before responding to the instructions to turn, simply because she has so much momentum. This is the importance of dropping excess baggage, such as assumptions, expectations, positionality, judgements, conclusions, resentments, stories, preferences, identity, needs, and so on. From the Alchemist's perspective, *all* baggage is excess baggage.

SACRED SPACE

In order to do his or her work, a Master Alchemist requires the appropriate tools of the trade. It is common knowledge that a surgeon needs an operating room to do surgeries, and a physicist needs a laboratory in which to do experiments. In this same way, an Alchemist has need of an environment with specific qualities in order to produce results. We refer to an Alchemist's workstation in its archetypal form as 'sacred space', and, when it is activated, and the Alchemist is at work, we call it a 'chamber'. What an Alchemist does is 'chamber work'.

~~An~~ One of the Alchemist's ~~only~~ primary 'tools of the trade' is attention, both his and others. Because an Alchemist knows where his own attention is and what he is and is not doing with his attention, he also knows where other peoples' attention is and what they are and are not doing with their attention. Out of attention an Alchemist fashions ~~everything else~~ other things he or she needs, including commitment, clarity, context, possibility, self-observation, will, integrity, reliability, mood, tone, intention, timing, purpose, definition, declaration, choice, inquiry, and so on.

Using attention ~~alone~~ as the base, an Alchemist can create, define, cleanse, protect, shift, navigate, and deconstruct chambers. In this way, the Alchemist can make sacred space whenever and wherever he or she needs, including in train stations, cafés, around the kitchen table, driving in cars, etc., although the Alchemist usually establishes one or more permanent refuges for sacred space called 'Sanctuary'.

Trained caretakers staff Sanctuary. Although, in general, the caretakers of Sanctuary are apprentices working without pay, part of their training is handling details of everyday life in Sanctuary for the Master Alchemist and his or her guests. Under the tutelage and guidance of the Master Alchemist, apprentices answer the telephones, repair the plumbing, wash the toilets, cook the meals, clean the dishes, run errands, shop for food, tend the gardens, wash and dry the clothes, get the mail, maintain the vehicles, prepare and clean up the various sacred spaces in Sanctuary, and manage all of these various operations, <u>not to mention formal processes for making the teaching available, or furthering the education of others, such as writing, books, articles, promotional materials, even propaganda, if needed, and the production of various arts, music, painting, sculpture, and so on.</u> The more responsibilities the staff can handle, the more profound is the Sanctuary for the Master Alchemist. When an alchemist is thus liberated to do the work he or she needs to do when and where he or she needs to do it, the greater the blessings which can manifest.

LOVE
There is no such thing as soul mates.
Love does not ~~go~~ grow by itself. It is continuously invented.

Love is not a feeling. Love is not an experience.

If we live our lives looking for the evidence of love in our feelings or in our experiences, then we are placing the existence of love into the hands of our psychological circumstances.

If we become aware that love exists only when we source it, then we become responsible for generating the context of love in our life. Love then becomes an ongoing act of non-linear creation, declared moment to moment for no reason.

Love is a commitment to ongoing nonlinear actions creating five-body intimacy offers in service of the Bright Principle of Love. Love is consciousness in action.

21. 2002: Lee Lozowick In His Own Words

1 September 2002 – Notes from a Lee Lozowick Seminar at *Terre du Ciel* in France

The job of spiritual master is not without its traps and temptations. If the illusion of reality is so apparent to a spiritual master, then avoiding reality is a simple matter of creating distractions and deferring to your own authority. No one can get through such subtle defenses. Most would not even recognize that defenses were active. This leaves the option of revealing your vulnerability and humanity to you alone. But why bother? Honesty is not necessarily the best marketing strategy, even if you are selling the truth. Still, some spiritual masters take the risk of guilelessness – not foolishly, but to demonstrate the possibility of living courageously on the spiritual path. Below are words of Lee Lozowick, disciple of Yogi Ramsuratkumar, lineage holder of the Western Baul tradition – sudden intimacies He shared with seminar participants during the summer of 2002.

Mostly I will be talking about myself. That's because I was once like you, and still am for the most part, except for one specific distinction. I ended up being a spiritual teacher – which is the worst thing that could happen to you if you set foot on the path, but the best thing that you could do with your life.

In 1975 Lee Lozowick [speaking of himself in the third person] had a shift of context, which has so far proven to be permanent. It was asked for, but the person asking had no idea what He was asking for. The person asking thought He was asking for a blessing. Now He thinks it was a curse. Fortunately for us, the person who asked has no power – only a big mouth and a questionable sense of humor.

The shift of context was about leaving a kind of ignorance where I had a lot of information but not a lot of knowledge. The shift produced knowledge that had no roots, no source, and was completely nonlinear – whereas my information was linear and traceable. After two months I realized that the new knowledge had to be offered to others. I had no options like art or making movies. It had to be through the master disciple relationship. This was the only form of communication possible under the circumstances.

At first I communicated with force and perfect clarity what was wrong, illusory, and unreal about everything, about what had built limitations around what everybody was doing. This was confrontive and controversial – shocking. Even if you study esoteric magic and become powerful, still the system has built-in limitations because it is based on information and technology from the human form – compared to working in multifaceted reality.

Students asked, "What do you have to be a master for?" I did not know why. But I had no choice. Teaching as a master is a very specific form.

Ken Wilbur makes a distinction between a pundit and a master. A pundit transmits information like an ordinary teacher through writing, speaking, art, etc. But he has no personal responsibility for the student. Students take it or not, use it or not, end of story. There is no cyclical progress or reciprocity. When the class is over, the relationship is over. The master, on the other hand, is responsible for the process and the progress of the student. The master gets involved. A limitation in this system is that the master cannot force anyone to do anything. Nothing happens without the consent and participation of the student.

Let me tell you how things work for masters. They don't know everything all at once. They only know what they need to know at any given time. However, the more successful a master becomes (meaning, the more adherence to practice in a body of students, integrity is an important word here) the more knowledge starts pouring through. The more water that pours down the river, the more stress put on the dam. The stress on the dam must be released to the body of students or it can actually break the master.

So here I am, this master giving seminars. Here comes all this knowledge and things are starting to back up. I find this summer that I have to pass on knowledge. My vehicle is straining at the edges. It is very uncomfortable. That is a big problem. The transmission of knowledge does not take place through a verbal exchange, as in a seminar format. Yet I cannot do dance or massage – absolutely not – this is not for masters. No staring in each other's eyes. I refuse. Or talking about our best orgasm. I have to give knowledge away.

We find the path. We fall in love with the Work. It is very powerful, very magnetic. I love the first Century Christian catacombs. If they wanted to meet and practice, they had to meet in the middle of the night in secret underground caves. What could be so powerful that people would risk their lives to get punished or crucified?

We think that we will find the path, step on the path, follow the path to completion and find realization (or whatever). We should think that. We should not step on the path without the commitment to complete it. Often the results of our actions do not bear fruit for long periods of time. A surgeon goes through regular school, medical school, internship and training in a specialty. This takes twelve years or more. We are not talking about radically altering our lives. There are certain times when that is appropriate. But ordinarily what we have to learn we must learn where we are, even if we are bored or uncomfortable. We must pay attention to our tendency to distract ourselves from what we can learn right where we are.

QUESTION: What can we do to get our energy back?

RESPONSE: We can stop adding random unnecessary information; stop adding to the burden of distractions. The cause of a lack of energy is often psychological. We often waste a tremendous amount of energy that does not need to be wasted. For example, think of the stress and worry that comes from wanting something that we cannot have. Right living lessens the onslaught of unnecessary impressions in our lives. Instead of trying to get more energy, stop doing things that eat up energy. Then we would have more energy than we would know what to do with.

QUESTION: What do you propose for transforming the tension of feeling angry about others?

RESPONSE: Twenty years of practice.

One of the essential elements of the Baul tradition is: use what works. Bauls are synthesizers. If something irritates us, so what? Let the irritations arise and subside and use what works. There is only the continuous reality of existence as it is. If one does not know that there is no suffering, one suffers as if it were real. Don't assume that the future has to replicate the past. We can use the inherent tension in enduring the unpleasant manifestations of others. Our heartbreak and pain can inspire us to act differently in relationship to others. The slightest little thing with our partner and we think, "Oh, my God! Is my relationship over?" The master does not think this way. Don't let your human desires get in the way of your master's Divine Inspiration.

I was not willing to allow small discomforts to interfere with the openness and continuity of my relationship with my teacher, Yogi Ramsuratkumar. The genuine master is not motivated by the same things that we are: sex, nice surroundings, hunger. The master is not moved by human motives. The true master has only one motivation: that the realization of truth be duplicated in the disciple. This is the same motivation as God. God's wish to be is itself a wish for creation to return the same wish to God. Every action of the master is motivated by one thing: to in some way catalyze the realization of the disciple.

Can the disciple know with certainty what will catalyze their own awakening? Absolutely not. So, what is your problem with obeying a master?

QUESTION: What is real and what is not real?

RESPONSE: In one sense, it is all real. But, so what? Every time we concretize something as if it were a truth that excludes other truths, we are wrong.

In the Tibetan literary traditions there is no such thing as fiction. Everything is real. Everything is literal. So what if we cannot see such things? It does not mean those things are not real and it does not mean we are handicapped. Everyone has strengths and weaknesses.

There is a story about Hakyusho, a Buddhist abbot who is getting old and wants to pass on the responsibilities of the monastery to someone else. He knows that there will be problems because there is already a natural hierarchy in the disciples as to who is next in line. It is the head monk. Hakyusho also knows that there is a great disciple lower in the ranks named Issan. So Hakyusho sets up a dharma competition. Whoever wins the competition becomes the new abbot. Now, as we know, the person who makes the biggest problem gets the most attention. Sometimes the senior student is the most aggressive, the biggest bully, the loudest. He may appear to be the best, but is he really? The competition day comes and Hakyusho places a pitcher full of milk on the floor in the center of the hall. He poses the question, "What is this?" The head monk stands up and says, "It is not a sandal." Then he sits down. None of the junior monks dare to get up to compete, because they know they will pay for their transgression later. But then Issan gets up, kicks over the pitcher of milk, and walks out of the hall. Hakyusho claps his hands and says, "The head monk loses."

If we see a living deity in a statue and we are one with the deity, then it is not an illusion. If we see a deity in a statue because we think that we are supposed to and we want to be accepted, we are under illusions. Illusion is about the implications that we give to what we see, the context, not the content. Just see. Do not interpret. Do not analyze. Do not associate with other things that you have already seen. Just see.

Soen Sa Nim, the Korean Zen master, always held the possibility of enlightenment for every human being. Many oriental traditions only consider that men can be enlightened. At a talk, someone asks Soen Sa Nim, "Are there any women teachers?" He responds, "There are no enlightened women." A woman student of his comes storming up to him after the talk and says, "What do you mean women can't be enlightened? What's going on?" And he says to her, "Oh, so you are a woman?"

QUESTION: What if you cannot be touched? What if no matter what the master says, you can respond in a way that is safe?

RESPONSE: Just wait around. Sooner or later the teacher will get to you.

QUESTION: Do we need a living master?

RESPONSE: My master died last year and I have not found a new master. For me, my master is still alive. One consideration is that I had twenty-seven years with my master to figure out what was coming from Him and what was coming from my own mind. That is a key point. I do not have much faith in human ability to discriminate. Our egos are so complex and sophisticated that they can convince us of anything. I used to be cynical about the human condition. Not as cynical as I am now... [laughter]

QUESTION: Do you think God is immanent or transcendent?

RESPONSE: Both. At the same time. But what difference does my answer make to your life? We have to be careful that we do not use 'right answers' as a buffer to self-awareness. That is the pathology of study – we have all the 'right answers'. When faced with the choice between inquiring for self-awareness and using 'right answers', we may tend to use the 'right answer'. It is great to have 'right answers' when they come from our experience. Teachers are having to find other ways to stop students' minds. 'Right answers' can be pernicious. They can stop us from seeing the truth.

The question is, can the mind be stopped? Are we willing to be stopped? The purpose of shock is to stop our mechanical behavior so that

we can realize how mechanical it was. We think we have choice in our lives. Be we don't have choice. It is all mechanical. When the Coca-Cola button gets pushed, Coca-Cola comes out. When the Perrier button gets pushed.
..

The ability to be willing to be stopped cold in our tracks and to observe what is going on is an extraordinary gift to bring to the master. To not be willing to be manipulated by the complex of internal reactions – to fight it instead of surrendering – it is a very quick and instantaneous decision. Just to stop. Just to see. And to choose not to react in a mechanical way. Habits are deep. Our willpower only goes so far to keep our habits at bay.

As soon as the mind is switched off – no defense, no justification, no argument – then blessings can get in. Let them in. If we do not plug the mental reaction into the physical emotional process, nothing happens. Stopping does not mean the mind will stop. It just breaks the chain of mechanical events.

Gurdjieff was believed to be harsh, critical, and without romantic sentiment. But Gurdjieff was a master and did not break the veneer. He did not lose character in front of his students. Here is a story about the real Gurdjieff, the real man unprotected by the role he played with students. Even when Gurdjieff was in his eighties, he would often give a feast in Paris. This particular evening a young man comes. He has an important business meeting the next day with a lot of money to be decided upon. Everyone leaves the party at 2 am and the young man rushes home to get some sleep. Halfway home, he realizes that his briefcase is back at Gurdjieff's apartment with all the papers he will need for his meeting. Does he go back and wake Gurdjieff up? He decides that he cannot improvise at his meeting. It is 3 am when he gets back to Gurdjieff's. He is afraid to knock on the door. Gurdjieff could be furious at him, kick him out of the study group. Finally he raps lightly. The door opens. Gurdjieff peers out, and breaks into a soft, warm, radiant smile. "Oh, you have come back to help this old man!" Gurdjieff takes him by the hand and leads him into the kitchen, where the young man is shocked to realize that Gurdjieff alone was washing up after the feast. He saw that all of them in the Work group had been so fixated on the ideas of the Work that every night after feasting, Gurdjieff washed up all of their dishes without any help! Of all the lessons, all the talks, all the shocks received, this night changed the young man's life. His night spent washing dishes with Gurdjieff was a pivotal experience.

QUESTION: How do we get a teacher to work with us?

RESPONSE: A teacher does not learn that we are ready to be students from a note in his mailbox, although the note is a fine gesture. It is actually the student who gives the teacher permission to work with him. Ego can effectively stop the benediction of God from entering the body. The Divine cannot get through ego unless ego makes itself vulnerable and passable. Ego has control. How do we give the teacher permission to work with our ego? Not only does the conscious mind need to give permission, but the unconscious mind needs to give permission also. How do we do that? It is unconscious! The master is sensitive to signs other than the linear and the verbal. The master knows who is really giving permission, who is ready.

When our life script is inconsistent with our ability to serve the work, we can give the master permission to interfere with our lives. The price to be paid is our attachments to the elements of our life script. We have to be willing to completely transcend those elements if necessary – to transcend our negative Enneatype characteristic. Changing the negative into the positive is an alchemical process. Alchemy is about one thing becoming something else – without moving. We can do this with our life script. The strongest characteristics of our neurosis get to be transformed into utility on the path. We are so easily seduced by the absolute brilliance of our minds, bodies, or emotions. Our illusions have a very big investment in convincing us that they should be entrusted with complete domination and control.

QUESTION: How do you know if a master has integrity?

RESPONSE: If they have no life but the Work. Once we cross that line, we cannot be self-centered again. Ego is not crushed, smashed, or murdered. Ego is turned to the service of the Divine rather than to the service of the separative self.

According to the Sufis there are three kinds of students, each with their unique motivation. The first kind of student assumes that the teacher has information and can pass it on. The student comes to collect information. They soon realize that the teacher does not know everything, get disappointed, critical, and aggressive, and then leave looking for another teacher, one who knows everything. They are never satisfied. The second kind of student comes to the teacher because the teacher meets the student's expectations about what a teacher should be. The image fits. Sooner or later the teacher will do something that is not quite right according to the student's image. The student will be disappointed and will leave, looking for another teacher who fits their image. They are never satisfied. The third kind of student comes to a teacher because they want the truth.

They are not willing to let anything create doubt or get in the way of their search for the truth. Even the lack of the teacher's faith will not influence the student's faith. They are satisfied from the beginning on.

QUESTION: There is a certain dimension of ourselves that is Divinely intelligent. We have other dimensions ready to guide us into hell. How do we discern between subjective and objective dimensions?

RESPONSE: The living master can help. But it is the disciple's task to surpass the master. What the master wants for every disciple is complete independence for the disciple. Perfect independence equals union with God. Thus the disciple must discover the true inner guide or they will be dependent on the master for praise, security, guidance, etc. Ultimately we need to leave the master like our children must leave our houses. The relationship with the master does not end. It cannot. The master is always our master, and it is our job to become completely independent of the master.

There are four types of teachers. The first type is the real thing. They can deliver what the real teacher is supposed to deliver. The second type is the decent person. They have basic social integrity. They are honestly trying to help people. They imagine themselves to be far more advanced than they really are. They are sincere, but they lack the skill to actually craft a student into a disciple. The third and most common type of teacher is so unaware of their own Underworld motivations that even though they believe themselves to have integrity and to be helping people, they are actually unconsciously manipulating people and trying to get power over others. The fourth type of teacher, not so common, intentionally lies, cheats, steals and manipulates people.

There are two ways people find a master. One way is we go look for one. We have done a certain amount of work and we realize that we need a guide. The other way is we stumble on one. We are looking for something else. We are stunned; every word out of the master's mouth makes perfect sense. It is crazy, but we have the feeling that, "This is what I have been waiting for my whole life!" Our mind screams, "No! No! Please don't feel this way." But there is nothing we can do about it.

Every master is looking for one thing: Disciples. Unfortunately, what they get are students. Disciples are quite rare. Every once in a while, a student magically turns into a disciple. One day, student – the next day, disciple! If you are already a good disciple, the master will find you. When the student is ready, the master appears. It is also true that when the master is ready, the student appears. The master disciple relationship is completely reciprocal.

QUESTION: What does it mean to be a good disciple?

RESPONSE: It means that you are good for your word. Do not commit to something if you cannot follow through on it. Be able to move quickly. Be able to shrink or expand quickly as the circumstance requires. When you make a mistake, do not try to fix it. In most cases, when we try to fix something, it just makes it worse. Do not jump to conclusions. Instead of jumping to conclusions with the master, just ask them, "What is going on?" The master is managing the universe. Who knows what is going through that mind! Before you jump to conclusions about what you are experiencing with a master, get a reality check. Develop discrimination. People think that someone close to me speaks for me. They ask people close to me questions instead of me. For many masters, half the work they do is damage control. Just because the master has a great regard and respect for someone does not mean that the person knows their ass from a hole in the ground. How can you develop discrimination? Be willing to learn from your experience. It is that simple.

QUESTION: How can I have a successful relationship?

RESPONSE: Your euphoric honeymoon period ends when you make the decision that you are unwilling to change to please your partner, and instead you expect them to change to please you. It ends when you are not big enough to include the unexpected, to embrace the surprise, to deal with things as they are, whatever they are. We are simply unwilling to include these little or big eccentricities of our partner. It is a decision that we make in the moment: "Yes, I am going to embrace this, without recoil, without argument."

At the core of Tantric practice is, "*Accept what is, as it is, here and now.*" Near the core is the practice of transforming useless or toxic substances into something useful or precious. When something negative arises, can you make positive use of it so that it provides some value? We may think we need to seek out circumstances of danger or toxicity to test our practice. This is not necessary – it is a misunderstanding or an illusion of Tantric practice. Just moving through life with its inherent tensions, struggles and difficulties is enough to work with.

If there is something about us that disturbs another person, it will keep disturbing them. Either we must change what disturbs them, or be willing to just keep on disturbing them.

QUESTION: How do I change?

RESPONSE: How do you change? You change! That is all! Could a five-year-old get this? Yes! Do we get it? No! What is our problem? The problem is, we are not ourselves. Our habits come from someone else. We cannot change the someone else, so we cannot change ourselves.

QUESTION: I don't know which context to move into to be a good student. Where is it?

RESPONSE: The mind of the context that we are in now cannot understand or perceive the context that we are moving into. It cannot. It is like Orson Wells said, "Audiences are not going to watch this movie. It is going to happen to them." If you are vulnerable to what a child is, it changes your world. There is only one way to prepare yourself for a change of context and that is to work in the context you are in now as if your hair is on fire. Work with more vigor, more totality, more intention, and more intensity. Discipline, concentration, and the ability to work quickly and efficiently are all required in the new context. Work on that in this context with more focus, more effort. We think that to prepare for the new context we should conserve our resources and wait to get ready, but actually we should keep pushing the limits. Shifting context does not happen progressively. It just happens to you. After all, whose business is it that you are a saint? Just keep practicing, keep practicing. Keep your spiritual progress to yourself – practice invisibility. My recommendation is to be as invisible as you can. It gives you a lot more options in every circumstance.

QUESTION: As my practice actually begins to take root in me, I meet with resistances that I did not realize that I had. They are stronger than I thought. What can I do?

RESPONSE: Typically we try to use force. We try to apply more pressure to practice. But as our practice deepens we are crossing dimensions. Using force is like trying to fight with weapons that are not effective in the domain we are trying to fight in. One thing that can help is the idea of drifting down through the levels, beta, alpha, gamma, delta. Just relax. How? Just stop struggling against the conflict. Our body wants one thing, our mind wants to practice. Relax the conflict. Pay attention. Trust yourself. Trust your intention as a spiritual student. Say to yourself, "I am not practicing now. I want to practice. I will practice when I can." The intention to practice will not go away. Our conscience provides a constant pressure. We don't have to know it or be aware of it. Sooner or later the pressure will be stronger than ego's habitual resistance. Our resistance is lowest when full out laughing, when praying, or when thinking that nothing is going on. Trust your own intention. You know what the goal is. You know what you are looking for. You will know when you meet it. We think that when we are not struggling with guilt we are not practicing. Relax about the guilt. Relax about the struggle.

Just look at how much effort you already have put into the path, the time, the energy, the money. Something is inspiring you to put forth that effort. Whether you articulate it or not, trust it. It won't let you down. It won't go away. Even if you put it in prison and torture it, it won't go away. It is too late. Whatever resistance arises in the moment, just reestablish your intention and relax.

Completing the path does not happen in two weeks. It is a lifetime affair. It can be basically exciting and enjoyable from beginning to end (except for a little despair and a few other unpleasant sensations).

QUESTION: How can the path be exciting and enjoyable?

RESPONSE: Do not have unrealistic expectations. Remember, everyone is different, absolutely unique – even identical twins. Do not compare yourself to someone else on the path. This adds frustration and more work unnecessarily. There is already enough work. To compare ourselves to others does a disservice to ourselves, our teacher, and our path. Usually when we compare ourselves to others it is just the most superficial level of psychology, and all it does is handicap us. When we compare, we do not take into account unique karmas, personality, or needs. The master regards each student differently, according to what they need and what is required. The master's respect for us is not defined by the usual social niceties. Praise of one person does not mean they are respected more than someone who is criticized. We need to develop the skill to encourage direct feedback from the master. We can say, "Tell me what is wanted and needed." Sometimes what is wanted and needed is that we learn on our own, without feedback from the master. We have to be allowed to struggle alone, make our own mistakes and experiences, and learn our lessons. We think, "If only the teacher would tell me what to do, everything would be fine." But sometimes the path is like this.

QUESTION: What is the goal of the path?

RESPONSE: To be surrendered to the will of God. The will of God is specific to every moment, so you cannot give it a definition, because each moment is different. You may call it truth, or life, or God, but whatever you call it, there is an intelligence at the source of the universe that is so profound that we could not hope to grasp its immensity, except to say that it is purposeful. The will of God is whatever serves the purposefulness of the universe.

QUESTION: Is there anything that could not serve that?

RESPONSE: Yes. Free will, because it is free. Free will can function in a way that serves itself rather than the purposeful process of the universe. The will of God is unique in each moment.

We can direct our intention to this question, "What can I do now that will serve this situation?" Never mind 'the goal of the path'. If a child is lost, do we help it find its parents? Of course we do! Serve what is wanted and needed in this minute.

Shortly before he died, Aldous Huxley was asked if he would review his life's research and boil it down to a simple phrase. He said, "Be kind to people."

I have friends for two reasons. I have friends to give help, and I have friends to get help. I would be glad not to see most of you again. I have enough students. It is just more work for me. But once you are in, you're in. I'll stand by you the whole way. I'll complain like hell, but I'll stand by you. 'Cause once you're in, you're in.

22. 2003: What's Love Got To Do With It?

1 August 2003 – She finds me

"I love these things. I really love these bronzes," says Lee Lozowick to one hundred and thirty people while sitting next to Arnaud Desjardins in the vast conference hall at Hauteville during his summer 2003 visit. "If I didn't love these things, I wouldn't have the confidence to sell them to you."

But what's love got to do with it?

The mind goes crazy with questions like this. Just like the mind goes crazy with trying to pick out a bronze to buy. Hundreds of pieces stand shoulder-to-shoulder, rim-to-rim, haunch-to-haunch, all tastefully arranged on eight square meters of antique oak table surfaces in the private formal dining hall in Hauteville's Grand Maison.

New, old, shiny, blackened, huge, miniature, pristine, damaged, stone, wood, bronze, silver, bowls, cups, implements, animal figures, goddesses and gods of every description and price, all available and waiting your decision.

The mind analyzes. "I wonder where this one came from?" "How much does this one cost?" "Where would I put it?" "What would this one do for my Work?" "Would the Guru like me more if I 'played the game' and added a zero to my debt?" "Wouldn't it be legendary to join the 'four zero club'?" "Why would I ever want another one of these?" Thinking, thinking, thinking, trying to make a choice. Trying to figure it out. Trying.

It is my third or fifth time around the table in as many days, each pass revealing pieces that I never saw before. Meditating on the bronzes is a training exercise. Their form modifies my form by some kind of imprint. They train my ability to perceive. The more I am formed by the bronzes, the more they can reveal themselves to me. Each pass causes new qualities to be sensed.

On my third time around I see pieces that were invisible on my second pass. How can they appear now? Where were they before? Behind my own barriers? Covered by my own fears? Does the process of gazing upon the bronzes cause my mind to momentarily slacken its rigid grip on my experience of reality so that more can appear? Or is Lee following me and placing new objects around the table when I am not looking?

In a distracted moment of random gazing upon the rich assortment of metallic geometries and forms, my breath catches in my throat. *What is that?* A strange experience. A warm gentle electric buzz tingles in my chest. The aftershock ripples out through my limbs. *What is that?*

Is this experience the result of some new factor? Or was it there all along and I just never noticed it before?

It is true that I have been investigating verbal reality. I was not aware that I was imprisoned in a verbal reality. In verbal reality, words lead. My experiences are limited to whatever I can squeeze into my prison cell of words. Since childhood I have been hammered and locked into verbal reality, and there I stay until I make a prison break.

If I dare to risk going crazy, I can escape verbal reality and enter experiential reality. In experiential reality, experience leads. Experience is wordless, being bigger, faster, richer and far more complex than words can ever be. Then, if I wish to communicate with words, I use the words as a bridge to cause an experience to occur within another person's body.

So here I am, stuck with an experience and no words for it.

My eyes search through the figures before me. Suddenly I find the source. It is her! The golden one! Four arms outstretched, sitting there, a scant twelve centimeters tall. Present. Waiting. (She seems so good at waiting.) And the sensation comes again, only more so. It is a smiling upon me. A quickening. The countenance of a goddess. I gaze at her and a circuit clicks home. It is now irrefutable: whatever it means, however it works, I have been touched by the bronze and the touch is good. A sentence that Lee recently spoke drifts into my mind.

Lee: "The purpose for the existence of the Universe is self-delight."

This is bizarre! (Yes, it is bizarre. The Sacred Bizarre!) Why this statue? Six others nearly identical to her sit side by side. I pick them up one by one and feel the hard, cold metallic weight of them. There is nothing illusionary about the bronze. I look at their labels: 'Durga', says one. 'Kali', reads another. 'Shakti', the next. "That figures," I think to myself. "Confusion as authority. Crazy wisdom." But as Shakespeare put it: "A rose by any other name is still a rose." These statues represent the same deity, but only one of the statues speaks to me. There is no logical reason but only one figure touches me at the core. That one.

I put them all back on the table and walk away. From across the room I surreptitiously watch other shoppers to see if anyone else notices her, to see if she is calling out to just anyone, to see if she is a prostitute.

No. No one else sees her.

But I do.

In the crowded melee of a shopping spree I carefully retrieve her from the table, cradle her in my hands, and walk over to Lee who is seated against the wall interacting with his clientele. I explain what happened. He pauses momentarily, looks directly into me with a rare knowing sparkle in his eyes and merely nods his head. Since I have experienced it, there is no need for any kind of confirmation from Him… The little deity gets wrapped in a wrinkled scrap of Indian newsprint, tucked under my arm and in a few days brought to her new home.

I place her on my desk in my office. Some more days go by. A week. The moment comes when I haphazardly remember that she is there. As I scrutinize the form and detail of her crossed legs, outstretched arms, bare chest, her torch, knife, ball and snake in her hands, her fancy hat and well-rubbed face, I make an internal observation. By experimentation I realize that I have a choice. Either my mind is there thinking, analyzing and judging, or, I can be with her. It is one or the other. Not both.

I can either sustain a distinct conscious space for experiencing her, or I can fill up that space with word salad from my mind.

This then is the first requirement: if I am to experience the deity then it must somehow be so that mind is not there.

To the mind, not being there is no different from death. So, to encounter the deity, I must first be prepared to die. This does not mean that I need to be little or to be adaptive; it does not mean that I need to give up my power. Of what use is an irresponsible admirer to the deity? She needs a sanctuary of intentionally devoted attention to work in. How can I put the mind out to pasture for a few minutes? With that challenge the goddess experiment begins in earnest.

At the same time Lee's guidance starts becoming crucial: (When was it ever not crucial?) (All quotes herein are personal hand written notes taken during Lee's talks and seminars during the summer of 2003 in France.)

"There is only God. To adore something is to recognize that thing's inherent Divinity. This recognition brings that thing to life. Adoration allows the light that is there to arise and radiate. The adored then becomes a doorway to all of reality. To go through the doorway we must be detached from form."

Lee has just outlined a complete technology for working with the bronzes. But detached from form? I am adoring her form! The beauty of her face, the cheekbones, her forehead, her knees, the curve of her breasts, the glow of her golden skin! No… actually that is not true. The form becomes beautiful through the adoration! At this expansion in my understanding the doorway suddenly opens wider for me and the experience of adoration gets far too intense to manage. I reflexively return to my office work. There are things to do, places to go and people to talk to you know…

A few days later I decide to stop flirting and instead make it formal. These are important experiments. The nature of reality is being revealed. The physical sensation in my chest is repeatable. Something is happening.

Lee: "What it boils down to is each person's individual personal experience, but we usually try to find answers outside of our experience, from our mind. Sooner or later, if we are really going to get the Teaching, we are going to get it essentially."

So I set aside specific amounts of time to practice encountering the Divine through the doorway of adoration. In doing so, I discover Countenance.

First, the word 'her' starts to become sacred, an exquisite precious sound. Forming the word 'her' becomes a holy experience.

The feminine needs to be cared for, such fineness, such delicacy. And when she experiences the care and dignity of my respect she becomes strong and indomitable, radiating her strength back to me.

The experiments continue. What is discovered? When I practice adoring the bronze, something else shows up. The space shifts. The most intense sensation of impersonal unqualified unconditional Love permeates every atom in the space, thicker and sweeter than honey. All doubts, all self-loathing vaporize in the intensity of this super radiant Love.

And she changes too. I am no longer looking at a bronze. No longer is it simply a womanly form. I am having Countenance with a Goddess, fully present, benevolent, eternal. Having the Countenance of a Goddess puts me on my knees.

How could she be so? A moment before she was just a small golden body, imperfect, mortal. Now behold! The Goddess in full blooming radiance and beauty, all wisdom gazing back at me with a Love that is so intense my breath stops, so compassionate that my heart no longer needs to beat by itself.

My body shudders. Neither laughter nor tears come although I think they must. Love burns through emotional indulgence like fire through straw. It is gone before I feel the heat. Emotionalism is without substance. All that is left in me is objective awe.

I do not want to turn away, ever. But if I keep gazing, all my secrets will be revealed, all my faults, all my failings. Then Love eats the thoughts and all I can experience is being totally, unconditionally accepted by the Goddess, just exactly as I am. It is inconceivable, immeasurable Paradise.

I ask myself, "Why me? Why do I receive such blessings?"

Lee: "The mood of wonder, awe, majesty and ecstasy when we behold the Goddess makes us more human. It does not separate us from others who do not feel these things."

I come to realize that I am being healed, made round and whole. What is healing me? Love. Not personal love but archetypal Love. Love as radiance. Love as the fundament. Love as pure consciousness. Where does the Love come from? The Love seems bi-directional. Love comes through me towards the Goddess and she recognizes and experiences that Love. At the same time Love comes through her towards me and I recognize and experience that Love.

Wave after wave, tide after tide. Endless Love that can never go away. The Goddess conducts what I conduct. As I become conscious of what she gives and receives and what I give and receive there is a recognition that completes a circuit and makes the Love conscious of itself. When Love becomes conscious of itself, creation comes to life. The reverberations caused by the shift of archetypal Love into conscious archetypal Love produces a substance in the world and a feedback sensation in the body called Countenance.

I could avoid Love, deny Love, covet Love, fear Love, subvert Love, but it is never Love that changes. It is me. Love is Love, impersonal, pure, powerful, and the most abundant thing in the Universe.

Lee: "Love is a completely free-standing radiance." (At some point I have to ask myself how He knows these things...)

How much ecstasy can I tolerate? Why should life be so delightful?

Lee: "God's wish for creation is that creation have the same wish for God."

Recognizing that my love of the Goddess is as strong, clear, true and as deeply irreducible as the Goddess' love of the God – that is ecstatic. Love consciously recognizing Love.

The recognition happens through two physical objects that are nothing more than mud that has been structured fine enough to become conscious of its own consciousness. Love is all there is. Love is already there. I am wrapping myself up with the Goddess to become conscious of Love, and she wraps herself up in me for the same thing. It takes both of us to complete the circuit. Love meets Love. Countenance.

Just as light shining through air is invisible until it hits something, consciousness only manifests when there is a piece of creation to manifest through.

Consciousness manifests according to the complexity and maturity of the matter through which it manifests.

A Goddess is elegant and sophisticated enough to recognize the Love I have of the Goddess, and my adoration makes me elegant and sophisticated enough to recognize the Love she has of me.

But what about between times? What about after this finishes? This is worrisome. *Because life is mostly spent between times.*

Longing for gazing at the Goddess with Love and having the chance that the Goddess could be delighted and gaze back at me with Love is strong longing. The longing may not go away.

Experiencing the lack of once having been in Paradise and not being there now may not be a pleasant experience, and it may stay with me forever. I feel the longing when I sigh. I feel the longing as a physical ache in my chest every time I remember. The words 'wistful', 'pensive', 'sorrow', and 'melancholy' take on new levels of meaning.

Lee: "Even when you have found the Beloved you are still yearning for the Beloved. This is the broken-heart. To Be is heartbreaking."

Lee: "How do you put your attention on the Divine? Look to what your attention is drawn to relative to the Divine – and then that is where you put your attention."

Anything could be used as a doorway if I put the proper kind of attention on it.

Here I have the paradox. What is the right kind of attention? What is the key? When Bugs Bunny comes to a solid rock cliff face, he can pull out a paintbrush, paint a doorway on the rock, open the door and walk right through. That is a high-level skill.

Painting doorways requires taking radical responsibility for sourcing the way things are. Elmer Fudd (representing me) cannot do that.

Elmer Fudd smacks his face into the rock wall no matter what is painted on it, because for poor old Elmer Fudd, a rock wall is not a door; it is a rock wall. I am faced with the same question that Lee poses: Is a bronze a bronze? Or is it a doorway?

Lee gives me some assistance for this experiment. He provides bronzes that have already been used as doorways for fifty or one hundred years, or more. These doors have greased hinges. They already know what to do. They can open almost all by themselves with the slightest flicker of attention. I ask for the key; I look for the key; I try to find the key with my mind. But it could well be that the key cannot be found with my mind. The key may be Love, and that key can only be found with my heart.

23. 2004: 8 Poems To Lee Lozowick

POEM 0

Dear Certainty,
Like a dust devil spinning out into nothing,
You died quietly,
The rustle of a few dead leaves in the wind,
Which was a surprise for me.
How precious I once thought you were.
You seemed solid as granite,
Fierce as a tax collector,
Deadly as a wounded vampire.
I almost didn't know you were gone
So engaged was I in the avalanche
Of new experience,
Liberated by your passing.
I used to hang all my finest possessions
On your robust branches:
My expectations, my superiority,
My resentments, my trust.
Only raise the temperature and the sturdiest wood
Transforms into ashes
That can hold nothing.
I have fleeting memories of a time when things fit together
Into nice, neat packages and made sense.
Oh, what a small, tight world that was.
By accident I meet you now,
Lurking in the bottom of a glass,
Behind a betrayal,
Beneath a mistake.
Like brushing against sheets hanging on a line to dry,
I slip past so as not to disturb,
Feeling gratitude that you escorted me safely
Into a vaster more mysterious world,
Not wishing to renegotiate.
Life is better raw and unprotected.

POEM 1

Dear Lee,
My Teacher,
My Guru
My Satguru
My Alchemist,
I have now satisfactorily figured out what you are.
You are an enigma.
Perhaps even THE enigma: that which cannot be figured out.
You who invite me to ingest the Golden Elixir
Five little drops that loosen my grip on known territory
(Of what value is security anyway?)
And bump me ready or not to the next level,
(Of course I are ready because I am webbed into the context
of transformation!)
But what if the next level is wordless?
What if Your existence on the physical plane is almost all
An illusion?
A mere convenience to keep the body alive?
And where You really live is here more now
In the etheric, astral, and aural planes
Where Your heart, Your guidance, Your Love
Is always present, always available in perfect clarity,
Boundary-less.
The only difficulty being confirmation for my logical mind
When the real mind is experiential, energetic, obvious, and non-
verbal.
It is so easy to fool myself.
And yet self-deception is itself obvious, plain as day,
So that going ahead means following the signs and doing the ex-
periments
Making mistakes so as to learn about Love and reality.
Expanding into the dimensionless,
Waiting, waiting for results, even through wild uncertainty.
You indicate that there is no way else now to really follow You
Except by growing up
In the bigger sense of the word.
There are no rules. All rules must be broken.
But there are laws, irreducible inflexible laws, to which everyone is subject.

No way to talk about them before, no way to avoid them after.
Make my mistakes small and fast and pay attention,
And remember what I learn forever.
Dear Teacher, Satguru, Alchemist, fellow lover of God,
I thank you for the price that You pay to make it safe for me to struggle,
And try, and make mistakes, and try again.
Because it is all You.
I work in Your laboratories, doing Your bidding.
Discipline is my only hope, my only prayer.
Please give me the discipline to discern Your reproach,
Your confirmation, Your need,
Even if it is beyond my imagined self-image and self-generated restrictions.
Please continue to let me be Your eyes, hands and mouth.
You are crafting vehicles to carry the possibility of Love.
I want nothing other than to be Your servant.

POEM 2

Dear Lee,
How else could You teach me the art of Love
Except by extracting Yourself from my reasoning mind?
Then I am left with nothing
But experience.
Very clever!
Your subtle gestures become apparent.
I sense Your invitations to risk vulnerability,
To risk nakedness and raw contact with Your soul
Without being personal.
It is true:
Without words
I can be closer to You.
Without needing to know
I can let You closer to me.
In the stillness
Unfolds Your tremendous presence.
Even now I explore with sensation first
To find out where You are,
Where You want to take me,
What to merely accept with gentle joy,
And what to reinvent instantly and without question.
You do not hesitate to indicate what comes next.
But I still resist.
I notice that I sometimes cringe rather than obey your instructions,
Because I still think that it is personal.
I think that Your words are coming
From somebody with their own desires.
At least now I can feel my resistance.
I regret each missed opportunity to simply move.
I still think that there is a me to have dignity, and
A me to protect.
I forget that the dignity is intrinsic.
I blind my knowledge that it is impossible
To separate the dignity from me.
I pray: Let me keep breathing and let me just move.
Let me reliably perform whatever You need
Now and next.
This dance is Yours.
I already have everything that I need.

POEM 3

Dear Lee,
Every day
At Your invitation
Sometimes every hour
I beseech God with all my heart
To be annihilated in Love…
Is this where You sit?
Annihilated in Love?
Is it like that?
Where each move feels exquisitely full colored and complete
Because it is orchestrated by God?
Where each breath is the same breath
That the Beloved takes?
Breathing in communion,
Breathing as the whole universe breathes?
Where each touch is so much Love
And never enough Love?
Where contact with any object
Floods the body with surging living current?
Where gazing at the little golden Goddess is the greatest pleasure
Because even the briefest devotional glance
Brings Her quiveringly alive
And She becomes more attractive than anything else in the world?
If this is so, if this is true,
If You awake each morning and go to sleep each night
And eat each meal, and sit at Your desk
Annihilated in love,
It is no wonder then that you might refer to yourself as
The Marquee de Sad.
The King of Sadness.
Because it is so sad, so sad,
That even a moment could go by
For anyone, anywhere in the world,
when they are not bathing in the wondrous oneness of
Being annihilated in Love,
When so much Love is so possible
For everyone.

POEM 4

Dear Lee,
I sit.
You sit with me.
You sit so closely I can feel You breathe.
You breathe me.
I breathe You.
If I am fortunate when sitting happens,
Then Shiva sits in my place.
A sitting Shiva attracts Shakti, Parvati – the feminine wave.
Remember that little bronze Goddess you sold me at Hauteville?
She is not so little, and hardly made of bronze!
Oh beautiful One! Oh Goddess!
The whole nervous system sings
With electric love
So strong
That breathing is barely necessary anymore.
You can sit forever like this, Goddess.
You Love, never go away.
Never.
But I have a body.
I stop.
Sooner or later I must stop,
And I go on about my human life.
Yet my cells remember.
In a short while my nervous system grows hungry
And aches for the moment
When I can sit again
That there may be a chance
That You, as the Goddess (such an inadequate word!)
That You, as the beautiful, radiant, pure, endless, love One
Might appear and sit with me
Once more.
Oh, please, just once more.

POEM 5

Dear Lee,
You have taught me to sit with You and
To sublimate sexual energy.
No reason was given back then.
"It is just an exercise," You said,
A practice.
Some years have gone by.
I keep placing this rare radiant stuff,
This sublimated sexual energy
At my heart,
As You have instructed.
Slowly, I guess,
I have built a cave full of treasure,
A sanctuary of precious riches that is
More and more attractive to certain beings.
Suddenly a Pirate has come.
She has noticed this treasure room,
This heart full of love nectar.
She has waited and waited, I guess, watching,
Attentive to my state, patiently waiting
Until I could not help but to
Recognize Her recognition
And invite Her to come just a bit closer,
To visit,
Finally, to sit with me.
Closely.
As close as possible.
And to drink of this nectar of Love.
It is amazing to experience
That the more She comes to bathe and drink
In the Love
The more Love is there,
The more It grows, on Her, the Goddess.
This nectar
Expands from my heart
Into my soul, my being,
And starts to be noticeable
Even when I am not sitting with You.
I remember when I walk, when I pause,
And I start wanting to go back and sit again with You.
Oh, You stealer of attention,
You Pirate,
You Thief,
Please come again and sit with me
And take all You can.
I can't wait to give You the treasure.

POEM 6

Dear Lee,
I think that You know what I am talking about.
I think that You know ecstasy (or bliss)
Personally (or impersonally)
On a daily basis.
You may deny it, but
I think that You know about this not theoretically but as an experience.
Or why else would You sit?
Why else would You guide us to practice?
Except as You know the value of doing as You do.
You live as a transformer.
The more we align ourselves
And resonate to Your resonance
With Yogi Ramsuratkumar
The more we are transformed
And the more we transform.
We don't even have to know what we are doing.
We only need to rest in Your field,
To lay in Your hands,
To move as Your whim moves us,
To handle what is wanted and needed by the School.
You are the School in action.
As above, so below.
Our school
The Western Baul Tradition,
Led by Lee Lozowick (the Alchemist)
Is modeled after, and a reflection of
The structure of consciousness at large.
Your school is God in action.
You are master of the invisible.
You are Love at work.
You are the son of a child of God.
And if we are willing to activate the blessings
That You shower upon us in unimaginable abundance
For no reason
The gates of Heaven burst open
In a flood of ecstasy.

Not once,
But endlessly.
And I think that You know what I am talking about.
I appreciate that You have kept it a secret
And played cool
And left it to be discovered by Your students one by one as a sur-
prise,
Because then it is unpredictable, unsought,
And, if it arrives like this, surreptitiously,
Then it is irrefutable and undeniable,
And rests on its own, stable and unaffected by other people's opin-
ions.
Oh, that I could emulate your care
Of the sublime.
That is my prayer.
I think that You know exactly what I am talking about.

POEM 7

Dear Lee,
The Lord giveth
And the Lord taketh away.
But He taketh away not everything.
He taketh away not the bodily memories
Of the experience of what it was
That He hath given.
And if what He gave was heaven on Earth,
If what He gave was so precious
That all other experiences pale in comparison,
Then all that remains
Is less than it was before the Lord gaveth.
Even the most magnificent sunset, the most satisfying dessert,
The most luscious orgasm, the best movie,
Has no worth compared to heaven on Earth.
I have discovered an exception to the rule
That all things are transitory.
The discovery is that all things are transitory
Except longing.
Longing remains.
Longing never fades away.
Even when heaven returns the longing for heaven remains.
Longing for heaven in heaven?
What? Am I crazy???
No.
I am ruined.
Ruined.
So let this be a warning to you.
The house of the rising sun
Looks so tempting from the outside,
But run away.
Run away before it is too late.
Heaven on earth can vanish
But your longing for it to come back won't.
And they do not tell you how much the longing hurts.
Ah, well.
You will not heed this warning.
(I did not.)

So I'll see you later,
Late in the night
After everyone else has gone home to something,
You and I will be sitting there together
With nothing
In the tavern of Ruin.

POEM 8

Dear Lee,
It hurts
When a door of golden opportunity slams shut in their face.
But by then it's too late to do anything,
Their bright trusting eyes already drop to the floor,
Shoulders slumped.
They turn away from me.
The magic is gone.
Just from the tone of my voice,
Or a moment of skeptical hesitation.
Their hope dashes against the hard cliffs of my reasons.
I can feel it.
Like a note in a bottle hitting a rock and going down,
Like the day after Christmas,
Like checking your ticket against the winning number,
And seeing it does not match,
The moment once so full of wild dreams and excitement
Becomes grey and worthless,
Life draining away like blood on the dirt,
Me knowing I killed it.
Murdered: another possible moment
Of laughter and joy,
Of glances bursting with unrestrained love,
Of a rest-of-your-life memory,
Of a Dad who was a "Yes!" for them.
It hurts when a door of golden opportunity
Slams shut in my face.
I remember quite precisely how it goes.

24. 2006: Being Alive In The Face Of Breakdown

31 December 2006 – From my talk during Baul Feast in Prescott, Arizona

The phrase *being alive in the face of breakdown* comes from Werner Erhard. It relates directly to Guru Yoga and the core process of spiritual work, insofar as spiritual work is a process at all.

Think of it this way: Yogi Ramsuratkumar is dead.

Janis Joplin is dead.

George Gurdjieff is dead.

Taizen Deshimaru is dead.

Harry Chapin is dead.

Paramahansa Yogananda is dead.

Mother Teresa is dead.

Irina Tweedie is dead.

Jan Cox is dead.

Jose Silva is dead.

John Holt is dead.

Chögyam Trungpa is dead.

M. Scott Peck is dead.

Ken Windes is dead.

Frank Herbert is dead.

Charles Bukowski is dead.

U. G. Krishnamurti is dead.

Deben Bhattacharya is dead.

Kurt Vonnegut Jr. is dead.

Michel de Salzmann is dead.

Dina Rees is dead.

Eric Berne is dead.

Robert A. Heinlein is dead.

Buckminster Fuller is dead.
Ozel Tendzin is dead.
Yvan Amar is dead.
Thomas Gordon is dead.
Elisabeth Kubler-Ross is dead.
Carlos Castaneda is dead.
You could name others.

Learning of their deaths reveals unconscious assumptions I have been making which you may have been making too. I have assumed that these people are the big ones, that they – or someone like them – will always be out there in front of me to carve paths in the chaos that I can then more easily follow. I assume that I can hide behind their courageous practice, that I can default to them.

These are the heroes I secretly count upon to keep fighting up there at the front lines.

And now they are dead. Killed in action.

My assumption fails. The battle lines creep ever closer.

The ominous question raises its serpentine head: Who is then to carry on? What then shall we do?

This question puts practice hard into my face. It makes me hope to God that practice eats me alive so thoroughly that there is *nothing* left, so when it is me on the front lines, and the challenges confront me in whatever form it pleases (my partner, my sangha mates, the newspaper reporter twisting my words in an interview) there is nothing left to be knocked unconscious and triggered into mechanical reactivity.

It is the *being eaten alive* part that I want to consider here – some ideas about being eaten alive with elegance.

Lee is a salesman for what He calls *the great path of divine evolution*. If we are in this salesman's company it would behoove us to recognize that evolution *lives* through the possibility of breakdown. Breakdown and evolution are the two faces of Janus.

Breakdown is the fluid state that permits things to rearrange themselves according to the influence of evolution; old things fall away; new things sprout. A proper sort of breakdown has its rightful place in spiritual work. Without breakdown there can be no evolution. Therefore, on an evolutionary path it is worthwhile becoming a student of breakdown.

From a simplified view, there are five distinct categories of breakdown, each associated with one of our five bodies, physical, intellectual, emotional, energetic, and archetypal. Each body has its own breakdown symptoms. If you know the symptoms of transformational breakdown, you do not have to go get a brain scan. You can simply go on about your day in the process of transformation, because you can trust the process.

Physical breakdown may include headache, flu, nausea, diarrhea, fever, sore muscles, bones out of alignment, deficiencies, infections, blockages, injury, or disease, but also may include physical ecstasy and being in the zone of magnificent performance.

Intellectual breakdown could include confusion, argumentation, not knowing, being lost, forgetting, being caught in lies, expectations, fantasy worlds or conclusions, but also may include revelation, insight and pristine clarity.

Emotional breakdown could include mixing emotions together, not distinguishing feelings from emotions, storming off, blame, vengeance, paralysis, panic, hysteria, catatonia, unworthiness, isolation, or despair, but also may include reasonless joy and saintly compassion.

Energetic breakdown might include loss of identity, loss of face, loss of centeredness, loss of sensitivity to spaces, forgetting protocols, bad timing, or inappropriateness, but also may include telepathic connection, prescience, and sublime creation.

Archetypal breakdown might include loss of dignity, loss of inspiration, existential angst, baseless doubt, faithlessness, giving up hope, overwhelm, or the so-called *dark night of the soul*, but also may include unbridled radiance and archetypal love.

What if physical, intellectual, emotional breakdowns turned out to be mere distractions from the spiritual path? What if energetic and archetypal breakdown was what you came to the spiritual path for? What if you committed to a spiritual tradition because being in the maws of evolutionary spiritual breakdown was the biggest turn-on in your life? What if you entered the School precisely to experience the chaos of evolution?

If so, then a counterintuitive secret of evolution may be to navigate *towards* spiritual breakdown rather than fortifying your defenses against it. Whether the breakdown lasts for three seconds or three weeks, it is the *Liquid State* inherent in the breakdown experience that allows for evolutionary change to take place.

Even though you may have been taught that *the show must go on*, you can ally yourself with the force of evolution and use the opposite strategy: *let the show fall apart*.

If you include evolutionary breakdown in your understanding of what it is to be a human, a couple, a family, a School, or a project, then nothing is wrong or bad about breakdown.

You are free to take a system intentionally into breakdown when it is called for, knowing that many little earthquakes may be better than one gigantic one.

Breakdown is the way.

If the purpose of relating is evolution, then when *authentic* breakdown arises it is evolution happening. *Authentic* breakdown means that if you are feeling emotions (as opposed to feelings which come from the present, are used to handle things, and are entirely gone from your body as an experience in less than three minutes), that you are consciously aware that they are emotions that come from others (including religions, society, politicians, and corporate sales programs), OR, from unhealed or incomplete feelings from your past, OR, from your Gremlin, OR, from a vampire demon, AND, that you tell people around you that you are experiencing emotions that do not come from the present so have nothing to do with them personally, AND, you go get a skilled emotional healing process spaceholder and actually do one or more emotional healing processes to get down to the core issues, including untangling your hidden purposes for keeping your resentment and reactivity alive. That is what is meant by an *authentic* breakdown. In *authentic* breakdown, evolution is happening.

But your comfort zone might not like the experience of breakdown. Your psychologically generated story about the breakdown / breakthrough evolutionary experience happening might tell you that this is bad or negative, disgusting, or unseemly. You might avoid breakdown because it was pounded into your head during childhood that you must keep that smile on your face, keep your act together, stay calm, stay in line, and maintain good form.

In most Western cultures human beings are taught to stay numb and avoid feelings. However, on a true spiritual path, avoiding feelings and breakdown will quickly become problematical. Blocked feelings can prove to be quite an impediment to participating in the great path of divine evolution due to extinguishing your life earlier than you might wish due to an emotion-repression-related disease. By the way, there are many, including many cancers, Parkinson, multiple sclerosis, and most forms of inflammation.

Breakdown may indeed be unavoidably frightening. But if your fear is blocked, then entering breakdown could be nearly impossible for you. It can be indicative of not entering breakdown often enough if you keep getting the same feedback. It could facilitate entering breakdown more gracefully if you simply changed your relationship to fear.

To change your relationship with fear, start by noticing what meaning you have associatively wired to fear in your thoughtware. If feeling fear is wired to threatening meanings such as *fear is bad, fear is dangerous, fear means approaching pain, or fear means possible death*, you may wish to do an experiment that rewires the meaning that is connected to the experience of fear in your mind. Re-wiring is a quick three step process. First, split away the old meaning from the experience so that in one hand you hold the meaning and in the other hand you hold the experience. Put the meaning on an energetic shelf to the side. Second, choose a new meaning for the experience, a meaning that empowers you rather than disempowering you. And third, test your new meaning. The most powerful new meaning we have discovered to attach to the experience of fear is that the experience of fear means that you are experiencing fear. Some people try new meanings such as: *fear is exciting, fear is fun, or fear is alertness*. In the end it may be most useful to rewire fear to its one true meaning, like this: *fear is fear*.

To test your new wiring, do a little something that ordinarily causes you fear, like go admit failure to someone, go appreciate your partner, or go talk to your Guru. As the fear comes up in your body, you can greet it. Say, "Welcome fear. Fear is fear. What do you have for me?" Let the fear persist in you so that it can download its intelligence for your benefit. It is a valuable resource you have long ignored. Keep doing what you were doing that was bringing the fear. See? You are afraid and you are still functioning. Great! For your next experiment, detect fear as fear when you are about to enter breakdown and, while feeling afraid, allow the breakdown. This quickly grows your capacity to elegantly and intelligently inner-navigate emotions during breakdown. Once you learn to do this for yourself, you can help others learn this precious new set of skills. These distinctions and skills are so valuable that you can make this your profession and quit your corporate job. Seriously.

Sadness may also block you from entering breakdown. If it is not okay for you to feel sad, then you cannot go through the natural grieving that permits old ways of being to slide away into the past, giving space for new ways of being to functionally emerge. To permit grieving, change your relationship to sadness. Rewire the meaning so that sadness equals sadness. Then let the breakdown come, and go ahead and feel sad so the wisdom and power of conscious sadness can nurture your life and relationships.

Anger too may be an impediment, if, as for most of us, anger was not an acceptable experience. Anger may appear just before breakdown for two reasons. One, because you are afraid, and you are angry about whatever it is that is making you afraid. And two, because you are about to lose control. If there is one thing you have fought hard for, it is control. Losing the fight for control can easily bring up anger. In that case, say, "Ah. This is anger. Welcome anger. Anger is anger. What do you have for me?". Write down the distinctions, boundaries, changes, and declarations your anger empowers. Afterwards say, "Thank you anger." Then you get to decide what you do with the information and energy from your anger. Your anger does not get to decide.

Breakdown is experience. Like all experiences, breakdowns come and breakdowns go. What are you going to do about it? That's what I want to know. Breakdown is temporary and *completely neutral*. It has no built-in implications. Breakdown is neither good nor bad, neither positive nor negative – it simply is what it is, and feels exactly like it feels. Breakdowns carry no implicit meaning.

The mind, however, is a meaning-making machine. Its job is to create an endless stream of meaningless thoughts, and it does its job well. The mind can generate and attach meaning to any experience, and it cleverly edits the news it reports to you according to the unconscious directives of your internal politics.

If you experience a breakdown, ego demands to know why it happened, what does it mean, what is the reason? The mind, noble servant that it is, produces reasons for you in abundance. After selecting a satisfying meaning you conclude that you now understand the breakdown.

Werner Erhard is (in)famous for relentlessly pointing out that *understanding is the booby prize*, the least valuable reward. Trying to understand breakdown may be gratifying to ego, but understanding is not the useful part of breakdown. Understanding may perhaps even interfere with evolution. For example, if you create an understandable enough reason for your breakdown, then the force that is trying to direct your attention to learning about what you assumed you already knew about, and assumed there was nothing more to learn about, is disabled. Understanding stops learning.

A more transformational approach to breakdown could be to go ahead and let yourself be truly broken down. (What is that *self* which gets broken down anyway? Is it your true self? What if 'self' is a superstition, believed in by many, ignored by the Universe? Try that one on for size…) Try to directly experience the various subtle and overt experiences of breakdown rather than trying to understand how or why the breakdown happened. If you do not permit yourself to truly be broken down then the breakdown may not be able to do its work on you to produce break-through. It could be a long time before circumstances arrange themselves to deliver this same transformational breakdown opportunity to you again.

It is crucial to know that *breakdown does not guarantee breakthrough*. You might indeed be in breakdown, but the breakdown might not be authentic. There is a difference between authentic and inauthentic break-down.

This is not meant to encourage you to dramatize your breakdowns to prove to others how authentic they are. "Oh my God! I am in break-down! I can't do the dishes now. Can't answer phones. Cancel all my appointments! Someone else has to take care of the kids. I have to fully experience this. For sure it's a major breakdown, a real one… maybe it's the big one!"

At first glance, many signs of irresponsible interaction can look as if they are authentic breakdown, but they are not. Your Gremlin has probably long ago learned how to imitate breakdown as a way of avoiding responsibilities. Remember playing sick to avoid going to school? Ah, hah! Yes. Sure you do! You created a healthy Gremlin even back then. Do you think it went somewhere and leaves you alone now? No chance of that! Determining the authenticity of breakdown requires looking at the total end results. If responsible changes result, then the breakdown was authentic. If nothing changes and the breakdown repeats itself at a future date, the breakdown was a Gremlin charade. How many times will you allow yourself to be fooled by the same trick?

A breakdown's intention can be detected. Inauthentic breakdown intends to manipulate others, to attract attention from the authority figure, to control things so as to continue being the same without having to change, to be taken care of, to get pity, to be rescued, to get revenge, ultimately, to prove that your way is the right way.

Authentic breakdown has no such agenda. Authentic breakdown rises out of a context of innocence. The future result of authentic break-down is unknown and unknowable. You do not get to manage your own evolution.

The next time breakdown is hovering in your vicinity, sense into the intention vector of the mood to determine instantly, at its beginning, if the breakdown is authentic or not. Feel out along the intention lines of your subtle positioning to find out where your gestures are aimed to land. You can listen to the level of responsibility in your tones of voice, in the momentum of your emotions, and in the quality of consciousness contained in the theatrics you are performing.

If you assess that the breakdown is *not* authentic, then make the decision to suddenly *not* go there. Go sideways instead. Admit that you were unconsciously generating pain and confusion. Put your dirty cards on the table and apologize. Then go sing show tunes, clean out the cupboards, and serve somebody else.

On the other hand, if you assess the breakdown as authentically headed for evolution, then trust your assessment and decide to take the dive; let yourself fall completely into the abyss (keeping 10% of your adult awareness present). Rely on the School itself to act as your safety net and to be the intelligent field that manages your reordering. Listen for feedback from sangha, and plan to learn quickly from your misjudgments.

Being alive in the face of breakdown depends first on living in the clarity of the above distinctions, and then on taking one more step: extemporize. If Lee Lozowick is a master of anything, He is a master of extemporizing. Lee demonstrates ongoingly what it is to be alive in the face of breakdown because, although He is a slave of the One Law, there is obviously no plan. He makes it up as He goes along. You have the opportunity to develop the faculty of extemporizing in the safety of Lee's presence. This is such a precious opportunity, one you may regret not using if you ignore the invitation. Through an abundance of artistic and business suggestions, practices, projects and tasks, while traveling on the road and at informal gatherings, Lee waits catalytically. He holds a particularly awakened space in which students can discover aliveness in groundlessness, and *feel the magic in each and every breath.* (lyrics from the Lee Lozowick, song All There Is To Say, on the *Transfestite* CD.)

Attempting divine improvisation requires your total participation. You take the highest risk. It may feel safer to stay absorbed in trying to puzzle out the Guru, trying to unravel his paradoxicality, to learn his teaching, to figure him out. But that's not it. That's just mind distracting you with an endless pointless thought loop. The Guru is paradox. He is enigma. He can never be figured out.

Forget about figuring him out. Take a bigger risk than trying to figure him out. Take the risk of *creating in the presence of the Guru* (a phrase I first heard from Lee in an After Dinner Talk upstairs in *Arrakis* in the early 90s). Creating in the presence of the Guru means to reveal what you are up to through being up to it. It's the opposite of being nice, adaptive and invisible. It involves you paying attention to spaces, timing and the laws of hospitality, and then, as soon as the door is open, create something astonishing. Join the conversation, chip in, tell a story, share an insight, go nonlinear by asking a real question. It will be like standing at the edge of the nest and flapping with maximum effort and precision until you are no longer supported by solid ground. This is what it means to create in the presence of the Guru.

Probably as soon as you try, your mind will interfere, demanding that you have a ready reason for each of your actions. Otherwise, how will you be able to explain yourself when an authority (one of those senior students…) requires justification? To approach your preconscious reticence, it helps to remember that for centuries witch hunts and inquisitions ruthlessly weeded out the extraordinary ones. Generation after generation, for thirty-five generations, the heretics were killed. It is in your cells not to be unorthodox. And that is the trap. How can you enter the Guru's divine play when it only takes place in what Pema Chödrön, student of Chögyam Trungpa Rinpoche, refers to as the groundless nature of reality, yet every action you make must, on pain of torturous death, be burdened with a logical reason?

You have learned to weld your choices to reasons, and you have learned this lesson impeccably. You can test this for yourself. Place two pens before you on the table. Choose one. Then honestly answer this question, "Why did you choose that one?" Your answer will be that you chose it, "Because it is red, because I like the shape of it, because it was on the right side and I am right-handed…" Whatever your answer, the answer is a reason, and you weld the reason to your choice as a defense against being killed for being unreasonable. If you cannot fabricate a 'good' reason for a particular choice, then, on a cellularly-remembered threat of death, you cannot make that choice.

Now answer this next question: "When you choose between the two pens for a reason, what had the responsibility, you? Or your reason?" You will be forced to admit that since you made the choice *for a reason*, then it is the *reason* that has the responsibility for your choice, not you.

Reasons are how we protect ourselves from the consequences of our choices (ask any politician or corporate profiteer). For example, if you come to school late and the teacher demands, "Why are you late?" if you say, "Uh, I dunno," you would be punished. But if you say, "There was an accident on South 47th Street and I carried the mother's baby to the hospital so she could take care of her other children in the ambulance…" you might instead be applauded. It is our reasons that determine whether we are seen as a hero or a villain.

Using reasons seems to function excellently in ordinary human domains. But what if you wish to enter the domain of radical responsibility, where it is required to move faster than the speed of mind and there is no time for reasons? If each choice has a reason attached, then you will be carrying a lot of extra baggage. A bundle of reasons makes you far larger than the eye of a needle, gives you too much mass to do right angle turns at light speed, and interferes with extemporizing in the service of something greater than yourself. If every choice must be welded to a reason, then you are far too sluggish to be moved by the will of God.

Not to worry. There is a piece of self-surgery you can do, privately of course. It's like grabbing a bottle of Scotch, a razor blade, and your mom's sewing kit, and removing your own appendix. A bit of a nasty job, for sure, but it can be done. Cut the weld. Separate your choices from reasons. Leave the reasons aside. Stand in your choices raw and unprotected. After the surgery there is no longer any deception. It's like when Richard Gere in the film *Sommersby* reclaims his true identity to protect the dignity and property of the woman he loves, even though it costs him his life. Without the contrivance of reasons, you become irrefutably responsible. That's actually how it is anyway, in reality, but now the situation is clear, and you stand on reality.

After the surgery of cutting your choices away from your reasons, choose one of those two pens again. When you are asked, "Why did you choose that pen?" you answer, "I chose it for no reason."

Voila! You have become unreasonable. No longer does a reason have responsibility for your choice. You do. You are completely exposed. In the film Last Samurai they call it, being alive in every breath.

What you will receive when you take radical reasonless responsibility for creating in the presence of your Guru is feedback.

Feedback is gold. The first feedback you get is that you will crash. Count on it. As noted in the first Matrix film, "No one ever makes their first jump."

If you do not crash then you are probably deluding yourself about having gotten off the ground in the first place. This exercise is about crashing, learning how to crash well, crashing with elegance, being alive in the face of crashing. It's like Aikido: the first thing to learn is how to crash without hurting yourself. Keep your center. Roll back onto your feet into ready position. Be grateful for the feedback. Then crash again, hopefully in a new way. Crashing creatively leads to rapid learning.

An important guideline when creating in the presence of the Guru is to start very gently. As Lee's buddy E. J. Gold wisely warns, *make no sud-*

den moves. Regardless of how gently you start, the feedback will seem to produce lethal pain. This is because when you create in the presence of the Guru instead behind his back, you make yourself into an easy target. As Mike McDonnell, a student of E. J.'s would say, "Be the bear in the woods who, instead of hiding behind the trees from the great Hunter, paints a circle on his chest and steps forward with both arms spread." You present yourself at maximum exposure to the Guru's gifts.

The fear of being completely vulnerable to what, from ego's perspective, looks like certain annihilation, is the source of your previous hesitations. It is a memory that originated in far different circumstances long ago when you had not yet learned the skills and distinctions you have now. Leave the past in the past. It is time to start over. You can choose a new option. Invention is possible, because now you can say, "Fear is fear," and attentively proceed with creating in the presence of the Guru.

It may help if you sensitively remind yourself about the name list at the very beginning of this article. How much time do you assume that you have with your Guru? The chance to practice being alive in the face of breakdown by creating in the presence of the Guru is not a permanent opportunity. Perhaps you should make use of it while you still can.

25. 2006: Requiem And Conscious Death In The Western Baul Tradition

30 October 2007 – A transformational proposal

Even if you consider yourself to be a Western Baul, you are perhaps more brainwashed by the American attitudes about death than you might want to believe. The American attitude towards death is that it will never happen to you. Death is clearly a mistake from God. Science is quickly repairing God's oversight. If natural healers can't cure you, then in the last-minute, allopathic medicine will step in and save your ass with its heavy hammer of technology and drugs. If you do happen to accidentally die then something went wrong. It was a glitch in the program. You are an American. Death is not part of your culture. You must struggle against death to your last breath.

Occluding death's certainty is a modern cultural trait, developed along with the industrial revolution of the 1850's. Observe old village churches in Europe and you will observe how death was historically an integral part of spiritual considerations. The pious (or the privileged) were actually buried on church grounds, as close to the church building as possible. And the church itself was located in the center of the village. Every time you attended a service you were also walking through the graveyard, a daily reminder of your ultimate physical demise.

A popular gravestone carving of the early 1800's reads:
Remember me as you pass by. As you are now so once was I.
As I am now so you will be. Prepare yourself to follow me.

You would not likely see such an epitaph today. In fact, you hardly see gravestones at all. Today's cemeteries are hidden miles out of town, well away from view. Cheaper and easier is to burn the corpse and toss away the ashes so there is no trace of the death at all. The modern result of death is not getting emails from someone for a very long time.

With SUVs, smart phones, credit cards, nightlife, Facebook, Netflix, Instagram, computer games, flat screens, and a gazillion channels of shit on the TV to choose from, the primary function of modern Western culture may be to distract you from the inescapability of your own death. For example, even the dire and declining physical condition of my parents does not bring them to separate from a lifetime's collection of consumer goods. Instead they talk of their next vacation to Europe.

It is not easy for the Western Baul subculture to retain its simple purity when continuously blasted by the Technicolor pretensions of whoever is imitating the great American archetype Mickey Mouse (who, by the way, never dies).

To stand in Western Baul cultural knowledge about death you may start by repeating Little Big Man's mantra, "It is a good day to die." You may recount how Don Juan implored Carlos to remember Death waiting incessantly over his left shoulder. You may subscribe to the Sufi teaching to 'die before you die'. You may have read E. J. Gold's *American Book Of The Dead*. You may even carry the Baul Death Prayer in your wallets for emergency use. But your formal relationship to death as Western Bauls is not well established. As a young community we have only been confronted with death in the last few years. Our death customs are just now being revealed. Let us ponder what it could be for Western Bauls to engage conscious death in community.

The predominant community thinking about serious diseases and the process of dying seems to be to withhold the existence of, or the details about, a person's condition from public knowledge to the point of total concealment. This is done for a good reason. The Chinese Law Of Secrecy is known to us. When an outcome is still uncertain, that outcome can be easily swayed by the subtle energetic contamination of unconscious projections, fears, and personal desires of people having even the best of intentions. Better to keep the delicate situation secret so Divine influence can do its work and a beneficial outcome occurs.

But what if the outcome is no longer in question? What if you give up the American fantasy-world of immortality and admit that Death is on a serious mission? At some point for all practical purposes the game is up. You know you are going to die. What is the point of continuing to maintain the charade? Perhaps there is a misunderstanding. Perhaps your present attitudes and actions surrounding an approaching death represent early experimental attempts at expressing your way of dealing with impermanence. Perhaps you are ready for the next level.

And that brings up the central question: what is to be the way of Western Baul dying? Does conscious death mean to spend your last few days desperately holding on to the chance that the laws of nature will somehow be radically reversed in your particular case? Perhaps this is not what was originally intended by the secrecy. Perhaps the current Western Baul tradition of dying secretly is a temporary aberration that actually contradicts the very fact that we are a community.

As a community we are one body. When one part of the body is ill and the other part does not know, this lack of communication causes a disharmony that could well even aggravate the illness. By keeping an illness secret, it is true that the victim is protected from burdensome sentimentality, nostalgic emotionalism, projected fears, and so on. On the other hand, keeping the dying process secret potentially cuts off the body from useful learning, and potentially cuts off the ailing person from healing resources that may be abundant in other parts of the body.

Sickness and death are evolution in action, a learning process for the whole of the community, no different from healing and birth. We already recognize and embrace the fact that one person's insight can inform and benefit the whole of our community. That is why we have Tawagoto, Hohm Press, After Dinner Talks, Celebrations and Study Groups. Could it be just as true that one person's pain and suffering also benefit and inform the body of the whole community?

Let us try a new experiment. Let us henceforward make it an option that when a student of the Western Baul tradition realizes that they are in the final stages of their death they can ask for a 'Requiem'. Let it become possible that a dying student can ask for a time of *being with* other members of the community, a day or more of coming together, of completion, of sharing and letting go. Let Requiem be a time for celebrating with gratitude the great Mystery of life through acknowledging that there is nothing we can do to prevent it from ending.

We could include in the Western Baul tradition that when a person comes to the point of recognizing that they are about to die, they can go public. They can call together an assembly of friends, a Requiem. Instead of keeping death private we could have the tradition of going out with a party. And in doing so we would not be in poor company. Paramahansa Yogananda for example, died on stage in front of hundreds of friends and devotees.

We are spiritual students, yes. And we are also human beings. I think that Lee has been telling us over and over that being a warrior of the path does not obviate our own simple humanity. Although we do not have so many powers as a human being, one power that we do have is the power to greet each other with a 'hello' and the power to part from each other with a 'good bye'. To leave without saying 'good bye' is a sneaky way of holding onto the fantasy of, "I am not really dying." The gesture leaves inelegant incompletions. It disrespects the depth of our connection and the interdependence of our lives together in this community. We are of one body. We are, if nothing else, friends. Friends usually do not leave for a great transition in their life without saying 'good bye'. Let us create the possibility of consciously saying 'goodbye' to each other before we die.

The choice of having a Requiem is not something that can be decided by someone else. Lee has said that we as a group cannot pronounce for someone else what they have not yet pronounced for themselves. It would be inappropriate to tell a person that it is Requiem time because they are soon dead, when they are not yet owning that their condition is just this. Great sensitivity and respect are in order.

To prepare yourself for the new experiment, all you have to do is memorize the following words: "I'm dying. I want a Requiem." Leave the rest up to us. We are Western Bauls. We know how to create celebrations.

But here's the catch. God works in mysterious ways. What if you're wrong?

What if you have a Requiem and then afterwards you don't die? Wouldn't that be the ultimate embarrassment? The little boy who cried, "Wolf!"

Wouldn't you be the laughing stock of the community? Everybody coming around to make their final farewells, and then you don't have the good manners to exit stage left!

I suppose that would be the occasion for starting another new ritual in the Western Baul tradition. We would then invite everyone back together again for a follow-up party. This time we would call it: Resurrection.

26. 2006: Handbook For Creating Ordinary Human Relating

13 December 2006 – *From Building Love That Lasts*, published in Tawagoto

Here are 122 specific instructions and practices for how to start, grow. and end Ordinary Human Relating. Study them carefully to improve your Ordinary Human Relating Intelligence.

1. Complain to your partner about anything that does not suit you. Use a whining, victimy tone in your voice when you complain. Respond negatively to any assurances given to you about anything. Make sure that the object of your complaints can never be resolved. You complain. Your partner tries to fix it. You create reasons why their solutions will not work. At least in this game you always have something to talk about.

2. Try to be right whenever issues arise. Argue your point. Do not give up until your partner concedes that you are right. Gloat to others on the phone about your victory, or your partner's incredible stupidity, so your partner accidentally overhears you.

3. In order to supplement being right, also try to make your partner wrong whenever there is an opportunity to do so. After all, you are not making them wrong. They actually are wrong. You are just doing them the favor of pointing it out to them. Also tell their mother about it, more than once.

4. Take a rigid position about everything and anything ("I have to wash my face before I go to bed!"). Be fanatical about your positions. Go for the throat. Take no prisoners. Justify your position

any way that you can. After all, this is a democracy! Everyone has a right to their own opinions.

5. Feel resentment about anything your partner ever did that offended or frightened or embarrassed you. Whenever you look at your partner, remember your resentments first. Never forget your resentment. Especially if your partner tries to touch you.

6. Feel resentment about your own childhood. Remember all of your old wounds. Assume that the people presently around you will wound you again in the same way. Project this onto your partner. Your partner then becomes your enemy with conscious or unconscious intentions to harm you. Stay little. Never grow up. Use the hatred you harbor to fuel your life.

7. Feel resentment about your children, your boss, your colleagues. Use resentment as a way to take care of yourself by feeling strong and righteous. Never question how you got your resentments, or how they cut off the possibility of intimacy with these people. After all, they are the ones who made you resentful.

8. Have a never-ending competition with your partner about who has the worst life. Dedicate yourself to proving to your partner your life is less fun than theirs is. If life seems momentarily good, hide it and hold up the shit end of the stick. Search for subtle evidence to demonstrate that your partner has it better than you do. This gives you permission to go shopping.

9. If your partner does have a little bit of fun, make them feel guilty as hell. They should have been working on something. There is so much that needs to be done or that needs to be cleaned up. Who do they think they are, having fun?

10. Confine your experience of love to the linear, personal, transient, conditional, minimized, localized, ordinary, verbal-reality of the three words: "I love you." That is what you can give. That is what you can receive. As soon as the echo of the spoken words fades out of the room so does your faith in your partner's love.

11. Give up about little things. Give up about life. Have no hope. Try to make your partner rescue you from this utter hopelessness. If they fail to rescue you, blame them for not caring and assume they are having an affair.

12. Get a nice car and keep it clean. Get a hi-tech smartphone and a slick computer. Live in your car, your phone and your computer. Look at your relationship and wonder why it is so messy compared

to your car, your phone and your computer. Obviously, the mess must be your partner's fault.

13. Be strong, try hard, be perfect, rush around, always keep pushing yourself on to the next thing. Push yourself until you break down psychologically, emotionally or physically and then make your partner pick up the slack for you so they can finally value all the work you have been doing for them.

14. Do not be happy. Do not enjoy life. Do not be powerful. Create complex excuses that blame other people or your life circumstances as your reasons for not being happy, powerful, and enjoying life. Consider yourself creative.

15. Give away your authority so you do not have to make decisions about your life. Give your authority to any authority figure: doctors, plumbers, computer guys, the phone company, the car mechanics, the government, your children, the tax people, anybody. Feel weak and used. Feel stupid. Complain about the bad service, high prices, and poor quality of your life. Nitpick to find ways that people are not taking care of you well enough.

16. Stay in your head. Think about things. Try to brag about all the things that you know. Righteously value intellectual and rational considerations above all else. Confine your life to your reasons. No matter what, do not feel. Feelings are irrational.

17. Stay in your bed. Sleep in. Each morning try to keep dreaming as long as they allow. Sleeping and dreaming are better than what is happening in your life. If you are sleeping and dreaming maybe people will leave you alone. Maybe things will change by themselves.

18. Do not be glamorous and sexy for your partner. Instead be glamorous and sexy for people who do not matter so you can maintain a cool image with them. Make those other people jealous about how your partner gets to be with someone so glamorous and sexy as you.

19. Conceive of 'here' as very big, covering everywhere that you have ever been. Regard 'now' as immense, extending far beyond this moment, back into the distant past and far away into the distant future. Ignore the obvious fact that you can do nothing to change anything that is not here, and nothing to change what happened to you or to assure what will happen to you. Include the past, the future, and everywhere into a gigantic 'here and now' and then feel

totally overwhelmed about how much you carry on your shoulders. Use this overwhelm as an excuse to eat more chocolate.

20. Never say just "Yes," or, "No," in response to 'yes or no' questions. Always go sideways instead. Nothing is simple. There are so many factors connected to so many details. Use complexity and confusion as a way to never get cornered into saying "Yes," or, "No". Suffocate your attackers in their own drivel.

21. Never answer the question that is asked. Always assume that your assumptions about the question and about the questioner are more correct than the questioner's. Dedicate yourself to answering questions that you are certain are more relevant to the questioner than the questioner's questions.

22. Always be worried that the worst thing that ever happened to you is any minute going to happen to you again. Make it your partner's responsibility to protect you from this worry, and your partner's fault if you ever have this worry. Always have this worry.

23. Limit your experience to your vocabulary. Have no experience that you do not have a name for. Regard every experience that does not fit into the pigeonhole meaning of a word that you know as ridiculous and irrelevant. Avoid admitting that you have experiences you have no words for. Teach rationality to your children.

24. Create and maintain the story in your mind that your partner is inferior to you or that your partner is an idiot. Consistently find little pieces of evidence to support that story. Whenever you look at your partner, see your stories about them instead of them.

25. To supplement the view that your partner is inferior to you, also create and maintain the story that you are superior to your partner. Find little ways to constantly remind your partner of your superiority, especially when in the company of relatives, business associates, or mutual friends. Insult their taste in clothing, food, entertainment, hobbies, investments, etc.

26. Have expectations about how your partner should act, about what they should feel, about where they should sit, about how they should dress, about how they should treat you, about what they should order to eat in the restaurant, about how they are driving, and so on. Get angry if their behavior ever fails to meet your expectations. Hold onto your resentments that they did not meet your expectations.

27. Feel afraid if your partner dares to express their feelings to you. As soon as they begin expressing their feelings to you, panic and

express your emotions about their feelings to them. After all, if they stop withholding their feelings it is only fair that they must listen to your emotions. Make sure that your emotions are bigger and stronger than their feelings.

28. Collect up evidence that your partner is out of integrity. After all, if they had integrity, you would be pleased. Blame your partner for everything that is not handled, everything that goes wrong, everything that ever went wrong, and everything that could possibly ever go wrong. What else are they there for?

29. Attack your partner whenever you feel any kind of discomfort. This way they know you are there. The squeaky wheel gets the grease. The more uncomfortable you are the more attention you might get. If your partner ever thinks that you are comfortable, they might not give you any more of their attention.

30. Be a public doormat. Worry that you might cause a problem for somebody else. Neurotically walk on eggshells around everyone. Keep imagining ways that you might be a problem for your partner and explain this to them. Keep giving many excuses and reasons why it is not your fault, and also blame your partner for the unfairness that they might ever think you are a problem.

31. Do not live your life. Feel resentment for having to be adaptive and for not being able to be yourself and live your life. Never clear your resentments so that you do not have to live your life.

32. Make assumptions freely about everything in your life. Assume things should or should not be a certain way. Do not tell your partner your assumptions. Instead, expect your partner to read your mind about what you have assumed. Expect your partner to make the same assumptions as you. If your assumptions ever turn out to be wrong, blame your partner for not correcting your assumptions.

33. Ignore the possibility of being an adult man or woman. Let your childhood thinking and feeling patterns take over and dominate your adult life. Center your identity on the script and emotions of a scared needy adaptive inner child. Give more importance to this fantasy than to your mate.

34. Project your father onto your man. Find any evidence you can to prove that he is your father and that he is doing to you what your father did to you. You somehow survived with your father, so if your partner is like your father, then you know you can survive with him too. Stay in survival mode.

35. Project your mother onto your woman. Be in bed with your mother when you are in bed with your woman. Look at other women and imagine being in bed with them because they are different from your mother. Blame your woman for this.

36. Be scared about everything that you do not know and cannot control. Use your fear to control your partner. Secretly threaten to make your fear bigger if you ever discover anything about your partner that you do not know or cannot control. Use this threat to force your partner to always stay the same as they have always been.

37. Whenever your partner is willing to listen to you, complain about the mobbing at work, complain about projects being prematurely terminated, complain about the incredible laziness of your colleagues or employees or your boss, describe people dying in bizarre accidents, describe what is happening in the war, describe what is happening in politics, complain about the housework, complain about the kids always interrupting you, complain about having too much to do and no time to complete anything. Keep talking about something dramatically bad. If you are talking, then you are relating.

38. Always keep the radio or TV on. Above all, do not be together with your partner in silence. Without making it obvious, distract your partner and yourself from ever entering spaces where it would be possible to speak together about love or beauty or grace, because you might not know what to say.

39. Be needy in such a way that your neediness can never be fulfilled. Express your neediness to your partner every chance you get. Make it your partner's impossible responsibility to fulfill your neediness. This way they will never be confident enough to leave you.

40. Be adaptive to the man who comes to your front door and asks for donations. Be adaptive at work. Be adaptive to the telephone sales lady. Be adaptive to your parents. Be angry with your partner for not protecting you from all the people with whom you are adaptive.

41. Let your parents' opinion about your life have more importance than your own opinion about your life. Let your parents' opinion about your partner's life have more importance than your own opinion about your partner's life. Be afraid that those who have

opinions about you have some secret power over you. Stay unsettled enough that it justifies having a drink at night.

42. Let your parents question and berate your decisions about child raising, vacations, housecleaning, and your job. Let your parents berate your mate. Give your parents controlling authority in your household. Decide that you will wait until your parents die before you start living your own life. Wait impatiently. Let the years go by without living, compensated by the knowledge that you have been a good child.

43. Draw conclusions about whatever you want in life so as to sustain your present view of things. Believe your conclusions in the face of contradictory evidence. Especially ignore evidence offered by your partner. Make the conclusion that life is like this.

44. Defend yourself from intimacy. Do not let anyone, especially your partner, closer to you than your mask. If they see that your mask is fake, they might not want to stay with you. You know how to keep your mask looking good, but you don't know how to take care of your Being. Never let your partner know this about you.

45. Do not trust your partner. Continuously collect evidence to prove that they are untrustworthy. Manipulate your partner to continuously try to gain your trust. This way you can get them to take you out whenever you want.

46. Defend yourself from evolution. Do not try to learn anything new. Think that your habits are you. Try to stay solid in your habits and persevere with the set of behaviors that you established for yourself long ago. Always serve the same menu for Christmas dinner. If your partner ever mentions wanting to evolve, immediately report them to the sect police.

47. Become an expert in avoiding responsibility. Procrastinate. Hesitate. Justify. Use your energy creating excuses rather than creating results. Take no risks. Leave things well enough alone. Do not rock the boat. Keep your hands clean. Relate to responsibility as if responsibility means fault, blame, guilt or a heavy burden. Do not live your life full out. As you get ready to die, feel joyful that none of the problems were your fault.

48. Do not negotiate intimacy. Do not make exact requests or make corrective boundaries. If you do make a boundary, make it so feeble or so late that you get hurt anyway. Feel justified in making ultimatums as a way of getting revenge.

49. Do not ask for what you need. Expect that by now other people around you should already know exactly what you need. Collect incidents of your unfulfilled needs like savings stamps from the grocery store. When your drawer is full of savings stamps books, turn them all in at once by getting divorced.

50. Be a nice person on the surface. Never let anyone know of the other people inside of you. When the people inside you do not get their needs met, let them take over and live your double life. Sneak out to get what you want somewhere else. What your partner does not know will never hurt them.

51. Withhold sex to punish your mate for not giving you what you want. Lie to them about why you are withholding sex. When you go to the relationship counselor, use the authority of the counselor to force your partner to give you what you want. Then start all over again.

52. Make your own personal comfort and security the highest priority. Make other people dance around you to make you feel comfortable and secure. After all, you deserve basic comfort and security, don't you? Other people are comfortable and secure, so they should know how to make you comfortable and secure. Be neurotic in ways that make it impossible to be comfortable or have security.

53. Attach yourself to your partner by getting into their space. Go in their drawers, read papers on their desk, open their email and message apps, cross-examine their friends and colleagues, check their receipts, listen to their phone messages, and snoop into their stuff. Know what they are going to do before they do. Be psychologically, emotionally, and energetically enmeshed with them. Think that fusion is closeness.

54. If your partner does not give you pleasure, if they do not cook you the right meal at the right time or the way you want it (too much salt, eggs too wet, salad is cut and not torn, etc.), if they leave messes, if they do not touch you the right way, if they play the music too loud, if they dress improperly, etc., then feel insulted and close up your love for them. If they do not please you the way you want, then obviously they do not love you. Why should you love them?

55. Try to change your partner. If your partner will not change, then complain about them to their mother. Maybe she can make them change.

56. Try to change your parents, your boss, your colleagues, your neighbors, and your relatives. Hate them for not changing. Hate yourself for failing to change them. Make it so if they do not change, you are not happy. Do not let your partner change you so you become happy.

57. Be involved in all the latest diet, exercise, and health fads. Secretly think that your partner has no life if they do not get excited about your diet, exercise, or health plans. Spend a lot of money. Change your plan when you get bored. Do not explain anything to your partner so you never have to look at your own paranoia.

58. Blame the faults of your children on your partner. Your children obviously inherited their bad characteristics from your partner or your partner's family. Side with your children in any fight against your partner to try to heal your partner's faults.

59. Guiltily buy expensive little things and put them away in your closet or in the garage. Wait. When you finally wear them or use them and your partner notices, say, "Oh, I've had this a long time..." This way you can secretly honor yourself without having to honor your partner.

60. Be a victim of time. Stay super busy. Chase after the clock. Always be in a hurry. Rush around. Do not have enough time to feel or to be relaxed. Do not make time to be present or connect with anyone. Starve yourself from deep, nurturing, adult human contact, and go to bed exhausted each night. Make your own life hell so that your partner cannot add to your troubles.

61. Do not keep your time commitments with your partner. Never arrive on time. Make them wait for you. Always pack your things at the last minute and be completely wiped out or even sick before leaving on any trips with your partner. Use this to prove how important you are to the world.

62. Feel overwhelmed about global warming, extinction of species, government psychopaths taking office, dying oceans, the corruption of corporations, the failure of modern culture to create a bright future for humanity. Attack anyone not feeling as overwhelmed as you for being irresponsible or unconscious. Then your relating problems become small by comparison.

63. Do sports. Use all your extra energy for athletic competition. Come home exhausted. Get hurt so your partner must respect your sport because it has the power to interfere with their life. Constantly talk about your sport whenever you get together with

friends even if your partner does not participate. Use sore muscles and exhaustion as an excuse to avoid physical intimacy. Get up early and run seven days a week because it is inarguable that everyone needs cardiovascular exercise! Then you don't have to face your fears that come up around having sex in the morning.

64. Suddenly become holy. Read spiritual books and do whatever they say. Do breathing practices, yoga postures, Buddhist meditations, and shamanic rituals. Fill your house with crystals. Take lots of ayahuasca. Tell your partner what they should or should not do by quoting from your books or your Shaman. Bring over weird friends who are not really your friends but at least they are holy. Then your partner has no chance to find out about your fears.

65. Surround yourself with persecutors and rescuers. Wake up in the morning and before you even get out of bed, count your enemies. Enter each day as if it has the same lack of possibilities as yesterday, like wearing dirty clothes. If you ever make a mistake it will be hidden in the smokescreen of low dramas in your life.

66. Make jokes about your partner's personality quirks at parties. This way they will remember that you have weapons and they will be nicer to you at home.

67. Be mean to your partner, but feel well justified that it is pay back for all the times when they were mean to you. Accept disrespectful behavior from yourself towards your partner, because everyone is already doing it to each other, at least on the Netflix series.

68. Expect your partner to be everything for you. Do not have friends. Do not let your partner have friends. Starve yourself from contact and make your partner starve themselves from contact so that you can prove that you have a 'monogamous' relationship. Stay with your partner even if your relationship is no longer alive so that you can have a relationship "'Til death do you part." Sacrifice your aliveness to the customs of your culture and times. If you stay inside the monogamy construct prison, at least it is predictable.

69. Mix your emotions from the past and future with your feelings from the present to create massive confusion for yourself and others. Suck as many people in as possible. Your swamp is so full of monsters and demons that no one can rescue you, and then you never have to be accountable for what is happening right now.

70. Indulge yourself in addictive sentimentality, nostalgia, depression, and melancholy. Expect your partner not to react or to need you to be present for them. They should maintain respect for your

deep sadness and grieving for a long-lost past that was so much better than now. Your burden is so heavy that your partner cannot grow strong enough wings to fly off and enjoy the present.

71. Use your relationship to feed psychological vampire entities. Pretend that you do not know what I am talking about. Try to stay unconscious about the fact that you host psychological vampire entities that feed on your partner as their main source of food. Let yourself be fed upon by your partner's psychological vampire entities. Call this reciprocal vampire feeding frenzy a 'relationship'.

72. Do not notice the predictable feeding patterns of your inner Gremlin devouring your life energy. Do not notice that you explode in rage and have an emotionally charged conflict once a month for five days, or once a week for a day and a night, or a few times a day. Do not notice that your partner is doing the same. Even if you are not having a good time in your relating, at least your Gremlin is.

73. Live in the world of "Me! Me! Me!" as if you are separate from everyone else and they are all separate from you. Make it obvious that others should care about you as much as you care about yourself. This way your partner can make up for your mother not loving you enough as a child.

74. Stay in survival. Live a minimal life. Do not indulge your personal whims for adventure, extravagance, new experience, generosity, learning, discovery, exploration, or expansion. Instead, watch television night after night. Have no imagination. Be timid, linear and predictable. Let your fears stay bigger than you so that you can remain in a life of survival. If you torture yourself worse than anyone else could ever torture you, you have nothing to fear.

75. Engage in an ongoing power-struggle with your partner. Struggle privately at home, about the children, about money, about timing, about making plans. Struggle publicly at meetings, at parties, at work, so that when you win, others can witness your great victory over your partner. Always make sure that your partner does not have more power or recognition than you do. If they do, figure out ways to undermine their power and partially destroy them. If they are totally destroyed how could you continue enjoying the power-struggle?

76. Be jealous of your partner's attractiveness or success. Resent them for it. Pull your appreciation away from them and minimize your love for them whenever they are successful, because they obvi-

ously get more than enough love and appreciation from other people.

77. Feel small. Feel weak. Feel like a failure. Feel unworthy. Feel unlovable. Find evidence to continuously prove the view that you are unlovable. This proves that your partner is stupid because they chose someone to love who is unlovable. This proves that life is bad. When life is proven to be bad, then you can continue to not really care about anything.

78. Twist everything your partner says so that you are sure they are telling you "You are wrong," "You are stupid," or "You are not good enough." Respond to your interpretation of what your partner says to you, not to what they actually say to you. Drag your friends and relatives into your arguments. Deny that you twist their communications inside out. Derive satisfaction from being able to confuse so many people for so long.

79. Use your fear to limit your partner's radiant exuberance. Obviously there needs to be a balancing force. When your partner is effervescing beyond your personal aliveness limit, then dump cold water on them. Keep your aliveness limit low so that you get to dump cold water on your partner a lot. This way you have job security about keeping your partner dead enough to be normal. Only be alive when your partner is not around to see.

80. Fight unfairly. Call your partner names (like: 'know it all', 'Mr. Independent', 'sad sack', 'Mrs. Prudence'). Use the words 'never' and 'always' in your accusations. Be aggressive. Hit or throw things. Threaten violence. Think that the conflict is all their fault and that you are not equally responsible. Use the children, money, and sex as weapons. Plan to write a book about your clever ways to win fights.

81. Conclude that you know who your partner is. Do not listen to your partner so that you can repeat back what you heard them say. Refuse to be-with your partner in any conflict. After a conflict cut yourself off from your partner for days and sulk until they apologize, because you were right about them the whole time.

82. Use intimate time with your partner to triangulate (to speak about someone who is not there). Complain about people to your partner rather than speaking only about that person to their face. Do not acknowledge that you again trivialized a moment that could have been profound. Other people's pain is so important.

83. Triangulate about your partner. Gossip about your partner to your friends, to your partner's friends, or to relatives, when your partner is not there. Let the others lead you on until you share intimacies that would embarrass or hurt your partner. Blame your partner for not sharing about themselves with their own friends.

84. Exaggerate when recounting stories about your partner to other people. Make your partner sound braver, stronger, and smarter, or weaker, slower and stupider than what actually happened. Live in your fantasy world of what happened rather than in the simplicity of what actually happened. This way you defend your fantasy world.

85. Use your partner as a garbage can for all the bad things that happen to you during your day. When you are finished unloading your psycho-emotional garbage into their heart and mind, then assume that your obligations for being intimate with them are over for the day.

86. Do not respect the natural inherent nobility, elegance and dignity of your partner as a man or a woman. Do not even see the possibility of such qualities in them or in their lives. Treat your partner as a child, or as a kind of monkey with the capacity for living only an ordinary low-grade animal life. This way you can avoid meeting the archetypal nature of the Universe.

87. Do not let your partner have their own problems. Do things for your partner because you are afraid that they are incapable of doing those things for themselves. Think that you are helping your partner. If they ever complain, get offended because if they do not want your help then they obviously do not want your love.

88. Secretly find evidence to support the story that your partner is a pig. Find a little piece of evidence each day. Even the tiniest piece of evidence is sufficient. After all, you have so much evidence already in the 'evidence sack' that you carry around with you on your shoulders that you actually do not need to find any more evidence to prove your point. The new evidence finding just helps you to remember that your partner is a pig so that you do not forget. You can also use the evidence on your partner in public so they do not forget their pigness either.

89. Live as if you are your psychology. Live as if the reality that your psychology paints for you to live in is the one and only true and actual reality of the world. Believe it like the sun shines. Live as if the views that you got from the news are solid as granite, and ob-

jective as well. Regard anyone who so much as hints that they doubt you as if they are an attacker. Make your life about defending what you perceive as normalcy so that you seem normal to your partner.

90. Live as if your partner is their psychology. Assume they are always going to stay that way, and that they are completely inflexible and rigid. Take what they say as a challenge that you must either destroy or become the slave of. Do not assume that your partner is anything but their arguments and reasons. Do not let love or relationship or acceptance or healing be bigger than your psychological differences. Never simply rest in the psychology-free communion of being together. You might not like it.

91. Try not to know that you are going to die. Live as if you have all the time in the world. Do not appreciate those rare moments of simple companionship as if they could be the last moments. When nothing is happening, it is wasted time. If one of you is sick, it is a problem. Something is wrong. It is a mistake in the program. Again, it is wasted time. If one of you dies or goes away, be shocked, but do not fundamentally learn anything about life.

92. Feed your addictions. Use part of your attention, even during the most intimate times, to crave videos, foods, drinks, self-gratification, complaining, being depressed, criticizing, staying in your head listening to buzz radio. Never learn to tolerate the ever-increasing intensity of being wholly with another human being. Get yourself a drink and turn down the volume of passionate love. Keep it boring. Only go where you already have been before. Then you do not have to be afraid of how magnificent and glorious life really is.

93. Do not speak about what matters to you. Do not dare to risk sharing from the depths of your heart. Never trust so deeply as to open your soul to reveal your deepest tender delicate incomplete uncertain desires to your partner. Even alone naked in bed together. Your partner will probably just laugh at you, or later on ridicule you in public. Instead of sharing your inner world, keep your desires secret. Do not allow life to be a creative playground in which you can unfold your being and create what really matters to you. Then you can take your secrets with you to the grave.

94. Try to be a good boy. You know what a good boy is. Your mommy taught you to be a good boy. So did the teachers. If you are not a good boy, the teacher will tell mommy and mommy will tell daddy

and daddy will whip you in the worst way. The rules for being a good boy are deeply imprinted and socially acceptable. Being a good boy is safe. If you keep being a good boy, even though the price is excruciating shame and gut-wrenching heartache about not being yourself, at least you are a good boy. Maybe a nice girl will approve of you like mommy and the teachers and then everything will be fine.

95. Dedicate yourself to being a nice girl. Give your authenticity over to the magazines and advertising media. Try to make yourself beautiful according to standards set by the makers of anti-aging creams, stylish clothing, and cellulite producing prepackaged cake mixes. Be a nice girl so deeply that you can no longer find the wickedly sensuous creature of whole-body orgasms skilled enough to keep a man at bay until she herself is satiated. Nice girls don't do that! At least your living room looks like an Ikea catalog.

96. Permit yourself to be repeatedly disrespected and dishonored. Use this as permission to get revenge. If you save up enough 'disgrace points' through silently eating disrespect and dishonor, perhaps you can cash them in for a wild spending binge, for an affair, or maybe even for a righteously justified divorce complete with lawyer enforced alimony payments.

97. Decide that since you went to school you know everything there is to know about being a man or a woman, being in a human body, being in a long-term committed relationship, and being a parent besides. Do not go outside of your culture to learn things that your culture is incapable of teaching you. Do not admit to the necessity of change. Do not use your relationship as a way to create a path of evolutionary development. Act as if everything is okay. Act as if things are as they are supposed to be, and make it clear that you are not responsible for making them any different. Then you are safe.

98. Surround yourself with 'eggshells'. Create a complex and sophisticated protective layer of ways that you can be offended. Maintain a hair trigger to threaten your partner with violent rage or other childish behavior so that you can control them. That is the way your mom did it, and her life was a great example.

99. Stay identified with the rules and views of your cultural, political or religious affiliation (I am Italian. I drive a Ford. I am from the Big Apple. I am a Dodgers fan. I am Buddhist. I am Republican. I am Vegetarian. I am LGBTQ friendly.). Hold on to your identi-

fication stronger than to your partnership. Attend gatherings of your false identity circle to sustain your illusion of self-knowledge, belonging and being accepted. Never find an intimacy that is more subtle or profound than the intimacy of a cheering football crowd or a bar song. It was all a dream, anyway.

100. Do not really care about the well-being of your partner. They are, after all, an 'adult' like you. They should be able to take care of themselves. Use your partner as the butt of your jokes. Feel glad when they lose. Feel superior when they are not strong. Feel arrogant when they are feeling pain. It is only fair that they too should suffer sometimes. Who cares about your own well-being?

101. Worry about what the neighbors think. Make your highest priority to be seen and classified as normal by your neighbors. Go into deep denial of yourself and endure a lack of connectedness in order to keep up the appearance of being in a happy relationship with your neighbors. Then they cannot turn you over to the Inquisitors, again.

102. Worry about keeping up with the neighbor's possessions or vacations. In addition to subtly competing with your partner for whose life is most difficult, subtly compete with your neighbors for whose life is more wonderful. Force your partner to join in the competition. Whoever dies with the most toys wins!

103. Complain about not having enough money. Buy things on credit. Live in terror and confusion about not knowing how you are going to pay all your credit card bills because your partner does not make enough money. This way you have your partner over a bed of coals any time your Gremlin wants to torture them about something.

104. Keep mementos and souvenirs of past relationships around the house and in your bedroom, such as photos, letters, gifts, clothes, etc. Keep putting attention on those objects as if they mean something. Do not give that attention to your partner. Why should they deserve all your attention? What if they leave?

105. Deep in your heart keep comparing your partner to past partners, to their parents, their siblings, their colleagues at work, their friends, and of course, to movie stars. Worry if you have found the 'perfect partner' for yourself. After all, this is your one and only life. Now and then tell your partner how wonderful the other people are as a way to force your partner to change.

106. Do not apologize to your partner. Do not accept apologies from your partner. Never forget what has offended you, even if it was a long time ago. Never forgive your partner. Keep your Santa Clause checklist up to date of all the times they were 'naughty or nice'. Then you have an excuse to be mean to them, just to balance things out.

107. Listen to the critical voices in your head. Keep an internal dialog going in your mind about how stupid your partner is, what they are doing wrong, how they will never get it, how they are so self-centered and never think about the wants and needs of anybody else. If you keep your critical voice inner radio station at high volume then you do not have to listen to them at breakfast.

108. Get offended or scared if your partner is ever unpredictable. Do not allow them any freedom for explorative expression. Require your partner to behave within strictly defined norms. Keep your 'kinkyness' detector on high sensitivity, and reject your partner if they ever get weird beyond what you think your mother would accept. (If you only knew your mother...) Try to act sane, and try to make your partner act sane also, especially in public.

109. Use your bed or your bedroom as a place to emotionally process your partner. Create no refuge. Protect no sanctuary. Permit no asylum free of your criticisms or complaints. Let there be no place in your home, or no hour in the day, that is a safe haven from the all-consuming emotional reactivity of Ordinary Human Relating.

110. Assume that your partner's potential is limited. Assume that your relating's potential is also limited. Assume that you have already achieved the maximum of that potential, perhaps years ago. This changes your relating into an endurance test. How long can you stand it? Whoever breaks first is clearly the bad guy. They were not really committed in the first place.

111. Assume that one of your children is a 'problem child'. Having a 'problem child' distracts you from having a 'problem relationship'. Focus all of your time and worries on managing the 'proper education' and 'proper socialization' of your 'problem child' and let twenty years go by, zippity doo-dah! Use your children as the reason to postpone learning how to create anything but Ordinary Human Relating until your learning faculty crystallizes into non-functionality. Then you don't have to think about it anymore because learning won't happen. (By the way, there is no such thing as a 'problem child'. However, this is the subject of a different book!)

112. Keep involved in conflicts in many areas of your life. Have fights with your boss and colleagues. Have fights with your partner's parents, siblings or relatives. Have fights with the labor union. Have fights with the butcher, the baker, and the candlestick maker. Have fights with the tax people, the mayor, the minister of the church, and the dog next door. Then by the time your day is over you are too worn out for sex and really fine kissing. It is not your fault that all those people are fighting with you.

113. Repeat your parents' neurotic relating patterns, whatever they are. Create a cult of pairs with your partner and stay isolated so that you have no friends at all. Then at Christmas time, invite many superficial friends over for dinner and act as if you are satisfied with this level of intimacy. While cleaning up the dishes, decide that this is enough socializing to last you until next Christmas. Then no one can blame you for not being monogamous.

114. Make sure that all of your life decisions are attached to very good reasons. Insist that your partner's decisions are too. Do not allow nonlinear or evolutionary influences to enter your life or the life of your partner. Protect your partner from questionable activities. Keep your lives squeaky clean and defensible. Watch the news so that you have something to talk about. When anyone asks how you are doing, say, "Fine." Do not ask how they are doing. Then change the subject to the news. Then your secrets are safe.

115. Flirt, in subtle and overt ways, to make up for what you do not get from your partner. Flirt because you have no discipline with your gluttonous greedy and insatiable appetite for sexual energy no matter where it comes from or how it contaminates you. Flirt with sexually overt billboards. Flirt through your computer. Flirt with singers on the radio. Flirt over the telephone. Flirt with the waitress, the postman or your tennis teacher. Flirt with total strangers and with your mother in law. Also flirt when your partner is around in order to make them afraid that you might leave so they shape up. Flirt to prove that at least somebody is sexually attracted to you.

116. Get worried if you start to feel something. Think that if you are having feelings then something must be wrong with you. Use addictive substances to stay away from your feelings. Use television, sugar, newspapers, alcohol, speeding, shopping, overwork, over exercise, videos, internet, and so on, to keep from being authentic about what is going on for you. Hide any feelings that leak out

sideways, or find external reasons to legitimize your internal feelings. Now and then you can blow up, or collapse. But everyone does that... right?

117. Allow relatives, neighbors, babies, salesmen or friends to have priority over your partner when it comes to having your full admiring attention or expressing love and joy. For example, be vivacious and cheery while talking on the telephone with anyone who calls, and then when you hang up, go back to being dull and contracted. Pretending to be happy is almost like being happy, so why not at least give this to yourself? Keep the 'at least' conversation going in your head to suppress the inner voices begging for more aliveness.

118. Limit your concept of intimacy so that it only includes sex. Forget that you can explore and completely enjoy other physical intimacies such as cleaning out the garage, dancing, gardening, hiking, washing hair, massage, singing, playing music, yoga, martial arts, cooking, eating, traveling, trying on clothes, painting the house, and so on. If opportunities for these other intimacies occur, stay in your head and consider them as merely chores.

119. Bring your work home so there is no time for intimacy. Stay late for work or meetings so there is no time for intimacy. Use any way you can think of to avoid intimacy. Always have a good excuse. As a back door, be hypochondriac. Always have some physical ailment to complain about. Make comments about your physical pains an important part of your daily conversations. Keep at least one illness alive so that you can use your illness if you ever run out of other excuses to avoid intimacy. Never wonder where your fear of intimacy comes from.

120. Assume that your partner has expectations of you. React to what you assume your partner's expectations are, even if your partner does not say that they have those expectations. Get offended about what you assume your partner expects of you. Do not believe your partner if they ever try to convince you that they do not have the expectations of you that you think they do. After all, your parents had these expectations of you so why would your partner not? Who would you be without pressure from other people's expectations?

121. Be a slave to your reactivity. Create no gap between your internal emotional reactions and your triggered external actions. Definitely do not develop the discipline to observe your own behavior patterns by splitting your attention so that you can use part of your

attention to become conscious of what you are doing with the other part of your attention. Instead stay identified with your re-actions as if you had no other choice. If you protect yourself from having free will, no one can blame you for your choices.

122. When you end your relationship, make it your partner's fault. (The asshole!) Live the rest of your life permanently scarred. Find evidence to prove that you were horribly betrayed. Take no responsibility. Learn nothing. Hate your partner for eternity. Distrust all men (or all women). Use lawyers, relatives, and the children to get all the money you can out of your partner just for spite! Tell incriminating stories to mutual friends about your partner before your partner can tell stories about you, especially to their family, and whenever possible to the media. Take a pound of flesh. Hit them where it hurts. How could they dare to do this to you? Teach them a lesson they will never forget so that this will never happen to you again. Then, arrange for it to happen to you again.

To make best use of this list, read it carefully and slowly once a week for three months. Each time you read the list new insights will reveal themselves. Let each insight bubble up slowly into your experience. Take the time to let each realization hit you with the full intensity of its shocking message that: *Something completely different from this is possible right now.*

People do not change until it hurts too much to keep doing things the old way. It may feel counterintuitive but if you want to change, then let it hurt intensely.

The above listed behaviors and attitudes are neither good nor bad. The above list is valuable because it allows you to acquire a more precise "X" for locating where you are on the *Map Of Three Kinds Of Relating* (ordinary, extraordinary, and archetypal).

When you are enacting to any degree even one of the above listed behaviors then you prove your commitment (no matter what else you might be thinking) to creating Ordinary Human Relating.

This is your "X" on the map.

Study this list until you are nauseated. Study it in a weekly meeting group. Study it with an online team. As painful as it might be, studying the *Handbook For Creating Ordinary Human Relating* gives you intellectual and emotional reference points which you can use for the rest of your life. These guidelines and hints help you detect what you are actually up to when your mind may be telling you that you are up to something very different.

Knowing what you are actually up to is clarity. Clarity provides alternative options in the exact moment when you can take a different action. Such options are priceless. The point is, if you do not know with accuracy what you are doing in this moment then you will have little success trying to do something different in the next moment.

27. 2010: Lee's Death

16 November 2010

I hear that a few days before Lee's death, Wolfgang Köhler (LeeKumar) my friend, was alone with Lee at a huge exposition in Los Angeles where together they set up Lee's Sacred Bazaar so Lee can do his Father's bidding: rescue sacred objects collected from around the world and place them into the hands and homes of those who would love them.

The two men drive to Los Angeles from Prescott, Arizona, in two vehicles, a van and a car. After setting up and doing business for a couple of days, Lee is coughing up a lot of blood. At last Lee says to Wolfgang, "You finish the show and pack up the van. I need to go back now." Wolfgang says, "Okay." That is the last time Wolfgang sees Lee alive.

Later, I hear that Lee dies in his own home, surrounded by intimate friends with a big smile on his face. I believe it.

Lee dies on a Tuesday. On Wednesday, a senior student of Lee's from Germany, my friend Thomas Young, is kind and generous enough to call me personally with the news. At that time, I am living in a suburb of Munich, Germany, with Marion Lutz, next to the SBahn 7 train tracks on the pine-studded plateau overlooking the Isar River. The phone rings. I am downstairs in the kitchen. I answer. Thomas identifies himself, and then says simply, "Lee died."

I say, "Just a minute." I walk upstairs, step into our tiny sacred artifact-packed sitting space, close the door, sit down, light a candle, then bring the phone back to my ear. "Could you say that again please?"

Thomas says, "Lee died yesterday."

My five bodies cry out. Huge sobs shake my chest and take me over. I never cried so long, so loud, or so authentically, not when my parents died, not when my brother died, not the two times I got divorced. The tears and snot pour from my face. My mind is gone. An entire lifetime of suppressed sadness pours out of me.

This amazingly miraculous chapter of my life is suddenly and absolutely ended, never to be repeated. There is nothing I can do about it.

For a guy who can move his family from Arizona to France, build an Ashram out of old farm buildings, repair plumbing and electrical, build dozens of simple but elegant wooden dining tables, bunk beds, and bookshelves, organize work teams, design and deliver transformational trainings in foreign countries without speaking the language, write publishable books, and so on, not being able to do something... well, it's devastating. I am utterly lost.

Thomas is compassionate enough to stay silently on the line and listen to me the entire time I sob. He and I are best buddies, trainers for the Event training together for years. We know the importance of the one who listens to someone else cry. Silent but completely attentive listening creates a space in which the emotional communication can complete itself. I worked years to learn to consciously feel my feelings and emotions. Thomas listens to my torrent of sadness as it hurricanes itself through me. In the end, I am present.

The entire Sangha moves as one organism. Steve Ball, the Sangha woodworker, builds a pine coffin for Lee's body. A funeral date is set. I could fly to Arizona from Europe, like so many others, to be part of the sure-to-be-momentous ceremony. All of Lee's friends will certainly attend. But the Maha Samadhi is set for the same weekend I am to deliver a fully booked-out Possibility Lab in Germany. I could reschedule the Lab, of course. Participants would understand.

I return to the sitting room, close the door and sit again. I try to connect directly with Lee, the same way I have been doing since 1995 when Lee sent me overseas to France. Lee is immediately there. I feel suddenly sad again to discover Lee just as present now as He was all during the time He was in his body, perhaps even more present now.

I explain my dilemma. He already knows it, as usual, yet listens anyway. His answer is clear. It is the same answer He always gave me before: "Don't try to fix it. Stick to your plans. Stay in Europe. Do your job. Serve your people. You won't miss anything important by not coming to the funeral."

This is what I do.

The familiar sense of being left out, of being far away from the center of Hohm Sahaj Mandir community action, the worry that people might make up the story in their minds that I care more about making money in my own gameworld than disrupting my schedule to fly to the funeral of my Teacher... these things fall away. They are not my problem.

In 2013, three years later, I get a chance to visit Lee's new Ashram with the Gaian Road Team. I make my way barefoot along the rocky trail through the sagebrush and mesquite to the roofed-over shrine where Lee's body lies encased in his casket but exposed to the sun and air. The place is so peaceful, utterly silent, elegantly radiant. Nothing is happening. I sit at Lee's feet, studying the beautifully crafted bronze plaque sculpture of his bare soles. I receive no download.

Senior students invite me to go upstairs in Lee's new Ashram house to visit a tiny artifact-filled shrine-room dedicated to Lee. I accept the invitation. I sit alone in the room in silence.

Not so long ago, Lee had called me up in France to say, "I cut off my dreadlocks."

I say, "I want one. I will put it into a Stupa that I will build here at La Ferme de Jutreau."

There is a pause on the line.

It is the only pause I ever hear Lee make in responding to any of my questions over all these years.

Lee finally says, "We want to keep them together. I will give you other sacred objects for the Stupa, if you want."

Here in this room full of memories and artifacts, carefully arranged on a tray on top of the central display cabinet, available to touch, are Lee's dreadlocks. I think the instructions were to not touch anything in the room. I used to be a good boy. Lee healed me of that. I gently touch the dreadlocks with one finger. Nothing happens.

On a shelf below the dreadlocks is another hand-wrought bronze tray. In the center of that tray are the pinewood sandals that I hand-carved for Lee, years before, and gave to him one Darshan for no reason. He never said anything about them to me. I never saw them again. Until now. Here they are, a central element honoring and praising the feet of the Guru.

I slowly shake my head in amazement. No one is there to witness the warm tears rolling down my cheeks.

So many secrets lie hidden in plain sight. So many things work themselves out perfectly in mysterious ways. There is a massive flow of 'shouldnesses', placid as the Mississippi River, rolling along silently through the world. Clearly somehow, I played a part in the high drama life and times of Lee Lozowick.

Can I stay in that flow? Lee repeats the Zen answer to me: "*Don't know. Go straight.*" It has worked so far. Perhaps it will keep working.

28. 1989-2010: Guru Feedback

This chapter relates precious, often inexplicable, teacher-student interactions.

ACKNOWLEDGEMENT

During the November 1989 Appearance Day Celebration at the old Prescott Ashram, Brenda and I are accepted by Lee as students. For the first of the grand meals under the huge blue canvas tent erected on the Ashram tennis court as our dining hall, Lee asks Brenda and I to sit across from him at the 'head table'. As one might expect, there is a point to such an invitation.

The point is to deliver to us a communication. Lee tells us, "It is a rare honor when an entire family comes to the school as a configuration." I do not understand what He means. I do not sense how deeply we had connected into E. J. Gold's I.D.H.H.B. school before shifting to Hohm Sahaj Mandir. I do not recognize how bringing our two daughters on Thursday nights every week for years to Mike McDonnell's Study Group in Santa Rosa, California, and also our commitment to homebirthing and homeschooling, has bonded us extraordinarily as a family to each other and to an evolutionary path.

Lee is acknowledging this for us. It is not praise. It is an 'X' on the map. Years pass before these distinctions make sense to me.

TRYING TO FIX IT

Two core principles of show business are: *Start off with a bang.* And: *Leave 'em laughing when you go.* As a young 'spiritual 'student, and at this early stage in my participation in the Hohm Community, a 'bang' seems in order. I use the last of my 'life savings' to pay for our four-person family to join Lee on the 1990 summer LGB Band and Baul Theater Company tour of Germany. By the time we depart, the sale of our California house is nearly complete. I figure that our capital gains will make the costs of our journey insignificant. What I do not figure is that exactly while we are on the road with Lee in the summer of 1990, the bottom drops out of the California housing boom. Our house deal falls through. We end up receiving $40,000 less for the house than originally agreed upon. I think of Milarepa giving his hard-earned bag of gold to his teacher Marpa as tuition, and Marpa tossing the bag into the deep cold Tibetan lake so that Milarepa can begin with nothing. Transformational forces are already at work...

The band gear has been loaded into the belly of the jetliner. Our tour members are in their seats... but our departure is being delayed. I look out my window and notice a piece of Liars Gods and Beggar's band equipment being offloaded. No one else sees. I think, "Oh, my god!" as I leap out of my seat. "This is a problem!"

I urgently call for a stewardess so she can intervene and reverse what is going on. They are 'stealing' our band equipment! The long metal tube may be mislabeled, but it is an essential element of band set-up during the tour and must accompany us to Germany! I begin exerting my will to 'fix the problem'.

At that point, Steve Ball literally grabs my shoulders to force me to look into his eyes so he can deliver a message from Lee: "Calm down. Stop trying to fix it. Let things go as they will." I do not understand. Not solving problems which I think I can solve is beyond my comprehension. But... I obey. I sit back down in my seat, irritated at the 'incompetence' of the loading crew. We fly off without the tube.

Later I see that I am 'right'. The part does not arrive with us in Germany. The lack is indeed 'a problem' for the band set-up. But the 'problem' eventually seems to fix itself. Lee's longstanding approach is simple: "*Don't try to fix it.*" Perhaps these logistical FUBARs fulfill a mysterious karmic purpose which I cannot perceive. Over and over I watch Lee being completely unruffled. My desire to use some kind of willful force to 'solve the problem' turns out to be the actual problem.

The sun sets quickly while flying eastwards from Phoenix towards Berlin. At one point I need to use the privy, but all toilets in the economy zone of the plane are occupied. I make my way forward, shooting through the stratosphere at nearly one-thousand kilometers per hour in the Business Class toilet. Stepping out of the cramped commode, I notice the stewardess passing out tantalizing desserts to the rich: dark swirling chocolaty concoctions with – no kidding – a cherry on the top. I pause a moment, make sure I have my center, grounding cord, and bubble, then I approach the stewardess with a forlorn look on my face saying, "Excuse me, ma'am. I am traveling with a group and it is our teacher's birthday today. With all the arrangements we forgot to get him a treat. He is the elderly man back there with gray dreadlocks sitting in seat 69G. Is there any way you would be willing to bring him one of these desserts? I would really appreciate it. I am willing to pay…" She smiles graciously and says, "No problem. I will bring him one. You don't have to pay."

I stroll back to my seat some rows behind where Lee is seated. The whole cabin is darkened except for the reading lights over Lee and a couple of the women, making Lee easy to spot. Perhaps they are playing Bridge.

A few minutes later the elegant stewardess arrives with the chocolate delicacy on a small plate, delivering it to Lee with a hearty, "Happy Birthday!" Lee says, "But it is not my birthday!"

The smiling stewardess instantly understands that there is love involved, and she gives Lee the dessert anyway, then departs. A few seconds later, Lee pops up on his seat, turns around onto his knees, looks me straight in the eyes a few rows back – how does he know it's me? – and says, "Next time I will be better prepared!"

TEAR DOWN THE WALL

It is 21 August 1990. The LGB tour in Berlin has begun. Instead of getting to attend Lee's public talk with the other students, I am assigned to be 'on childcare'.

I gather up the children and head out into the afternoon sun, meandering around the German streets with one daughter on my back. My other daughter trudges at my side with several other children. We have no idea where we are, or where we are going, but we start to follow different groups of excited people in a general direction.

By sunset the crowd has become so large that the guards simply open the gates wide and allow everyone to come in. The only thing is, we do not know what we have been let into!

At a far distance we can see a gigantic Styrofoam construction being erected with cranes on an immense outdoor stage. The crowd grows unusually reverent, then, in incredibly high fidelity and on dozens of huge video screens, we get to experience Pink Floyd's *The Wall* concert, live in Berlin, with guest singers Sinéad O'Connor, Joni Mitchell, Van Morrison, and more! Tens of thousands of us heartfully celebrate the miraculous collapse of one of mankind's most bizarre and neurotic inventions: the Berlin Wall.

I am in tears of amazement and joy at Lee's 'childcare' gift to us. As we finally return to our sleeping quarters, the children are all so nourished and ecstatic that the parents do not complain about our coming home so late.

POSSIBLE FUTURES

Around the year 2000 I recognize that even by focusing everything I can on trying to grow my *Expand The Box* training business in Europe, I am unable to bring in enough cash to cover my family's simple living expenses. I surrender to the obvious and make a list of alternative money-earning possibilities.

My list includes such options as taking a corporate job as a research-lab assistant, starting an online 'Liberty Card' bank through which purchases cannot be traced (of course, charging extra for the service of anonymous transactions), reconnect with my previous electronic engineering partner to continue developing our programmable Polymerase Chain Reaction Thermal Cyclers (yes, the now famous 'PCR' devices that are used world-over for COVID testing – I could have been rich!), and about ten additional futures. To make the list complete I add one last item: 'Continue delivering *Expand The Box* trainings'.

I fax my list from La Ferme de Jutreau's office in France to the dedicated fax machine in the Hohm Sahaj Mandir office in Arizona, and nervously await my fate.

Clearly this is a Flux Point in my life. Several of the ideas are sure-fire millionaire makers. Yet I vow to follow Lee's guidance on this decision, rather than trying to use my force of will to create my personal preferences.

A couple hours later Andrea Sürth hands me a rolled-up fax paper. Before unrolling it, I sit down. It turns out to be the very list I sent to Lee, faxed back with one single item circled, followed by the formidable little signature 'lee'.

The item Lee circles is the least reasonable and most impactful I can imagine: 'Continue delivering *Expand The Box* trainings'.

My throat tightens up. My heart aches. I am unable to speak for a couple of days. I circumambulate the La Ferme de Jutreau meditation path fifty times. I wash a lot of dishes. I pull weeds in the garden. I visit with the horses, all the while trying to integrate.

Lee stands strong in his wish that the Possibility Management work continue being developed, even if he never recommends any of his students to participate. Somehow Lee senses the importance of my stand to 'upgrade human thoughtware', to the extent that he asks Hohm Press to publish two of my Possibility Management contexted books (*Radiant*

Joy Brilliant Love / Building Love That Lasts, and *Conscious Feelings*) both of which are still in print with revised and updated editions.

FEEDBACK IS GOLD

I am a student of Lee Lozowick for thirteen years before he finds it worthwhile to give me feedback. It begins suddenly one summer Monday morning in 2001, after my all-night train ride home from Germany. I 'accidentally' meet Lee in the courtyard lawn outside of the big house of La Ferme de Jutreau. Lee asks what I have discovered during my recent *Expand The Box* training. I excitedly tell him how our cutting-edge research is proving that fierce solid clear feedback is truly gold, because it provides a person with that incredibly valuable little 'X' on the map that says, "You are here!" without which even the most accurate map is utterly useless.

Lee smiles at me and says, "Please find Michael Siciliano and meet me in the Darshan Hall in five minutes." I easily find Michael and we sit silently together on cushions in the Pujari position at the foot of Lee's raised dais. Lee strolls in, sits next to us and says to Michael, "Please ring the meditation bells."

Michael unwraps the twin brass cymbals from their cloth bag and rings the bells as he would to commence our morning sitting practice. Lee waits until the sweet ringing diminishes to silence, then looks at me and says, "You ring the bells too loud."

Without effort He rises to standing position and departs from the Darshan Hall. Michael says nothing and also leaves.

I sit startled, although not emotionally reacting. It is new that Lee would give me fierce solid clear feedback. I practice ringing the bells as Michael had done.

It takes me a full half hour to realize that there was a direct connection between my conversation with Lee in the lawn, and our interaction in the Darshan Hall. Lee has just given me gold!

Something deep inside me rearranges itself. It feels proper, yet somehow terribly serious and consequential… almost like growing up.

THE DIFFERENCE BETWEEN POSITIVE FEEDBACK AND PRAISE

From time to time during longer seminars, Lee might spontaneously ask one of his students to give the next talk. In the summer of 2002 at *La Source Bleue* in Central France this happened to me.

As I look into the listener's expectant faces, it comes to me to distinguish the difference between feedback and praise. If this difference is not clear in one's practice, then one is not reliable to receive positive feedback from the Guru. Each time it is offered, ego reinterprets positive feedback into praise. The Guru must then withhold positive feedback from you.

The practice around this is simple. Whether the Guru gives you positive feedback or negative feedback, you treat them both the same. Your answer is always, "Thanks for the feedback."

Other questions are raised by the participants. One man, in particular, is making assumptions which he would believe to be true, thus changing the assumptions into expectations. When his partner does not fulfill his expectations, then he feels resentment towards her. This resentment, of course, blocks intimacy between them. I am very clear and specific with him about how creating the resentment is his actual aim, or rather, the aim of his Gremlin, starting from his first assumption onwards. He does not want intimacy at all. He wants Gremlin food.

More people ask questions. People seem inspired. The talk is energy-packed.

Just afterwards I sit on the floor in a passageway back behind a display case, trying to find my way back to ordinary.

At that moment Lee strolls by. "Whoa!" he says. "That talk was great. Especially when you took that guy through his process!" Before Lee is hardly finished speaking I enthusiastically blurt out, "But I can do that with anyone! It is because of all this training I've gotten from delivering *The Event* and *Expand The Box*! I could do a lot more of this!"

A vacuous, pregnant, non-sequitur pause emerges between us, during which time Lee simply stares at me. Then He walks slowly away.

Later, while eating lunch, I suddenly can no longer taste my food. I stop eating. A realization emerges. The scene in the passageway with Lee replays itself in my mind's eye like a film. It feels like my heart stops beating. Because right there, just after my grand distinction between positive feedback and praise, just after I explained the practice for becoming reliable enough to receive positive feedback from the Guru, Lee gives me a mountain sized compliment about my talk, and I do not say, "Thank you for the feedback." Instead, I blurt out a blob of self-aggrandizing bullshit that twists his positive feedback into praise.

I unconsciously exemplify the vital difference between pontification and practice.

I make myself unreliable to receive praise from the Guru.

Indeed, it is a long time after that before anything like positive feedback comes out of Lee's mouth in my general direction.

LOOK AT THAT

One special evening during the five days that Lee answers questions from Arnaud Desjardin's students at Hauteville is reserved for the occasion of LGB band playing a public gig in a small bar up in the nearby French hills. Lee's wish is that if a student comes to a gig, you dance. Making uninhibited moves around the dance floor while Lee sings and the band plays gets us out of our minds enough that we can receive the gifts of the space Lee is creating for us.

This evening I am unusually brave. I move close to the stage and dance in plain view of Lee rather than hiding out behind the other dancers. As if this experiment is not disturbing enough, directly next to me a barely-dressed nubile blonde-haired French woman gyrates in weird sensual sexual psychotic moves toward any man nearby. Some psychological distortion disinhibits her flinging raw sexual energy everywhere. I try my best to ignore her.

In the middle of the next song, Lee steps down off the stage with his tambourine in hand, steps over to me with a big smile on his face, and says, "Look at the way she dances! Isn't that something?"

Well, yes. It is indeed something... especially it is something that my Spiritual Teacher finds it necessary to dance over to me in front of the band and all the dancers in the bar, in the middle of singing a song, to encourage me to escape enough of my 'nice boy' 'good spiritual student' charade to gaze upon this woman as a way of participating less constipatedly in the night's delights that Lee is offering us.

TATTOOS

As less and less of Lee's skin remains free of tattoo ink, when He sees bare skin strutting down the sidewalk exposed on some beautiful creature, instead of saying, "Nice legs!" or "Nice tits!" He says, "So much virgin territory...".

During the summer of 2003 I call La Ferme de Jutreau from Germany where I am delivering trainings. Brenda excitedly says, "Lee just showed us Nara's new tattoo designs. Dasya and I picked one out for you. It costs eight hundred euros. Should I get it for you?"

You have to understand that the idea of having a tattoo permanently impaled anywhere on my body has for my whole life been the farthest thing away from my mind's ability to imagine. Notwithstanding, my answer is, "Yes."

That Fall we are visiting the Ashram in Prescott, Arizona. Lee invites us to an exclusive coffee experience at Christina Sell's café in town. Lee indicates I should sit directly across the long narrow table from Him. Christina comes by and asks Lee, "Your regular?" He says, "Yes." I say, "Me too!" having, of course, no idea what I am in for. It turns out to be some kind of triple-shot steam-extracted espresso, dark as shoe polish. He knocks His back. I knock mine back. I don't know what it does to Lee, but as we get down to business, I am jittering from the caffeine rush. Lee says, "That tattoo design from Nara? I want it on your back." My mind says, Yes, sure, but of course, I mean… I am planning to do it… someday. But which 'I' is making the plans? I accept Lee's proposal.

Not long after I fly alone into Los Angeles and visit my parents on the Palos Verdes Peninsula. I say, "Dad, can I borrow your car?" He says, "Sure. What for?" I say, "I am going to go get a tattoo." Wordlessly he hands me the keys.

I park in front of *Tattoo Revolution* in Redlands, California, just as they open. Lee's favorite tattoo artist, Aaron Funk, is waiting there for my appointment. I show him Nara's incredibly inspiring artwork titled: Auspicious snow lions victoriously holding aloft a tray of radiant dharma jewels. Aaron studies it and makes preparations while I go sit nervously at his workstation. I notice a five- or six-year-old boy wandering around in the shop. Aaron keeps nagging at him to stop touching things, mentioning that his ex-partner lost her babysitter this morning so the kid would be sticking around.

This does not bode well for an undistracted session. I feel anxious. I have limited time in Los Angeles, and I'm freaking out about having a million pin holes punched into my back. I make contact with the boy, ask about a few things he likes, and while Aaron traces the tattoo outline onto my bare back that he will soon follow with the needle, I establish the context for a fabulous tattoo space, weaving it full with an amazing story-world. Together we encounter dinosaurs, giant mushrooms, aliens, volcanoes in the jungle, and plenty of unexpected but dangerous action. The boy is the star of the adventure. Four-hours of work zip by when suddenly the son begins adding in his own version of what happens next in the story. Aaron instantly says, "Shhhhh! I want to hear HIS story. I will listen to your version later." The son acquiesces and I continue exploring this exciting and mysterious universe with them. Previously I did not know I had two listeners.

When the outline is tattooed to my back, we make a short pause. Aaron decides he has enough stamina to ink in the colors. After eight full hours of painful buzzing on my back we are finished. I shakily stand up in an altered state of consciousness, both from the exhausted endorphins and the identity-shift liquid state. I am now a man with an astonishing tattoo on his back for the rest of his life. I never thought this would occur.

Aaron wraps his arm warmly around his son's shoulders and says, "It was an excellent inking session!" clearly proud of his superb work and his son's cooperation. I pay him twice the amount he asks for, in cash.

Upon my return to Palos Verdes, both my father and mother confront me in their kitchen. Something is seriously amiss. It seems they have been arguing over something. My father demands, "Where did you really go?" I say, "To the tattoo parlor in Redlands." Then he nearly shouts at me, "C'mon! Stop lying to me!" The idea of me getting a tattoo is just as far away from his picture of me as it recently was for me.

I slowly, carefully, painfully, turn my back towards them while lifting the rear of my shirt by its lower hem. There is silence behind me.

I glance over my shoulder. My mother is smiling. "It's beautiful!" she says. With tears in his eyes my father says, "I'm sorry I did not believe you. I never saw anything like this. The only tattoos I know about are from the Navy." I turn around, put the keys back into his hand and say, "Thank you for trusting me with your car."

IT IS NOTHING 'TIL HE CALLS IT

There is a story of three baseball Umpires sitting at the bar sharing perspectives about their craft. The novice Umpire says, "The pitcher throws that baseball and it either flies over the plate, or it does not. I call it the way it is." The ten-year professional Umpire interrupts and says, "Well... actually there is no scientific proof of whether the baseball comes over the plate or not. I call it the way I see it." That is when the veteran Umpire of thirty years' service speaks up. He says, "I am the Umpire. When the pitcher throws that baseball, the whole world waits, because it is nothing until I call it."

One December afternoon in France in 2003, I stand outside the immense Auchan grocery store in Chatellerault where Brenda and I purchase cartloads of food to feed the thirty-five students who will be attending our Baul Feast at La Ferme de Jutreau. From a phone booth I speak with Lee who sits in the office of the original Arizona Ashram. I ask Lee for a few logistical clarifications, after which Lee asks me to give Him a quick report of how things are going. It is basically all positive news.

At that point Lee says, "Someday, instead of people asking, 'Who is Clint Callahan?' and the answer being, 'He is Lee Lozowick's student,' people will ask, 'Who is Lee Lozowick?' and the answer will be, 'He is Clint Callahan's teacher.'"

I cannot assimilate the implications of Lee's comment. What is His actual intention? Is He teasing me about my ego? Is He trying to encourage me to keep going? Is He reframing my future, again? I do not know. I cannot conceive how His prediction could ever come to pass, even now... Nonetheless, I do report the conversation as accurately as I can.

SECRET NAME

Lee enacted so many startling behaviors that it was difficult to decide if these were His own personal practices, or if they were demonstrations intended to transform the crystallized patterns and limiting beliefs of his students' worldviews.

At different phases in His life, Lee would eat a whole fresh grapefruit after every single meal (supposedly at the recommendation of his Mother), eat mainly celery, wear wild clothing that he pulled out of the Hohm Community Give-Aways Box, peel garlic without cutting off the hard little end that attaches the clove to the stem, drive barefoot, always travel with the same ratty old woven cotton shoulder bag but stuff it full of books and CDs as gifts for others and almost no personal belongings, instantly memorize the name of each person he met, compare the prices of gasoline in different countries by converting currencies in his head, and so on. Lee would also voraciously recycle things.

This is why it is no big surprise when Lee responds to one of my written letters by using an envelope upon which someone else has already written the word 'lee'. He cleverly incorporates the 'lee' into my French address by writing my name as 'Cleent Callahan'.

I laugh out loud when I first see this, marveling at Lee's ingenious recycling techniques.

Some months later I receive a second letter similarly addressed. This time I do not laugh. I wonder what is actually going on. But I wait, making no conclusions.

The third time I receive a letter from Lee with his name nested inside of my own name, I get the message. It is not an accident. It is not simply for recycling. It is not humorous. When I write back to Lee next, I sign my name 'Love, Cleent'. I finally understand that Lee has secretly given me the name which is commonly pronounced in the French accent as 'Cleent'. Lee never writes me another letter with the secret name, nor does he ever speak a word about this to me. Neither does anyone else.

MAY I ASK YOU A QUESTION

It is early spring of 2004. I am working at one of the desks in the tiny cramped La Ferme de Jutreau office. The office phone rings. Andrea Sürth answers it professionally, as usual, then hands the phone to me, saying, "It's Lee." I say, "Hello." Lee says, "May I ask you a question?" Without hesitation, but with tremendous consternation about Lee's adamant tone of voice, I say, "Yes." He says, "Are you a pathological liar?"

Since I trained for ten years delivering over one-hundred 'The Event' trainings across the USA and Europe, during each one of which I receive 'The Demand' from the participants and any other Trainers in the space, a chaotic diabolical loud 'ratpacking' process that shreds ego to a quivering puddle of undefended mush in a matter of moments... I manage to remain vulnerable to the possible truth of Lee's demanding question. After a memorable moment of careful consideration I say, "I don't know. I will check it out and get back to you about that." Lee says, "Okay," then hangs up the phone.

Some months later I am sitting shotgun next to Lee in the front seat of his white van on the uphill drive from the Phoenix airport to the Prescott Ashram in Arizona. It is a two-hour drive, and already dark outside. Most of the drive is silent. Finally I say, "Remember you asked me if I am a pathological liar?" Lee says, "Yes." The question had set me into a deep introspection into what felt like every corner of my life. I discovered sleazy habits of untruth-telling almost everywhere, almost all the time, ever since I was a baby trying to be a 'good boy'. I recognized that every word I use is a lie because words are mere symbolic approximations of sloppily agreed-upon meanings. I discovered that speaking the truth was impossible. Each message I concocted – spoken or written – is wrapped in and motivated by both conscious and unconscious survival strategies, always. I learned that a 'pathological liar' is someone who cannot not lie, someone who lies in every word without remorse, someone who lies as if their survival depends on avoiding any admission of truth. Yes. I am a pathological liar. I say, "I figured out that I am."

A few moments of silence go by as the road slides underneath us. Then Lee says, "You don't have to worry about that anymore."

I say nothing. I also understand nothing.

I wonder to myself, "What changed? Did I change? Did Lee decide that whatever stories he heard from others about me were somehow distorted?"

My personal journey with the Bright Principle of Integrity has been long and tedious, starting with adopting my father's superficial hero's halo, "Of course I have integrity. You can always trust me..." to a period when my Gremlin gains a grip on 'integrity' and neurotically uses it as a weapon against any detectable imperfections in the words or deeds of others around me so he can viciously attack them with the accusation, "See, you did not do it perfectly. You are bad, wrong, and evil. You have no integrity! I win! You lose!"

After this car ride with Lee, months go by. Never another word about this comes from Lee, either directly or indirectly through the comments of other students. I sigh now... remembering the ordeal. So often I asked myself, "What was that all about?"

The next year during a public talk in Freiburg, Germany, Lee opens up a rare opportunity for his students to also ask Him questions. I raise my hand and am called upon to speak. I remind Lee of his question to me, "Are you a pathological liar?" and ask him "What about that?" Lee repeats what he told me in the van, "You don't have to worry about that anymore." No further explanation follows.

To this day I do not understand it at a logical level. The process seems to have occurred for no reason.

Yet this 'Pathological Liar Inquisition Initiation' served me well. It shattered my false self-esteem. It lost me all 'face'. It killed my fake show of 'being confident'. It devoured my delusions of grandeur, dissolved my source of superiority, my arrogance, and my insane hubris. In the end I trusted Lee's statement, "You don't have to worry about that anymore." But this does not mean I forgot about Lee's question!

DEPARTURE

It is summer 2010 at Hauteville. Andrea Sürth, LeeKumar (then Wolfgang Kohler), and I are taking down Lee's Bazaar Sacré in the 'petit salon' of Château Hauteville, a room with windows overlooking the rear gardens shaded by ancient sycamore trees. Only a few days before, we had helped Lee unpack and set out the artifacts. The days have flown by. This morning was Lee's final Q&A session in the grand meditation hall, sitting on the dais shoulder to shoulder with Arnaud Desjardins.

Now Lee and Arnaud dine with a few select students while everyone else serves themselves from the luscious buffet and eat joyously together at the surrounding tables.

Andrea, LeeKumar, and I would have been enjoying Hauteville cuisine with the Spiritual Masters except that tension and confusion has emerged in the van-packing team. I am merely the sweeper. I have no idea what built up to this. I only recognize my powerlessness to make things go quicker. Each artifact has its particular protective carton, and all the cartons must be stacked safely and efficiently in the cargo van. But who has the authority to decide all this?

Time ticks by. Lunch is served and eaten. Dessert is served and eaten. Covered in sweat and dust, the three of us load the myriad odd-shaped boxes into their proper places.

Over the years of Lee's summer visits to Hauteville, a tradition developed where Lee's passenger van and the artifact van are already waiting in position before the lunch begins. At that special moment when Lee and Arnaud look into each other's eyes to acknowledge that their precious time together has come to an end, they stand up from the table and walk gracefully over towards the transports while sharing hugs with everyone. By the time they finish, all of Lee's students have buckled into their seats, and all of Arnaud's students stand gathered with Arnaud in a semicircle of loving respect around Lee, making silent heartfelt goodbyes.

This year our difficult van-packing has set things out of kilter. Finally we shut the cargo van's loading doors. LeeKumar and Andrea buckle-in to pilot the cargo van to Lee's next destination. I am still sweeping out the last of the packing debris from the salon and setting chairs back in their places. By the time I get outside, all eyes are full of tears and directed at Lee who stands gloriously next to his white van in his white meditation outfit, radiating blessings, ready to depart. I want nothing more than to hug Lee goodbye before I drive alone back to Germany, but I am too dusty, too sweaty... and too late. Lee glances briefly in my direction then steps into his driver's seat, shuts his door, waves with a grand smile out his window, starts the engine, leads the caravan of vehicles down the driveway, and roars off into the sunset.

I stand there devastated. I did a good job, yes... but it cost me what everyone else will probably celebrate: one last parting hug with their dying Spiritual Teacher.

My chest is compressed into a huge knot. Arnaud's students silently and efficiently move to clean up the lunch space. I do not belong here anymore. I sigh and try to swallow it all down. There is nothing left but to walk alone back to my car in the parking lot and drive away.

I keep my eyes to the ground so no one can see my grief and loneliness. I turn to depart... and bump directly into Arnaud's big chest. His arms are spread full wide. He pulls me to him in a strong loving embrace.

Arnaud sees the whole thing from start to finish. He sees what happened and what did not happen, then moves without thinking to help his friend Lee Lozowick deliver what is needed in that moment to one of

Lee's devoted students. Arnaud gives me a Spiritual Teacher's hug of gratitude and farewell.

I can no longer hold back the flood. I sob into Arnaud's arms. Dust, sweat, and tears, all go into Arnaud's suit. My heart is well met. My soul is accompanied.

After an appropriate while, Arnaud holds me out at arm's length by my shoulders. His face radiates with his authentically rich, healing, and joyful 'Arnaud Desjardins' smile. Then he sends me on my way.

Not a word passes between us.

None is needed.

I never see Arnaud again. He dies in France 10 August 2011, a mere 268 days after the death of his true-heart friend, Lee Lozowick.

My mother dies the same year as Lee Lozowick.

My father dies the same year as Arnaud Desjardins.

What does all this mean? Nothing. We are humans, being.

29. 2014: Circular Meetings

2014 Summer Seminar at Emmendingen, Germany – Written 4 February 2015

During thirty-five years of bodacious psycho-emotional-energetic ego-stone-sculpting Lee Lozowick built an immense intelligence into the global Hohm Sahaj Mandir Sangha body. It is not that Sangha members have become individually more intelligent, so much as that the design of each person Lee so majestically and nonrationally reshaped, the shifts He made in each one's energetic body, optimizes the transduction of general intelligence into daily-life applications.

Lee reshaped student after student from an antenna for modern culture's neurotic self-obsessive adolescence, to an antenna for next culture's collaborative adulthood. Like invisible TV waves, the signals for both contexts will forever be around us. What matters is the design of the antenna, and which signals your circuitry decodes.

What a treasure to leave behind! An intelligent and empowered Sangha!

I feel continuously more gratitude and respect for what Lee has crafted. Now I am pondering our current predicament. Specifically, I refer to the 'meeting technologies' we were shown for accessing and applying our Sangha's intelligence.

By the term 'meeting technology' I mean the group sharing sessions – those times we come together to interact and exchange. The forms we have been given include Bordello meetings, formal talk spaces (Darshan, After Dinner Talks, Celebration talks), ritual spaces, bridge playing spaces, road travel spaces, tea spaces, Hohm Sahaj Mandir 'board of director' meetings, study group spaces, men's and women's support group spaces, and public talks and 'seminars'. These, of course, all still function for us, because we have learned to fill the Guru chair with what could be called 'speakers for the Guru', or from another perspective, 'those who are sacrificed at the altar of the Sangha's scrutiny'.

This 'hot seat' will persist due to its 'matrix building' efficiency. The Guru chair role will be filled through wisely-chosen volunteers (or innocents) such as various of Lee's family, Bordello leaders, original Sangha, Ashram residents, specially invited guests, and occasionally well-selected new students.

Although the Guru-chair meeting structure will continue, a condition has arisen that never arose before Lee's transition. The new condition is that the authority figure has vanished. Our foolproof compass has flicked away into the spiritsphere. We are left with two futures: either we eventually crust-over into scripture-quoting dogmatists politicizing personally-remembered teaching lessons, or, we go through a process of reinventing ourselves as a Sangha.

As might be imagined, this article investigates the latter.

Me writing this article may be the result of an insurance policy Lee secretly invested in for twenty-one years by insisting that I persist with the personal-development-process research-and-development work of Possibility Management even if it did not make the Sangha rich and famous. Of course, me writing this letter could well be complete self-deceiving bullshit. As always, the Secretary disavows any knowledge of my actions. Risking everything, I continue.

By the term 'reinventing ourselves' I refer to what I witnessed during the Hohm Sahaj Mandir meeting last summer in Freiburg when we experimented with implementing a new meeting technology to serve certain specific meeting purposes. The new meeting technology is the circle.

A few distinctions could help to build the clarity out of which further experimentation may be more productive.

Every meeting takes place within the space of a consciously or unconsciously held context. Being able to consciously establish and elegantly navigate a consciously contexted meeting space is one of Lee's basic teachings to us.

It is? But He never said so!

Reminds me of Lee's story about the impetuous American Zen student in Japan insisting on taking his third Zen Bow test even when he so seriously failed two previous tests, and his Teacher recommends against it. Test day comes and the pugnacious white-boy gets his way. By the end of the test the student hits the bull's eye with his arrow (as he had failed to do in the first test), and his kimono does not fall off his shoulder (as it had done in the second test) and yet the judges sadly proclaim that he fails the test. His Teacher's eyes fall to the floor in embarrassment (or the conscious-theater enactment of embarrassment…). The student breaks protocol and demands in outrage to know why he failed this time. One of the judges takes pity on the student's hurt ego and explains, "As you lay your bow back down across your knees after the shot, the tip of your bow was five centimeters above the floor instead of the proper form of fifteen centimeters." To which the student turns and glares directly at his Teacher and accuses, "But you never told me!"

Ah, yes. How often does what *"Lee never told me"* slap me up-side the head…

The context of a meeting space is constructed out of a specific set of distinctions. The spaceholder would ideally be conscious of and dexterous with sourcing the distinctions of the meeting context as an aid to effectively navigating the space for the benefit of everyone.

Lee both adamantly and sweetly, and in any case incessantly, landed distinctions of the Hohm Sahaj Mandir context in the energetic body of anyone around him bearing a matrix that was practice-toughened enough to hold them. He landed distinctions *directly* through both private (Sangha only) and public talks, plus week-long question-and-answer seminars (mostly in Europe during the summers), and *indirectly* through spontaneous uncontrollable unstoppable multi-branching stories (some still unfinished…), and through immediate alchemical process.

Lee would deliver the five basic tenets of the Western Baul Tradition, plus guru yoga distinctions, George Gurdjieff distinctions, José Silva distinctions, Werner Erhard distinctions, Robert Svoboda distinctions, Arnaud Desjardins distinctions, Hindi distinctions, Bhakti distinctions, Tantric distinctions, Women's culture, Men's culture, and Children's culture distinctions, parenting distinctions, adulthood distinctions, transformation distinctions, reality distinctions, diet and health distinctions, sexuality distinctions, spiritual tradition distinctions, esoteric practices distinctions, and occasionally even sheep-jokes. Then He continued unfolding, deepening, widening, and effervescently expanding facets of these distinctions for over thirty-five years. By the end of Lee's life, the distinctions He worked with sizzled like radiant suns of shining clarity, diamond-sharp, white-hot and transformationally flaming.

It had to be so, because the Hohm Sahaj Mandir gameworld emerges from a living evolving context.

This school is an organism which thrives on the energetic configuration of our commitments to holding and navigating our personal life spaces in this context. But since the circumstances have changed, the school's necessity has changed. It looks now as if a circular meeting technology may from time to time, for specific purposes, be useful.

The principal difference between a circular (to be more accurate: toroidal – meaning a 'donut shaped' mapping of energy flows) meeting technology and the meeting technologies demonstrated to us by Lee Lozowick as mentioned above, is that in a circular meeting technology there is no 'Guru seat'.

The Guru seat has been easily mistaken for and twisted into the 'cock on the dunghill' power position in the patriarchal empire's hierarchical business, political, education, and religious meeting technologies, within which the bulk of the Sangha were born and embedded. But, it is not the same. The Guru seat is not removed in circular meeting technologies because it is thought to be hierarchical. It is removed to shift the energy flow to access a different quality of intelligence.

In circular meeting technologies the center of the circle is open, void of typical new-age-style artifacts such as candles, flowers, peace-inducing crystals, 'meaningful' objects, and calming rainbow-colored silks. If the circle center is not free of debris then the contents of the center take over as the context-setting authority.

The circular meeting space includes a regal and abundantly appreciated altar, but the altar is positioned at the altar spot, not in the middle of the circle. The circular meeting depends on the nothingness of not knowing through which what is wanted and needed is called into the space.

The function of the Guru role is exchanged for several ingredients in the circular meeting technology, namely: a spaceholder, one or more context holders, the nothingness of the void, the blessings of the lineage, and the resources from the Bright Principles of Kindness, Generosity and Compassion.

For properly running circular meeting technologies in Hohm Sahaj Mandir contexted gatherings, it is crucial to get it that the space holder – the person nominated to hold and navigate the spaces of this particular meeting – need not be and is often not the same person as the context holder. When you make the spaceholder and context holder the same person it is difficult not to subtly return to the Guru seat format.

It is equally important to get it that the context holder role cannot be faked. That is, *everybody already experiences who the context holders of a circular meeting are* and those people cannot be replaced by anybody else. Until you rest tacitly in knowing that context holding cannot be faked, ego may generate fear of itself becoming un-exceptional. This tragic egoic maneuver is visible to all, and therefore preferably self-noticed and sidestepped. The sidestepping can be empowered by recognizing that imagining (in the Gurdjieffian sense) that authentic context holders can be replaced by someone merely asserting themselves to be an authentic context holder is like imagining that the ending of the (very) short film titled *Bambi Meets Godzilla* could ever turn out differently…

Matrix cannot be faked and is completely visible to everyone in the space who can scan for matrix. As Lee used to explain, when you scan for matrix you can see people who are sleeping but you cannot see people who are awake. You can see people with less matrix than you but you cannot so well see the matrix of people who have more matrix than you. Experiment: If you ever scan someone and cannot see their matrix, consider going to talk with them and find out what they are up to.

Context is held in each person's matrix, caught by the hard-earned distinctions that weave together to catch and hold more consciousness.

That the structure and possibility of each person's matrix is so visible makes it irrelevant to pass out colored belts as 'dans' to indicate 'achievement' in the Western Baul Tradition. Each person's condition is tacitly evident. A big-Being person trying to sit invisibly in a room is like a crocodile standing in line for ice cream. You must drown yourself in serious denial not to notice it.

By now it should be clear that many people in a circular meeting can function as simultaneous context holders as long as they have the same purpose.

Circular meetings get particularly interesting when the context of the meeting includes *feedback* (Feedback is: a clear and neutral report of what just occurred, what worked, and exactly what did not work.) and *coaching* (Coaching is: clear proposals with distinctions about precisely what to try next time to cause better results). In a feedback and coaching context, less-experienced individuals can safely be nominated to publicly improve their space-navigation skills at the fastest possible rate benefitting the entire Sangha.

That is benefit #2.

Benefit #1 is that by assembling people in a circular formation around an empty space, with context holders giving feedback and coaching and a spaceholder getting support to more elegantly navigate the space, everyone, meaning everyone, can freely and naturally unleash their intelligence during the discovery journey. This procedure is called 'parallel play'.

The typical gut-fear about implementing circular meeting technologies is that if 'Daddy' isn't there being the almighty authority keeping peace and order, then participants with hidden competing commitments, with unhealed childhood projections, with uninitiated (adolescent) reactivity, with unconscious Gremlins, or with only rudimentary knowledge and experience of the Hohm Sahaj Mandir context, will 'take over' the space and ruin the pristine possibilities of the meeting. This fear vanishes, however, once the circular meeting technology is appropriately put to use because a fresh level of attentiveness blossoms. People wake up and slide forward to the front edge of their seats when they directly experience how proficiently and humorously the context-coached spaceholder (who could be any one of them in the next moment) navigates the abundance of free-play intelligence collaborating to fulfill long-term commitments for the benefit of the School and all Beings everywhere.

One might ask oneself why this has not shown up so much before? What has been in the way until now? Certainly Lee was not suppressing students' contributions to spaces. The opposite was true – He was ongoingly asking, "Any questions or considerations?" And certainly the matrix of Western Baul students has grown overall as a result of Lee's decades of alchemical artistry causing the quality of each person's contributions to increase. So then, what stopped it?

Think about it. The format of having a Guru chair at the front of a meeting space establishes a certain protocol. It formats a time for listening and receiving, not for speaking. It promotes a time for being 'internally active and externally passive'.

Co-creating is not triggered because, quite frankly, how can there be a 'co' thing happening with the Guru?

Group intelligence is not liberated because when intelligence resources flow through whoever sits in the Guru chair, group intelligence becomes irrelevant.

These days in the Hohm Sahaj Mandir we harvest abundant fruits of Lee's decades of soil-tilling, seed-planting, and weed-pulling. Witness the elegance and unspeakable power and beauty unfolding at Triveni in Arizona. Experience the loving presence at Triveni II in India, Kripa Mandir Ashram in Canada, R.A.M.J.I. Association in France, Trimurti in Montana, the bands, the art, the books that keep pouring out of Hohm Press, and the creative bondedness of the European Sangha. The blessings of the tradition are indeed bountiful.

But endless harvesting cannot continue without further tilling, planting, and nurturing. How should the Hohm Sahaj Mandir become regenerative? How can we thrive now, without someone sitting in the Guru chair?

Here is an insight. One calm summer Sunday morning at La Ferme de Jutreau in France around the year 2003, the Teaching meeting is over and brunch is not yet ready. The sun shines through the windows of the now-quiet and nearly empty multi-purpose meeting room of the main house, where the entire back wall of pinewood shelves radiates blessings from irreplaceable artifacts for sale in Lee's Sacred Bazaar.

Between the gigantic stone fireplace and the dark hardwood door to the foyer sits Lee Lozowick, waiting.

I squat next to him with a question that has been burning in me for some time. He is willing to engage.

My quandary goes like this: What is, is, as it is, here and now, without judgment, with no stories attached. Yes. I can accept that, with full responsibility. And… I cannot do what I need to do with it.

I cannot be responsible for creating whatever is needed or wanted next through mere acceptance of what is, as it is, here and now. My job is to serve evolution, in other words, to cause change, to cause transformation, at least as far as creating physical objects, spaces, and conditions in which Ashram-appropriate activities can continue to unfold.

What is, as it is here and now, is a meeting between potential and necessity. At this intersection, where actions can occur, is the Mage Interface. The accurate assessment of current reality is required for generating useful new results. But how do I escape from, or transform, 'what is', if 'what is' is all there is?

Nonacceptance of 'what is', must be required to break free of the current 'what is' in order to cause change. Orthogonal, nonlinear, unconventional actions are essential to escape the current conventions. In order to invent the next 'what is', I must be consciously and responsibly at source for navigating the current 'what is' here and now into 'what could be' here and now, taking everything into account so that the next 'what is' has more value than the currently existing 'what is'.

My actions must destroy one 'what is' and replace it with a more useful 'what is', or else things will always stay the same, and things obviously do not always the same! What gives?

Lee pushes back on me. I persist with further precisions.

Lee counters. I am terrified of demanding an answer that I can use, but even more afraid of never getting one. I reformulate my urgency by entering unknown territory.

Lee stays right with me. After half-an-hour Lee suddenly hands over the gold. He says, as if he has known it all along:

"There are two forms of what is: the passive form and the active form.

"The passive form of what is, is simply, what is.

"The active form of what is, is creation."

The practice of the *passive* form of what is, is to accept what is, as it is, here and now in the moment, without judgment.

The practice of the *active* form of what is, is taking radically responsible actions for pulling the rug out, for transforming the what is, whatever it is, (step-by-step if necessary… without excuses, without turning away…) into whatever 'what is' can support whatever is wanted and needed next. This opens up an entire universe of new skills, distinctions, tools, responsibilities, explorations, practices, and possibilities.

Crunch, bang, sizzle, kaboom, pop, fizzzz… Right then and there my world falls apart and catalyzes into an upgraded and more elegant format. I can feel my memetic constructs reordering from the heavens to the hells.

In that moment, the entire domain of creating, transforming, and destroying Possibility – the human capacity for managing Possibility, in other words, 'Possibility Management' – takes an intensely transformational turn. Whole new dimensions open up. I am so excited I can hardly breathe. I bow with unspeakable gratitude to Lee and go help set the table for brunch…

Evolutionary gameworlds – that is, gameworlds that provide or cause evolution – must also evolve. In that moment, Lee Lozowick delivered general principles that could be applied everywhere, even within the evolutionary gameworld of Hohm Sahaj Mandir.

During the summer of 2014 in Freiburg, unexpected questions naturally although somewhat suddenly surfaced: Could there be times when shifting to a circular meeting technology best serves the emergent needs and intentions of Hohm Sahaj Mandir?

Do we have the self-reflective flexibility to get good at this? Or would we be submerging ourselves in a 'devil's workshop'? Betraying the trust of a Tradition? Subverting an authentic Context?

On the other hand, would suppressing these questions steer us away from an appropriate and valuable development? Could this be a true way that our School continues to flourish and evolve even without a Guru successor?

This is intended to be the beginning of a long and interesting conversation. May we be annihilated in Love.

30. 2015: Self-Deception

26 August 2015 – Finding your way when the Guru is ex-carno.

The term 'self-deception' equates to 'fooling yourself', usually to serve some unconscious purpose. To give an example, a belief is self-deception. Anyone can believe anything about anything, because beliefs have no connection to reality. You could believe that hotdogs are sacred and the greatest sin is to waste them by eating them. You could just as well believe that hotdogs are sacred and the greatest sin is to waste them by not eating them. In either case you are fooling yourself. The 'pay dirt' question is, why?

A belief is different from a thought. A belief is a Band-Aid used to cover over a hole in your worldview where you have no thoughts, where the true answer is, "I don't know…" For example, "I don't know what happens if I waste a hotdog…" Your Band-Aids can have any logo on them you want, but as Lee put it, "A belief and fifty-cents will get you on the bus."

Are you holding any beliefs about the dead Guru? List your Guru beliefs.

If you peel away a belief, what is behind it? Write down your answers.

Whatever beliefs you harbor can be ferreted out and inquired into until the belief-mirage dissolves into oblivion. Then you discover the unconscious fears which the belief was hiding from you.

This brings you one step closer to reality. Probably your Guru would be glad about this. After a while you might be glad about it also.

The term *self* is intended to distinguish your *essential* Being from the *world-interface Construct* you cobbled together out of personality, psychology, comfort zone, self-image, worldview, rules, customs, stories, conclusions, assumptions, expectations, opinions, beliefs, mindset, philosophy, old decisions, etc., so that your Construct can function as your survival strategy. Your Being remains imprisoned inside this Construct until you make an *experiential distinction* (in contrast to an intellectual distinction) differentiating your Being and your Construct Box by inserting a thin gap of nothingness between them.

The optional initiatory self-surgery of relocating your point of origin to the gap of nothingness, allows you to disidentify your Being from your Construct, and thereby gain the option of choosing which is in charge, your Being or your Construct. The freedom of movement between Being and Construct comes from the nothingness in the gap which serves as a lubricant. (What is possible when you enter and learn to navigate the nothingness would be the subject of a different essay...)

Being around a Guru in the flesh makes it almost irresistible to imagine that your Guru has His hands on the steering wheel. The Guru has His informers everywhere, and it seems obvious that one way or another, sooner or later, directly or indirectly He will give you clear, radically-honest feedback guaranteed to keep you on track. It is equally tempting to think that the physically closer you are to the Guru the more completely you will be taken care of.

Such beliefs are core elements in FIVE tricky self-deceptions as follows:

FIRST SELF-DECEPTION: Assuming that the closer your physical presence is to the living Guru the more you can rest-assured that you are on track.

Actually, the track does not care if you are on it or not. Probably also the Guru does not, in reality, care if you are on track or not. It is not actually His problem. However, due to the seeming abundance of course-corrections from the living Guru, it is difficult to imagine that it is even possible to get off track. You could be fooling yourself about this.

SECOND SELF-DECEPTION: Concluding that since the Guru gives you feedback, you are protected in His special safety net.

These two are killer naïvetés.

For a while it was rumored that the Guru gives you enough rope to hang yourself. Lee was careful to explain that this is not the case. It turns out that we live in a responsible universe. What this means is that every action and inaction, conscious or unconscious – regardless of your mastery at justification – has real consequences, visible and invisible, short-term and long-term, local and distant...

Actions like what? Like wearing blue-jeans in the Darshan hall, whistling while you work, subtle cynicisms in your facial expressions or tone of voice, minuscule power-struggles in the timing of your speech, entering – even if only peripherally – into someone else's energetic space, leaving soap on the washed dishes, table talk while playing Bridge, attracting negative attentions to feed your Gremlin, thinking that 'feeling someone else's emotions' is compassion, believing any of the conclusions that your mind makes, waiting without generosity, putting on the act of being a 'good student', keeping a blank stare so others volunteer to do the dirty work and you don't have to, energetically competing for speaking time, not distinguishing which culture you support with your purchases, exaggerating how bad it really is for you, eating two instead of one, letting your Gremlin loose to take over a space because you 'know better', disrespecting a child, being unkind to yourself, on and on. Like dropping a stone towards your foot, all these – and their opposites – have real consequences.

Modern culture intensifies intellectual skills while eradicating authentic initiations into the emotional, energetic, and archetypal domains. Empaths and Alchemists were systematically killed during the seven-hundred years of Catholic Inquisitions. This does not mean your feelings-body, energetic-body, and archetypal-body do not exist. It means that whether you recognize it or not, your human experience can be severely handicapped by your culture and times. Since modern culture's crippling is indiscriminate and ubiquitous, its institutions and customs regard the resultant crippling distortions as ordinary, also in presidents, billionaires, priests, and movie stars.

THIRD SELF-DECEPTION: Thinking that Hohm Sahaj Mandir is somehow part of modern culture. It is not. At all.

Yes, you pay taxes in Caesar's coin to avoid being sent to their prison camps. But modern culture's rule of law is illegitimate because it leads directly to global ecocide. Anyone obeying the rule of law of modern culture is criminally insane. Anyone defending that law has already sacrificed their life.

Triveni, Triveni II, Ramji, Trimurti, and Kripa Mandir are context-bonded nanonations, internally following a set of laws wildly different from the rule of law of modern culture. How can you be a servant of Hohm Sahaj Mandir if you behave as a slave of the capitalist patriarchal empire?

Being fit and creative as a Western Baul requires gaining capacities that modern culture prohibits. These include: taking your energetic center, authority and voice back from external authority (as is modeled in Silat, Aikido, and unschooling), completing childhood with your parents and shifting into authentic adulthood (modeled by The Event, Landmark Forum, Possibility Management, etc.), healing technopenuriaphobia – the fear of losing technology – by learning to live in small autonomous groups directly on the Earth (modeled by Ashram gardens, growing, harvesting and preserving foods off-grid, and by shifting into cultural-relativity during extended international travels in 'un-developed' countries), holding and navigating space (modeled by Lee Lozowick, Arnaud Desjardins, Robert Svoboda, Llewellyn Vaughan-Lee, E.J. Gold, and other teachers Lee has exposed us to), being unhookable (modeled in Women's Groups, Men's Groups, Barbershop Quartets, Bordellos, group households, Ashram Steering and Business Committees, etc.), being able to go nonlinear and unreasonable to create possibilities beyond the options provided by modern culture and our personal comfort zones (modeled by the music bands, Baul Theater, Sacred Bazaar, Celebrations, building and running the Ashrams, etc.), and being the space through which Bright Principles and your Archetypal Lineage can do their work in the world rather than being the space through which your psychological aberrations can do their work in the world (for example, the Bright Principles of Hohm Sahaj Mandir are *Kindness* (heart related), *Generosity* (soul related), and *Compassion* (sword related)).

Elizabeth Kübler-Ross found that it can take a human being two to five years to digest and integrate the five perturbation states of sudden change:

1. Fear-fueled denial
2. Anger-fueled outrage
3. Gremlin-fueled bargaining
4. Sadness-fueled grief
5. Joy-fueled consciously and responsibly accepting what is, as it is here-and-now in the moment without judgment.

Not being able to consciously distinguish and communicate your feelings and emotions extends or even blocks these five steps for re-entering reality. This means learning to vulnerably and consciously feel is central to Baul Sadhana.

The necessity for Western Baul fitness does not decrease in the least when the Guru dies.

To prove it, the Guru dies.

Game over.

Both foreground shit and background shit hit the fan.

Now you must viscerally decide: Do you duck into self-deception and try to stay clean? Or do you stay standing and get lambasted with your own self-deceptions?

This might be the moment to re-evaluate what it means to 'eat shit and die':

VALUE 1: What dies is not real.

VALUE 2: Shit fertilizes dormant seeds that are valuable uncivilized potentials within you.

VALUE 3: Since you can only die *now*, the experience of virtual death shatters your illusion that you are actually involved 'anywhen' other than now.

VALUE 4: Since, *"The nature of reality is groundlessness."* (P. Chodron) exposure to the groundlessness of virtual death can increase your reality-navigation skills.

VALUE 5: The Gremlin-feeding games of 'trying to look good for the Guru', or 'trying to be unworthy enough for the Guru to save me', or 'beating myself up with self-hatred so the Guru does not have to reprimand me', etc., have become useless and are unambiguously exterminated... because the Guru has unambiguously died.

VALUE 6: When the shit hits and your psychological defense strategy gets killed, you can practice how to get killed and not die, which is especially useful for men learning to be with women.

Yeah, and then what?

FOURTH SELF-DECEPTION: Thinking you have vanquished the Four Enemies of a student on the path.

The Guru dies, but the dharma remains the same. And the sangha body? It simply remains.

The frontliners have almost all died off. There is no one out in front of you to do the dirty work anymore. Just like Lee Lozowick was, you are now left with distinguishing between the personal Guru in the flesh who is gone, and the personal Guru who is archetypal, who was actually always there and has become even more available now.

Relating to the archetypal Guru is learned through experiential discernment, the same way relating to the road while driving a car is learned through driver's education training. Hopefully you learned to drive in a simulator where crashes only elicit the snickers of your peers instead of painful months in the hospital and karmic baggage.

But how do you simulate disincarnated Guru discernment? Lee sponsored this abundantly by encouraging each of us to speak out during After Dinner Talks, Darshans, Celebrations and in Bordellos. How? If you speak out, you die.

Further de-carnated Guru discernment muscles are developed by submitting completed written pieces to Hohm Press, by being a Yes to whatever instructions were received through studying Lee's poetry, prose and music, by delivering on any promises you make, by washing more than your share of dishes by hand, and by putting your shoes on the shoe-shelf no matter what kind of 'hurry' you imagine yourself to be in.

Bauls practice 'til our last breath. Yes, *but how now, brown cow?*

The archetypal is directly accessible through your energetic body, not through your mind. Try this: Assume that Lee is here, right now, with you, closer than your own thoughts. Start getting that He never wasn't there. Right now, one-on-one visceral communion between you and Lee Lozowick ex-carnated is happening. Ask him a real question. Shut up your mind and write down the answers you get. Do this enough that you can discern bullshit from brilliance until you can radically rely on the source. There is an impersonal bright ally standing at your elbow, waiting for your check-in, your question, your praise, ready to collaborate with you in your Sadhana.

Connecting-in with the personal ex-carnated archetypal Guru depends on you turning on your own internal archetypal structures, the ones that were hard-wired into your body since birth, and sit there waiting for you to unwrap the plastic and put the batteries in.

- The Warrioress is turned on through 100% intense anger, consciously experienced and expressed, starting and stopping for no reason.
- The Lover is turned on through 100% intense sadness, consciously experienced and expressed, starting and stopping for no reason.
- The Sorceress is turned on through 100% intense fear, consciously experienced and expressed, starting and stopping for no reason.
- The Baul Practitioner student of Lee Lozowick is turned on through 100% intense joy, consciously experienced and expressed, starting and stopping for no reason.

Through 'stellating' your four feelings, your tubes are blown clean of a lifetime of debris and expanded wide open. None of these feelings are negative. None are bad. It is an entirely new thoughtmap of feelings, where feelings are the neutral energy and information that you need if you are to deliver what is wanted and needed in this moment.

FIFTH SELF-DECEPTION: Thinking that if there is a voice, it must be Lee.

How do you tell the difference between a voice in your head and Lee? This is simple: Presence has no voice.

Stories exist in time. The present is timeless. Lee can only be with you in the present. The present is too small to contain voices and stories.

Some have tried arranging for the equivalent of a séance with 'Madame Sylvia' to 'connect in with and get the download from' the ephemeral Guru. Have you tried it? You should try it. The problem comes when you are in a fix, because that is when 'Madame Sylvia' is on holiday... and you come to wonder who she is talking to really?

Perhaps you had the luck of interacting with a living-in-the-flesh Guru for a time. That may be lucky, but is not necessary. In any case, it is a chapter that is over for all of us in Hohm Sahaj Mandir. You may carry memories of interactions with Lee, or from seeing videos or listening to talks of Lee. You may have read his books, or made notes from talks. You may even have a photograph of you and Lee together. These are all dead recordings – memories included – like dancing alone to a CD rather than dancing in a crowd at a live music performance.

True, as a result of mulling over your memories you may from time-to-time puzzle-out a new understanding, as when Lee famously described having a new insight about what Yogi Ramsuratkumar had told Him nineteen years earlier.

Your challenge is to start over from the beginning.

What about doing that now?

The field-effect Guru remains as potent as He was when He was alive and in your face. Perhaps because your Gremlin survival strategies have no physical form of Lee that they can try to manipulate, Lee may be even more immediately available than He was before.

Lee does not become more present when you fantasize that you hold in your fingers the same beads that Lee once held in His fingers. This is imagination, like Dumbo the elephant imagining that he can fly because he carries a feather with his nose. It is not the feather – nor his belief in the feather – that causes Dumbo to fly. It is going through the actual trials and tribulations of learning how to flap his huge ears that he can learn to efficiently fly.

I think human beings are designed to fly. I think Lee was running a flying school. The Guru dying does not make learning to fly impossible. When aluminum is shaped into the form of a jet plane and is pushed down a runway at a certain velocity, it cannot be kept on the ground. That shape automatically flies.

I think human beings are the same. We can take many shapes. Some of those shapes can fly.

As Lee Lozowick passionately writes in his LGB band lyrics *All There Is To Say*:

Would you be free from all pain, and the hurt you don't need to feel?

Would you live free as the wind in the trees, and take time that you did not steal?

Do you want to feel the magic in each and every breath?

Would you reach beyond the stars, to laugh in the face of death?

Dropping extraneous physical, intellectual, emotional, energetic, and archetypal baggage, clearing up misidentifications, dis-attaching from triggers, gaining conscious choice over unconscious purposes, becoming spacious, connecting to and using inner and outer resources, taking radical responsibility, becoming consciousness in action, stopping feeding parasitic entities, serving something greater than yourself, loving love, becoming love, noticing what you are noticing, entering reality as a collaborator, this and so much more is still your work.

Once there was a feather you could hold onto named Lee Lozowick. You got the idea somewhere that if you held tightly onto this feather you could fly along with the Guru.

The Guru was already flying. Maybe the Guru let you believe in the feather for a while because He enjoyed your company.

Then suddenly the feather disappears into infinity. Were you actually flying before? Or was Lee carrying you?

Can you keep flying without a feather in your hands?

Shaping yourself through practice into a form that flies by itself… this is your work.

It always was.

Jai Guru Lee Lozowick

Jai Guru Yogi Ramsuratkumar

Jai Guru Papa Ramdas

Jai Jai Jai Guru

31. Diving Deeper

Here are a few recommended sources for diving deeper:

https://westernbaul.org

https://westernbaul.org/podcast

http://hohmsahajmandir.org

https://hohmpress.com/authors-hohm-press/lee-lozowick.html

https://en.wikipedia.org/wiki/Lee_Lozowick

http://www.leelozowick.com

https://www.hohmpress.com/collections/clinton-callahan

...further precisions and experiments for deepening the distinctions in this book can be found in more than six-hundred-and-fifty interlinked websites at http://startover.xyz